T0295518

THE HISTORY OF EIBA

THE HISTORY OF EIBA: A TALE OF THE CO-EVOLUTION BETWEEN INTERNATIONAL BUSINESS ISSUES AND A SCHOLARLY COMMUNITY

BY

VÍTOR CORADO SIMÕES
ISEG – Lisbon School of Economics and Management,
University of Lisbon, Portugal

JOHN CANTWELL
Rutgers University, USA

AND

PHILIPPE GUGLER
University of Fribourg, Switzerland

United Kingdom – North America – Japan
India – Malaysia – China

Emerald Publishing Limited
Emerald Publishing, Floor 5, Northspring, 21-23 Wellington Street, Leeds LS1 4DL.

First edition 2025

British Library Cataloguing in Publication Data
A catalogue record for this book is available from the British Library

ISBN: 978-1-83608-665-9 (Print)
ISBN: 978-1-83608-664-2 (Online)
ISBN: 978-1-83608-666-6 (Epub)

INVESTOR IN PEOPLE

CONTENTS

LIST OF FIGURES

LIST OF TABLES

LIST OF ABBREVIATIONS – GENERAL

AEIB	Association for Education in International Business
AES	Academy of Economic Studies (Romania)
AI	Artificial intelligence
AIB	Academy of International Business
AIB-WE	Academy of International Business Western Europe Chapter
BF	Belgian Franc
BRI	Belt and Road Initiative
CESA	Centre d'Enseignement Supérieur des Affaires
COST	European Cooperation in Science and Technology
CSA	Country-specific advantages
DTT	Doctoral Think Tank
EC	European Commission
EEC	European Economic Community
EFMD	European Foundation for Management Development
EIASM	European Institute for Advanced Studies in Management
EIBA	European International Business Academy
EIBA LAA	EIBA Lifetime Achievement Award
EU	European Union
FAIB	Federation of Associations of International Business
FDI	Foreign direct investment
FPI	Foreign portfolio investment
FSA	Firm-specific advantages
GATT	General Agreement on Tariffs and Trade
GDPR	General Data Protection Regulation
GVC	Global value chains
HBA	Home base augmenting
HBE	Home base exploiting
HOS	Hecksher Ohlin Samuelson framework
IB	International business
IJVs	International joint ventures

IPR	Industrial property rights
I-R	Integration-responsiveness
LBS	London Business School
MAI	Multilateral Agreement on Investment
MERIT	Maastricht Economic Research Centre on Innovation and Technology
MIT	Massachusetts Institute of Technology
MNC	Multinational company (or corporation)
MNE	Multinational enterprise
M&A	Mergers and acquisitions
NAFTA	North American Free Trade Agreement
NGO	Non-governmental organisation
NR	National representative (at the EIBA Board)
OECD	Organisation for Economic Cooperation and Development
OLI	Ownership Location Internalisation
PDW	Paper development workshop
RA	Regional Association
SDG	Sustainable Development Goals
TPP	Trans-Pacific Partnership
TTIP	Transatlantic Trade and Investment Partnership
UK	United Kingdom
UN	United Nations
UNCTAD	United Nations Conference on Trade and Investment
UNCTC	United Nations Centre on Transnational Corporations
US	United States of America
USD	US Dollar
WIR	World Investment Report
WTO	World Trade Organisation

LIST OF ABBREVIATIONS – JOURNALS

AMJ	*Academy of Management Journal*
AMP	*Academy of Management Perspectives*
AMR	*Academy of Management Review*
ASQ	*Administrative Science Quarterly*
BJM	*British Journal of Management*
CJE	*Cambridge Journal of Economics*
CMR	*California Management Review*
CR	*Competitiveness Review*
EMR	*European Management Review*
ETP	*Entrepreneurship Theory and Practice*
GSJ	*Global Strategy Journal*
HBR	*Harvard Business Review*
IBR	*IBR, International Business Review, Int Bus Review*
ICC	*Industrial and Corporate Change*
IMR	*International Marketing Review*
JDE	*Journal of Development Economics*
JEG	*Journal of Economic Geography*
JIBP	*Journal of International Business Policy, J Int Bus Policy*
JIBS	*Journal of International Business Studies, J Int Bus Stud*
JIE	*Journal of International Entrepreneurship*
JIM	*Journal of International Marketing*
JMS	*Journal of Management Studies*
JoM	*Journal of Management*
JPIM	*Journal of Product Innovation Management*
JWB	*Journal of World Business*
LRP	*Long Range Planning*
MIR	*Management International Review, Manag Int Rev*
MS	*Management Science*
OBES	*Oxford Bulletin of Economics and Statistics*

OEP	*Oxford Economic Papers*
OS	*Organization Science*
RP	*Research Policy*
SMJ	*Strategic Management Journal*
SMR	*Sloan Management Review*

ABOUT THE AUTHORS

Vítor Corado Simões has served for many years as Professor at ISEG – Instituto Superior de Economia e Gestão (University of Lisbon) until his retirement in 2020. His research addresses two main fields: international management and innovation management. He has published in Portuguese and international journals. He has been a Visiting Professor at the following universities: Complutense (Madrid, Spain), PUC Rio (Brazil) and Toulouse (France). Besides his research activity, he worked at the Foreign Investment Institute of Portugal, provided international consultancy on foreign investment and innovation policy and has actively cooperated with international organisations, namely OECD, UNIDO (missions in India, Philippines, Senegal and Venezuela) and the European Commission. He has been a committed EIBA member since 1986. He served as President of EIBA in 1993 and is now Fellow of this Academy. Since 2015, he has convened the EIBA History Panel at every EIBA Annual Conference.

John Cantwell is Distinguished Professor of International Business at Rutgers University, NJ, USA since 2002. He was previously Professor of International Economics at the University of Reading in the UK. He has also held various visiting professorships, including at the University of Rome 'La Sapienza' in Italy. His research focusses on technological innovation and international knowledge networks. His published research spans the fields of international business, economics, economic history, philosophy, economic geography and innovation studies. He has been President of EIBA, Dean of the EIBA Fellows, Program Chair of the AIB and he is an elected AIB Fellow. He served as Editor-in-Chief of the *Journal of International Business Studies (JIBS)* from 2011 to 2016. In 2019, he was named the PWC Strategy & Eminent Scholar by the International Management Division of the Academy of Management. He received an honorary doctorate (honoris causa) from Complutense University, Madrid, in December 2021.

Philippe Gugler is Director of the Center for Competitiveness at the University of Fribourg. He holds the Chair of Economic and Social Policy in the Faculty of Management, Economics, and Social Sciences (FSES) at the University of Fribourg, Switzerland. He serves as President of the Department of Economics at FSES and is a former Dean of FSES. Additionally, he is a Microeconomics of Competitiveness (MOC) Affiliate Faculty Member and Co-Chair of the Research Council at the MOC network established by Professor Michael Porter of Harvard Business School. In 2010, Professor Michael Porter inducted him into the Hall of Fame at the Institute for Strategy and Competitiveness at Harvard Business School. Since January 2014, he has been Editor-in-Chief of the scientific journal *Competitiveness Review*, published by Emerald in the United Kingdom.

ACKNOWLEDGEMENTS

This book is the result of a knowledge excursion taken by three people, but it would not be successful without the contributions from many others, inside and outside the perimeter of EIBA. We express our recognition to all those who made possible for us to take this journey through the history of EIBA as well as to complete this book, starting with a reference to Tilo Halaszowitch, who is also a member of the EIBA History Committee and responsible for the EIBA History website (https://history.eiba.org/). We would like to note from the outset that we have intended the website to act as a companion to this book, so some of the more detailed accounts of the contents of past conferences, and a wider array of photos from the past, can be found on the website.

The first words of thanks must go to the EIBA Fellows – that, at the Rio de Janeiro-2015 meeting, warmly supported the idea to write a history of EIBA and nominated the authors to form the EIBA History Committee – as well as to the EIBA Board, that, besides expressing its full backing, took the decision to provide funding to carry out the project in early 2016. More specifically, we thank the Deans of the Fellows – Francesca Sanna-Randaccio, Juán Durán and Sarianna Lundan – for their interest in and continuous support of a project that has taken longer than originally anticipated. We also thank the EIBA Chairs for their sustained encouragement and availability to facilitate our work. We are particularly grateful to Lucia Piscitello for carrying out the preliminary contacts with the publisher. We warmly thank the Executive Secretaries of EIBA, Ene Kannel and Anne-Laure Marteaux, for their spirit of cooperation and commitment to this project, including the support provided to the team in our stays in Brussels to carry out archival research.

Our interviews with the EIBA 'Founding Fathers', who had been at the original setting up of our organisation in 1974, were the first big step along this journey. We wholeheartedly thank Jim Leontiades, Michel Ghertman, Lars-Gunnar Mattsson, Sylvain Plasschaert, the late José de la Torre and Pål Korsvold for being available for lengthy interviews aimed at recalling their remembrances of an event that had taken place more than 40 years earlier. Besides this, they have been always available to support and respond to our questions. Jim, Michel, Lars-Gunnar, Sylvain and José also participated at the memorable online session of the EIBA History Panel in 2020. Pål was kind enough to attend the EIBA History Panel in Oslo-2022 and to share further memories of EIBA conferences. José commented on the very first draft versions of Chapters 2, 3 and 4. Lars-Gunnar provided further support in identifying those pictured at the famous Uppsala-1977 photo (Fig. 2).

We also thank other EIBA pioneers who have agreed to be interviewed to share with us information about the origins of EIBA, in particular the following: Peter Buckley, who has also expressed his engagement in this project since inception, at the

Rio de Janeiro-2015 Fellows meeting; Alain Chevalier, who participated in the first EIBA conference; the late Reijo Luostarinen, who handled us personal information about his EIBA proposals (at this juncture, we also enthusiastically thank Kirsti and Jukka-Pekka Luostarinen for going through Reijo's EIBA archives and sending us the most relevant information); Gerry Van Dyck, who served as Executive Secretary of EIBA for about 20 years, kindly agreed to come to Brussels for a long interview; and Liliane van Hoof, who was one of the few women in EIBA in the late 1970s. Filip De Beule shared with us the enormous collection of photos taken by Danny Van Den Bulcke, most of which are now available on the EIBA History website, and accompanied us to interview Sylvain Plasschaert. We also thank other EIBAians from different generations, who have kindly responded our questions and demands for information: Anze Burger, Jorge Carneiro, Davide Castellani, Juán Durán, Jean-François Hennart, the late Seev Hirsch, Lars Håkansson, the late Jorma Larimo, Ana Teresa Tavares-Lehman, Sarianna Lundan, Klaus Macharzina, Bernard Marois, Krzysztof Obloj, Torben Pedersen, Lucia Piscitello, José Plà-Barber, Jonas Puck, Francesca Sanna-Randaccio, Grazia Santangelo, Örjan Sölvell, Marjan Svetlicic and Jan-Erik Vahlne. We thank Nuno Crespo for kindly introducing in the survey addressed to the EIBA Lisbon-2023 participants, a question to indicate the first EIBA conference in which they participated. Besides Lars-Gunnar Mattson, Peter Buckley, Pervez Ghauri and Mats Forsgren also supported us in the identification of those depicted in the Uppsala-1978 photo. Our deep gratitude goes to the colleagues who have written the text boxes about outstanding figures and events/awards of EIBA (see https://history.eiba.org/people-and-events-that-have-marked-the-history-of-eiba/): Filip De Beule and Alain Verbeke (Danny Van Den Bulcke); Rebecca Piekkari, Denice Welch, the late Lawrence Welch and Catherine Welch (Reijo Luostarinen); Francesca Sanna-Randaccio (Danny Van Den Bulcke Best Paper Prize); Jeremy Clegg (Danny Van Den Bulcke Doctoral Tutorial); Lars Håkanson, Örjan Sölvell and Udo Zander (Gunnar Hedlund Award); Andreja Jaklič (EIBA and Eastern Europe); and Jonas Puck; and Stefano Elia (remembrances of their first EIBA conferences). We also thank all those who have participated at the successive EIBA History Panels, since 2015, sharing with us relevant information about their EIBA experiences. We have strived to do justice to recognise all the persons who have played a scientific and/or institutional role, but it is entirely possible that some individuals have not been mentioned by name, and if this is the case, we apologise.

Other people, outside the EIBA umbrella, have also contributed with information and ideas, namely with regard to the contextual sections; that is, especially the case of Mário Romão and Vítor Martins.

Excellent research and editorial assistance were provided by Dinis Macedo, Gonçalo Martins and Pedro Simões. A word of gratitude goes also to João Pedro Magalhães for his committed research assistance over what has been a long period for this research.

The last word of recognition goes to our families and friends who have been deprived of our company due to our long-term commitment to the EIBA History project.

CHAPTER 1

THE EMERGENCE OF THE INTERNATIONAL BUSINESS SCHOLARLY COMMUNITY IN EUROPE AND BEYOND

1.1. THE ANTECEDENTS OF THE SCHOLARLY COMMUNITY, IN THE 1950s

The international business (IB) scholarly community today is global in nature, but this was not always the case. The IB field has developed considerably since its early beginnings in the late 1950s to the early 1970s, and this book tells the tale of that development. In doing so we focus in particular on the emergence and then growth to maturity of the European International Business Academy (EIBA), an organisation that has become genuinely pan-European, and nowadays also includes the participation of IB scholars from many other countries around the world. The origins of the IB field of scholarship can be traced to some selected parts of Europe and North America, and so while focusing on EIBA we will refer occasionally as well to a companion association, the Academy of International Business (AIB), which began as a US-based organisation, but today positions itself as a global academic grouping, with chapters around the world. So our story begins in Europe and North America, and we must begin by making some reference to the parallel yet independent emergence of a scholarly community on each side of the Atlantic, which eventually became represented through EIBA and the AIB. Later in the book, we will return at times to what has been a shifting relationship between EIBA and the AIB.

The IB scholarly field originated through independent seminal contributions on either side of the Atlantic. The new ways of thinking were stimulated by a wave of transatlantic investment that began in the 1950s, in the aftermath of the

The History of EIBA: A Tale of The Co-Evolution Between International Business
Issues and a Scholarly Community, 1–6
Copyright © 2025 by Vítor Corado Simões, John Cantwell and Philippe Gugler
Published under exclusive licence by Emerald Publishing Limited
doi:10.1108/978-1-83608-664-220241002

Second World War, and in the context of what had become a close relationship between Western Europe and the US after the war. These academic contributions became the foundational cornerstone for the identification of IB as a field of study in its own right, rather than as just a specialist branch of the disciplines of economics, finance or management. As a steadily expanding group of scholars came to identify themselves and their work with the IB field as such, and not only with whatever had been their mother discipline, this new scholarly identity became institutionalised in the formation and growth of the academic associations, EIBA in Europe and the AIB in North America.

It is only a slight exaggeration to say that the IB scholarly field emerged as a distinctive research area through the doctoral work of two brilliant young intellectuals in the mid- to late-1950s, namely John Dunning in Europe and Stephen Hymer (a Canadian) in North America. John Dunning was then a recently appointed lecturer at the University of Southampton on the South coast of England (in those days in the UK it was quite common to complete a PhD after having obtained one's first academic appointment), while Stephen Hymer was a student of Charles Kindleberger at MIT. Both Dunning and Hymer were interested in examining the nature of the US foreign direct investment (FDI) that had begun to grow rapidly in Western Europe. This expansion of FDI, and the later wave of European FDI in the US which followed in response, was mainly of a local market-seeking character. This fast-growing form of FDI contrasted with the predominantly natural resource-seeking type that had run mainly from developed to less developed countries, and which had accounted for the largest share of worldwide FDI before 1945 (see Dunning, 1983a). The shifting landscape for FDI raised new questions, especially with respect to its driving forces, and its likely impact on industry in the host location, which Dunning and Hymer were inspired to address.

John Dunning's research was supported by funding from the Marshall Plan, arranged through the US embassy in the UK, in the light of questions about how US inward FDI might affect the industry in the UK (see Dunning, 2008). Dunning found compelling evidence that US FDI in the UK tended to raise productivity in local industries, and he suggested that this was attributable to effective international technology transfer between US and UK plants, and the role of local knowledge spill-overs and competition effects (Dunning, 1958). Instead, Stephen Hymer was to provide a somewhat more sceptical account of the likely local impacts of inward FDI, paying more attention to the possibilities of expanded forms of collusion and market power by large, dominant corporations. With particular reference to the question of why US firms set up foreign facilities, especially in Europe, Hymer was the first to draw a clear analytical distinction between FDI, in which multinational corporations exercise operational control over subsidiaries, and foreign portfolio investment (FPI), in which arms' length investors held only a financial interest (Hymer, 1976/1960). Previously, FDI and FPI had been more simplistically grouped together in generic theories of foreign investment as a whole, which is why IB had been considered as essentially just a subdomain of international finance or international economics. These new lines of thinking now set IB apart as a separate, legitimate field of study in its own right.

Both Dunning and Hymer stressed the vital nature of what might now be called by economists micro–macro relationships in an IB system, between firms, industries (and their populations of firms and other supporting actors in a host location), and home and host countries and their respective sets of national institutions. Understanding how IB interacts with domestic actors, and with national institutions, both in the home and host locational environments, became critical for the new subject area. Such interactions below the surface between the underlying elements of the IB system get lost if one deals solely with aggregates of foreign investment at the country level, or with industries regardless of differences in the origins and international linkages of firms.

Stemming from this early work, and moving through the 1960s through to the early 1970s, a gradually but steadily increasing number of scholars came to identify with this nascent IB field. While the AIB in the US was formed very early in 1958, being motivated more by teaching and education in IB (it was originally created as the Association for Education in IB, or AEIB), by 1974 the emergence of EIBA was more inspired from the outset essentially by the newly emergent IB scholarly research community. Unsurprisingly, in those early days for the community, the EIBA grouping brought together a somewhat disparate set of avenues for research into IB, each of which had its own focus of attention. These new research trajectories were driven not just by specificities associated with the national origins of scholars (which were indeed more distinct at the time), but also by the disciplinary foundations of the line of inquiry. Scholars grounded in economics (as Dunning and Hymer had been), finance, management, marketing, business history, international relations and economic geography among others, all had some role to play in building the IB field in the early days.

1.2. THE EMERGENCE OF IB RESEARCH IN EUROPE AND NORTH AMERICA, FROM 1960 TO 1974

During the 1960s and early 1970s, both Dunning and Hymer spent significant periods on the opposite side of the Atlantic, encouraged by the gradual emergence of a transatlantic scholarly IB community. John Dunning followed his work on US FDI in the UK with a project on British FDI in the US (Dunning, 2008), and in 1964 he moved from Southampton to the University of Reading, where he established a new Department of Economics, and he built a flourishing IB group within the department. In the 1980s he moved across the Atlantic to Rutgers University, and so he had a career which like his own research interests spanned Europe and North America. From the 1970s onwards, he came to be involved continuously throughout his life in leadership roles in both EIBA and the AIB, and he enjoyed a well-deserved recognition as one of the founding fathers of the IB research field.

After MIT, Stephen Hymer taught at Yale and then at the New School for Social Research in New York. He was a research visitor at Cambridge in the UK in 1968, and being originally from Montreal, while he was in Europe that year he worked on an article on IB that appeared in a French journal (Hymer, 1968).

Some years later, that article came to be seen as anticipating subsequent developments in IB theory (Horaguchi & Toyne, 1990). Sadly, we lost one of the brightest lights of our IB field when he died far too young in a car accident in a snowstorm in upstate New York in early 1974, just a few months before EIBA was founded. Both Dunning and Hymer were representative of a wider IB field in this early era, in which many of the foundational ideas were published in books (e.g. Dunning, 1970; Hymer, 1972) rather than in journals, as they would be most often nowadays – books that were at least as likely to be published in Europe as they were in the US, in this field.

In the aftermath of the seminal contributions to IB thought of Dunning and Hymer, some selected pockets of scholarly interest and expertise in IB began to spring up in various parts of Europe and North America. Indeed, as individual scholars moved, some after completing their doctorates on an IB topic, linkages gradually began to be formed between some of these places, and thus a recognisable research community emerged. Such centres of IB scholarship became critical to the formation of EIBA in Europe, and the expansion of the AIB in North America. In the UK, apart from Dunning's IB group at Reading, some very important and influential research on IB and economic development from the 1960s onwards was conducted by Sanjaya Lall at Oxford and by Vudayagi Balasubramanyam (Balu, for short) at Lancaster. Peter Buckley was a doctoral student of Balu in Lancaster who moved to Reading, and after leaving there he established new centres of IB scholarship in Bradford and later Leeds. Another critical figure from the early days was John Stopford, who had returned to the UK from his doctoral studies as part of the Multinational Enterprise project group at Harvard, initially moving to Manchester, but from 1971 taking up a new chair at the London Business School (LBS).

An IB scholarly tradition also emerged early in Scandinavia. Among those involved were Jan Johanson in Uppsala, who was working on firm internationalisation processes from an international marketing perspective. He was joined by Jan-Erik Vahlne, who did his doctoral work in Uppsala in the early 1970s, before moving to Stockholm. Having studied in Munich, with a background in international accounting, Klaus Macharzina had been a faculty colleague of Balu in Lancaster in the early 1970s, before he returned to a professorship in Germany at the University of Hohenheim. Also in Germany, Hans-Günther Meissner did his doctoral work in Cologne on the anthropological foundations of international economic transactional relationships, before becoming a Professor of International Marketing in Dortmund in 1973. In Belgium, Sylvain Plasschaert, a professor at the University of Antwerp from 1971, was working on the relationship between tax regimes and multinational firms, especially in economic development contexts.

Meanwhile, in some of the centres for IB scholarship that had emerged around this time in the US, various younger scholars were developing IB research interests that led them to academic careers in which they would come to have a substantial impact on the IB field in Europe. This was especially true of the Multinational Enterprise project group under Ray Vernon at the Harvard Business School in the 1960s and early 1970s. We have already mentioned John Stopford of LBS, who wrote a pioneering book with Harvard IB Professor Louis Wells (Stopford & Wells, 1972) on international strategic management. Wells was one of a number at

Harvard who developed the fundamental principles of the product cycle model, which adapted the received theories of international trade and investment in light of the contributions of Dunning and Hymer to offer a better understanding of the growth of US FDI in Europe in the late 1960s, and to which a critical contribution was made by the doctoral research of a young Seev Hirsch (Hirsch, 1967). After returning to Israel following his PhD, Hirsch visited the IB group in Reading in the 1970s, and he became a very active member of the IB community in Europe. Another key figure among the Harvard IB doctoral group during this period was José de la Torre, who came to INSEAD in France in 1975, and who played a leading role during the early years of EIBA.

Apart from the activities of Hymer himself, a number of associations also began to arise between the IB scholarly community in New York and Europe. Jean Boddewyn came to the US from Belgium as a Fulbright scholar in the 1950s, and he began his post-doctoral academic career at NYU in 1964, and then in CUNY from 1973, as a professor of International Marketing, while retaining some links with Europe. Meanwhile, Ingo Walter became a professor of International Finance at NYU from 1970, and he later also held positions at INSEAD, Berlin, Mannheim, Zurich, Basel, and IESE in Barcelona, among others. Another scholar who studied International Finance in the US in the early 1970s was Juán Durán, who was a fellow graduate student of Attila Yaprak (who later served as the AIB Executive Secretary) in Indiana University. Juán Durán returned to an academic position at the Autonomous University of Madrid in Spain, and he was later to become a key figure in EIBA.

1.3. THE STRUCTURE OF THE BOOK

Having now set the scene of a new, young IB scholarly community in the early 1970s, it was natural that members of this community began to consider some more formal, institutional forum within which to meet and exchange ideas more regularly and to promote the interests of the field. This became the basis for the formation of EIBA in 1974. In this book, we will look in more depth at the emergence, and the subsequent evolution and growth of EIBA and the IB field in the ensuing 50 years (as of the time of writing). During this time the real world of IB has itself changed enormously, just as has scholarship about IB. Therefore, our approach is to relate the three facets of the changing character of IB in the real world, the state of IB scholarship in each period and the growth of the IB scholarly community in Europe as represented by EIBA. Overall, we will examine how these three elements (the IB context and actors, the scholarly analysis of IB and the professional community of researchers in Europe and beyond) have co-evolved over time.

In this book we follow a chronological approach to the co-evolution of these inter-related vectors: the changes in IB issues over time, the profile of key IB research in each period and the growth of an epistemic community in IB studies. So, in each of Chapters 2 through 8, we examine the three dimensions of our story and the connections between them. We suggest that this co-evolutionary process has had seven distinct phases or stages, which we consider in turn.

The next chapter, Chapter 2, deals with the first phase, the creation of EIBA in 1974–1975. The second phase, considered in Chapter 3, encompasses the second half of the 1970s, when EIBA was still finding its feet. Moving into the 1980s, Chapter 4 reviews a more turbulent third phase. While the first half of the 1980s witnessed an increase in EIBA membership, this was followed by a more troubled period, between 1985 and 1988, when membership declined and the survival of the organisation appeared to be at risk. We argue in Chapter 5 that the turning point for the fourth stage of EIBA development came in 1989 with the conference in Helsinki organised by Reijo Luostarinen, after which EIBA was stabilised and better anchored, and managed to successfully pursue geographic expansion to Southern and Eastern Europe. The fifth stage, addressed in Chapter 6, may be characterised as the maturing of EIBA into adulthood and the building of a stronger institutional foundation. This began with the EIBA conference in Scandinavia (Stockholm, 1996) and ended in Southern Europe (Athens, 2002), a phase that saw the creation of the EIBA Fellows in 2001, and an increase in the diversity of the scholarly community and its leadership. These trends were further consolidated during the sixth phase, discussed in Chapter 7, during which the change of the statutes in 2004 transformed EIBA governance. This sixth phase, from 2003 to 2012, witnessed the transition of EIBA into a mature organisation and was a period that also saw the last conference attended by John Dunning (Catania, 2007). In Chapter 8 we reach a seventh phase, from 2013 onwards, by which time many of the 'founding fathers' had left us, but a new generation took the helm of the academy, keeping its spirit and making it stronger and more vibrant. The book concludes in Chapter 9 with a brief overall assessment of the evolution of EIBA and the prospects and challenges for IB research in the future.

CHAPTER 2

THE ESTABLISHMENT OF EIBA (1973–1975)[1]

This chapter covers the period between 1973 and 1975. It addresses the initiatives that led to the establishment of EIBA, in 1973 and 1974, and the first EIBA conference, held in Jouy-en-Josas (France), in 1975. The intention is to show the reader how EIBA was born, while highlighting those who have championed the establishment of the new organisation. This chapter will also provide a perspective of the wider context, including the international environment and especially the main issues driving IB thinking at that time.

2.1. THE INITIATIVES LEADING TO THE CREATION OF EIBA: THE ROLE OF EIASM, EFMD AND CESA

We need hardly remind you that last December at Jouy-en-Josas a new European professional association was formed dedicated to research and education in international business. These were the introductory words of the message sent by Jim Leontiades (Manchester Business School, UK), Michel Ghertman (Centre d'Enseignement Supérieur des Affaires – CESA, France) and Lars-Gunnar Mattsson (University of Uppsala, Sweden) to a set of colleagues announcing the first annual Conference of EIBA, held in December 1975. It was the beginning of a long path, though it was not really the starting point. In fact, the first EIBA conference was preceded by two meetings aimed at putting together the community of scholars working in the IB field in Europe.

In December 1973 and 1974, two conferences on 'Recent Research on the Multinational Corporation' were held at CESA, jointly by the European Institute for Advanced Studies in Management (EIASM) and CESA (Ghertman & Leontiades, 1978). Before those there had been informal contacts among IB scholars, including a trip made by Lars-Gunnar Mattsson to England to meet with Jim Leontiades

The History of EIBA: A Tale of The Co-Evolution Between International Business
Issues and a Scholarly Community, 7–14
Copyright © 2025 by Vítor Corado Simões, John Cantwell and Philippe Gugler
Published under exclusive licence by Emerald Publishing Limited
doi:10.1108/978-1-83608-664-220241003

and Michael Brooke, and at a conference in 1973 in Rennes, organised by Gilles-Yves Bertin (Mattsson, 2017). The purpose of these conferences was to create a 'communications network' of scholars and researchers in the IB field (Ghertman & Leontiades, 1978, p. v). This was expected to lead to IB research *on a European wide basis* (Leontiades, 2017). The creation of an association was envisaged as an instrument 'to further expand and institutionalise' such a network (Ghertman & Leontiades, 1978, p. v). Jim Leontiades and Michel Ghertman championed the initiative. The support provided by EIASM and the European Foundation for Management Development (EFMD) played a key role in this endeavour.

Michel Ghertman expressed his *gratefulness to EIASM and the Ford Foundation* [since] *they gave the money* and actively promoted the initiative (Ghertman, 2016) to develop management education in Europe, including IB education. EIASM provided the list of IB researchers and scholars to be invited to participate and financed the organisation of the conferences.

Established in 1971 with support from the Ford Foundation, EIASM was originally aimed at promoting post-graduate education in management, following the approach taken by American universities. According to Engwall, Pahlberg and Persson (2018, p. 1082), EIASM was 'originally intended to provide a US-type doctoral programme in management but instead became first a research institute with visiting faculty and doctoral students, and later a hub in a European network for research cooperation through professional organisations, workshops and doctoral seminars'. EFMD, the sister organisation to EIASM, was created in 1972, and originally its *motto* was 'acting as a catalyst to promote and enhance excellence in management development' in Europe (Wikipedia, 2018).

EIASM was successful in assembling a set of distinguished American and European management scholars. Many of the European faculty had received their doctoral degrees in the US and lectured in American universities. Several of the very early members of EIBA temporarily served on the EIASM faculty, including Anders Edström, James Leontiades and Lars-Gunnar Mattsson. Both EIASM and EFMD significantly contributed to the emergence of EIBA as well as other European disciplinary research organisations. Their support was essential for EIBA, not just in the early years but also in the 1980s and 1990s when the Association ran into successive deficits. We will come back to this issue in later chapters, but it is important to recognise here how EIASM companies played a key role in bearing EIBA deficits and, therefore, in keeping it alive (Van Dyck, 2017).

It is interesting to remark that the initiative taken by EIASM and CESA, which led to the creation of EIBA, took place at a time when public opinion in Europe and elsewhere was critical of the power that multinational companies (MNCs) were achieving in the international economic scene. In particular US firms were subject to increasing criticism.

2.2. THE CONTEXT

In 1973, the first enlargement of the European Economic Community (EEC) increased its membership from six to nine countries as a result of the accession of

Denmark, Ireland and the UK. This generated a surge in the enthusiasm for a more pan-European approach instead of keeping to traditional national perspectives.

However, the increase in oil prices and the dollar devaluation in 1974 led to an economic crisis in Western economies, which translated into a shrinkage in FDI flows (OECD, 1981). The criticism against MNCs was growing. In Continental Europe, Jean-Jacques Servan-Schreiber's book *Le Défi Americain*, first published in France in 1967 (Servan-Schreiber, 1967), was very influential. It argued that American firms were gaining increasing ground namely due to their advantages in management and technology. This was translated into market power, an issue that researchers such as Stephen Hymer, Sanjaya Lall and Paul Streeten had also been arguing in their writings (Hymer, 1970, 1972, 1976/1960; Lall & Streeten, 1977). The involvement of the firm *International Telephone & Telegraph Corporation (ITT)* in the process leading to the *coup d'état* which overthrew the democratically elected Salvador Allende in Chile further spurred the negative reaction towards MNCs. Multinationals were envisaged as a challenge for the nation-state, and many thought that their power should be curbed (Ordonneau, 1975; Vernon, 1971). This perception, together with the transformation of former colonies into independent countries, led to several United Nations decisions aimed at curbing the power of MNCs as well as the creation of the United Nations Centre on Transnational Corporations (UNCTC) in 1974. One of the first initiatives launched by UNCTC was aimed at the establishment of a Code of Conduct on Transnational Corporations. However, this never became a reality.

John Dunning (1982) labelled this period as the 'Confrontation stage'. He argued that (Dunning, 1982, p. 361):

> In the first half of the 1970s MNEs came under increasing scrutiny and attack. Not only were they criticised on the grounds of their unacceptable behaviour, and uneven contribution to economic development, but as an expression of a no longer acceptable international economic system; if the system could not be changed, inter alia because of the inadequate bargaining strength of developing countries, then, at least, some redress might be taken against one of its institutions viz. the MNE.

A change in MNC organisation and management also played a role in the process (Dunning, 1982). More centralised structures and decision-making processes emerged. After an initial period of internationalisation, MNCs became increasingly concerned with the establishment of coordination procedures to ensure consistency, economies of scale and standardised international procedures (Bartlett & Ghoshal, 1989). Multidivisional organisations developed and matrix structures emerged (Chandler, 1962, 1977; Stopford & Wells, 1972; Williamson, 1975). 'The trend towards the international standardisation of some products, and specialisation of processes and markets, placed an increasing premium on quality control, the continuity of output, the protection of proprietary rights, and transaction cost economising' (Dunning, 1982, p. 361). This enhanced national policymakers' suspicion about the declining concern of MNCs with their contribution towards host countries' economic and social welfare.

According to Dunning (1982, p. 362), 'the early 1970s were the 'high noon' of confrontation between several nation states and MNEs'. It is against this backdrop that EIBA has emerged. Of course, EIASM was aimed in part at diffusing the American managerial principles in Europe and European research on IB. However, the majority of the scholars involved in the 1973 and 1974 conferences intended *to develop 'a European way' of teaching* [and researching on] *international business* (Marois, 2018).

Drawing on the pioneering work of Dunning (1958), Hymer (1976/1960) and Vernon (1966), research on international production in the late 1960s and early 1970s followed four main strands (Dunning, 2001): the formalisation and testing of 'Hymer-type hypotheses' (Dunning, 2001, p. 38), in which Caves (1971, 1974) played an important role; the extension of Vernon's US approach to encompass other countries (Franko, 1976; Stopford, 1974, 1976); the strategic behaviour of firms, including the work by Knickerbocker (1973) and Graham (1978); and financial issues, including multi-currency effects (Aliber, 1971) and risk diversification (Rugman, 1975, 1979). Other authors in the economics field stressed the political and economic role of MNCs in shaping developing countries' policies (Santos, 1970; Sunkel, 1972; de la Torre, 1981). Some of the research contributions in these times, especially those by John Dunning, followed what Nelson (1995, 2005) called 'appreciative theorising'; instead of drawing on formal models, the analysis was based on conceptual, historically grounded reasoning. They were designed to better address the complexity of the IB system as a whole.

Managerial issues also started to be addressed, especially those dealing with organisational structures (Stopford & Wells, 1972), and internationalisation processes (Aharoni, 1966), leading to the Uppsala model (Johanson & Vahlne, 1977). The purpose was to learn more about how firms were managed and to understand processes, namely with regard to decision-making, and the increase in foreign market commitments (Ghertman, 1978; Johanson & Vahlne, 1977, 1978). The fact that the majority of the participants in the early conferences came from the management field (29 out of the 45 participants in the 1975 EIBA conference) is a possible explanation for the approach taken. Even those with an economics background, while recognising the existence of market power and calling the attention to political issues, were increasingly concerned with explaining why MNCs exist (Buckley & Casson, 1976, 1978; Dunning, 1977, 1981), and so they were moving to a focus on the firm as such, rather than the wider IB system.

In the early 1970s, IB research in Europe emanated mainly from three main clusters. One was Reading, where John Dunning played a key role as an intellectual leader of this newly emergent field; he was able to attract to Europe some of the leading scholars from the US, such as Vernon and Hymer. The second was Scandinavia, especially the research team in Uppsala, including Jan Johanson, Lars-Gunnar Mattsson, Mats Forsgren, Jan-Erik Vahlne, Erik Hörnell, and Finn Wiedersheim-Paul (Mattsson, 2009). The Paris-Brussels area corresponded to the third cluster, encompassing the work carried out by Michel Ghertman at CESA, by Edith Penrose, José de la Torre and Yves Doz at INSEAD and by the EIASM faculty, both with a significant share of American colleagues.

Be that as it may, though being aware of the *esprit du temps* with regard to MNCs, the early EIBA members focused much more on analysing and understanding behaviours and processes than on taking sides in the political debates of the day. Probably this is the reason why some of their contributions have become classics in the IB field, still being referenced today (for instance, Buckley & Casson, 1976; Dunning, 1977; Edström & Galbraith, 1977; Johanson & Vahlne, 1977; Stopford & Wells, 1972).

2.3. THE BIRTH OF EIBA

2.3.1. The Decision to Create EIBA

The two pre-EIBA conferences were both held at Jouy-en-Josas, near Paris, where the CESA headquarters were located. The number of participants was small by today's standards: around 20 in 1973, and 25 in 1974 (Marois, 2018). It was in the second, in 1974, that the decision was taken to launch EIBA. The process was not without controversy, however. When the issue was raised, two currents emerged. One, led by the Nordic participants, argued in favour of having an independent pan-European organisation, separate from the AIB, founded in the US in 1959. Another, led by the British, namely Michael Z. Brooke, and Jean-Jacques Boddewyn (a long-term AIB member) was in favour of creating a Western European AIB chapter, similar to AIB UK. Following a debate between the proponents of each of these two options, it was decided to create an organisation independent of the AIB.

The next step was to elect the President of EIBA. While several names were voiced, the vote was for James Leontiades. Michel Ghertman and Lars-Gunnar Mattsson were elected as Vice-Presidents. With a view to structure the Association, it was then agreed that the first Vice-President would become President, being in charge of organising the next conference. By that time, like today, having a succession of annual conferences was considered essential to hold the organisation together, to attract new members and to achieve a pan-European status.

AIB was envisaged as providing a role model: it was more developed and already well-established. But there was simultaneously a recognition of the advantages of having a specific, independent, European approach to IB research and education. While following a European way, links with the AIB have been established, mainly through those scholars who were members of both organisations. This kind of co-opetition has shaped the relationships between EIBA and AIB, with cooperation prevailing on most occasions (including the launching of joint conferences in 1981 and 1986) in spite of some tensions at specific moments, such as in 2004. While AIB continues to be much bigger, they may be regarded as sister organisations (Engwall et al., 2018).

2.3.2. The 1974 EIBA Statutes

EIBA was legally established on 1st December 1974. Its purpose was defined as being: 'to provide a professional society for faculty and practitioners with interests in International Business research and education' and a 'focal point of communication for its members residing in Europe or abroad'. While headquartered in Brussels, it was pointed out that EIBA had 'no citizenship requirements nor official language' to underline its pan-European nature. Membership might be individual or institutional, the membership fee being set in the statutes: 250 or 5,000 Belgian francs per year, respectively (that is, €6.20 or €124.00).

The main thrust of the Statutes was obviously to provide for the governance of the newly created Association, including the duties of the officers. The management of EIBA was assigned to an 'Executive Committee, which shall consist of one representative of each country, where the association has members, as well as the President, the two Vice-Presidents, the previous President and, *ex-officio*, the Director General of' EFMD (article V). A Steering Committee was also established, including the President, Vice-Presidents and the Executive Secretary, which 'will be responsible for the day-to-day affairs of the association' (article VII). The first members of Executive Committee were the following: President – James Leontiades; Vice-Presidents – Michel Ghertman and Lars-Gunnar Mattsson (see Fig. 1). National representatives (NRs) were the following: Cornelius Botter (Netherlands), Michael Z. Brooke (UK), Hans-Günther Meissner (Germany), Naoto Sasaki (Japan) and Jan-Erik Vahlne (Sweden); the EFMD representative was Jean-François Poncet.

It is interesting to mention the role given to the NRs. No minimum membership requirements were defined for a country to be represented on the Executive Committee. This may be envisaged as an expression of EIBA's intent to have a pan-European scope from its inception. However, this introduced a bias in favour of those countries with limited membership (even just one member as was the case of Japan), which were entitled to voting rights in the Executive Committee equivalent to countries with larger membership. This effect might have been, however, countervailed by the fact that, at least in the early days, the President and the Vice-Presidents came from countries with a significant number of members (UK, France and Sweden). Another curiosity is the absence of an NR from France.

Fig. 1. The Members of EIBA's Executive Committee (1974): Jim Leontiades, Michel Ghertman and Lars-Gunnar Mattsson. *Source*: Photos supplied by Michel Ghertman (middle) and the authors.

2.4. JOUY-EN-JOSAS, 1975: THE FIRST EIBA CONFERENCE

The call for papers issued in April 1975 by the President and the Vice-Presidents of EIBA invited interested scholars to send 'research papers or a one-page summary' to Michel Ghertman. In another call with more detailed information, it was stated that the conference will include a seminar on recent research on the international firm, aimed at identifying 'promising new fields of investigation as well as to give participants a more accurate idea of the state of research in Europe in their respective areas'.

The conference was held on 15th and 16th December 1975 at CESA. The programme extended for slightly more than one and a half days, combining plenary sessions and small group discussions, and closed with the EIBA annual membership meeting. The conference was attended by 45 people, coming from 11 countries, including Canada (3) and the US (2). Not surprisingly, France had the largest share (17), followed by Sweden (10). The other countries were scarcely represented: Belgium (3), UK (3), Germany (2), Spain (2), and the Netherlands, Norway and Switzerland (1 each). A striking feature is the dominance of men: only one female colleague (Monique Lejeune, who became a specialist in the marketing of services) is mentioned in the list of participants. The participants also included other names which became well-known in the IB field and/or Presidents of EIBA (such as José de la Torre, Anders Eckström, Jan Johanson, Pål Korsvold, Bernard Marois, Hans-Günter Meissner, Sylvain Plasschaert, Barto Roig, John Stopford and Jan-Erik Vahlne). Although not being in the list of participants, a reference is due to three colleagues (Peter Buckley, who attended one of the pre-EIBA conferences, Reijo Luostarinen and Klaus Macharzina) who have been involved in the process since the early days and became regular attendants of EIBA conferences. Klaus Macharzina was recently awarded an EIBA Lifetime Achievement Award (EIBA LAA).

According to the programme, 17 papers were presented; the large majority were in English, but a couple of them were in French. The main subjects addressed in those papers included strategy and organisational structure (3), international finance (2), internationalisation processes (2), international marketing (2) and international human resource management (2). Some papers presented became the basis for future books. Others were later published in high-calibre journals.

2.5. EIBA's PROFILE IN 1975

The story we have just told shows that by 1975 EIBA was still in its infancy, trying to become a magnet for IB research and education in Europe, while taking the AIB as a reference point. In retrospect, it may be said that the pre-EIBA initiatives were successful in building a group of IB researchers that have walked together for a long time. At a moment when IB as a field was in its infancy in Europe – only in Sweden were there the embryos of IB departments at the time (Marois, 2018; Mattsson, 2009) – EIBA played a key role in forging ahead and in contributing to the organisation of the scientific field in Europe (Engwall et al., 2018).

EIBA was confined in terms of geographical breadth and depth. As mentioned above a large number of countries were not covered by the newborn organisation, as is the case of Southern European (both representatives of Spain were from Barcelona) and small countries, such as Denmark or Ireland. Even in countries which were, so to say, represented in the initial conference, participation was very limited, namely from the UK, Germany, the Netherlands or Switzerland. To a large extent, there was a need to bring together the identities of EIBA and IB research in most countries and Europe. This was an issue to be addressed in the coming years.

NOTE

1. The authors thank José de la Torre and Teresa da Silva Lopes for comments on earlier versions of this chapter. The usual disclaimer applies.

CHAPTER 3

TEETHING TROUBLES: THE LATE 1970s (1976–1981)[1]

The six years following the first EIBA conference were focused on the stability and expansion of the newly founded organisation through the convening of annual conferences and the setting up of a newsletter to distribute information about EIBA's activities and foster membership networking. EIBA got off to a promising start, with a sustained increase in membership: from 85 in 1976[2] to 184 in 1978. However, this was followed by a decline to 149 in 1982.[3] The 1981 conference, organised together with AIB in Barcelona, was not a success for EIBA, and many members did not show up. This fact reflects the difficulties confronted by a very young, conference-based organisation. In the absence of stronger institutional instruments (such as a longer-term leadership and a journal), its fate became closely linked to the way in which successive conferences were organised, and the people they could attract and retain.

This chapter addresses these early times in the process of establishing EIBA as an organisation, from 1976 to 1981. It is structured in five parts. A broad picture of the context is provided in the first two parts. It starts with a perspective of the general political and business climate at the time. Then, it moves to a brief account of the main developments in the IB literature, highlighting some key research topics. The third part delivers a summary of the EIBA conferences held in this period. The next section provides an account of the main initiatives taken on the organisational front as well as of the membership pattern and evolution. The chapter closes with a summary of the main developments of this period.

3.1. THE CONTEXT: ATTITUDES TOWARDS FDI

The international investment climate in the second half of the 1970s was not much different from the one presented earlier: the confrontation between nation-states,

The History of EIBA: A Tale of The Co-Evolution Between International Business
Issues and a Scholarly Community, 15–28
Copyright © 2025 by Vítor Corado Simões, John Cantwell and Philippe Gugler
Published under exclusive licence by Emerald Publishing Limited
doi:10.1108/978-1-83608-664-220241004

especially developing countries, and MNCs was still prevalent, though it had gradually been fading. Developing countries were arguing that the world economic order was uneven, and that their resources were appropriated by foreign players, leading to dependency (Cardoso, 1980; Ernst, 1980; Katz, 1976; Sunkel, 1981; Wionczek, 1981). Control over international resource allocation became a key consideration (Dunning, 1979). MNCs were key players in this context, often exploiting monopolistic or oligopolistic positions, so that a need was felt to regulate their activities. The launch of the negotiations towards UN Codes of Conduct on Transnational Corporations and on Technology Transfer was an expression of the intent to establish a new world economic order (Rubin, 1995; Sagafi-Nejad & Dunning, 2008; UNCTAD, 1977). The UNCTC published in 1978 *Transnational Corporations in World Development: A re-examination* (UNCTC, 1978). Although more balanced than the work published by other UN agencies at the time, this report was still very critical about the contribution of MNCs towards economic development. It argued that the control of resources, including technology, the use (and abuse) of market power and the 'conversion' of local business elites were elements of the tool-kit of MNCs to increasingly dominate the international economy. As Perlmutter and Sagafi-Nejad (1981) put it, with regard to the technology transfer regulation, there was a 'muffled quadrilogue', involving MNCs, local firms, developing and developed countries.

Import substituting policies were prevalent in the larger developing countries, including India and Brazil. In India, following the Foreign Exchange Regulation Act of 1973, which forced the conversion of foreign subsidiaries' equity into minority holdings, the Industrial Policy Resolution of 1977 established industries in which foreign participation was not allowed. In Brazil, the import substitution policy was still dominant, though in the second half of the 1970s, a new policy initiative promoting the establishment of joint ventures between foreign investors and private and public Brazilian firms was launched (Motta Veiga, 2004). In the other Latin American countries, with the exception of Chile, strict controls on FDI were the rule. The instruments used to deal with foreign investors became increasingly sophisticated, especially in Latin America and East Asia (Dunning, 1982). Even in Southern Europe, the climate was not easy. In Greece, a transfer pricing control system was established; in Portugal, the 1977 foreign investment law was marked by a position of distrust towards foreign companies; this law was, however, replaced by a less restrictive one in 1978. Meanwhile, in Eastern Europe, while in the forefront of the Cold War, cooperative business developments were still taking place behind the scenes, labelled by Charles Levinson (1977) as *vodka-cola*.

By the turn of the decade, the recognition of the limited achievements in 'unbundling the package of resources offered by MNEs' (Dunning, 1982, p. 363) together with the growth of the East Asian economies that were more involved in international trade and investment flows, gradually led to a change in the attitude towards FDI. This was increasingly perceived to have a potentially positive contribution towards host country development through their effects in the fields of employment, technology acquisition and exports. As suggested by Kojima (1978), FDI might play a tutorial role in promoting the growth and international competitiveness of local business initiatives. Therefore, by the early 1980s, the confrontational tone was giving rise to what Dunning (1982, p. 363) called a 'reconciliation phase', in which 'the focus of bargaining has moved to promoting a more harmonious and mutually beneficial relationship between the parties'.

3.2. THE CONTEXT: IB LITERATURE

The academic production in the years under review (1976–1981) was paramount in shaping IB theory for decades to come. In fact, this period witnessed the emergence of four key perspectives in the IB field: internalisation theory; the eclectic (OLI) paradigm; the Uppsala model; and Hofstede's analysis of culture dimensions.

The *Future of the Multinational Enterprise*, co-authored by Peter Buckley and Mark Casson (Buckley & Casson, 1976), launched internalisation theory, although there had been antecedents in McManus (1972). Internalisation is aimed at explaining why companies replace (internalise) markets, across national boundaries. As Buckley and Casson (2003) explain, their thrust was two-fold: to challenge the conventional economic wisdom at the time, and to contribute to the political debate about MNCs' behaviour.

Two further voices in favour of internalisation, though with some differences from Buckley and Casson (1976), were Jean-François Hennart and Alan Rugman. In his doctoral thesis, Hennart (1977, published in 1982) draws on Coase (1937) and especially on McManus (1972) to argue that markets enable decentralised adaptation through prices while firms follow managerial directives 'to coordinate and constrain the behaviour of resource owners' (Hennart, 1977, p. 93). Alan Rugman, who had been invited by Dunning to spend a sabbatical in Reading, published *Inside the Multinationals*, a book that brought together his work on internalisation (Rugman, 1981). There, internalisation was defined as 'the process of making a market within a firm' (Rugman, 1981, p. 28).

An interesting feature of this pioneering literature on internalisation is that the main contributions were published in books. This shows how the format of IB research has changed over the years. In the 1970s there were expansive topic areas waiting to be explored while supporting extant literature was scarce. As Buckley and Casson (2003, p. 220) put it:

> Books are influential because the author has a chance to expand on his or her ideas. There is enough space to explain new concepts and put them through their paces. The space constraints imposed by journal publication usually condemn you to start where other writers have left off, rather than strike out on a path of your own.

Cognizant of the research by Peter Buckley and Mark Casson, both associated with Reading at the time, John H. Dunning combined internalisation theory with his own research on the determinants of international production (Dunning, 1973) to frame the Ownership Location Internalisation (OLI) paradigm, hereinafter the eclectic paradigm. The first presentation of the paradigm, initially called a theory, was made in 1976 at a Nobel Symposium in Stockholm, and published in 1977 (Dunning, 1977). Further work was published in the period under analysis to refine or extend several aspects of the paradigm (Dunning, 1979, 1980, 1981). The main tenets of the paradigm are well known. Suffice to recall here that, in the initial formulation, the eclectic paradigm argued that the determinants of MNC activity rely on the juxtaposition of three elements (Dunning, 1977): O advantages *vis-à-vis* firms of other nationalities in serving particular markets; internalisation advantages (I), meaning that it is more beneficial to use such advantages (or their output) than to sell or lease them to foreign firms; and the utilisation of the advantages provided by factor inputs, including natural resources, and other favourable local conditions in foreign host countries (L advantages).

The third key perspective is the so-called Uppsala model, presented by Jan Johanson and Jan-Erik Vahlne (Johanson & Vahlne, 1977). Based on earlier empirical research on the longitudinal internationalisation process of Swedish companies and drawing on behavioural approaches (by those such as Aharoni, or Cyert and March), the authors developed a model of the internationalisation process. As mentioned in the title of the article, the model depicted a process 'of knowledge development and increasing foreign market commitment' (Johanson & Vahlne, 1977). The acquisition of experiential knowledge from business activities in foreign markets was placed at the centre of the model. This process of learning was translated into an incremental approach with two dimensions. The first is the development of the establishment chain. The second corresponds to a gradual process of moving from psychically closer countries to more distant ones.

Geert Hofstede's first book on culture dimensions, entitled *Cultures Consequences: International Differences in Work-Related Attitudes*, was published in 1980 (Hofstede, 1980). His initial four dimensions model was a result of a factor analysis applied to the results of a worldwide survey of IBM's employees' values, carried out between 1967 and 1973. The national cultural dimensions were: individualism versus collectivism; uncertainty avoidance; power distance (that is, the strength of social hierarchy); and masculinity versus femininity. Though Hofstede's contribution has withstood several criticisms and has been challenged by alternative approaches (see for instance the JIBS special issue on Hofstede and GLOBE in cross-cultural research, published in 2010), it has had a strong influence in IB studies.

Besides these seminal and long-lasting contributions, other research streams were salient during this period. In the economics field, the relationships between trade and investment (Hirsch, 1976), technology trade and international investment (Teece, 1976, 1977, 1981a) and cross-investment flows (Graham, 1978). In the management area, the following deserve a reference: the foreign investment decision process (Ghertman, 1981; Hedlund, 1980); other Nordic research on internationalisation processes (Luostarinen, 1979); licencing (Contractor, 1981; Killing, 1980; Teece, 1981b); human resource management (Edström & Galbraith, 1977[4]); and MNC strategy and organisation (Chandler, 1977; Stopford & Haberich, 1976). Having in mind the characteristics of the international investment climate in this period, it comes as no surprise to see the publication of a host of research addressing the issue of MNCs versus host countries from different perspectives, including Baranson (1978), Cardoso (1980), Doz and Prahalad (1980), Emmanuel (1981), Ernst (1980), Kaplinski (1976), Katz (1976), Mytelka (1978) and Stewart (1979).

It is interesting to point out that all the authors associated with the four key perspectives mentioned above have participated in EIBA conferences between 1973 and 1981, with the exception of Mark Casson and Jean-François Hennart (whose first EIBA was in Rotterdam in 1984). Relevant contributions were presented at the early conferences: in 1976, Jan Johanson and Jan-Erik Vahlne, together with Lars-Gunnar Mattsson and Peter Sandén, delivered 'The role of knowledge in the Internationalization of Business'; 1977 corresponded to John Dunning's first EIBA conference, with an address on 'Recent developments in research on MNEs: An Economist's Viewpoint', while Peter Buckley presented the first findings of his research with G. D. Newbould and Jane Thurwell on the foreign direct investment behaviour of smaller UK firms; Alan Rugman and Geert Hofstede have both attended the EIBA conference in 1980 in Antwerp, presenting papers on 'The Multinational Enterprise, Internationalization and the Transfer of Technology to Canada' and 'In praise of ethnocentrism', respectively. This shows how EIBA conferences have been able to attract, from the early days, the main European (and sometimes non-European) authors in the IB field.

3.3. EIBA: THE CONFERENCES

In the period under analysis, EIBA conferences were held in Brussels (1976), Uppsala (1977), Dortmund (1978), London (1979), Antwerp (1980) and Barcelona (1981). A longitudinal perspective on the evolution of EIBA conferences is provided below.

EIBA was a conference-based organisation. Annual conferences were the 'heart' of EIBA. They were aimed at providing an environment in which members could socialise and exchange ideas about IB issues. As pointed out by Jim Leontiades and Michel Ghertman, the purpose was to develop a pan-European forum to promote the development of IB research and teaching in Europe. After the initial conference in 1975, at Jouy-en-Josas, the second EIBA conference was held on 16 and 17 December 1976 at the EIASM premises in Brussels. The President of the Association was Michel Ghertman, and the Programme Chair was Anders Edström, who was a member of EIASM's faculty at the time. The announcement of the Conference recalled that EIBA was created 'to provide a professional society for faculty and practitioners with interests in international business-research-and-education'.

The Brussels-1976 Conference was attended by 48 people, from 14 countries. France held the largest group (13 people) followed by Germany (6), Sweden and the UK (both with 5). Looking at the lists of participants in the first two EIBA conferences it becomes clear that a core group of attendants, going beyond the members of the EIBA Executive Committee, was taking shape: 19 members have attended both the 1975 and 1976 conferences.

The 1977 conference was held in Uppsala, organised by Lars-Gunnar Mattsson (University of Uppsala), who had been involved since the beginning in the process of EIBA creation, and was one of the Vice-Presidents of EIBA.

The conference was integrated in the commemorations of the 500th Anniversary of the University of Uppsala. The number of attendants reached a record: 85, coming from 16 countries. Not surprisingly, Sweden accounted for about half of the participants. As mentioned in the last section, this was the first EIBA conference attended by John Dunning, who addressed the following question, is there room for further research on the multinational enterprise? The answer was positive, and avenues were suggested on this regard. With the exception of John Cantwell, the other three members of the original EIBA Fellows 'founding fathers': Reijo Luostarinen and Seev Hirsch, as well as John Dunning, were EIBA debutants in Uppsala. Unfortunately, of these only John Dunning received a well-deserved EIBA LAA. Uppsala was also the first EIBA conference for Mats Forsgren, who became an EIBA Fellow, and Yves Doz, one of the most influential IB scholars. An important remembrance of this conference is the famous photo featuring the participants, with Lars-Gunnar and John Dunning in the first row (see Fig. 2).

The Conference was very well organised. Although there was no formal selection of papers, only papers in English were accepted. It was the first time that a common format and cover was given to most of the papers presented. A volume with the Conference proceedings was later edited by Lars-Gunnar Mattsson and Finn Wiedersheim-Paul (Mattsson & Wiedersheim-Paul, 1979).

From Sweden, EIBA moved to Germany. The 1978 conference took place in Dortmund and was chaired by Hans-Günther Meissner (University of Dortmund), another EIBA pioneer. The conference theme was 'Big and small enterprises in the international competitive environment'. The number of participants declined to 57, from 11 countries. The smaller attendance may be due to two reasons: the lower participation by the local research community in comparison to the previous conference (22 German-based participants in Dortmund as against 44 Swedish-based in Uppsala); and the limited attractiveness of the host city. Leaving local participants aside, the decline is less sharp: from 44 to 35. Interestingly, this was the first EIBA conference attended by Danny Van Den Bulcke, the future 'Mr. EIBA'. It also marked the EIBA debut of two very influential Scottish IB scholars: Neil Hood, who organised EIBA 1985 in Glasgow, and Stephen Young.

In 1979, EIBA crossed the Channel for the first time. The fifth conference was held in London, under the chairmanship of John Stopford (London Graduate School of Business Studies). This was envisaged as an important move to attract further members from the UK, conveying the idea that joint membership of both AIB UK[5] (which had existed since 1973) and EIBA was compatible and desirable. With hindsight, this was confirmed by the fact that two presidents of AIB UK (Fred Burton and Peter Buckley) have also been at the helm of EIBA. Attendance increased, reaching 72 people from 15 countries. However, contrary to Uppsala or Dortmund, the largest share did not come from the home country (12 participants only) but rather from Sweden (16). Nonetheless, EIBA London was a successful conference, reaching the second-highest attendance of the conferences in the 1976–1981 time-window. It was the first EIBA conference for Ian Jones, who organised EIBA London 1986, and for Pat Joynt, who was for many years Norway's NR.

Fig. 2. Participants at EIBA Uppsala (1977). *Note:* First row: Tom Huston, Dick Ramström, John H. Dunning, Lars-Gunnar Mattsson and Kia Walner. Other people featured include the following: Gerry van Dyck, Sylvain Plasschaert, Erik Hornell, Peter Sandén and Björn Wootz (all in the second row); Gianni Lorenzoni and Mats Forsgren, respectively, on the left and right of the third row; Deo Sharma, on the extreme right of the fourth row; Reijo Luostarinen, on the middle of the fifth row; Peter J. Buckley and Gunnar Hedlund, respectively, on the middle and the right of the sixth row; and Klaus Macharzina and Jan Johanson, respectively, on the left and right of the seventh row.

In 1980, EIBA moved to Belgium again. Chaired by Sylvain Plasschaert (University of Antwerp), the sixth conference took place in Antwerp, attracting 47 participants from 11 countries. Klaus Sahlgren, a Finnish diplomat, then Vice-President of the United Nations, was invited as keynote speaker. While the attendance drop was partly due to the lack of a large IB research community in Belgium, one might expect that a conference at the heart of Europe might attract more people. Interestingly, the largest group came from the UK. It seemed as if EIBA's appeal was fading, in particular among the French and Swedish IB research communities, while the UK powerhouse was showing its strength. Alan Rugman, who was to become a very influential IB scholar and US NR on the EIBA Board, and Eugene Jaffe, organiser of EIBA Jerusalem-1998, made their EIBA debuts in Antwerp.

The 1981 conference was organised in cooperation with AIB, probably to profit from the partner's established image to entice more participants. However, the analysis of EIBA archives did not yield much evidence about the precise reasons leading to this decision. EIBA 1981 was held in Barcelona, organised by Barto Roig (IESE, University of Navarra). Presented as an 'AIB/EIBA Joint International Meeting', it featured 72 papers, of which 21 were presented by EIBA members. It was the first EIBA conference for Pervez Ghauri, who later became the editor of *International Business Review* and an EIBA Fellow; it was also the debut of Angela da Rocha, a well-known Brasilian IB scholar, who was then a PhD student in Barcelona. However, attendance by EIBA members was limited: 33 only.[6] The minutes of the general EIBA business meeting suggest that this was partly due to registration fees perceived as excessive. The result was a drop in EIBA membership: from 159 for 1981 to 149 for 1982. Teaming up with AIB had not achieved the intended outcome. It did not foster EIBA's attractiveness; on the contrary, the conference seems to have been perceived as negatively affecting EIBA's identity. The need was felt for renewal. The 1982 conference in Fontainebleau was key to respond to this concern. It will be addressed in the next chapter.

3.4. EIBA: ORGANISATIONAL DEVELOPMENTS

This section deals with EIBA's organisational evolution in 1976–1981. As a newborn organisation EIBA was facing two main challenges: (1) to ensure growth, by creating a core group of scholars committed to the organisation; and (2) to establish a sound organisation that might reduce the dependence on annual Conferences. EIBA leaders in those early years were clearly aware of this double challenge. As shown below, several initiatives, with different degrees of success, were undertaken to respond to both challenges. This section is organised into six parts: statutory changes; development initiatives, EIBA newsletter, EIBA accounts, membership evolution and EIBA officers.

3.4.1. Statutory Changes

The main change to the EIBA constitution in this period was the amendment to its article VI. The new version, approved in Brussels in 1976, provides that 'upon termination of their tenure of office <u>one of the current Vice-Presidents</u>

will be elected President by the Association's membership, present at the annual meeting'.[7] The purpose of the change was two-fold: to strengthen the role of Executive Committee and the commitment of Committee members to organise a conference in the near future and to elect the Committee at the annual meeting. The changes were also intended to ensure the continuity of a governing body and to provide stability for the organisation. This was especially important at a juncture in which the men who were behind the creation of EIBA, namely Jim Leontiades and Michel Ghertman, would no longer be at the helm of the organisation.

3.4.2. Development Initiatives

The recognition of the need to lay a solid foundation for EIBA's development beyond annual conferences is evident in the minutes of EIBA's annual meetings. In the 1976 meeting in Brussels, three important issues were addressed: the location and role of the EIBA secretariat; the launching of a journal or the association with an existing one; and the creation of an EIBA newsletter. Other initiatives, reported in the minutes of later annual meetings, include the establishment of a working papers series in IB, and the setting up of a European International Business Clearing House for cases and teaching materials (EIBA, 1979, p. 5). Since the latter two were short-lived, we focus on the first three issues.

The proposal to have an EIBA secretariat housed at EIASM was accepted at the 1976 annual meeting. With hindsight, this proved to be a wise decision, which provided a sound support basis for EIBA. In particular, the fact that between 1977 and 1996 Gerry Van Dyck continuously served as EIBA secretary was very fortunate. Her commitment to the organisation, her savoir-faire and her long tenure ensured a stability which proved paramount in overcoming the problems felt in the early years, as well as providing the continuity that the absence of a multi-year Presidential team left unresolved. She also played a key role as editor of the *EIBA Newsletter* (see below), which has been for many years the key tool for diffusing information among EIBA members. Gerry deserves a strong word of recognition from the EIBA community for her professionalism and dedication to EIBA.

A suggestion to create a new European Journal of Management, co-sponsored by the various associations, was discussed at the general EIBA meeting in Brussels. A committee (Lars-Gunnar Mattsson, Jim Leontiades and José de la Torre) was elected to explore the possibilities in this regard. However, negotiations have been unsuccessful, and 'the idea was abandoned', as mentioned in the minutes of the 1977 annual meeting (EIBA, 1978, p. 3). The setting up of a journal was envisaged as an anchor for EIBA, reducing the over-reliance on the annual conferences. The idea would be revisited about 20 years later when the possibility of teaming up with an existing IB journal was considered by the EIBA Board.

The earliest reference to the idea of launching an *EIBA Newsletter* was found in the minutes of the 1976 EIBA meeting in Brussels. Our talks with Jim Leontiades and Michel Ghertman indicate, however, that the idea was germinating even before the first conference in 1975. In the pre-internet age, the establishment of tools to promote the diffusion of information throughout the IB community was felt to be critical for the new organisation. The launching of the *EIBA Newsletter* was one of the main achievements of the period. It deserves closer analysis.

3.4.3. The EIBA Newsletter

The first *EIBA Newsletter* was published in May 1978, less than one and a half years after the decision was taken. At a time of difficult communications, this may be considered an example of fast implementation. It can be explained by two main factors: the perception of the importance of the newsletter to strengthen the young organisation as well as to build and develop a European IB community; and the steering role played by the EIBA secretariat.

The *EIBA Newsletter* was published twice a year (Spring and Fall) and became a key networking tool for EIBA members. It provided information both about EIBA conferences and initiatives as well as about developments in IB research (by that time working papers were very important in diffusing research work). It also facilitated the identification of common interests among members, which in some cases gave rise to joint projects. Together with the annual conferences, the newsletter was critical to nurture the establishment of an EIBA community.

3.4.4. EIBA Accounts

The accounts are available from the year 1977 onwards. They show that the young organisation incurred successive deficits between 1977 and 1981. The lowest was recorded in 1979 (almost 162,000 BF[8]) but deficits significantly increased in the next years, to reach 209,000 BF in 1981. Membership fees declined from 55,000 to 45,000 BF between 1980 and 1981, in spite of an increase in the annual fee to 750 BF.

These financial problems are not surprising for a young organisation. They were envisaged as inherent to the process of establishing and stabilising EIBA. As we have seen, the growth in conference attendance (which was to a large extent reflected in membership) recorded in the late 1970s was not sustained in 1980–1981. The efforts to attract institutional members, which would be charged an annual fee of 10,000 BF, were not successful. Fortunately, EFMD and EIASM took a cooperative stance. As mentioned in the minutes of the Barcelona business meeting, 'Mr. Poncet [director of EFMD] commented that it would be appreciated by the sponsoring bodies if something could be done to diminish' the deficits (EIBA, 1982a, p. 4). The wording 'the shortage [...] have been carried by both the EFMD and EIASM' became standard in the presentation of EIBA accounts.

3.4.5. EIBA Membership

It was pointed out at the beginning of this section that EIBA membership increased sharply between 1976 and 1978, from 85[9] to 186. To a large extent such growth was due to the very high number of members from Sweden (66) as the local hosts, as a result of the participation at the 1977 conference in Uppsala. Be as it may, membership figures exhibited a declining trend after 1978.

Fig. 3 provides information about the average membership and membership shares of those countries accounting for at least 2% of tital membership in this period. The main point is the concentration of membership in a few countries. Five countries (Sweden, France, the UK, Germany and the US) accounted for about 65% of EIBA membership for 1977–1982. Their share hit the maximum

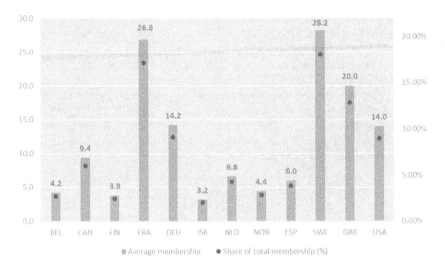

Fig. 3. EIBA Membership per Country (1977–1981). *Source*: EIBA archives.
Note: The figure includes those countries with at least 2% of total average membership
in the period concerned.

for 1978 (70%[10]), and has steadily declined since then, corresponding to 58% for 1982. The leading position of Sweden is very much influenced by the very successful Uppsala-1977. Interestingly, the weight of seven countries with an average of three to nine members (Belgium, Canada, Finland, Israel, the Netherlands, Norway and Spain) constantly increased, gaining 10 percentage points in five years (from around 20% for 1978 to 30% for 1982).

This geographical excursion leads to four main conclusions. First, EIBA membership was heavily concentrated in a small group of countries: the top-5 held about two thirds of total. France and Sweden (which accounted for almost half of the initial membership) were joined by other countries, namely the UK, among EIBA powerhouses. The second is the increasing share of those countries in the second tier. Third, several countries were underrepresented or had no members; this was the case of Italy, Ireland and Portugal, and East European countries (mostly for political reasons). The fourth conclusion concerns EIBA's openness to the world. Membership from the non-European countries was welcomed. Especially relevant was the weight of North American countries (US and Canada), which reached almost 18% of total membership for 1980–1982.

3.4.6. EIBA's Executive Committee

EIBA was managed by an Executive Committee, which included the President, the two Vice-Presidents, the past President, NRs, and *ex-officio* a member nominated by EFMD. It is interesting to remark that then it was enough to have one member for a country to be represented at the Executive Committee.[11] However, not all countries were represented. Some countries that had just one member (always the same person, as was the case of Japan or Libya) had a NR on the Executive

Committee while others, even with more members, were not represented. This suggests that there was a kind of 'old-boys-network' in the process of nominating NRs: only trusted members were nominated.

Table 1 provides information on the composition of the Executive Committee between 1975 and 1981. In 1981, 15 countries were represented on the Board. An unwritten rule that became 'common law' and later enshrined in the statutes (see 3.4.1 above) was that the Vice-Presidents were responsible for organising the next couple of conferences. This ensured the location of EIBA conferences to be decided two years in advance, thereby allowing for a minimum time lag in the preparation of future conferences.

3.5. SUMMARY

The period under review comes immediately after the first EIBA conference in 1975. It corresponds to the setting up the Association. This was a time characterised by a confrontation between Member States and MNCs, which gradually changed towards a more peaceful coexistence. As a result of this, much IB research had a political tone. Between 1976 and 1981 several of the pioneering contributions to the IB field were published, and some of them had been presented beforehand at EIBA conferences. EIBA made a promising start, responding to the need felt by European IB researchers to have a forum for networking as well as for sharing the results of their work.

In fact, EIBA experienced a significant increase in the numbers of both members and conference participants in 1976 and 1977. However, the 1977 record was very much due to the mobilisation of the strong research community in Sweden, whose participation declined in the following years. Since then, EIBA was not able to maintain its growth, in spite of the well-attended EIBA 1979 in London. The 1981 conference had the lowest EIBA attendance (33 members only) and membership for 1982 declined to 149, from 184 in 1978.

In contrast to this grim picture, positive developments took place on the organisational front. Some initiatives to respond financial constraints, in particular the promotion of institutional membership, were unsuccessful. The idea to launch a European Journal of Management, encompassing different associations under the EFMD aegis did not materialise either. However, it was possible to launch the first *EIBA Newsletter* in 1978. This was a major achievement for the young EIBA, since it provided a basis for interaction, diffusion of information and networking at a time of slow communication.

In spite of the lack of growth in terms of membership and Conference attendance there were reasons to expect a revival of the association. While in many countries academic IB communities were still to be established and the support for academic research was limited and erratic in several countries, there was a growing interest in IB issues and a new generation of IB researchers was emerging. There were prospects for EIBA to achieve a turnaround and to resume its growth. The convening of the next EIBA conference in Fontainebleau and the intention to revise the EIBA statutes were envisaged as key steps towards achieving this objective.

Table 1. Composition of the Executive Committee (1975–1981).

Officers	1975	1976	1977	1978	1979	1980	1981
President	James Leontiades	Michel Ghertman	L.-Günnar Mattsson	H. Günther Meissner	John Stopford	Sylvain Plasschaert	Barto Roig
Vice-Presidents	M. Ghertman	L. G. Mattsson	H. Meissner	J. Stopford	S. Plasschaert	Barto Roig	J. de la Torre
	L. G. Mattsson	H. Meissner	J. Stopford	S. Plasschaert	B. Roig	J. de la Torre	P. Korsvold
National Coordinators							
Belgium	–	S. Plasschaert	S. Plasschaert	S. Plasschaert	S. Plasschaert	D. Van Den Bulcke	D. Van Den Bulcke
Canada	–	G. Leroy	G. Leroy	H. C. Jain	J. Picard	J. Picard	J. Picard
Finland	–	–	–	R. Luostarinen	R. Luostarinen	R. Luostarinen	R. Luostarinen
France	–	A. Chevalier	B. Thiry	M. Ghertman	M. Ghertman	M. Ghertman	M. Ghertman
Germany	H. Meissner	M. Strötmann	M. Welge	M. Welge	M. Welge	EPausenberger	EPausenberger
Israel	–	–	–	T. Weinshall	T. Weinshall	T. Weinshall	T. Weinshall
Italy	–	G. Bisoni	G. Pellicelli	G. Pellicelli	G. Pellicelli	G. Pellicelli	G. Pellicelli
Japan	N. Sasaki	N. Sasaki	N. Sasaki	N. Sasaki	N. Sasaki	N. Sasaki	N. Sasaki
Lybia	–	–	–	A. Buera	A. Buera	A. Buera	A. Buera
Netherlands	C. Botter	FDerkinderen	FDerkinderen	C. Van Dam	J.W.R. Schuit	J.W.R. Schuit	J.W.R. Schuit
Norway	–	P. Korsvold	P. Korsvold	P. Korsvold	P. Korsvold	P. Korsvold	P. Joynt
Spain	–	B. Roig	B. Roig	B. Roig	B. Roig	B. Roig	B. Roig
Sweden	J.E. Vahlne	A. Edström	A. Edström	A. Edström	A. Edström	A. Edström	A. Edström
UK	M. Z. Brooke	M. Z. Brooke	J. Leontiades	J. Leontiades	S. Young	S. Young	S. Young
US	–	–	–	M. Hochmuth	M. Hochmuth	M. Hochmuth	M. Hochmuth

Source: EIBA Newsletters.

Note: New EIBA officers are elected in December of a given year. Although we know they may immediately start their functions, we assume here that their service as President, as Vice-President or as NRs starts in the next year, to avoid overlaps and make easier for the reader to follow the sequence of officers and the time of their duties.

NOTES

1. The authors thank José de la Torre for comments on an earlier version of this chapter. The usual disclaimer applies.

2. The membership figure for 1976 corresponds to written information provided by Reijo Luostarinen. We have not been able to confirm this figure in our analysis from the EIASM and EIBA archives. The figure may seem a bit high, having in mind that the number of participants in the 1975 initial conference was 45. However, to this figure one may add the colleagues which, in the 1974 workshop, expressed the intention to join the association and those which became members meanwhile, though not participating in the 1975 conference.

3. It is important to note that at that time membership was paid for the incoming year. This means that the membership figure for 1982 includes the participants at the 1981 conference.

4. As mentioned earlier, one of the first versions of this article was presented at the first EIBA conference.

5. Ireland was only included in the chapter some time later.

6. The number of AIB attendants was 49.

7. The changes are underlined in the original.

8. 1,000 Belgian Francs correspond to €24.79.

9. This figure was provided to us by Reijo Luostarinen in 2016. We have not been able to confirm it. In fact, in the EIBA archives, membership data is available only from 1977 onwards. Remember that, as mentioned in endnote 2, membership fees were paid for the incoming year, meaning that, for instance, the membership figure for 1982 includes the participants in the 1981 conference.

10. Mainly due to the very high attendance of participants from Sweden at Uppsala in 1977.

11. As will be explained later, the condition for a country to have a NR was changed by new statutes approved in 1982; these provided that it was necessary to have at least five members for a country to have a representative on the Executive Committee.

CHAPTER 4

BRIDGING TROUBLED WATERS (1982–1988)

The Fontainebleau Conference, in 1982, marked an EIBA revival, to a large extent due to the upswing in attracting new members from the US. However, in spite of the initiatives aimed at ensuring its stabilisation, EIBA was still a one-conference-a-year organisation. It was far from financial balance, with successive deficits inhibiting bolder initiatives. At a time when financial support for IB research was limited and the IB profession was in its youth, location played a very important role in attracting participants. Nevertheless, after Fontainebleau, EIBA looked ready for taking off. The 1983 and 1984 conferences were held in Oslo and Rotterdam, respectively. The Rotterdam Conference reached an attendance of 212 people, the second highest so far in EIBA history, after Fontainebleau.[1] However, EIBA membership experienced a continuous decline between 1983 and 1987, when it dropped below one hundred.[2] After the Glasgow Conference, in 1985, dark clouds were emerging on the horizon again, announcing another troubled phase. Faced with AIB's decision to hold its annual conference in London in 1986, EIBA followed its senior partner, locating its conference also in London, immediately before AIB's. This might have minimised losses, but in practice it was a blow to the young Association. In the next two years, the dearth of applications to organise EIBA conferences led committed EIBA members to take charge of them: Danny Van Den Bulcke organised the Antwerp Conference in 1987; and Hans-Günther Meissner managed EIBA Berlin, in 1988. But this was also a time of discovery and network-building: discovery of diverse local scholars and research streams hitherto insufficiently known; and networking, to the extent that bridges between scholars were built or further strengthened. This chapter spans along a seven-year period (1982–1988), when, in spite of some very successful and enjoyable conferences, EIBA struggled for survival. But, with hindsight, one may also argue that this was a time to build EIBA's resilience, to launch cooperative initiatives and to consolidate the 'EIBA family'.

The History of EIBA: A Tale of The Co-Evolution Between International Business Issues and a Scholarly Community, 29–44
Copyright © 2025 by Vítor Corado Simões, John Cantwell and Philippe Gugler
Published under exclusive licence by Emerald Publishing Limited
doi:10.1108/978-1-83608-664-220241005

The present chapter is structured in five parts. The first two provide contextual perspectives regarding the political and business climate and the evolution of IB research. The third addresses the seven Conferences held during this period, from Fontainebleau (1982) to Berlin (1988). Then, organisational and membership development trends are presented. The final section delivers a brief synthesis and the main conclusions.

4.1. THE CONTEXT: ATTITUDES TOWARDS FDI

This time period is characterised by a gradual improvement in the relationships between nation-states and MNCs, which was emerging at the beginning of the 1980s. As *The Economist* put it, public opinion towards MNCs had changed, from the 1970s' dragon to a large, though not so dangerous dinosaur, in the 1980s; this was anticipating the 1990s' honeymoon (The Economist, 2000). As mentioned in Chapter 3, the 'confrontation' stage was over, giving rise to a 'reconciliation' and then to 'a mature relationship' between Governments and MNCs (Dunning, 1982).

Reflecting changes in governments' stance towards MNCs, the UN efforts to establish international codes of conduct regarding MNCs and technology transfer were abandoned (Sagafi-Nejad & Dunning, 2008). The 1983 *Transnational Corporations in World Development* (UNCTC, 1983) recognised that MNCs might have a positive contribution towards host countries' economic development. Policies towards MNCs were envisaged to be increasingly pragmatic, flexible and sophisticated (Dunning, 1982; UNCTC, 1983). Developing countries were changing their stance on the establishment of performance requirements regarding MNCs' behaviour, moving towards more realistic policies, focussed on a limited set of relevant issues, namely local content and export targets. In spite of the nationalisation of large industrial groups in France, in 1982, the EEC experienced a new dynamic in the mid-1980s, with the enlargement to Portugal and Spain. This provided new opportunities for MNCs to profit from the intra-European division of labour, by drawing on the Iberian countries, especially Portugal, as export manufacturing bases (Alonso & Donoso, 1989; Cantwell, 1987; Deubner, 1981, Donges, Krieger-Boden, Langhammer, Schatz & Thoroe, 1982; Durán, 1992; Martin, 1989; Martinez & Jarillo, 1988; Simões, 1992; Taveira, 1984); this effect was especially felt in the automotive industry, in which corporate integration overlapped with regional integration (Fernández-de-Sevilla, 2016; da Silva Lopes & Simões, 2020; Simões, 2003; Van Tulder, Ruigrok & Baven, 1991; Vickery, 1997).

The 1980s may be envisaged as the dawn of globalisation in the contemporary sense of the emergence and growth of global value chains (GVCs) and more complex cross-border interdependencies. Following Levitt (1983), the words 'global' and 'globalisation' became part of the IB lexicon. Enabled by technological developments in the fields of transportation and especially information and communication technologies, the establishment of international value chains based on the segmentation of production stages gained further energy (Baldwin, 2012). The Uruguay Round, a new spurt of trade liberalisation negotiations, started in 1986, led to the establishment of the World Trade Organisation (WTO) almost 10 years later. Throughout the 1980s 'FDI has grown at a faster pace than either world trade or world production' (BenAissa, 1993, p. vii).

The period under analysis is also characterised by three further IB features. The first is the emergence of Japanese MNCs. According to Dunning (1993), the outward stock of Japanese FDI increased about three-fold between 1980 and 1988, enabling Japan to reach the top-three outward investors, overtaking Germany, Switzerland and the Netherlands. With almost 10% of the World FDI stock in 1988, Japan was behind just the US and the UK. Japanese companies became increasingly envisaged as challengers to American MNCs, especially in the fields of the automotive industry, semiconductors and machine tools (Reich & Mankin, 1986). The second concerns the increasing role of FDI in service industries. Dunning (1993) provides evidence of the increasing share of services in FDI flows between the late 1970s and the late 1980s. For a sample of the biggest origins of FDI, services accounted for an average of 47% of FDI stock in 1988 as against 33% in 1975. The third trend is the diversification of foreign entry modes. Contractual forms have developed, including subcontracting, licencing, franchising and contractual joint ventures (Oman, 1984).

The confluence of these features led to a new IB pattern in which non-Western players were emerging. This generated a double-edged perception of the challenges for MNCs: on the one hand, opportunities to profit from an increasing similarity of perceptions and aspirations were increasing while, on the other, national institutional differences remained strong. It was not just a matter of following Levitt's (1983) preaching. There was a need to balance global integration with local responsiveness to differentiated demand and environmental conditions (Prahalad & Doz, 1987). On the national FDI policy side, recognition of the potentially positive MNCs' contributions regarding foreign exchange, employment and technology was leading to more pragmatic negotiation approaches.

4.2. THE CONTEXT: IB LITERATURE

The 1982–1988 period witnessed the emergence or development of five strands which significantly influenced IB literature. The first was the consolidation of the transaction costs approach with the publication of *The Economic Institutions of Capitalism* (Williamson, 1985). In connection with this, it is interesting to recall that Oliver Williamson was the keynote speaker at the EIBA 1992 conference in Reading. The second strand corresponded to evolutionary economics perspectives. Nelson and Winter's (1982) *An Evolutionary Theory of Economic Change* came to have a profound effect on IB theory, from the late 1980s. This was especially evident in the work of John Cantwell (1989a, 1995b) and Cantwell, Dunning and Lundan (2010) as well as from a more sociological perspective of Bruce Kogut and Udo Zander (1992, 1993, 1995, 1996) and Zander and Kogut (1995).[3] Economic sociology comes next, with the concept of embeddedness, introduced by Granovetter (1985). It played a role in shaping the analysis of both the MNC as a multi-unit/multi-embedded entity and the headquarters-subsidiaries inter-action (Andersson & Forsgren, 1996; Andersson, Forsgren & Holm, 2001).

The two last strands concern corporate strategy. The fourth was the further development of Michael Porter's (1985) approach to strategy, expressed in his *Competitive Advantage*. The final strand is the launching of the resource-based view, particularly the works by Wernerfelt (1984) and Rumelt (1984), which assumed various shapes in the following decade (e.g. Barney, 1991, 1999; Peteraf, 1993; Spender, 1996). This came to exercise a significant influence on IB thinking, especially in the fields of internalisation (Hennart, 2009), cooperative agreements (Arora, Fosfuri & Gambardella, 2001; Mowery, Oxley & Silverman, 1996, 1998, 2002; Madhok & Osegowitsch, 2000; Tallman, 1999) and born globals (Gassmann & Keupp, 2007; Mort & Weerawardena, 2006; Weerawardena, Mort, Liesch & Knight, 2007).

More specific contributions to the IB literature also emerged in this period. They may be clustered along four main, and interrelated, axes: FDI theory and trade; technology and IB; cooperative strategies and entry mode choice; and globalisation and international strategy. The literature on FDI theory comes in the wake of the seminal work developed in the second half of the 1970s, and includes contributions by Buckley and Casson (1985), Hennart (1986, 1988) and Rugman (1982, 1985), aimed at expanding and providing empirical applications to internalisation approaches. Particularly relevant is Dunning (1988a), focussed on two issues: (1) responding to the criticisms of the eclectic paradigm; and (2) providing some extensions, including inter alia an increased formalisation, the introduction of dynamics, the inclusion of different forms of IB transactions, and divestment. Helpman (1984, 1985) and Helpman and Krugman (1985) introduced relevant developments regarding FDI and trade. This period also witnessed further research on IB history, including Dunning (1983b), Wilkins (1982, 1988) and Geoffrey Jones' longitudinal case studies (Jones, 1984, 1985, 1988).

The second axis has to do with technology and IB. As mentioned in the previous chapter, technology issues gained increased relevance since the early 1980s, not just as a key ownership advantage of MNCs but also in terms of technology trade. Two books dealing with these issues were written by Lall (1985) and Dunning (1988b). Other relevant contributions encompass the works by Davidson and McFetridge (1984, 1985) on technology trade, the framework developed by Teece (1986) on the options faced by innovators to profit from their innovations, and the case studies on Swedish MNCs' international R&D management by Håkanson and Zander (1988). It is interesting to remark, in connection with this, that the paper contributed by Cantwell and Dunning (1982) to the EIBA conference in Fontainebleau addressed the effects of US inward investments and the UK's technological competitiveness.

It was pointed out above that the 1980s were characterised by the expansion of new types of IB transactions besides the traditional FDI approach. This led to a spurt of research on cooperative strategies and entry mode choices. Relevant contributions on the latter include Anderson and Gatignon (1986), providing a seminal analysis of the application of transaction costs to entry mode choice, and *Entry Strategies for International Markets*, the nowadays classic book by Franklin Root (Root, 1994). The literature on licencing established a link between entry modes and technology trade, especially Davidson and McFetridge (1985), mentioned above, Caves, Crookell and Killing (1983), Carstairs and Welch

(1983), Contractor (1985) and Welch (1985). Joint ventures gave rise to a plethora of research, to a large extent anchored in Canada (Beamish, 1984, 1985, 1988; Beamish & Banks, 1987; Geringer, 1988; Killing, 1983, 1988; Schaan, 1983) but also in the US (Harrigan, 1985; Kogut, 1988) and Europe (Artisien & Buckley, 1985). *Cooperative Strategies in International Business*, an edited volume by Contractor and Lorange (1988b), put together important research on strategic alliances. The literature shows a divergence between those who envisaged cooperative deals as a win-lose (Porter & Fuller, 1986; Reich & Mankin, 1986) or as a win-win approach (Buckley & Casson, 1988; Killing, 1988). The concept of forbearance, coined by Buckley and Casson (1988), became a key contribution to understand how to build trust in inter-firm alliances.

The fourth axis concerns globalisation and international strategy. Stimulated by the work of Doz, Bartlett and Prahalad (1981), on global competitive pressures, and Levitt (1983), a wide stream of research on globalisation emerged. While some argued that globalisation was a myth (Douglas & Wind, 1987), most authors underlined that globalisation entailed a significant shift in demand, requiring MNCs to espouse new strategic approaches (Ghoshal, 1987; Hamel & Prahalad, 1985; Hood & Vahlne, 1987; Kogut, 1985; Ohmae, 1985; Porter, 1986). This led to taxonomies of international strategies, which became classical in IB literature (Bartlett & Ghoshal, 1987, 1989; Porter, 1986; Prahalad & Doz, 1987). The book *The Multinational Mission: Balancing Local Demands and Global Vision* (Prahalad & Doz, 1987) argued that MNCs should follow multi-focal strategies in order to balance the contradictory forces of global integration and local responsiveness (I-R). Bartlett and Ghoshal (1987) pushed the I-R framework further by introducing another requirement: firms' international learning ability, envisaged as the capacity 'to transfer knowledge and expertise from one part of the organization to others worldwide' (Bartlett & Ghoshal, 1987). This became the basis for the concept of transnational organisation (Bartlett & Ghoshal, 1989), to be addressed in the next chapter. In this context, it came as no surprise that the theme of MNC organisation and control turned to be a key IB research issue. The main contributions on this regard include the following: Chandler (1982), on the M-form; Doz (1986) and Doz and Prahalad (1984), on strategic management and control in MNCs; Egelhoff (1982, 1984), on information-processing and control patterns in MNCs; and Hedlund (1986), introducing the concept of heterarchy. By the same token, new avenues were opened in the research on headquarters–subsidiary relationships, recognising the advantages of granting more room for subsidiaries to respond to local requirements (Hedlund, 1984) and developing the first taxonomies of subsidiary roles (White & Poynter, 1984). Some of the key scholars in this field (Yves Doz, Bill Egelhoff, Gunnar Hedlund, Bruce Kogut and Thomas Poynter) were active EIBA members throughout the 1980s and 1990s.

Besides these four main axes, a reference is due to other research themes in IB literature. These include the emergence of Third World multinationals (Lall, 1983; Khan, 1987; Wells, 1983), later labelled as emerging market MNCs (EMNCs), further developments regarding internationalisation processes (Luostarinen & Welch, 1988), the design of quantitative metrics to assess inter-cultural distance (Kogut & Singh, 1988; Ronen & Shenkar, 1985), and the above mentioned publication of a new volume on *Transnationals and World Development* (UNCTC, 1983), reflecting a more positive view of the UN regarding the contribution of MNCs towards development.

4.3. EIBA: THE CONFERENCES

As mentioned in Chapter 3, the Barcelona conference (1981), held in cooperation with AIB, was a disappointing experience, in terms of both the number of EIBA participants and their contributions. The main thrust of the next EIBA President, José de la Torre, then at INSEAD, was to make EIBA more resilient as an organisation, by changing its statutes (see below), and to resume membership growth. The Fontainebleau conference, held in 1982, was able to achieve the latter objective. However, the dependence on a single event (the annual conference) and the perception of being a junior association in relation to AIB continued to constrain the EIBA's development in the following years, as will be shown below. It is worth to remark that, reflecting EIBA's membership pattern, all the conferences in this time period were held in Northern Europe: Oslo (1983), Rotterdam (1984), Glasgow (1985), London (1986), Antwerp (1987) and Berlin (1988). With hindsight, it may be said that 'as the people often didn't come to EIBA, so EIBA had to go to where the people were!'.

The 1982 conference was held at the INSEAD premises in Fontainebleau, under the general theme of 'Empirical Research on International Business Problems'. The conference was very successful both in terms of the quality of the sessions and the attendance level. Profiting from INSEAD's reputation and network, José de la Torre made a remarkable effort to attract wide participation, especially from America. The conference was attended by 143 participants, corresponding to an increase of almost 70% with regard to the previous maximum (85, in Uppsala, 1977). An innovative feature of this conference was a new conference structure, organised by themes (production and technology issues in international operations; managing cultural diversity; managing the international financial function; and strategic responses to international environmental changes). Sessions had 'fewer papers but more in-depth discussion' without putting into jeopardy the 'participation by as wide a cross-section of our membership as possible' (de la Torre, 1982, p. 2). Several well-known scholars have participated in this conference (John H. Dunning, Geert Hofstede, Bruce Kogut, Charles Albert Michalet and Yves Doz); a special reference is due to the presence of Edith Penrose, who chaired one session together with John Stopford. The conference structure was used as a template for the following conferences. It was to some extent the embryo of the separation between competitive and interactive papers, introduced from 1991 onwards. This was the first EIBA conference attended by John Cantwell, who was to serve EIBA for many years, namely as EIBA President (1992) and as Dean of the Fellows (2016–2018).

The 1983 EIBA conference was convened by Pål Korsvold and was held in Oslo, between 18 and 20 December. The dates are relevant, since, according to some observations, they appear to have negatively influenced attendance level. In fact, a couple of interviewees conveyed the message that a snowy Oslo was not the most attractive place to travel, so close to Christmas. In fact, the number of participants was 70 only, more than two-thirds coming from Norway and Canada. This means that attendance declined to the figures recorded in the late 1970s. The main sessions focussed on three issues: the firm's internationalisation process; the firm's international environment, and managing the international firm. Participants included Mats Forsgren. Gunnar Hedlund, Thomas Poynter, Lawrence Welch, and Roderick White. This was the first EIBA conference for two future EIBA veterans: Carl-Arthur Solberg and Lawrence Welch.

The 10th EIBA conference was held in Rotterdam in 1984. Organised by J. W. Roland Schuit, from Erasmus University, who had been involved with EIBA since 1976, the conference reached a high participation level: 112 (EIBA Board, 1985). The largest host came from the US, with 32 participants (i.e. almost 30% of 112); other relevant contingents came from the Netherlands (14%), Canada and France (8% each). This was the first EIBA conference for two EIBA Fellows: Jean-François Hennart and the late Jorma Larimo. An innovative feature of the Rotterdam conference was the convening of the 'EIBA meets Practice – Practice meets EIBA' session, covering a whole day. Its goals were 'to discuss recent research results with representatives of the business and government community and to generate topics to be put on the research agenda of the EIBA members' (Schuit, 1985, p. 3). However, participation from the business side was disappointing: 12 people only. According to Roland Schuit, this was due to the fact that the outside world does not appear to be accustomed to approach the University 'to solve their (potential) problems' but rather considers the University as a 'neutral place to demonstrate company opinions' (Schuit, 1985, p. 4). This session aside, the 1984 conference followed the Fontainebleau template, assigning the mornings to the presentation and discussion of selected papers on five specific themes: changes in multinational financial management and control; international strategic responses; the international firm and its markets; the firm's international environment, and international production and technology management. The social programme was very attractive, with plenty of Gouda cheese, as portrayed by Danny Van Den Bulcke's photos.

From Rotterdam, EIBA moved further north, along the North Sea, to Glasgow. The 1985 conference was organised by Neil Hood, from Strathclyde University, then one of EIBA leaders. The format was similar to the previous conferences. Five themes were selected for the core sessions (Chairmen indicated in parentheses): international technology management (Arnoud De Meyer, INSEAD); strategy and competitiveness (Gunnar Hedlund); finance and strategy (Bruce Kogut); international environment (Danny Van Den Bulcke); and impact of MNCs (Thomas Poynter). Attendance declined with regard to Rotterdam, dropping to 80. The conference enabled the establishment of stronger links with the IB research group at Glasgow, then one of the strongest in the UK. Glasgow was the first EIBA conference for Örjan Solvell, who became to organise EIBA 1996 in Stockholm, the most visible face of the Gunnar Hedlund Award for years, and an EIBA Fellow.

The location of the 1986 conference had been a concern for EIBA long since. It was decided 'to take-up D. van den Bulcke (sic) on his previous offer to organise the 1986 conference in Belgium' (EIBA Board, 1985). However, a new turn was in the making. The AIB decision to hold its first general conference outside the US in London, in November 1986, was the reason for the turn. The EIBA Board felt that it would not be wise to have two conferences so close in different locations. Therefore, after an intense discussion at the Board, it was decided to approach AIB to link both events.[4] So EIBA came back to London, just seven years after the 1979 conference.

Instead of spanning for three days as usual, the conference lasted one and a half days only, and it was held at Café Royal, a conference centre close to Piccadilly Circus. It was a way to renew acquaintances and to attract new members. In fact, London was the first EIBA conference for two EIBA Fellows (Vítor Corado Simões and Udo Zander) as well as for two EIBA veterans (Leo Sleuwagen and Bernard Wolf). Attendance was similar to Glasgow: 79 participants. The closeness to the AIB conference (1986) did not entail higher overseas participation, as attendance from the US and Canada was 13 and 2, respectively, much below the figures recorded in Paris or Rotterdam. The UK had the largest contingent (20% of total), though a significant share was accounted for by publishers. Attendance from most European countries declined in comparison to Rotterdam, the main exceptions being Denmark, Norway and Spain.

EIBA was kept alive, in spite of the shade of the senior IB organisation. However, two negative features ineludibly emerged. The first was the very significant decline in EIBA affiliation, from 198 to 91 members only,[5] as it will be shown below. The second was the sinking commitment to EIBA from the communities of traditional IB powerhouses in Continental Europe, such as France, Germany and Sweden. A new boost was needed for EIBA to come back to the participation heights of Fontainebleau and Rotterdam. That was the main challenge faced by Danny Van Den Bulcke in organising EIBA Antwerp.

The future was to mirror the past: London plus Antwerp in 1986–1987 inevitably reminded London plus Antwerp in 1979–1980. The conference's theme was 'Multinational Enterprises and Developing Countries: A changing relationship?'. The second day of the Conference was focussed on this issue. Danny Van Den Bulcke proved to be up to the challenge. He put a lot of effort in making Antwerp 1987 a memorable conference. Although still below the Fontainebleau record, attendance increased, exceeding the one-hundred-participants mark (101, more precisely). First-time EIBA attendants in Antwerp included two EIBA Fellows (Alain Verbeke and Juán Durán, the organiser of EIBA Madrid 1990). Danny introduced a very important innovation which became a long-lasting feature of EIBA conferences: the launch of a Doctoral Tutorial. It is now called the John H. Dunning Tutorial.[6] The rationale behind the initiative was to contribute towards the development of IB education and research by enabling a group of selected PhD students to interact with other members of the IB community and to get 'some help from a friend' to steer their doctoral efforts (EIBA, 1987). The Doctoral Tutorial is now a key feature of EIBA conferences, and has played an outstanding role in expanding networking as well as in rejuvenating the Academy. In Antwerp the faculty included Peter Buckley, Geert Hofstede, John Stopford and Danny Van Den Bulcke. The winner was Andreas E. Ziegler, whose thesis project was about 'Success factors of international joint ventures (IJVs): The German experience in the U.S.A'.

Hans-Günther Meissner, who had been in charge of the 1978 EIBA conference in Dortmund, volunteered to organise the 1988 EIBA in Berlin, with the support of Klaus Macharzina (University of Höhenheim) and Martin Welge (University of Dortmund). Very well organised, the conference took place at the West-Berlin International Congress Centre under the theme of 'East/West business relations'. At the welcome reception, while looking at the troops patrolling the wall, conference participants could not imagine that it will fall less than one year later. EIBAians in Berlin had a snapshot of the history of Europe, when Germany was divided. The conference attracted 89 participants, including several from Eastern Europe, especially from Poland, who were given special registration conditions; Krzysztof Obloj, who later organised EIBA Warsaw 1994 and became EIBA Fellow, was a member of the Polish host.

Between 1982 and 1988 new steps were taken to improve paper selection. Submission in English was already taken for granted. However, quality standards were still highly variable. According to José de la Torre (de la Torre, 1982), there was a balance to be struck: on the one hand, the need to attract new members, to enlarge the IB community and to increase conference attendance (and the corresponding income); and, on the other, upgrading papers' quality, and enhancing the reputation of EIBA conferences as the appropriate setting to submit high standard papers. This led to a two-tier structure: discussion of top-quality contributions focussed on specific themes and selected by high-reputation academics, in the morning sections, and afternoon sessions, open to all IB subjects, following less strict selection criteria.

4.4. EIBA: ORGANISATIONAL DEVELOPMENTS

The Barcelona experience highlighted the need to develop further action to improve EIBA's governance and sustainability, with a view to both reduce the dependence on the annual conference and strengthen the association, escaping from the 'old-boys network' bias. Additionally, EIBA was still far from financial stability: in spite of the initiatives taken to attract institutional membership, successive deficits continued to be supported by EIASM.

The main developments in the organisational and management front are addressed below. They encompass six interrelated dimensions: statutory changes, EIBA publications; the relationships with AIB; EIBA accounts; membership evolution; and the composition of the EIBA governing bodies.

4.4.1. Statutory Changes

After a first approach to the issue at the December 1981 meeting in Barcelona, EIBA's Steering Committee met in Brussels in September 1982, under the leadership of José de la Torre, to design a proposal for changing EIBA statutes. The statutes dated back from 1974, when EIBA was still to have its first conference, with slight changes introduced in 1976. The need was felt to adjust them in the light of the experience gathered since the launching of the Association. It became clear that EIBA's governance needed to be streamlined to become more effective, and that a closer link should be established between EIBA's management bodies and its members. The proposal was approved at the annual meeting held in Fontainebleau in December 1982.

The 1982 statutes went further than a revision of the original 1974 EIBA statutes (EIBA, 1982b). They provide a more appropriate governance model for EIBA, avoiding the risk of overlapping responsibilities that existed beforehand. Clear orientations regarding governance, responsibility and the representation of what became known as country chapters were defined. The Board became the key governance body. In line with this, it was decided to have two meetings per year: one at the EIBA conference, and another by Spring. This contributed to enhance EIBA's management and the discussion about relevant issues. The requirement for a country to have at least five members to nominate a representative was also envisaged as a tool to promote membership. With hindsight, it may be argued that this revision, though very positive, was not enough to solve EIBA's problems. The changes introduced did not allow EIBA to escape from the one-conference-a-year trap. While enabling top Board members to stay on for four years, as a rule, the composition of the Executive Committee changed every year. Furthermore, the same happened with the President. As President-Elect, one's focus was on organising the next conference. Only when he/she would become President the opportunity to delve into EIBA's strategic issues would emerge. In a nutshell, while corresponding to a very positive change, it was not enough to provide the organisational continuity needed to ensure EIBA's medium- to long-term stability.

4.4.2. EIBA Publications

This section addresses two issues: the changes introduced in the *EIBA Newsletter*, and the initiatives regarding the creation of an EIBA journal.

One of the issues discussed at EIBA's Steering Committee meetings was the reshuffling of the *EIBA Newsletter* to make it more attractive. It was decided to mandate Gerry van Dyck, the newsletter editor, to work on this. The result was a new series of the *EIBA Newsletter* starting Spring 1984. The traditional periodicity (two issues, in Spring and Fall) remained unchanged as well as the difficulty in getting contributions from EIBA members.

As mentioned in Chapter 3, the idea had been floated to establish a link with a journal or alternatively to participate in the launching of a new journal. This was the start of a one-and-a-half decades-long process which only materialised with the teaming up with *International Business Review* (IBR) in the early 2000s, as it will be shown in Chapter 6.

4.4.3. EIBA/AIB Relationships

As explained in previous chapters, the relationships between EIBA and AIB have been, since the beginning, somewhat ambivalent. Larger and longer-established,

AIB was envisaged as a role model for EIBA. For some groups within AIB, EIBA was seen as a regional organisation that should rather be put under the AIB umbrella by 'merging' it with AIB Western Europe. This generated some misunderstandings, although the dominant mood has been characterised by cooperation rather than confrontation. The 1981 Barcelona meeting was an example of cooperation, through the joint organisation of the conference. However, as shown in Chapter 3, the experience was clearly negative for EIBA, whose image became faded when compared to a larger and wealthier AIB. This was confirmed in 1986 when EIBA tied up again with AIB.

The lesson was learnt: for EIBA to stabilise and prosper, an independent strategy had to be developed. EIBA should not be so much dependent on AIB decisions. A string of conferences should be defined in advance, to allow time for appropriate preparation as well as for EIBA members to plan their participation. In 1987, when John Dunning became President of AIB, the idea of establishing a Federation of Associations of International Business (FAIB), emerged. FAIB would be an umbrella organisation, acting as the governing body, of Regional Associations (RAs). It was decided to ask all EIBA representatives their opinions about the collaboration with AIB. John Dunning (then AIB President) and Peter Buckley (then President of AIB-UK Chapter) were invited to attend the December 1987 EIBA Board meeting in Antwerp. This was a diplomatic way to turn the idea down, given that AIB itself was largely unsympathetic to the proposal, and so it had become an impractical suggestion. However, the EIBA/AIB relationship was still pervaded with equivocal positions, taken even by the EIBA Board itself, as shown by the following quote from a Board meeting: EIBA 'is the European representation of AIB' (EIBA Board, 1990).

An important decision on that regard was taken in 1994 when the EIBA Board, faced with AIB's decision to hold its 1998 conference in Viena, decided to follow a different path, choosing Jerusalem as a venue for EIBA 1998.

4.4.4. EIBA Accounts

The deficits reported in Chapter 2 persisted between 1982 and 1988. No major changes were observed with regard to the previous period. With the exception of the 1988 Berlin Conference, which generated a small profit, EIBA conferences closed with a deficit. Again, EIASM provided EIBA with the required safety net, carrying out the successive deficits. Probably as a way to countervail these deficits, EIASM launched in the late 1980s a series of training initiatives focussed on IB. The responsibility for the design of the training courses was assigned to Neil Hood, then one of the key EIBA champions. Several EIBA members have participated in the faculty of these courses. However, their life was relatively short, not extending after the 1990s.

4.4.5. EIBA Membership

The evolution of EIBA's membership was to a large extent influenced by the one-conference-a-year approach that characterised EIBA in the 1980s. When conferences were held in attractive locations and/or when the organiser developed significant efforts to stimulate attendance, membership increased (with a one-year delay, since conference participants in year x paid their membership fees for $x+1$).

The maximum membership figure for the whole period was 257, recorded for 1983. This corresponds to a significant increase as against 1982, when membership was 149 only. The initiatives taken by José de la Torre to recover from the Barcelona drawback were successful: EIBA membership overcame the 250 mark for the first time ever. France and the US took the lead in the membership drive, accounting together for about 35% of the total. However, it was not possible to sustain this achievement, and EIBA membership steadily declined since then. The annual drops were noticeable for 1985 (almost 16% with regard to the previous year) and especially 1987 (54%). By 1987 EIBA membership was at its lowest level since 1976. Fortunately, Danny Van Den Bulcke's efforts to make the Antwerp conference the launchpad for EIBA's recovery were successful: membership increased to 108 for 1988; the trend since then has been clearly positive, in spite of the emergence of a decline around the turn of the century, reported in Chapter 6.

Although EIBA members came from at least 24 countries (30 for 1986), membership structure was relatively concentrated, as may be seen on Fig. 4. Two countries alone had consistently been in the top five throughout the 1982–1988 period:

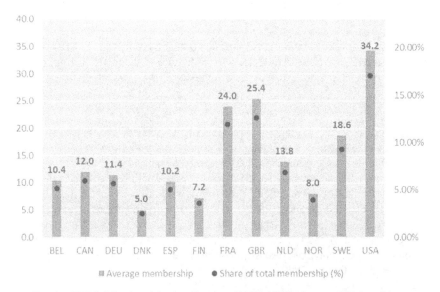

Fig. 4.   EIBA Membership per Country (1982–1988). *Source*: EIBA archives.
Note: The figure includes those countries with at least 2% of total average membership
in the period concerned.

the US and the UK; the former accounted for 18% of membership for the whole period, while the latter had a 12% share. The other countries in the top five were France, Sweden and the Netherlands, with shares of about 11%, 8% and 7%, respectively. Germany dropped from the top five.

The generalised drop of membership from the main Continental Europe countries contributed to reduce EIBA membership concentration. The countries in the second tier were the following: Canada, Germany, Belgium, Spain, Norway, Finland and Denmark. For the first time, all the four Nordic countries held shares above 2%. Most of these countries have increased their shares in the last years of this period. It is relevant to remark again that some countries' shares increased as a result of the convening of EIBA conferences, as was the case of the Netherlands, Norway or Belgium after the Rotterdam, Oslo and Antwerp conferences, respectively. In contrast, Eastern and South European countries, except Spain, had very low involvement in EIBA.

The additional findings from the whole analysis may be summarised in four points. The first concerns the weight reached by non-European countries, especially in 1985–1986, when the US and Canada combined accounted for almost one-third of EIBA membership. The second refers to the declining role of several countries that were the leaders in 1977–1981 (France, Germany, Sweden and the UK). The third has to do with the continuation of the very small contingents from Italy, West (Ireland and Portugal) and East European countries; the exception is Portugal which reached five members for 1988. The last finding is the trend towards declining membership. As a result of this, in 1987 EIBA was at the crossroads: further decline risked to make the Association less relevant to an increasing IB community. Fortunately, EIBA was able to reverse the trend, starting a recovery that enabled to overcome the 300-members mark by the second half of the following decade.

4.4.6. The EIBA Board

One of the main changes introduced by the 1982 statutes was the creation of the EIBA Board, replacing the former Executive Committee (EIBA, 1982b). The new statutes provided that a country should have at least five members to be represented at the EIBA Board. This implied that, from 1983 onwards, Israel, Italy, Japan and Libya had no longer a seat in the Board. As mentioned above, this was an important step towards enhancing the link between EIBA's membership and management.

Table 2 provides a tentative picture of the Board's composition between 1982 and 1988.[7]

The word 'tentative' is used because it was not possible to find in EIBA's archives the names of all the Board members for 1986 and 1987. An exercise of filling the holes was carried out on the basis of the analysis of General Assembly and Board decisions as well as of participation in Board meetings for 1986 and 1987. To make the table easier to read, the members of the 1982 Executive Committee whose countries were no longer represented at the Board, according to the new statutes, were not included.

Table 2. Composition of the EIBA Board (1982–1988).

Officers	1982	1983	1984	1985	1986	1987	1988
President	J. de la Torre	Pål Korsvold	Pål Korsvold	J. W. R. Schuit	Neil Hood	D. V. D. Bulcke	H. G. Meissner
President Elect			J. W. R. Schuit	Neil Hood	D. V. D. Bulcke	H. G. Meissner	R. Luostarinen
Vice-President		J. W. R. Schuit	Neil Hood	D. V. D. Bulcke	H.G.Meissner	R. Luostarinen	*Juán Durán*
Past President.			J. de la Torre	Pål Korsvold	J. W. R. Schuit	Neil Hood	D. V. D.Bulcke
National Coordinators							
Belgium	D. V. D. Bulcke	D. V. D. Bulcke	D. V. D. Bulcke	D. V. D. Bulcke	D. V. D. Bulcke	D. V. D. Bulcke	D. V. D. Bulcke
Canada	J. Picard	D. Ondrack	T. A. Poynter	T. A. Poynter	T. A. Poynter	Bernard Wolf	Bernard Wolf
Denmark			Ole Wiberg		H. Vestergaard	H. Vestergaard	H. Vestergaard
Finland	R. Luostarinen	R. Luostarinen	R. Luostarinen	R. Luostarinen	R. Luostarinen	R. Luostarinen	R. Luostarinen
France	M. Ghertman	B. Marois	B. Marois	G. Hirsch	G. Hirsch	G. Hirsch	Sabine Urban
Germany	E. Pausenberger	H. G. Meissner	H. G. Meissner	H. G. Meissner	H. G. Meissner	H. G. Meissner	H. G. Meissner
Netherlands	J. W. R. Schuit	Ben Bakker	Ben Bakker	Ben Bakker	Ben Bakker	J. W. R. Schuit	J. W. R. Schuit
Norway	Pat Joynt	Pat Joynt	Pat Joynt	Pat Joynt	Pat Joynt	Pat Joynt	Pat Joynt
Portugal							V. C. Simões
Spain	Barto Roig	Barto Roig	Barto Roig	Barto Roig	Barto Roig	Barto Roig	Juán Durán
Sweden	A. Edström	G. Hedlund	G. Hedlund	G. Hedlund	G. Hedlund	G. Hedlund	G. Hedlund
UK	Stephen Young	N. Campbell	N. Campbell	John Cantwell	John Cantwell	John Cantwell	John Cantwell
US	M. Hochmuch	M. Hochmuch	M. Hochmuch	M. Hochmuch		Bruce Kogut	Bruce Kogut

Source: Built on the basis of the following information: 1982–1985 – EIBA Membership Lists; 1986 and 1987: Minutes of the General Assembly and EIBA Board meetings; and further EIBA documents.

Notes: (1) Information for 1982 refers to the composition of the Executive Committee. Representatives of countries with less than five members (Israel, Italy, Japan and Libya) are not included. Information for 1983–1988 refers to the composition of EIBA Board. Ex-officio members (Executive Secretary, Director of EFMD, Director of EIASM and, for 1988, AIB President) are not included.
(2) Names in italics refer to information based on secondary sources, and not based on formal EIBA information about the composition of governance bodies.

4.5. SUMMARY

These were tough years for EIBA. The young Association was looking to over-come the Barcelona failure, to forge a strong IB research community by increas-ing the linkages between the main IB research centres in Europe (and in North America), and eventually to stabilise its finances. The Fontainebleau confer-ence, in 1982, was a major achievement. Drawing on INSEAD's resources, reputation and international connections, José de la Torre was able to attract almost 150 participants, including a large American contingent (more than 15% of the total). Simultaneously, a new template was established for EIBA conferences, with the setting up of key themes, and the implementation of a best papers' selection process. After Oslo, the Rotterdam conference in 1984 was another landmark for EIBA, consolidating overseas attendance (almost 38% of participants came from Canada and the US), while launching an ini-tiative, not fully successful, to foster interactions between IB researchers and practitioners: the 'EIBA meets Practice' session. While very positive in terms of quality and fostering research networking and rewarding for the Scottish hospitality, EIBA Glasgow fell short the organisers' goals on what attendance was concerned.

The EIBA Board's hasty decision to hold the 1986 conference together with AIB in London reduced the potential harmful effects of competition with AIB. However, it also entailed negative consequences, despite the efforts put by Danny Van Den Bulcke and Neil Hood in its organisation. Participation was low, and administrative problems strained the relationship between EIBA and some of its members. The second initiative to team up with AIB led an outcome similar to the first: a decline in participation and membership. Therefore, the 1987 and 1988 conferences (Antwerp and Berlin) were mostly intended to keep EIBA alive and to recover membership levels. This was especially felt in those countries that had been among the main sources of EIBA attendance (France, Germany, and Sweden). While open to the world, there was a concern to strengthen European membership and networking, since for 1985–1986 the US and Canada accounted for over 30% of membership. The Antwerp conference in 1987 introduced a very important and transformative innovation: the launching of the Doctoral Tutorial. This became a landmark in EIBA activities, providing a key contribu-tion to improve IB education as well as to rejuvenate EIBA.

On the organisational front, this period was marked by the revision of the stat-utes, the successive deficits and membership decline. The new statutes, approved in December 1982, were intended to contribute to stabilise EIBA's management as well as to establish a closer connection between EIBA's governance bodies and membership.

Taking the various elements together, the picture that emerges is a young organisation struggling for survival, in face of a much larger senior fellow: the AIB. The 1980s were hard times for EIBA, and its sustainability was at stake. However, by the same token, the difficulties faced have gave rise to a melting pot in which different IB research traditions interacted and a new generation of EIBAians was able to forge further capabilities and to take the baton from its elders. These developments provided the enabling conditions to establish in the next decade a fully blown and forward-looking European IB research community, open to the world.

NOTES

1. Attendance at EIBA Rotterdam was 252 if the participants in the 'EIBA meets practice' session and the students engaged were also considered.

2. See details in Section 4.4.

3. This will be developed in Chapter 5.

4. This theme will be dealt with more in detail below, in the EIBA–AIB relationship sub-section.

5. It is important to remark, in this connection, that evidence was found about 40 missing members in the EIBA membership files who have nevertheless attended the EIBA London Conference. This issue will be addressed in more detail below.

6. Interestingly, after Danny's passing away, the other tutorial originally called the EIBA Doctoral Symposium was relabelled as the Danny Van Den Bulcke Doctoral Symposium from the Milan Conference (2017).

7. To be more precise, the Board started functioning in 1983, after the approval of the new statutes. Therefore, the column for 1982 refers to the 'old' Executive Committee, while those between 1983 and 1988 refer, in fact, to the EIBA Board.

CHAPTER 5

STABILISING AND EXPANDING EIBA TOWARDS SOUTHERN AND EASTERN EUROPE (1989–1995)

This period is characterised by EIBA expansion, in terms of both membership and geographic scope. EIBA was able to withstand the difficult times faced between 1982 and 1988. The 1989 conference in Helsinki heralded EIBA's recovery. With a record number of participants, it gave EIBA a boost to face a changing Europe, stemming from the fall of the Berlin wall, and a new, more open World. These were times of hope for EIBA: globalisation was taking shape and the IB field was increasingly perceived as relevant in a widening Europe and a more connected world. EIBA was able to profit from such opportunities, and made significant efforts to expand towards Central and Eastern Europe, especially to Poland. As membership increased, EIBA's financial situation improved, achieving a surplus in 1994; the burden of accumulated deficits was not eliminated, however, and it would rebound later. In 1995, EIBA changed its name: as a result of Reijo Luostarinen's initiative, the A of Academy replaced the A of Association. The idea of creating the EIBA Fellows, also championed by Reijo Luostarinen, started to germinate, replicating the approach followed by AIB. However, the launch of the EIBA Fellows had to wait until the next decade. While still being chiefly a one-conference-a-year organisation, EIBA was growing, becoming more robust and looking ahead with renewed optimism. Gradually, identifying the location for future conferences became more an opportunity than a challenge.

The tone of this chapter is therefore much more positive than the previous ones. It shows how EIBA made the turnaround, becoming a well-established and self-confident organisation. In Helsinki, the number of participants reached 174, the highest ever, from 89 participants the year before, in Berlin. EIBA's first inroads into Southern Europe, since 1981, led to a new record number of participants (234 in Madrid-1990), a figure almost matched three years later in

The History of EIBA: A Tale of The Co-Evolution Between International Business
Issues and a Scholarly Community, 45–64
Copyright © 2025 by Vítor Corado Simões, John Cantwell and Philippe Gugler
Published under exclusive licence by Emerald Publishing Limited
doi:10.1108/978-1-83608-664-220241006

Lisbon (230). EIBA was exploring, and profiting from European diversity: in 1994 EIBA's annual conference was held for the first time in Poland, thanks to Krzysztof Obloj's efforts; and the long-awaited travel to Italy finally occurred the next year, in Urbino, led by Roberto Schiattarella with the support of Francesca Sanna-Randaccio, then the President of EIBA. Therefore, EIBA membership exhibited a steady increasing trend to exceed the 300 mark, in 1991 and 1994. The gender imbalance was significantly attenuated, with the surge in the female share to about 20%, from 6% only between 1982 and 1988. Meanwhile, the academic standard of the conferences has significantly improved, with the implementation of blind review procedures and the distinction between Competitive and Workshop papers, pioneered by Harald Vestergaard, in Copenhagen-1991.

The structure of this chapter is similar to the previous one, including five parts. The contextual perspectives about the overall political and business developments and the evolution of IB research are provided in sections one and two respectively. Section three highlights the main features of the seven Conferences (Helsinki, Madrid, Copenhagen, Reading, Lisbon, Warsaw and Urbino) held in this period. The next part is devoted to the evolution of EIBA's governance, including information on membership and financial issues. The chapter concludes with a summary of the main findings.

5.1. THE CONTEXT: ATTITUDES TOWARDS FDI

In December 1998, at the EIBA reception cocktail held at the Reichstag, while looking at the wall, closely patrolled by Eastern German troops, one could hardly imagine that the wall was to fall abruptly on November 9th the following year. The fall of the Berlin Wall accelerated the transformation process, together with the 'Velvet Revolution' in Czechoslovakia. Those who profited from the Helsinki Conference to visit Saint Petersburg (then, Leningrad) went to a Soviet Union where the signs of political and economic change, under the leadership of Mikhail Gorbachev, were evident. While EIBAians were attending the Helsinki Conference, further change was happening in Timisoara (Romania), leading to the overthrow of Ceausescu's dictatorship.

1989 was a key milestone in Europe's history, only paralleled by 1789 and 1848. Of course, there were multiple question marks about the likely developments of East-West relationships, some of them addressed at EIBA Helsinki 1989. However, the dominant expectation was that a more open Europe, though not probably 'from the Atlantic Ocean to the Ural Mountains' as once suggested by De Gaulle, might emerge, starting with the prospects for German reunification (completed *de jure* in 1990). It was really a chance that EIBA successively met in two privileged places to watch East-West interactions: Berlin and Helsinki.

The changes were not limited to Europe. International relationships also improved in 1989, particularly relationships with China. The 1989–1995 period was characterised by an increasing trend of FDI towards China. In South Africa, the nomination of Frederik de Clerk as president generated an accelerated change of a regime strongly condemned by the international community, leading to the end of apartheid and the election of Nelson Mandela in 1994. 1989 also witnessed the election of F. Collor de Mello in Brazil, the first winner of free presidential elections since 1960 to take office.[1] Further, the election of Fernando Henrique Cardoso in 1994 created the conditions for a significant improvement in Brazil's attractiveness as investment location as well as for Brazilian investments abroad. In 1991, India abandoned autarky and launched a programme of economic liberalisation, which included also the attraction of foreign investments. This led to an upsurge in inward FDI, from an average of around USD 150 million in 1990–1992 to around 1,750 million in 1995 (UNCTAD, 1996).

Significant changes occurred also on the international organisations front. The process of European integration experienced an acceleration, under the direction of the late Jacques Delors. The process of European integration became a reference model for many other regional integration experiences around the World. Six interrelated developments were particularly germane to that process. The first was the launch of the Single European Market in 1993, in the wake of the Single European Act of 1986. The second was the beginning of a string of policy initiatives leading to the creation of an Economic and Monetary Union (EMU) and the launch of the Euro in 1999. In this vein, exchange controls were abolished on July 1st, 1990, fully liberalising capital movements in the then EEC. The third move was the signing of the Maastricht Treaty, creating the European Union (EU), that came into force on November 1993. The following was the 1995 enlargement of the EU, extending membership to Austria, Sweden and Finland. The fifth change regards the liberalisation of the movement of people: the Schengen Agreement was signed in 1995 by seven members (Belgium, France, Luxemburg, the Netherlands, Portugal, Spain and West Germany) and by 1997, all member states, except the UK and Ireland, had joined it. Finally, comes the support to the transition process of the Central and East European countries, which were formerly under Soviet domination or were part of Yugoslavia (Slovenia was the first to get independence, in 1991). The 1993 Copenhagen criteria provided the rules for new countries to be eligible for EU membership. Most of those countries entered the EU in 2004.

In the wake of the signing of the Canada–US Free Trade Agreement in 1988, the idea to foster North America's trade integration led to the signing of the North American Free Trade Agreement (NAFTA) in 1992, coming into force on January 1st, 1994. Meanwhile, the Uruguay Round of multilateral trade negotiations ran between 1986 and 1993. These led to the creation of the WTO by the Marrakesh Agreement, signed by 123 nations on 15 April 1994, replacing the General Agreement on Tariffs and Trade (GATT).

The change in the international FDI climate is also evident in the behaviour of the United Nations organisation, and especially the UNCTC. Taking a more positive stance towards MNCs (called Transnational Corporations in the UN jargon), the UNCTC launched in the early 1990s a series of initiatives aimed at diffusing statistical information about FDI and stimulating the discussion regarding the contribution of MNCs towards development and the design of appropriate economic policies towards FDI. In 1991, the first issue of World Investment Report (WIR) series was published. The theme of the first WIR was *The Triad in*

World investment (UNCTC, 1991), echoing the concept introduced by Kenichi Ohmae (Ohmae, 1985). The team in charge of the first edition was led by Karl P. Sauvant, a future EIBA Honorary Fellow.

The 1989–1995 period has also witnessed important developments in the process of technological convergence, namely between computers and communications, from which we profit today.

In a nutshell, the 1989–1995 period was characterised by a pro-democracy movement and the emergence of new nations. On the economic front, there was a significant expansion of pro-market reforms (Cuervo-Cazurra, Gaur & Singh, 2019) and the liberalisation in economic policy. Multinationals were 'lauded in the 1990s (including by third-world leaders in Davos) as the bringers of foreign capital, technology and know-how' (The Economist, 2000). While a decoupling between the location of production and consumption was emerging, leading to the development of GVCs (Baldwin, 2012; Buckley & Strange, 2015; Gereffi, 2014, 2019), a stiff competition among countries was emerging to attract an increasingly volatile FDI. The inward-looking perspective that dominated most of the 1980s gave rise to an increasingly globalised world, in which MNCs were the key players.

5.2. THE CONTEXT: IB LITERATURE

In the 1989–1995 period, two landmark contributions towards an improved understanding of IB issues were published. Chronologically, the first is the book *Managing across Borders: The Transnational Solution*, by Christopher Bartlett and Sumantra Ghoshal (Bartlett & Ghoshal, 1989). It provides a new perspective about MNCs, going further than the I-R framework (Prahalad & Doz, 1987). Based on clinical case research, they argued that such organisations need to simultaneously respond three managerial challenges: to achieve global efficiency, to adapt to locally differentiated conditions, and to profit from worldwide learning. While it comes in the wake of earlier works (Bartlett & Ghoshal, 1987; Hedlund, 1986), the book led to a significant change in the way in which internationally dispersed organisations were perceived. Responding the challenges required decentralisation and the replacement of a 'command-and-control' view by a perspective of the MNC as an integrated network. Bartlett and Ghoshal's (1989) approach had a significant and lasting influence on IB literature on several dimensions, especially with respect to organisation models (Ghoshal & Westney, 1993; Gupta & Govindarajan, 1994; Harzing, 2000; Leong & Tan, 1993; Macharzina, 1993; Rugman & Verbeke, 1992; Schmid, Schurig & Kutschker, 2002; Westney & Zaheer, 2001), innovation and knowledge management (Ambos & Schlegelmilch, 2007; Bartlett & Ghoshal, 1990; Cantwell & Mudambi, 2005; Doz, Santos & Williamson, 2001; Foss & Pedersen, 2004; Minbaeva, 2007; Régner & Zander, 2011), and subsidiary management (see below).

The second landmark contribution was the first version of John Dunning's *magnum opus Multinational Enterprises and the Global Economy* (Dunning, 1993). This is an encyclopaedic work, providing an encompassing view of the state of the art of IB scholarship at the beginning of the 1990s.[2] The thick

687-page volume summarised John Dunning's readings (he was an avid reader and became the lighthouse for generations of IB scholars, many of which he systematically encouraged to engage in IB research) and his own view about the key IB issues. While addressing multiple facets of IB, the effects of MNCs' activities stand as a dominant feature of the book, very much in line with John Dunning's concerns with the welfare consequences of MNCs on various dimensions, from technology and innovation to competitiveness, employment, and business practices. *Multinational Enterprises and the Global Economy* is still today a must read for all those who enter the field, enabling them to understand the evolution of IB literature, the main tenets of John Dunning's thinking and the characteristics of MNCs as key players in our economies.

Beyond those landmark contributions, the 1988–1995 period witnessed some very relevant developments in the IB field. With respect to the theoretical domain, there was the emergence of the evolutionary perspective of the MNC. It developed along two distinct, though interrelated streams, both rooted in the original work of Richard Nelson and Sidney Winter (Nelson & Winter, 1982). Knowledge and innovation are envisaged in both strands as key drivers of MNCs' behaviour and competitiveness.

The first stream was championed by John Cantwell, based on his research on the historical patterns of patenting by large international firms. In his book *Technological Innovation and Multinational Corporations*, Cantwell (1989a, p. 10) argues that MNCs 'have become global organiser[s] of economic systems, including systems for allied technological development in different parts of the world'. The process of creating technology-based ownership advantages is strongly 'associated with the research and production experience accumulated within a particular firm' (Cantwell, 1989a, p. 216). The MNC becomes therefore a worldwide orchestrator of knowledge, anchored on experience and combining insights from different locations (Cantwell, 1995a). The focus therefore shifts towards the role of international knowledge networks in sustaining or diversifying paths of technological accumulation in MNCs.

The second was led by Bruce Kogut and Udo Zander in a series of papers published in the first half of the 1990s (Kogut & Zander, 1992, 1993, 1995, 1996; Zander & Kogut, 1995). For our purposes, the key reference is Kogut and Zander (1993), which advances an evolutionary theory of the MNC. Similarly to Cantwell, they argue that the key capability of MNCs is anchored in the combination and integration of knowledge. They highlight in particular the knowledge about how to manage internationally dispersed operations and to launch new products and business lines, as a result of international learning. Since the MNC has developed such combinative capabilities, the international market for technology is not considered as an option to exploit firms' knowledge capabilities. This leads the authors to provide a sociological capabilities-based explanation of the internalisation leg of the eclectic paradigm, in contrast to the traditional transaction cost economics account (Kogut & Zander, 1993, 1995).[3]

The transnational perspective together with the evolutionary theory led to an increased concern with subsidiaries' capabilities and roles as well as with their contribution towards MNCs' competitiveness. As an orchestrator of geographically dispersed capabilities, the MNC needs to pay increased attention to the combination of headquarters-based and subsidiary-generated knowledge assets (Cantwell, 1995a). The development of 'combinatory capabilities' (Kogut & Zander, 1992) is essential to integrate knowledge from inside and outside the firm as well as from the headquarters and the various subsidiaries, leading to Kuemmerle's (1997, 1999) typology. Therefore, a new strand of literature on subsidiaries emerged (Andersson & Forsgren, 1996, 2000; Andersson, Forsgren & Holm, 2002; Birkinshaw, 1996, 1997; Birkinshaw & Hood, 2001; Birkinshaw & Morrison, 1995; Gupta & Govindarajan, 1991, 1994; Holm & Pedersen, 2000; Pearce & Tavares, 2002).

Other relevant developments on the theoretical front include the initial steps in the distinction between firm-specific advantages (FSAs) and country-specific advantages (CSAs) by Rugman and Verbeke (1992), in an edited volume in honour of John Dunning (Buckley & Casson, 1992a). Also in this volume, Buckley and Casson (1992b) drew upon the internalisation theory to venture into future developments regarding the organisation of innovation processes inside MNCs. Jean-François Hennart provided empirical application of his earlier transaction cost theory of equity joint ventures (Hennart, 1988, 1991), arguing that most economic transactions involve a mix of market and hierarchy (Hennart, 1993). Considering that traditional hierarchical capitalism was being superseded by an 'alliance capitalism', John Dunning proceeded to a reassessment of the eclectic paradigm (Dunning, 1995). He suggested that the combination of inter-firm resources and capabilities was likely to have effects on both the Oa (property rights and/or intangible asset advantages) and Ot (advantages of common governance) vectors of ownership advantages.

In fact, the development of international cooperative strategies became a central feature of the IB literature in this period. The reasons for collaboration were mostly based on transaction costs (Chi, 1994; Hennart, 1991; Parkhe, 1993) but, as time went by, they were combined with resource-based strategy, learning and relational considerations (Barney & Hansen, 1994; Foss, 1994; Gugler, 1991; Gulati, 1995; Hamel, 1991; Kanter, 1994; McGee, Dowling & Megginson, 1995; Mowery et al., 1996). Some approaches addressed strategic alliances in general, aimed at providing guidance to their management (Brouthers, Brouthers & Wilkinson, 1995; Gugler, 1992; Hamel, 1991; Hamel, Doz & Prahalad, 1989; Kanter, 1994; Lorange & Roos, 1992; Yoshino & Rangan, 1995), while others focussed on the choice of the specific cooperation mode (Chi, 1994; Contractor, 1990; Hagedoorn, 1990, 1993; Hill, Hwang & Kim, 1990; Kim & Hwang, 1992; Osborne & Baughn, 1990). Research has also highlighted particular aspects such as cultural fit (Lane & Beamish, 1990; Parkhe, 1993), trust (Cullen, Johnson & Sakano, 1995; Gulati, 1995; Madhok, 1995), and learning (Ciborra, 1991; Inkpen & Crossan, 1995). Hamel (1991) showed that alliances might be envisaged as 'learning races', in which individual benefits might be at odds with joint benefits.

The development of less hierarchical perspectives, stemming both from Bartlett and Ghoshal (1989) and from earlier work along similar lines (Hedlund, 1986; Prahalad & Doz, 1987), led to new perspectives on international management, some of them included in edited volumes such as Bartlett, Doz and Hedlund (1990) and Ghoshal and Westney (19932). Hedlund and Rolander

(1990) further developed the heterarchical approach, showing how it worked in practice, while White and Poynter (1990) introduced the concept of 'horizontal firm', highlighting how the development of information technologies might open new opportunities for horizontal, inter-peer subsidiaries cooperation. Doz and Prahalad (1991) put the diversified MNC in context and concluded that increased interaction between organisational theory and international strategic management was needed.

Regarding the cultural dimension, the 1989–1995 period was still dominated by Hofstede's (1980) thinking. However, beneath Hofstede's dominance, other approaches were taking shape. Fons Trompenaars, another Dutch scholar, intended to provide new insights on how to ride the waves of culture (Trompenaars, 1995). This period also witnessed the launch of the research, led by Robert House, leading to the GLOBE metrics (House, Hanges, Javidan, Dorfman & Gupta, 2004; Javidan, Dorfman, Sully de Luque & House, 2006; Javidan & Dastmalchian, 2009). However, Venaik and Brewer (2013) argued that both the Hofstede and GLOBE culture scores are averages of items that are unrelated and do not correspond to valid and reliable scales for cultural dimensions at the level of individuals or organisations.[4]

The research on internationalisation processes was pursued, still largely anchored on the work of Nordic scholars. Reijo Luostarinen published his doctoral dissertation (Luostarinen, 1979/1989). Benito and Gripsrud (1992) envisaged internationalisation as a cultural learning process. Johanson and Vahlne (1990, 1992) revisited their earlier model at the light of more recent developments with a view to address new aspects, including the relationships with the eclectic paradigm, industrial networks and international entry modes; the literature on internationalisation in industrial networks, especially Johanson and Mattsson (1988), would play an important role in the subsequent revision of the model (Johanson & Vahlne, 2006, 2009, 2020). Buckley and Ghauri (1993) made an interesting contribution by putting together some of the key pioneering papers on firms' internationalisation processes.

A final reference is due to Michael Porter's book *The Competitive Advantage of Nations* (Porter, 1990). It introduced the concept of the 'diamond' to highlight the interaction between different factors impinging upon a country's competitiveness. This work generated a vivid debate among IB scholars. Some of them cooperated with Porter in applying the approach to specific countries, such as Sweden (Porter et al., 1991). Others, instead, took a critical stance, as was the case of Robert Grant and Alan Rugman, pointing out several shortcomings or mistakes in Porter's diamond (Grant, 1991; Rugman, 1991; Rugman & D'Cruz, 1993; Rugman & Verbeke, 1993). Dunning (1993, p. 86) took a more nuanced view, arguing that the diamond drew 'heavily on the work of internalization scholars', and made use of it, together with stages-of-growth approaches, the Environmental/Systems/Policy (ESP) paradigm (Koopman & Montias, 1971) and insights from Pavitt (1988) and Cantwell (1989a), to design a general model of the interaction between FDI, asset accumulation and economic development (Dunning, 1993, p. 268). This reasoning led, with significant changes, to Dunning and Lundan's (2008, 2010) institutionalist approach as well as to the co-evolutionary view of Cantwell et al. (2010).

5.3. EIBA: THE CONFERENCES

After the troubled period experienced since 1986, the Helsinki Conference in 1989 heralded new, brighter times for EIBA. Reijo Luostarinen made a significant effort to organise a landmark conference. Its success paved the way to a string of conferences from which the eldest EIBA members still have pleasant remembrances: Madrid and the ceremony of assignment of the *Honoris Causa* doctorate to John Dunning; Copenhagen and the launch of a formalised procedure to distinguish between competitive and workshop papers; Reading and the keynote lecture by Oliver Williamson; Lisbon and the welcome evening at St. George's Castle; Warsaw and the opportunity to listen to Gunnar Hedlund and Marina Papanastassiou playing piano at Jablonna Palace; and Urbino, under the shade of the Palazzo Ducale and the spirit of Federico da Montefeltro. The attendance of EIBA conferences reached new heights. Conference venues successfully spanned out over space: West and South, to Madrid, Lisbon and Urbino; and East, to Warsaw. As Europe was becoming more integrated, so too EIBA was becoming more European. Below, a brief presentation of the main features of the EIBA conferences held between 1989 and 1995 is provided.

The Helsinki Conference's theme was 'Dynamics of International Business'. As pointed out above, it took place at a time of intense change in Europe, after the fall of the Berlin Wall. The effort to attract colleagues from Eastern Europe was pursued, with the participation of East European scholars.[5] The conference took place at Hotel Kalastajatorppa, a five-star hotel at the outskirts of Helsinki. Attendance reached a new record: 175 participants, from 28 countries. This was the first EIBA conference for some now well-known EIBA members, such as Francesca Sanna-Randaccio, the first woman to serve as EIBA President (1995) and later Dean of the EIBA Fellows, Rebecca Piekkari (*née* Marschan), now an EIBA Fellow and then a student who was about to start her PhD and responsible for the spouses' programme (Piekkari, 2023) and Ingmar Bjorkman. The third edition of the Doctoral Tutorial, chaired by Danny Van Den Bulcke, included nine PhD candidates, including some that later became respected scholars such as Liisa Välikangas and Helen De Cieri. The winner was Karin Fladmoe-Lindqvist (University of Minnesota) with a project on 'Ownership and control patterns of international service companies'.

Reijo Luostarinen had made a perfect contribution to revive EIBA spirits. Juán Durán, who took the baton to organise the EIBA 1990 in Madrid, pursued this by putting together an excellent conference. The pre-conference event of awarding John Dunning an *Honoris Causa* Doctorate by the Autonomous University of Madrid set the tone for the whole Conference. Under the theme 'Changes in International Business', EIBA Madrid started with a plenary session chaired by S.A.R. El Principe de Asturias, D. Felipe de Bourbon y Grecia, now King Felipe VI, who had been a member of the conference's Council of Honour. Attendance achieved a new height: 234 registered participants. The drive to attract participants from Eastern Europe continued; the organisation released funds to pay the expenses of participants from Hungary, Poland and Russia. The list of those who had their first EIBA experience in Madrid includes two EIBA Fellows (Gabriel Benito and Ulf Andersson).

The Doctoral Tutorial was becoming an EIBA tradition. 1990 was the first time that Danny was not at the helm, being replaced by John Cantwell. In contrast, John Dunning made his formal debut at the event, which now honours his memory, as Special Adviser. There were two winners: Jeannette Capel, from the Tinbergen Institute (The Netherlands), with a project on 'Exchange Rates and Foreign Direct Investments', and Ivo Zander (Stockholm School of Economics) that was researching about 'Technology and Technological Change in Swedish Firms: 1965–1990'.

EIBA 1991 took place at the Copenhagen Business School (CBS), organised by Harald Vestergaard, under the *motto* 'An Enlarged Europe in the Global Economy'. This was the first EIBA conference in which a blind refereeing process was established to select the contributions suitable to be presented at the conference. This innovation was a very important step to enable EIBA conferences to achieve higher academic quality standards, thereby attracting further top IB scholars. Although exhibiting a slight decline with regard to Madrid, the number of participants was still above 200. Bent Petersen, Marian Gorynia, Torben Pedersen and Trond Randoy made their EIBA debut in Copenhagen 1991; the first is now managing the tutorial and the last two became EIBA Fellows. The Doctoral Tutorial, chaired again by Danny Van Den Bulcke, had two winners, both from the US: David Parkinson, from Wharton, on 'Innovation Processes and International Competition', confirming the increasing relevance of international technology and innovation issues; and Dorothee Feils, from South Carolina, on 'Shareholder Wealth Effects of International Mergers and Acquisitions'.

The next year, EIBA crossed the channel again, going to Reading to show how successfully it had recovered from the 1986 drawback. John Cantwell organised the conference whose overall theme was 'Multinationals in Europe'. The ceremony of John Dunning's official retirement from the University of Reading was held in conjunction with the EIBA conference. This was emotionally moving, especially for those EIBA members who had been Dunning's students or had been deeply influenced by his ideas. However, on the other side of the Atlantic, at Rutgers, he remained very active in research and in supporting PhD students and participated in almost all EIBA conferences until he was hit by disease.

The Reading conference was also marked by Oliver Williamson's keynote lecture. The 2009 winner of the Nobel Prize in Economic Sciences address was entitled 'The logic of economic organisation, with applications to International Business'. Participants were also offered two recently published books: *Multinational investment in modern Europe*, edited by John Cantwell (Cantwell, 1992); and *Multinational Enterprises in the World economy, Essays in honour of John Dunning*, edited by Peter Buckley and Mark Casson (1992a). Despite the quality of the programme, the number of participants declined to 185. Several colleagues who are now EIBA Fellows made their EIBA debut in Reading: Lucia Piscitello, Marina Papanastassiou and Marjan Svetlicic. This conference was also the EIBA debut for other long-term commited members, including the late Bob Pearce and Mo Yamin. Reading was a further step towards the consolidation of the Tutorial. Chaired by Danny Van Den Bulcke, the faculty included inter alia John Stopford and John Dunning. The award was granted to Monika Weber-Fahr

(University of Trier, Germany) for her project on 'Segmentation of European Labour Markets: A Consequence of Multinational Firms' Investment?'.

The 1993 conference was held in Lisbon, organised by Vítor Corado Simões, under the theme 'International Business and Europe after 1992'. Going to a country with a small IB community was another test for EIBA. Although the academic programme did not meet the standards recorded in Reading, Portuguese warmth and friendliness enabled a successful conference. EIBA Lisbon was attended by 230 people, very close to the Madrid record. First-time EIBA participants included Lars Oxelheim, who became an EIBA Fellow, and Marin Marinov.

An innovation introduced in Lisbon was the organisation of a pre-session dinner for the Doctoral Tutorial faculty and students to get together in a more relaxed mood. The core faculty was the same as in previous sessions (Danny Van Den Bulcke, John Dunning, John Cantwell, Gunnar Hedlund and Jean-François Hennart), this time joined by Jean-Claude Usunier. The prize was granted to Thomas Puetz (University of Strasbourg, France), for his project on comparative analysis of 'Decision Processes in Research and Technology Management' between France and Germany.

K. Obloj offered to organise the 1994 EIBA conference in Poland. The Warsaw conference became a landmark in EIBA's expansion towards Eastern Europe. The conference was held in mid-December 1994 under the 'High Speed competition in a new Europe' theme. The number of participants declined with regard to the previous conferences, reaching 162. This is not at all surprising considering the shallowness of Polish IB community at the time and the fact that December is not the best time to visit Poland. Warsaw was the first EIBA conference for Philippe Gugler, who later became EIBA President, EIBA Chair and EIBA Fellow, as well as for other committed EIBAians, such as Joachim Wolf, Rudolf Sinkovics and Stefan Schmid.

The 8th Doctoral Tutorial was again chaired by Danny Van Den Bulcke. Several changes were introduced in the faculty. While John Dunning and J.-F. Hennart retained their positions, Stephen Young, Andrzej Kozminski and Krysztof Obloj participated for the first time. The winner was Anne-Wil Harzing (University of Maastricht), with a project on 'Organizational Bumble-Bees: International Transfers as a Control Mechanism in Multinational Companies'.

Meanwhile some developments were taking place on the Italian front. With the support of Francesca Sanna-Randaccio, then the Italian representative at the EIBA Board, it was possible to convene a conference in Italy, a long-cherished EIBA intention. In May 1993, Francesca informed the Board that her contacts with Bocconi (Milan) had not led to a structured proposal. However, Roberto Schiattarella, from the University of Urbino, showed interest in organising the EIBA conference. Francesca became EIBA President in 1995 and Roberto Schiattarella was nominated Conference Chairman.

The conference was dedicated to the memory of two former EIBA Presidents who had passed away in 1995: Barto Roig and Harald Vestergaard. Conference attendance was around 200, a figure which broadly corresponds to the average attendance throughout the 1989–1995 period. Urbino was the first EIBA experience for Sarianna Lundan, who became a very influential EIBA member and Dean of the Fellows[6]; other first-time participants were Tamar Almor, now EIBA Fellow,

Rajneesh Narula and Davide Castellani, then a PhD student at the University of Urbino, who served as a staff member. The Doctoral Tutorial was held at Palazzo Corboli, a 16th-century palace. A heavy-weight faculty participated in the Tutorial, with Yair Aharoni and Peter Buckley (who had been in the 1987 Tutorial faculty), joining three long-term members (Danny Van Den Bulcke, John Dunning and Jean-François Hennart) plus Stephen Young. The award was assigned *ex-aequo* to Tommaso Perez (University of Ancona, Italy) and to Omar Toulan (Massachusetts Institute of Technology, US), for their projects on 'Multinational Enterprises and Technological Spill-overs' and on 'Market Liberalization, Competitive Behaviour and the Internationalisation Strategies of Firms: The Case of Argentina', respectively.

Taking a longitudinal perspective, this was the period in which EIBA conferences achieved a significant average attendance and consistent quality standards, by establishing a proper refereeing process and by distinguishing between competitive and workshop papers. EIBA was sounder, but still very dependent on the yearly conferences. At the Urbino December Board meeting, a string of four future Conferences was already established: Stockholm, Stuttgart, Tel Aviv and Manchester. These will be addressed in the next chapter.

5.4. EIBA: ORGANISATIONAL DEVELOPMENTS

The developments on the organisational front between 1989 and 1995 will be addressed in 10 sections: general perspective; initiatives to increase membership; expansion towards Eastern Europe; EIBA special interest groups; relationships with other organisations; EIBA publications; statutory changes; EIBA accounts; EIBA membership; and the EIBA Board.

5.4.1. General Perspective

From the analysis of EIBA archives, namely the Board meeting minutes, the evolution of the perspectives about the future of EIBA emerges very clearly. While in 1989 there was a serious concern with EIBA's capacity to face the challenges ahead, expressed in the convening of a 'strategy' Board meeting in March 1989, in 1994–1995 the mood was different, reflecting an increasingly self-confident organisation, whose accounts had moved from red to black. The transition in Europe and the development of globalisation opened new opportunities for IB research and contributed to increasing the clout of the IB scholarly community.

On the organisational front, besides the membership issue, two proposals were presented by Reijo Luostarinen in 1992: one concerned the change of EIBA's name, from Association to Academy, and the other had to do with the creation of the EIBA Fellows, as AIB had already done.

The success of the Helsinki conference, the Copenhagen improvements in the paper selection procedure, the expansion towards Southern and Eastern Europe and the membership increase enabled EIBA to envisage the future with renewed confidence. In 1995, the Academy was preparing to reach adulthood. This would, however, require further organisational changes for EIBA to be less dependent on its annual conferences.

5.4.2. Initiatives to Increase Membership

As a result of the problems mentioned in the previous chapter, namely the low attendance of the 1986 London conference, in 1988 EIBA had 137 members only. There was a consensus about the need to attract more members to enhance the Association's dynamics as well as to improve its financial situation. It was thought that enticing company participation in EIBA might be the way to achieve a stabilisation in income, making it less dependent on the ups-and-downs in individual membership.

The 'Membership drive' project was aimed at addressing four objectives: to get 'drop-outs' back and to attract new members; to foster West European attendance; to get East European countries' scholars to join; and to increase the number of (individual) members to 200. It called for a joint effort involving the EIBA Secretariate, NRs and individual members. Every member was invited to 'bring one new member' (Luostarinen, 1989). It also included the initiative 'Knights of EIBA', championed by Roland Schuit. However, it did not achieve the desired results. Several companies were approached, but none of them became a corporate member.

As a result of EIBA Board members' efforts, EIBA membership reached 224 by the end of 1989, corresponding to an increase of more than 60% with regard to 1988. In the following years, increasing membership continued to be envisaged as an important goal. It was also felt the need to provide members with additional products aimed at increasing the value-for-money of continued EIBA membership. Ideas voiced in this regard included the publication of an edited book with the best papers of the previous conference, improving the *Newsletter* with texts contributed by members, especially Board members, launching a book on 'Who is Who in IB in Europe', and increasing lobbying within the European Commission (EC) (EIBA Board, 1995). With hindsight, it is interesting to remark that some of those ideas were turned into reality in the following decade, namely the book with selected papers, which became the Progress in International Business Research (PIBR) series, and the upgrading of the *EIBA Newsletter*, which became the *EIBAzine* in 2004, thanks to Danny Van Den Bulcke and Tamar Almor's efforts. The possibility of using the *Management International Review (MIR)* to circulate the EIBA leaflet evolved into negotiations for *MIR* to be the EIBA's journal. However, as it will be seen in Chapter 6, they were not successful. In 2001, *IBR* became EIBA's journal.

A relevant dimension of the 'Membership drive' project was EIBA's expansion towards Eastern Europe. Poland was the spearhead of this move, although efforts have also been pursued to attract scholars from other countries. Having in mind their importance for the geographic configuration of EIBA in the future, these initiatives are briefly presented below.

5.4.3. Expansion Towards Eastern Europe

As mentioned above, EIBA was concerned with expansion towards Eastern Europe even before the fall of the Berlin Wall. We have noticed, in the previous chapter, the establishment of contacts and the support provided to Polish scholars to attend the 1988 EIBA conference in Berlin. A dialogue with colleagues from the Baltic countries was launched by Reijo Luostarinen in connection with the Helsinki conference.

The political developments in the following years created new opportunities for attracting East European colleagues to the IB field. EIBA was able to get two TEMPUS grants to provide training to Polish scholars and to stimulate them to attend EIBA conferences. As a result of these initiatives, Krszysztof Obloj, one of the leaders of the Polish host, offered to organise the 20th EIBA conference in Warsaw.

In 1995, the EIBA membership list included colleagues from the following Eastern European countries: Czech Republic (1), Poland (6), Russia (1), and Slovenia (5). Poland was ahead but Slovenia was following suit, under the leadership of Marjan Svetlicic. It would still take almost one decade for the conference to come to Ljubljana.

5.4.4. EIBA Special Interest Groups

Having in mind the diversity of issues addressed by IB, it is not surprising that some groups of scholars might cluster around specific themes. In the period under analysis, two strands have developed as interest groups, though with different levels of formalisation: the EIBA working group on the Internationalisation of Small and Medium Sized Enterprises (EIBA-WISE); and the working group on Small and Medium-sized Open EConomies (SMOPECs). Both had their EIBA Board 'champions': Roland Schuit and Reijo Luostarinen respectively; however, while the first was formalised, the second proceeded in an informal fashion. Unfortunately, EIBA-WISE was discontinued after Roland Schuit's untimely death in 1997.

The SMOPEC group was focussed on promoting research on the internationalisation of small open economies and their firms. Led by Reijo Luostarinen, it encompassed colleagues from Austria (Christian Bellak), Denmark (Steen Thomsen), Finland (Jorma Larimo), Israel (Seev Hirsch and Tamar Almor), Portugal (Vítor Corado Simões) and Switzerland (Philippe Gugler). It was felt that small open economies faced specific issues that impinged upon their internationalisation patterns. The SMOPEC group had annual meetings coincident with EIBA conferences. However, there were few joint papers involving researchers from different countries, and the group lost strength and became diluted.

5.4.5. Relationships with Other Organisations

Relationships with AIB were pursued. The number of IB researchers who were simultaneously members of both organisations increased, and the bridges between them were active, especially after 1987, when John Dunning became President of AIB. However, AIB's decision to periodically convene its annual conference in Europe raised serious headaches for EIBA, since there was the risk that this would seriously curtail EIBA conference's attendance. That was the case in 1992 when AIB had scheduled its annual conference for Barcelona. This led John Cantwell to initially suggest to hold the EIBA Reading conference in

September 1992 'to avoid any clash with the AIB meeting in Barcelona in late
November 1992' (Cantwell, 1989b). London 1986 was still very fresh in EIBA
Board members' memory.

In practice, EIBA's position was rather orientated towards maintaining some
distance from AIB. The final decision regarding the Reading conference is a clear
testimony of EIBA's commitment to follow a path independent from AIB. This is
probably one of the reasons why the attendance at EIBA Reading 1992 was below
the two previous ones. This may be understood as the price to be paid for keeping
autonomy from the AIB.

Links needed to be kept, but being too close might raise troubles. The agreement reached in the early 1980s that each organisation would nominate a representative to attend the other's Board meetings was still in place.[7] However, Danny
Van Den Bulcke's report on EIBA activities to the AIB 1991 Annual Conference
Miami (October 1991) is an expression of the need for such an exchange.[8]

The 1994 decision to follow a path distinct from AIB, by choosing Jerusalem
as the venue for the 1998 conference, shows that EIBA was more confident on its
capabilities to keep independent from AIB, while maintaining a continuous dialogue, in which key individuals, belonging to both organisations, played a central
role as gatekeepers. However, by 1998 the conflicts over the timing of the EIBA
conference and the AIB conference when it was in Europe had anyway eased, since
the AIB conference in Vienna was held in early October, and from 2002 onwards
the AIB conference has been held in June or July. A gap of months between these
conferences became easier to handle than was a gap of weeks, which it had been
historically when the AIB conference was held in late November (in the American
Thanksgiving week).

Simultaneously, AIB was still serving as a role model for EIBA. The dual relationship with AIB is expressed in Reijo Luostarinen's proposals regarding EIBA's
organisational changes. On the one hand, the fact that AIB had changed its name
to Academy was used as a reason for EIBA to do the same, and the creation of
the EIBA Fellows closely followed the structure of the AIB Fellows.

5.4.6. EIBA Publications

The *EIBA Newsletter* was continued to be published on a bi-annual basis, Gerry
Van Dyck kept her editorial role. The contents were very much the same as in the
previous period. Information was also provided about other subjects relevant for
the EIBA membership, namely the development of the TEMPUS grant project
and the twin projects launched in 1989 by Reijo Luostarinen and financed by
the Helsinki School of Economics: the studies on EIBA membership and on IB
Education in Europe.

The EIBA membership study was aimed at providing a general picture
of EIBA members' activities and interests. The final report drew on a survey
responded to by 96 members and was circulated to EIBA members. In the
Foreword, Reijo Luostarinen underlined that it is 'a good start to strengthen the
possibilities for future cooperation' and expressed the wish that 'this kind of service would become a permanent part of the implementation of EIBA's mission'
(Luostarinen, 1990).

5.4.7. Statutory Changes

At the December Board meeting in Reading, Reijo Luostarinen presented two proposals: changing the name of EIBA from Association to Academy and establishing the EIBA Fellows. However, the proposals were not discussed since there were many points in the agenda requiring fast decisions, namely the venues for the 1994 and 1995 conferences. Therefore, Reijo Luostarinen put forward his proposals again at the May 1993 interim Board meeting in Lisbon.

Regarding the EIBA Fellows, it was felt that this move might contribute to provide a better balance between the need for injecting 'new blood' in the Board while mobilising the accumulated stock of experience/knowledge in profit of the organisation. It was also argued that this higher-level but semi-autonomous body might foster members motivation to devote their time and energy to EIBA. The Board's reaction was not overtly positive. The consequence was the postponing of the issue. It only came back by the end of the decade.

Arguments for changing the name of EIBA from Association to Academy included the following: Academy shows more clearly that EIBA is an academic and professional organisation; Academy has a higher status and provides the enhanced capacity to attract new members; it is likely to generate an increased thrust for high-level business managers to consider their firms to become EIBA members; and similar organisations associated with EIASM are already Academies, as happened with EMAC, the European Marketing Academy. It was approved by the General Assembly in Warsaw, and enshrined in the 1995 revision of the EIBA statutes.

5.4.8. EIBA Accounts

The continued deficits that were a consistent feature since EIBA foundation were reversed, EIBA's accounts showing modest surpluses for 1994 and 1995: BEF 22.5 and 38.5 thousand (corresponding to €560 and €950), respectively. Of course, these were much far from solving the accumulated debt to EIASM.

For 1994 and 1995, membership fees alone were sufficient to cover the expenditures. This indicates that the efforts taken to increase individual membership were paying off, enabling EIBA to become financially sustainable. Also, in this regard, the conditions for EIBA to reach adulthood, escaping from the dependence on EIASM's support, were being developed.

5.4.9. EIBA Membership

The one-conference-a-year continued to be a distinctive feature of EIBA. Membership figures were still very contingent upon a set of conference-related factors, including inter alia location attractiveness, the conference organisers' effort to attract participants, and the level of development of local IB communities. In fact, in spite of the initiatives to promote three-year membership, the decision to renew was very influenced by each member's interest to attend the next conference.

A longitudinal analysis the 1989–1995 period shows that, in spite of ups-and-downs (a maximum of 307 members for 1994 and a minimum of 204 for

1990[9]), an increasing membership trend emerges along the period. The 200 members target set up at the 1989 Strategy Board meeting (EIBA Board, 1989) was clearly exceeded. EIBA was increasingly attracting more members. EIBA conferences became known for their friendly atmosphere, the welcoming attitude towards newcomers and young researchers, and the improved paper selection process which have, in our opinion, played an important role in shaping this trend.

Although it has never been made explicit as an objective of the membership increase campaign, this period has witnessed a very significant upsurge in female membership. While until 1988 it had never reached 20, in 1989, 30 women were EIBA members, and the figure exceeded 70 in 1994. As a result of this, the share of female EIBAians jumped to an average of almost 20% for 1989–1995, with a maximum of 26% for 1995. A number of well-known members of the EIBA community joined the Academy in this period; that is the case of Francesca Sanna-Randaccio, Rebecca Piekkari, Tamar Almor, Marina Papanastassiou, Lucia Piscitello and Sarianna Lundán. This was also translated, although to a much lesser extent, in the main governing EIBA body: leaving the Secretary General aside, the number of women at the EIBA Board reached three (Sabine Urban, Francesca Sanna-Randaccio and Denice Welch) in 1995, from one only in 1989.

The trend towards a less concentrated membership structure country-wise, already observed in the previous period, was reinforced in 1989–1995 (see Fig. 5). The top-5 countries were responsible for 65% of total membership in 1977–1982, and 56% in 1982–1988. In 1989–1995 they accounted for slightly less than half (49.4%), and their share has shown a sustained decline from 1989–1991 (52%) to 1992–1995 (48%). This was due to the development of IB education and research communities in an increasing number of European countries. The efforts made

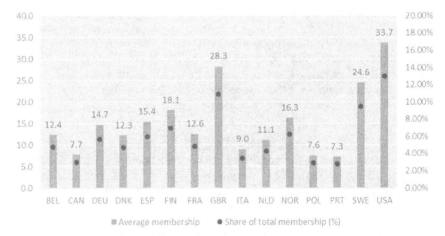

Fig. 5.   EIBA Membership per Country (1989–1995). *Source*: EIBA archives.
Note: The figure includes those countries with at least 2% of total average membership in the period concerned.

to attract more members were translated into three features: members were based in more countries (23 for 1988 versus 30 for 1995); new EIBA communities were developed, not just in Poland but also in other countries such as Denmark, Portugal and Italy[10]; and already established chapters have grown along the period, as is the case for the UK, Finland, Germany, and even Sweden. A remarkable feature is the increase in Nordic countries' share, which soared from 19% for 1982–1988 to 28% for 1989–1995.

The top-five included the US (13%), the UK (11%), Sweden (10%), Finland (7%) and Norway (6%). The US was until 1992 the top ranked country, as it had been since 1984. As time went by, however, the US share has dropped: from 14% for 1989–1991 to 12% for 1992–1995. This was due more to an increase in several European countries' hosts than from an absolute decline in US members. The UK evolution is very interesting, since the fall recorded in the late 1980s was followed by a significant growth in 1991–1993 and then a slight decay in 1994–1995; this is translated by the following figures: 6% for 1989, 16% for 1993 and 13% for 1995. Of course, the Reading conference, in 1992, played an important role in this growth: the teaming-up with AIB-UK enabled EIBA to attract scholars that had been so far in the AIB orbit only. The contrast of UK shares for 1989–1991 and 1992–1995 is striking: 8% against 13%. In the last time window, the UK became the leading membership country.[11]

Summarising the analysis, four interesting features emerge. First, there was a decline in membership concentration: the top-five's share dropped from 52% for 1989–1991 to 48% for 1992–1995. Second, there was a recovery of earlier EIBA powerhouses, namely Germany and especially the UK, which returned to the first place. Third, the dependence on members from America (the US and Canada) significantly declined with regard to the 1982–1988 period, from 24% to 16%, but it was not accompanied by a decline in absolute numbers. Fourth, EIBA's geography expanded towards East (Poland) and South (Portugal and Italy), where engaged EIBA communities emerged. But there was still much room for EIBA to expand, in particular in Eastern Europe (where Slovenia and Estonia followed Poland), Central Europe (Austria and Switzerland) and Western Europe (Ireland), as well as outside Europe (the decision to hold a conference in Israel in 1998 was taken in 1994). There were other opportunities for EIBA's growth waiting to be explored.

5.4.10. The EIBA Board

The list of the EIBA Board members for 1989–1995 is provided in Table 3. Most of the names included there have already been mentioned earlier on different roles, from conference organisers to sponsors of initiatives to promote EIBA.

The key finding from browsing the above list is stability. In fact, there have been very few changes in the core group that was at EIBA's helm. This has two contrasting implications: on the one hand, it expresses the commitment of a multinational team of scholars towards the development of EIBA; on the other hand, this entailed the risk of 'freezing' EIBA's leadership, limiting the inflow of 'new blood' and more diverse visions.

Table 3. Composition of the EIBA Board (1989–1995).

Officers	1989	1990	1991	1992	1993	1994	1995
President	R. Luostarinen	Juán Durán	H. Vestergaard	John Cantwell	V. C. Simões	K. Obloj	R. Schiattarella
President Elect	Juán Durán	H. Vestergaard	John Cantwell	V. C. Simões	K. Obloj	F. Sanna-Randaccio	Gunnar Hedlund (+ Ö. Sölvell)
Secret. General	G. Van Dyck	G. Van Dyck	G. Van Dyck	G. Van Dyck	G. Van Dyck	G. Van Dyck	G. Van Dyck
National Coordinators							
Australia						Denice Welch	Denice Welch
Belgium	D. V. D. Bulcke	D. V. D. Bulcke	D. V. D. Bulcke	D. V. D. Bulcke	D. V. D. Bulcke	D. V. D. Bulcke	D. V. D. Bulcke
Canada	Bernard Wolf	Bernard Wolf	Rolf Mirus	Rolf Mirus	Rolf Mirus	Rolf Mirus	Rolf Mirus
Denmark	H. Vestergaard	H. Vestergaard	H. Vestergaard	H. Vestergaard	H. Vestergaard	H. Vestergaard	Laurids Hedaa
Finland	R. Luostarinen	R. Luostarinen	R. Luostarinen	R. Luostarinen	R. Luostarinen	R. Luostarinen	R. Luostarinen
France	Sabine Urban	Sabine Urban	Sabine Urban	Sabine Urban	Sabine Urban	Sabine Urban	Sabine Urban
Germany	H. G. Meissner	H. G. Meissner	H. G. Meissner	H. G. Meissner	H. G. Meissner	H. G. Meissner	H. G. Meissner
Italy				F. Sanna-Randaccio	F. Sanna-Randaccio	F. Sanna-Randaccio	F. Sanna-Randaccio
Netherlands	Roland Schuit	Roland Schuit	Roland Schuit	Roland Schuit	Roland Schuit	Roland Schuit	Roland Schuit
Norway	Pat Joynt	Pat Joynt	Pat Joynt	Pat Joynt	Pat Joynt	Pat Joynt	Pat Joynt
Poland		Jerzy Cieslik	Jerzy Cieslik	K. Obloj	K. Obloj	K. Obloj	K. Obloj
Portugal	V. C. Simões	V. C. Simões	V. C. Simões	V. C. Simões	V. C. Simões	V. C. Simões	V. C. Simões
Spain	Juán Durán	Juán Durán	Juán Durán	Juán Durán	Juán Durán	Juán Durán	Juán Durán
Sweden	G. Hedlund	G. Hedlund	G. Hedlund	G. Hedlund	G. Hedlund	G. Hedlund	G. Hedlund
UK	John Cantwell	John Cantwell	John Cantwell	John Cantwell	John Cantwell	John Cantwell	Fred Burton
US	Bruce Kogut	Bruce Kogut	Bruce Kogut	J.-F. Hennart	J.-F. Hennart	J.-F. Hennart	J.-F. Hennart

Source: Analysis of EIBA archives.

With hindsight, it may be argued that the positive implications overshadow the negative ones. The work carried out by the core team was essential for EIBA to make the turnaround, after the London 1986 experience. To respond to the problems, the Board started to meet three times per year, always with a significant participation.

5.5. SUMMARY

The period under analysis was a time for EIBA recovery and expansion, in terms of both membership levels and geographic spread. EIBA profited from political and economic developments in Europe, from European integration to the fall of the Berlin Wall and the subsequent transition in Eastern Europe, to become truly pan-European. While the 1986–1988 troubles were still present in Board members' minds, the 1989 Helsinki conference was critical to achieving the turnaround. The setting up, from Copenhagen-1991, of a blind-review process to select conference papers significantly contributed to strengthen EIBA's legitimacy, reputation and attractiveness. The early 1990s were times of optimism and growth for EIBA. It was the first time that EIBA ventured clearly outside the well-beaten paths of EEC-founding countries, Britain and Scandinavia. It went South and East, reaching the Western tip of Europe and crossing the Alps. Significant efforts were made to foster expansion towards Eastern Europe, especially Poland. The organisation was still very much dependent on the attractiveness of the locations and the quality of conferences but the group of loyal EIBA members steadily increased, and conference attendance reached an average of about 200 people.

These developments cannot be separated from the commitment of core Board members. To respond to the challenges faced and to design the organisation's strategy, the periodicity of Board meetings increased, as mentioned above, to three per year. Achieving financial stability was a key concern, and multiple initiatives were taken to increase membership, both individual and organisational. While on the latter front, no results were obtained, on the former they were very positive: the average EIBA membership in the 1989–1995 period reached around 260 as against less than 170 for the 1982–1988 period. As for conference locations, the geographical spread of EIBA membership expanded, and new chapters were established (Australia, Italy and Poland). The share of the top-5 countries (the US, the UK, Sweden, Finland and Norway, taking into consideration the whole period), collectively experienced a steadily declining trend.

Reijo Luostarinen's initiative led to the change in EIBA's name: the A for Association was replaced by the A for Academy. In contrast, the proposal to establish the EIBA Fellows took longer to mature, and became a reality in 2002 only. EIBA's 1994 and 1995 accounts recorded positive results; but these were insufficient to offset the historically accumulated deficits supported by EIASM. This financial burden was to emerge as an urgent problem in the 2000s, when EIBA was fully established.

The constancy of the Board's members enabled EIBA to survive and to get more firmly established. But longer-term sustainability required additional moves.

EIBA was facing new challenges on how to balance stability with change. If the first half of the 1990s was the time for growth and geographical expansion, the period ahead was to a large extent a transitional phase, before the development of a series of statutory changes, between 2003 and 2012, which led EIBA to achieve a more consistent governance model, less dependent on conference locations' ebb and flow. The period between 1996 and 2002 witnessed several important changes in EIBA's life: technological, with the first edition of conference proceedings in diskette instead of paper; organisational, with the creation of the Fellows; and in gender, with women playing an increased role in shaping EIBA's activities, leading to the nomination in 2002 of the first woman who combined the functions of President and conference organiser, Marina Papanastassiou.[12]

NOTES

1. In fact, the first presidential election after the overthrowing of the military dictatorship was won by Tancredo Neves, in 1985, but he died before taking office, being replaced by José Sarney. Ironically, Collor de Mello was impeached due to misconduct in 1992.

2. An updated version was published in 2008, in cooperation with Sarianna Lundan, Dunning's former doctoral student and another committed EIBA member (Dunning & Lundan, 2008).

3. It is interesting to remark at this juncture that John Cantwell, Bruce Kogut and Udo Zander have all been active members of EIBA. Many of their three-way intellectual interactions took place at the EIBA conferences. The two first were Board members in the 1989–1995 period. Later, in the mid-2000s, John Cantwell and Udo Zander have jointly led the Doctoral Tutorial.

4. See also Tung and Verbeke (2010).

5. It seems that Reijo relied on barter trade (vodka to pay the conference fee) to solve the currency exchange problems faced by Eastern European scholars (see the text on Reijo Luostarinen and EIBA by Lawrence Welch, Denice Welch, Catherine Welch and Rebecca Piekkari, available at the EIBA History website: https://history.eiba.org/eiba-and-reijo/).

6. At the time of writing, Sarianna was the Dean of the EIBA Fellows.

7. See the letter from Danny Van Den Bulcke to John Cantwell dated 25 September 1992 in that regard (Van Den Bulcke, 1992). It seems that AIB had not exactly followed the terms of the agreement.

8. Formally, EIBA's representative on the AIB Board was Harald Vestergaard, and not Danny Van Den Bulcke. Most probably, Harald had delegated that specific responsibility to Danny.

9. The annual analysis needs to be carried out with caution, since usually membership refers to the year following a conference and not to the current one.

10. Of course, the fact that these countries have hosted EIBA conferences played an important role in increasing membership.

11. This may be also related to the fact that the UK scholarly IB community itself became increasingly internationalized. See Cantwell, Piepenbrink, Shukla and Vo (2016).

12. Recall that in 1995 Francesca Sanna-Randaccio became the first EIBA female President. However, she was not responsible for the organisation of the Urbino conference.

CHAPTER 6

CHANGE AT THE TURN OF THE CENTURY: DIGITAL MEDIA, THE EIBA FELLOWS AND RISING FEMALE PARTICIPATION (1996–2002)

1995 corresponded to the end of a period of consolidation and expansion of EIBA, towards South and East, in connection with the very process of European integration. It may be argued that EIBA reached adulthood. It continued, however, to be a one-conference-a-year organisation, very dependent on the commitment of a small group of 'champions'. EIBA was able to generate profits in a few years; but the burden of accumulated debt was yet to be solved. Francesca Sanna-Randaccio was the first woman to serve as EIBA President, although she was not the principal conference organiser.

The period covered in the present chapter, from 1996 to 2002, may be characterised as transitional. While making inroads towards the Mediterranean (Israel and Greece), the expansion of geographic scope became less relevant. A strong need to improve governance, to develop further instruments to make EIBA membership more enticing, and to adjust to what was then called the 'information age' emerged. The establishment of the EIBA Fellows, in 2001, was a very important step to consolidate the organisation while fostering the required change in EIBA Board. The setting up of a link to an established journal (*IBR*) was a further move to make EIBA membership less dependent on the attendance of annual conferences. The role played by women has steadily increased, leading to gradual but sustained changes in an organisation so far dominated by men. However, a qualitative leap took place: in 1995, EIBA had its first woman President (Francesca Sanna-Randaccio); in 2000, a woman co-organised a conference

The History of EIBA: A Tale of The Co-Evolution Between International Business
Issues and a Scholarly Community, 65–92
Copyright © 2025 by Vítor Corado Simões, John Cantwell and Philippe Gugler
Published under exclusive licence by Emerald Publishing Limited
doi:10.1108/978-1-83608-664-220241007

(Sarianna Lundan); and in 2002, for the first time, Marina Papanastassiou combined both roles: being EIBA President and organising the EIBA conference. Interestingly, this period begins and ends with the two piano soloists who played for the EIBA family in 1994 at Jablona Palace in Poland: Gunnar Hedlund and Marina Papanastassiou.

The structure of this chapter comprises six sections. First, a perspective of the main political and economic environmental changes with implications for IB activities is provided. Then, an overview of the main developments in IB research is presented. The next two sections focus on the key features of EIBA's life at the turn of the century. Section three is intended to provide a view about the main features of the string of Conferences going from Stockholm (1986) to Athens (2002), through Stuttgart, Jerusalem, Manchester, Maastricht and Paris. Section four deals with organisational developments. The creation and the early years of the EIBA Fellows are addressed next. The chapter closes with a general picture of the main developments occurred in this transitional period, which ended with a woman at EIBA's helm.

6.1. THE CONTEXT: ATTITUDES TOWARDS FDI

After Berlin, EIBA's encounters with history happened again in the 1996–2002 period. In 1998, the EIBA conference took place in Jerusalem at a time when the Israeli state commemorated its 50th anniversary, and the prospects for solving the Middle East conundrum looked rosy. It was a period of *détente*, marked by the visit of Bill Clinton, then President of the US, to the Middle East, meeting Yasser Arafat in Gaza and making a historic address to the people of Israel. The EIBA conference, held between 13 and 15 December, partly coincided with Clinton's visit. Conference participants could feel the tension in Jerusalem. It was possible to identify snipers placed at the roof of some buildings, prepared to shoot if any unpredicted event happened. Later, in 2000, the EIBA conference took place at Maastricht, an iconic place for the history of European integration: the treaty establishing the EU was signed there in 1992.

The string of developments in the economic and business fields recorded in the early 1990s, mentioned in the previous chapter, were pursued, sometimes at a fast pace, until the turn of the century. The opportunities opened by the internet looked so bright that many people believed in the advent of an information or knowledge society.

This outlook also led to a boom in mergers and acquisitions (M&A). According to the World Investment Report 2000,

> cross-border M&As are growing so rapidly in importance precisely because they provide firms with the fastest way of acquiring tangible and intangible assets in different countries, and because they allow firms to restructure existing operations nationally or globally to exploit synergies and obtain strategic advantages. (UNCTAD, 2000, p. xxi)

This played an important role in shaping the pattern of FDI flows in the period under analysis.

The generally positive attitude towards FDI held through to the late 1990s, although a backlash movement, led by non-governmental organisations (NGOs), gradually emerged (The Economist, 2000). Demonstrations against globalisation took place at various G7 meetings. Part of the protests were addressed to the alleged exploitative power of MNCs as well as to the intended Multilateral Agreement on Investment (MAI), a draft agreement negotiated in secret between members of OECD between 1995 and 1998. According to the OECD (2020), the objective was to 'provide a broad multilateral framework for international investment with high standards for the liberalisation of investment regimes and investment protection and with effective dispute settlement procedures'. Opponents argued instead that it was intended to establish a new body of universal investment laws that would grant corporations unconditional rights to engage in financial operations around the world, without any regard to national laws and citizens' rights. After an intense global campaign against the MAI, France withdrew its support, leading the process to an end (for an analysis, see Neumayer, 1999). In 2001, the WTO initiative to launch the Doha round on trade liberalisation also raised a wave of complaints.

China undertook a double move. On the one hand, a strong push was taken to recover the sovereignty over the former European outposts in the Sea of China: the handovers of Hong Kong (under British rule since 1842) and Macao (settled by Portuguese merchants in 1535) took place in 1997 and 1999, respectively. On the other, it became more integrated into the world economy, particularly since 2001, when it became a member of WTO.

In South America, the development of Mercosur, established in 1991 and changed into a customs union in 1994, stimulated both intraregional and extraregional FDI in the late 1990s. However, there was a steady decline since then: in 2000–2002, Latin America's share in world FDI fell to the levels recorded in 1990–1995 (around 4.3%). The emergence of the Corralito crisis in Argentina further contributed to hamper FDI in the region. In contrast, investments in Africa increased in 2001, after an erratic behaviour along the late 1990s, to reach 2.3% of worldwide FDI; however, this was not sustainable, since it largely resulted from two big M&A operations in South Africa and Morocco (UNCTAD, 2003).

After the tectonic change which occurred in 1989, Europe continued to witness significant moves in 1996–2002. These followed four interrelated axes. First, the change in governance, through the revision of the Maastricht Treaty. Together with all pre-existing treaties, this was amended by the treaties of Amsterdam (1997), Nice (2001) and Lisbon (2007). The second was the launching, in 1999, of the single currency – the Euro – intended to strengthen growth and economic integration and to leverage Europe's clout in the World economy. However, in 1999 only 11 countries (Austria, Belgium, Finland, France, Germany, Ireland, Italy, Luxembourg, the Netherlands, Portugal and Spain) adopted the Euro as their currency, followed by Greece in 2001. The third axis is related to the intention to prepare Europe for the envisaged knowledge society, through the so-called Lisbon strategy, enacted in 2000; this was aimed at combining innovation-led economic growth with social balance. The fourth axis concerns the expansion of the EU membership. Though no further enlargement took place in 1996–2002, this period witnessed the laying down of the foundations for integrating Central and Eastern European countries in the EU. Demands for accession mushroomed, after the formal applications of the Czech Republic and Slovenia in early 1996. In 2002, the EC considered that 10 countries (Cyprus, the Czech Republic, Estonia, Hungary, Latvia, Lithuania, Malta, Poland, the Slovak Republic and Slovenia) would be ready for EU membership in 2004. Enlargement finally took place in 1 May 2004, as it will be seen in the next chapter.

The developments reported above had significant implications for the way how IB was perceived by political, social and economic players as well as for the patterns of IB research. These will be briefly summarised in the following section.

6.2. THE CONTEXT: IB LITERATURE

In contrast to the previous period, the present one did not witness the publication of landmark additions to IB literature. A couple of contributions deserve, however, a reference. The first edition of *The Oxford Handbook of International Business* (Rugman & Brewer, 2001) provided an encompassing perspective of IB issues, addressed by a set of top-level academics. While being an influential book, with a second edition in 2009 (Rugman, 2009), by its very characteristics it did not have a significant effect in shaping the evolution of IB research. More relevant from that perspective was another book, also published in 2001: the challenging *From Global to Metanational: How Companies Win in the Knowledge Economy* (Doz et al., 2001). They argued that 'geography is no longer destiny' (Doz et al., 2001, p. 54), heralding how globalisation might enable worldwide knowledge management. It introduced a new label in the IB lexicon: the metanational company, i.e., a firm that learns from the World to be globally competitive. A reference is also due to the seminal article by Teece, Pisano and Shuen (1997) on dynamic capabilities.[1] Anchored on evolutionary approaches to strategy and innovation studies, it points out the need for companies to continuously adjust their capabilities, bearing in mind the three Ps: evolutionary Paths, competitive Positions, and organisational Processes. It significantly influenced future IB research, mainly on what regards the theory of the multinational enterprise (Dunning, 2000; Lessard , Teece & Leih 2016; Teece, 2014), international expansion (Luo, 2000), knowledge management (Madhok & Osegowitsch, 2000) and international new ventures (Keupp & Gassmann, 2009; Weerawardena et al., 2007).

The advances in globalisation generated various streams of research. Three deserve a mention here. The first concerns the new economy, the knowledge economy or the information age (Castells, 1996; Evans & Wurster, 1997), entailing implications for IB (Dunning & Wymbs, 2001; Petersen, Welch & Liesch, 2002; Teece, 1998; de la Torre & Moxon, 2001).[2] The second addresses the globalisation of technology and innovation, largely driven by MNCs (Archibugi & Iammarino, 1999; Archibugi & Michie, 1997; Florida, 1997; Granstrand, 1999; Lall, 1997; Zander, 1999; Zanfei, 2000). The third corresponds to the launching of research on global commodity chains and GVCs, led by Gary Gereffi (Gereffi, 1999; Gereffi, Humphrey, Kaplinsky & Sturgeon, 2001; Humphrey & Schmitz,

2002); this came to influence IB approaches, including Peter Buckley's global factory (Buckley, 2009; Buckley & Ghauri, 2004). Meanwhile, a discussion about the effects of globalisation on welfare and development was emerging; Stiglitz (2002) and Dunning and Hamdani (1997), including contributions from some EIBAians (Yair Aharoni, John Cantwell and Seev Hirsch). This line of thinking would become fully blown in the 2000s with the books by Dunning (2003) and Stiglitz (2006), to be presented in Chapter 7.

Strategic alliances attracted a large host of research in this period. Two sets of edited books, putting together different streams of research, were published. The first, entitled *Cooperative Strategies*, encompassed three volumes providing perspectives from North America, Europe, and Asia-Pacific (Beamish & Killing, 1997a, b, c). The second, *Cooperative Strategies and Alliances*, (Contractor & Lorange, 2002) came in the wake of an earlier book by the editors on the same subject (Contractor & Lorange, 1988b). Partially drawing from Gulati (1998), the literature on international alliances may be addressed from three perspectives: (1) the formation and the choice of alliance governance structure (Buckley & Casson, 1996; Chi & McGuire, 1996; Hagedoorn, 2002; Narula & Dunning, 1998); (2) the dynamic evolution of alliances, including a focus on trust and relational dimensions (Ariño, de la Torre & Ring, 2001; Dunning, 2002; Dyer & Singh, 1998; Dyer, Kale & Singh, 2001; Inkpen & Currall, 1997), but also on power (Yan & Gray, 2001); and (3) performance issues (Khanna, Gulati & Nohria 1998; Lane, Salk & Lyles, 2001; Zollo, Reuer & Singh, 2002).

The attention assigned to subsidiaries' capabilities and their contribution towards MNCs' overall competitiveness further increased in 1996–2002. Julian Birkinshaw coined the concept of subsidiary initiative and showed how subsidiary entrepreneurship might contribute to enhance MNC's competitiveness. He cooperated with Neil Hood, a very influential EIBAian at the time[3] (Birkinshaw, 1996, 1997, 1999, 2000; Birkinshaw & Hood, 1998, 2000, 2001). Birkinshaw, Hood and Jonsson (1998) provided empirical evidence that subsidiary initiatives may foster MNC's firm-specific advantages. The theme was revisited by Rugman and Verbeke (2001), who argued that subsidiaries are key actors in MNCs' capability development processes; they identified 10 types of MNC–subsidiary linkages leading to capability development. To understand the multi-faceted nature of such linkages, the concept of embeddedness is central. Drawing on both Polanyi and Granovetter, Ulf Andersson and Mats Forsgren took this concept to the IB field. MNCs are embedded in different national contexts, and each subsidiary is embedded in a specific local system of social, economic and technological relations; the idiosyncratic, contextual nature of such relations endows subsidiaries with particular advantages that may be leveraged to benefit the whole MNC (Andersson & Forsgren, 1996; Andersson, Forsgren & Holm, 2001, 2002). This led to a multi-country project on Centres of Excellence (CoEs), aimed at understanding the reasons why some subsidiaries were assigned such role as well as their scope (Andersson & Forsgren, 2000; Forsgren & Pedersen, 1998, 2000; Fratocchi & Holm, 1998; Holm & Pedersen, 2000). Further work on CoEs includes Frost, Birkinshaw and Ensign (2002) and Moore (2001). The research on subsidiaries' competences contributed to shape a new vision about subsidiaries' roles: instead of passive pawns, just implementing headquarters decisions, they came to be seen as active players to foster MNCs' innovation and competitiveness, as suggested by Kuemmerle's (1997, 1999) HBE (home base exploiting) versus HBA (home base augmenting) contrast.

Knowledge management and innovation also gained importance. Remind that EIBA Stockhom-1996's theme was 'Innovation and International Business'. Some research in this field concerned the use of alliances as tools for knowledge sharing and learning, as mentioned above. Another research stream addressed knowledge-sharing processes among different MNC's units.

The latter research is linked to the development of institutional approaches. Institutions matter, influencing IB behaviour (Mudambi & Navarra, 2002) and MNCs' management processes (Kostova & Zaheer, 1999; Xu & Shenkar, 2002). This research stream has also included work on international expansion (Guillén, 2002; Meyer, 2001). The concept of institutional distance (Kostova, 1996) influenced the design of the CAGE model (Ghemawat, 2001), which posits four institutional dimensions of distance: cultural, administrative, geographic and economic. Ghemawat (2001) argued that 'distance still matters', in contrast to Doz et al. (2001) and other globalisation champions.

Having in mind the spurt of M&A in the period under analysis, this theme might be expected to have enticed IB research. This did not appear to be the case, partly reflecting the delay between the emergence of business phenomena and academic research. Extant literature on M&A took different directions: the effects of acquisitions on innovation and learning (Ahuja & Katila, 2001; Bresman, Birkinshaw & Nobel 1999); technology integration (Ivarsson & Vahlne, 2002); connections with strategic alliances (Hagedoorn & Sadowsky, 1999); and the influence of cultural differences on acquisition performance (Morosini, Shane & Singh 1998). At this juncture, one may remark that further literature on culture emerged in this period, besides the ongoing GLOBE project (whose first results were to be published in 2004) and another book by Hofstede (1997): *Cultures and Organizations: Software of the Mind*. Interesting contributions addressed the rethinking of cultural distance (Shenkar, 2001), the effects of culture on ownership decisions (Hennart & Larimo, 1998), and the impact of psychic distance on international retail operations performance (Evans & Mavondo, 2002).

The analysis of internationalisation processes underwent significant changes. The main contributions may be clustered around two axes: the internationalisation of non-Western companies (Guillén, 2002; Henisz & Delios, 2001; Padmanabhan & Cho, 1999; Young, Huang & McDermott, 1996) and internationalisation towards emerging markets, often related to entry mode choice (Gaba, Pan & Ungson, 2002; Lin, 2000; Luo, 1998; Luo & Peng, 1999; Meyer, 2001; Pan & Tse, 2000). Petersen and Pedersen (1997) reappraised the Uppsala model, pointing out its relevance but also its limitations.[4] This model became subject to criticism from a new research strand, focused on fast internationalisation strategies, often followed by technology/knowledge-intensive firms, labelled international new ventures and/or born globals (Coviello & Munro, 1997; Jones, 1999; Lee, Lee & Pennings, 2001; Madsen & Servais, 1997; McDougall & Oviatt, 2000; Oviatt & McDougall, 1997; Yli-Renko, Autio & Sapienza, 2001; Zahra, Ireland & Hitt, 2000). Innovative approaches to operation modes were taken by Benito, Pedersen and Petersen (1999) and Petersen, Welch and Welch (2000), paving the way for later research on operation mode switching (Benito, Petersen & Welch, 2009).

The literature on international management lost impetus. Besides Doz et al. (2001) mentioned above, outstanding research on this topic was limited. Worth reference are Egelhof's (1997) edited book on transforming organisations, the evolutionary perspective on established MNCs transition from decentralised to network-based structures (Malnight, 1996), and the analysis of the challenges faced by diversified MNCs (Prahalad & Oesterveld, 1999).

We conclude with a brief account of IB theory developments. Though less remarkable than those recorded in the two previous periods, some relevant contributions emerged. In his relentless concern to adjust the eclectic paradigm to changing times, John Dunning introduced two important novelties in the paradigm: first, by envisaging it as an envelope for economic and business theories of the MNC, as a result of the developments in the knowledge-based economy and the relevance of resource-based approaches (Dunning, 2000); and second, by identifying relational assets as a key element of firms' ownership advantages (Dunning, 2002). A reference is due to Cantwell and Narula's (2001) article on the eclectic paradigm and the global economy, anticipating their edited book on the evolution of the OLI framework (Cantwell & Narula, 2003). As mentioned previously, Buckley and Casson (1998a, 1998b) modelled entry mode choices, drawing on internalisation theory. Hennart (2001) argued that the transaction costs theory of the MNC is based on comparing the costs of organising international interdependencies in firms and in markets, and the initiative to respond to such interdependencies may come from either of the firms involved, an insight leading to his *Down with MNE-centric theories* claim (Hennart, 2009). While recognising the merits of transaction costs/internalisation approaches, Madhok (1997) argued that resource-based and organisational capability views appear to better adjust to the business context of the late 1990s (see also Madhok, 2002).

6.3. EIBA: THE CONFERENCES

At the turn of the century, EIBA was facing significant challenges. They were no longer related to survival, but rather to improving governance, enticing younger scholars to join, and adapting to technological changes. Between 1996 and 2002, EIBA travelled East and West, North and South. However, this time it ventured much less on unchartered lands: while for 1989–1995, 5 out 7 conferences corresponded to countries' debuts (Finland, Denmark, Portugal, Poland and Italy), for 1996–2002, just two conferences had such characteristic, both in the East Mediterranean (Israel and Greece). The Stockholm-1996 and Stuttgart-1997 conferences contributed to enhance EIBA's attractiveness and reliability. In 1998 EIBA went to Israel. It was the first time that EIBA ventured outside Europe's geographical borders; this feat would be replicated later in 2015, at much longer haul, by holding the annual conference in Rio de Janeiro, Brazil. The Jerusalem conference was also the first to have digital, instead of paper, proceedings: it meant EIBA's entry into the information age. In 1999 and 2000, EIBA conferences moved closer to the Atlantic: Manchester and Maastricht. It was the second conference in Britain in the last decade of the 20th century, after Reading-1992. It took longer for EIBA to come back to the Netherlands: 16 years had elapsed since Rotterdam-1984. It took even longer to return to France. However, the Paris-2001 conference was not a landmark as had been Fontainebleau-1982, when a series of initiatives were taken by José de la Torre to strengthen the academic quality of EIBA conferences (see Chapter 4). The Mediterranean welcomed EIBA again, in 2002, when the conference was held in Athens. For the first time ever, a woman – Marina Papanastassiou – took the double job of serving as EIBA President and conference organiser. This heralded a new trend: female EIBAians were becoming increasingly important to shape the organisation's activities and governance. It was a long road for EIBA. By 2002, it was a healthier and more diverse organisation, while keeping its friendly, familiar and generation-bridging identity.

Gunnar Hedlund had on several occasions expressed Stockholm School of Economics' availability to host an EIBA conference. That turned into reality in 1996. Unfortunately, Gunnar was not able to attend it as he had undergone a surgery shortly before the conference; this was not enough to stop the progress of the disease that led to his untimely death. Therefore, Stockholm-1996 was pervaded by mixed feelings: on the one hand, it was a superb conference, very well organised on both the academic and social fronts as a result of the efforts of a group led by Örjan Sölvell; on the other, there was a feeling of discomfort and unease since Gunnar could not join us in a conference that he had inspired.

The conference theme was 'Innovation and International Business'. This expressed well the turn observed in IB research at the time. It was attended by about 250 people, a new record for EIBA, though a short-term one, since next year's conference in Stuttgart attracted almost 320 participants. A change, much welcomed by young (and some not so young EIBAians), was introduced in the traditional EIBA format: a DDD –Dine (light), Drink (in moderation) & Dance (as much as you can) – Monday evening event. This was to become a must of EIBA social programmes for some years. Stockholm was the first EIBA conference for now well-known EIBAians, such as Filip de Beule (NR of Belgium and editor of the *EIBAzine* between 2010 and 2013), Ulrike Mayrhofer (NR of France) and Antonio Majocchi (among the best reviewers in different occasions). On the social side, it has also been a memorable conference, with two events that old EIBAians even today remind one another of: the dinner at Vasa museum; and the closing banquet at Stockholm's City Hall, the place in which the dinner after the Nobel Prize award ceremony takes place.

As usual, the Doctoral Tutorial was chaired by Danny Van Den Bulcke. Besides John Dunning, the faculty included Yves Doz, Jean-François Hennart, Bernard Yeung and Stephen Young. Among the 10 students participating in the tutorial, a reference is due to Niklas Arvidsson, who wrote a very interesting PhD thesis on 'the ignorant MNE', Lin Lerpold, who attended several EIBA conferences in the following years and became a very influential scholar in the field of sustainability, Namrata Malhotra, who became known for her research on internationalisation processes, and Ulrike Mayrhofer, who was mentioned already. The winners were

Odile Janne, from the University of Reading (UK) and Georgine Kryda, from the University of Illinois at Urbana-Champagne (US). Their PhD proposals were, respectively, on 'The Geographical Spread of Corporate Technological Activity in Europe', and on 'Modeling the Bargaining Game between Multinational Firms and Britain's Monopolies and Mergers Commission'.

In 1997, EIBA moved to Germany again, less than a decade after the unforgettable 1988 Berlin Conference. Klaus Macharzina was strongly committed to make EIBA Stuttgart a landmark for EIBA's development. He put a lot of effort in enticing IB researchers worldwide, but especially from German-speaking countries, to attend the conference. Several well-known EIBAians made their debut in Stuttgart, namely Ana Teresa Tavares (now Tavares-Lehman), Grazia Santangelo, Catherine Welch, the late Pavlos Dimtratos, Teresa da Silva Lopes, and Ursula Ott. The former two became EIBA Presidents in 2010 and 2007, respectively, being now EIBA Fellows.

The conference success helped to countervail the unhappy news of the passing away of two former EIBA presidents: Roland Schuit (Rotterdam-1984) and Gunnar Hedlund (Stockholm-1996). For this reason, the proceedings of the Stuttgart conference were dedicated to the memory of both. Also following the proposal by the Institute of International Business (IIB), which had been led by Gunnar Hedlund for about 10 years, a decision was taken to launch the IIB Dissertation Award in Memory of Gunnar Hedlund (Gunnar Hedlund Award) to the best dissertation in IB.[5] The first winner was Anthony S. Frost (MIT Sloan School of Management, US), for his PhD thesis on 'The Geographic Sources of Innovation in the Multinational Enterprise: US Subsidiaries and Host Country Spillover, 1980-1990'. The 1997 conference theme was 'Global Business in the Information Age'. This was the last year in which the Conference proceedings were printed on paper. The conference also featured four panels. The opening session was focused on the implications of services, globalisation and the information age for company strategies, with interesting presentations by Klaus Mangold, then Chairman of the Board of *Daimler-Benz InterServices*, John Stopford (London Business School, UK), and Klaus Macharzina. The closing plenary addressed similar themes; the panel included Eugene Jaffe, the incoming EIBA President, Hermann-Josef Lamberti, Chairman of the Board of *IBM Germany*, and William Egelhoff, Fordham University, US.

Chaired by Danny Van Den Bulcke, the Doctoral Tutorial included 10 presentations, out of 25 applications. Peter Buckley, Jean-François Hennart, Bernard Yeung, Stephen Young and John H. Dunning, as special adviser, completed the faculty. Two well-known EIBAians presented their PhD proposals in Stuttgart: Grazia Santangelo, mentioned above; and the late Pavlos Dimitratos, who became a leading specialist on international entrepreneurship, and NR of Greece at the EIBA Board.[6] With a project on the 'Role of Corporate Headquarters and Cooperation among Subsidiaries during Global Product Launches', Andreas Gast (MIT, US) was the winner.

When leaving Stuttgart, most participants were really happy with the quality of the conference on both academic and social dimensions. They might be also thinking about the next Conference in Israel, remembering the enthusiasm of Eugene Jaffe in welcoming EIBA to Jerusalem on the 50th anniversary of the establishment of the State of Israel. The decision regarding the proposal to hold the conference in Israel (initially in Tel Aviv) generated an intense debate, with some Board members, having in mind the instability that characterised (and unfortunately still characterises) the Middle East region. Locations such as Manchester and Vienna were voiced as alternatives 'in case the situation would further deteriorate' (EIBA Board, 1996a). The final go-ahead was taken at the December 1996 Board meeting in Stockholm (EIBA Board, 1996b). Fortunately, the fears did not become reality. On the contrary: the conference was held at a time when a lasting peace looked feasible.

Not surprisingly, attendance significantly declined (185 participants) with regard to Stuttgart. But those who have been in Jerusalem will never forget this special event. It was the first EIBA conference with digital proceedings, on a CD-ROM format and the first EIBA conference for Michael Mol, Niron Hashai and Svetla Marinova. The Conference *motto* was 'International Business strategies and Middle East regional cooperation'. The opening session, chaired by Seev Hirsch, addressed a lively theme: 'How can Economics contribute to the Middle East peace process?'; the speakers included academics from Israel, Jordan and the Palestine Authority. The most remarkable session was the closing one, chaired by the Rector of Bar-Ilan University, about 'Religion and Global Capitalism'. The perspectives of the three religions (Judaism, Christianity and Islam) were addressed by eminent persons, John Dunning representing Christianity. This session was a launchpad for Dunning's edited book *Making Globalization Good*, very much influenced by religious and moral values (Dunning, 2003). The city tour of Jerusalem was one of the Conference's cornerstones. The possibility to visit personally several places that one was aware of through the Bible, such as the Mount Olivet, was a moving personal experience for many participants.

The 1998 Doctoral Tutorial had two winners: Elvira Haezendonck (University of Antwerp-RUCA, Belgium), with a project on 'The International Competitiveness of Maritime Industrial Development Area (MIDA) based Clusters' and Jeffrey E. Johnson (University of Strathclyde, UK), researching about 'Firm-Specific Determinants of Success for Small Global Start-ups: A Performance Study of US and UK Firms'. The student host had very high quality, some of them becoming high-standing scholars, well-known to the EIBA community (such as Filip de Beule, Niron Hashai, and Michael Mol), or policymakers (Francisco Castro, now adviser to the European Commissioner Elisa Ferreira). The faculty included Örjan Sölvell, Bernard Wolf and Bernard Yeung, besides John H. Dunning and Danny Van Den Bulcke as chair.

A long trip of almost 4,000 kms was made to travel to the 1999 conference venue: Manchester. Unfortunately, Manchester –'a place where it can rain cats and dogs'– did not appear to be an attractive location in December: the number of participants was 172, slightly down with regard to Jerusalem. The high conference fee may have played a dissuasive role. According to Fred Burton, 'the conference certainly suffered in a sense from the AIB conference being so close, which meant that a number of Europeans opted for the conference in the USA' (EIBA Board, 1999); in fact, AIB 1999 took place in Charleston, South Carolina,

US, in the second half of November. Manchester was the first EIBA conference for two EIBA Fellows (José Plá-Barber and Roger Strange) as well as for Alvaro Cuervo-Cazurra, a well-known scholar and regular EIBA participant. In spite of this, the conference was very successful on both academic and social grounds. The opening plenary, chaired by Alan Rugman, featured a keynote address by Peter Buckley on 'what do we know about international joint ventures?'. The social programme was marked by two events: the visit to Old Trafford, the Manchester United stadium; and the Gala Dinner at the Manchester Town Hall.

The Doctoral Tutorial award for 1999 was granted to Jan-Hendrik Fisch, from the University of Höhenheim, supervised by Klaus Macharzina. Jan-Hendrick had already served as a member of the organising committee of EIBA Stuttgart in 1997. His project was focused on the international location of R&D activities by MNCs. The faculty included, besides Danny Van Den Bulcke and John H. Dunning, Peter Buckley, Jean-François Hennart, Bernard Yeung and Stephen Young.

The 2000 EIBA conference was held at Maastricht, an iconic place due to the homonymous Treaty, and was jointly organised by John Hagedoorn and Sarianna Lundan,[7] then associate professor at the University of Maastricht. Sarianna was the first woman to serve as co-organiser of an EIBA conference. The conference *motto* was 'Maastricht 2000 – European business in the global network'. This theme was addressed in the opening plenary by John Dunning and Luc Soete, founder and director of MERIT, the Maastricht Economic Research Centre on Innovation and Technology. The links between IB and innovation and technology studies were a hallmark of the Maastricht conference. In spite of the difficulties in reaching Maastricht, the organisers were able to ensure a high attendance level: about 225 participants. Maastricht was the first EIBA conference for several EIBAians: Bo Bernhard Nielsen and Jens Gammelgaard, who participated at the Doctoral Tutorial and later became NRs at EIBA Board; Ilan Alon, who served as conference co-chair of Oslo 2022; Rian Drogendijk, who organised the Uppsala-2014 conference; Ram Mudambi, who became EIBA Fellow; and Rob Van Tulder, for many years the editor of *PIBR* and recently elected as EIBA Fellow.

Danny Van Den Bulcke chaired an increasingly attractive EIBA Doctoral Tutorial, with a record of 31 applications. The faculty included as usual John Dunning, as special adviser, Peter Buckley and Jean-François Hennart, together with a newcomer – Timothy Devinney, who came to organise the Leeds-2019 conference and is now an EIBA Fellow. The winner was Olivier Irrmann (University of Vaasa, Finland), whose PhD project focused on 'International negotiations in cross-border acquisitions: an analysis of intercultural communication during the post-acquisition integration process'.

The 27th EIBA conference took place in Paris, organised by ESCP-EAP. This was for sure a challenge faced by the conference organisation, led by Alain Chevalier, an EIBA veteran who had participated in the pre-EIBA workshops and in the first EIBA conferences in the 1970s. The EIBA Paris *mot d'ordre* was 'Alliances and Confrontations: Globalisation and the logic of trading blocks', a theme still relevant two decades later. The refereeing process and the conference organisation were subject to several criticisms. Following this conference, a decision was taken to prepare 'a template on the organization of the conference'

(EIBA Board, 2002a, p. 2). This materialised in 2003 in a key document prepared by Lars Håkansson and Torben Pedersen (see Chapter 7). Attendance was below expectations: 185, according to the list of participants.[8] The US involvement was very small, due to September 11th events, and the participation by French IB scholars outside ESCP-EAP was surprisingly low.

Following the tradition started in Antwerp in 1987, Danny Van Den Bulcke organised and chaired the Doctoral Tutorial. The faculty included a set of influential IB scholars: Yair Aharoni, Peter Buckley, Timothy Devinney, Yves Doz, Jean-François Hennart and John Dunning; this was the last time that John H. Dunning participated at the doctoral event that now holds his name. The award was assigned to Rekha Khrishnan (Tilburg University, The Netherlands) for her research project on 'International Alliance Outcomes: The Moderating Effect of Process'.

Marina Papanastassiou was waiting to welcome the EIBA community in Athens-2002. It was EIBA's debut in Greece. The conference theme was 'Regional integration, agglomeration and International Business'. Attendance was above two hundred (215 participants) again, as a result of the efforts made by Marina's team to entice IB scholars to submit papers and, of course, of Athens appeal. This was the first conference for some members of the EIBA community, namely Andreja Jaklic, who served at the EIBA Board as NR of Slovenia, Antonella Zucchella, Mika Gabrielsson, and Nuno Crespo, who came to serve as EIBA President and organiser of EIBA 2023 in Lisbon.

Several innovations were introduced in the Conference programme. Besides the traditional competitive and workshop sessions, poster sessions were included for the first time ever. This was a feature that proved to be lasting, since it enabled to accommodate academic quality with the attraction of younger scholars while contributing to the financial stability of EIBA conferences. Another important innovation was the convening of executive sessions, organised by Tamar Almor. The idea was to invite bridge-builders, people who worked simultaneously in Academia and in business. The keynote speaker at the opening plenary was Stephen J. Kobrin (The Wharton School, University of Pennsylvania, AIB Fellow),[9] who addressed the theme of 'The Trans-Atlantic Information Privacy Dispute and Regulatory Spillover'. The social side of the conference included three events: the welcome reception, the Gala Dinner, and a wine reception and tour at the Cycladic Museum. The welcome reception took place at the rooftop of the Divani-Caravel, the conference hotel; it was wonderful to meet again old EIBA friends and make new acquaintances with such an amazing view over Athens, including the Acropolis.

The winner of the Doctoral Tutorial was Arjen Slangen (Tilburg University, The Netherlands), who later became a regular participant at EIBA conferences, and co-chair of the John H. Dunning Doctoral Tutorial, as mentioned earlier; his project dealt with 'Cultural Distance and Foreign Direct Investment: The Impact of National Cultural Differences on Entry Mode Choice and Subsidiary Performance'. The faculty was led by Danny Van Den Bulcke, and included Peter Buckley, Timmothy Devinney, Jean-François Hennart, Stephen J. Kobrin and Bernard Wolf.

The Athens conference marks the end of a period of change and consolidation of EIBA, encompassing several memorable conferences that are still recollected today with pleasure. EIBA ventured outside its traditional boundaries: it went outside Europe's geography; it entered the information age, with digital proceedings; and it became more balanced, with women playing leading roles in EIBA. As an organisation, EIBA achieved more stability and attractiveness, the link to a major IB journal enticing IB scholars to become EIBA members. Gradually, EIBA was becoming less dependent on the ebb-and-flow of annual conferences. The creation of the EIBA Fellows also paved the way for further organisational changes. Time was ripe for a leap forward, now on the governance front. That was the challenge faced when Athens-2002 was over, and Copenhagen-2003 was emerging on the horizon.

6.4. EIBA: ORGANISATIONAL DEVELOPMENTS

As mentioned in the introduction, this period marked EIBA's adulthood. 21 years after its creation, EIBA became more confident and solid, with successive surpluses, in spite of the 'sword of Damocles' stemming from the accumulated debt.

The account of the main developments happened over the 1996–2002 period in the organisational front will be structured in 10 sections: general perspective; initiatives to increase membership; relationships with other organisations; the digitalisation of EIBA; EIBA publications; EIBA accounts; EIBA membership; the EIBA Board; gender diversity; and preparing for further organisational change. A special sub-chapter will be assigned to the process of creating the EIBA Fellows.

6.4.1. General Perspective

The 1996–2002 period corresponds to EIBA's transition towards the 21st century, involving several changes both to adapt to external challenges and to forge ahead in the organisational front. Although EIBA has extended towards the Mediterranean, going to Israel and Greece, geographic spread was no longer a central concern; it would emerge again in the following period, with further venturing towards Central and Eastern Europe. As mentioned previously, a set of landmark developments was recorded, from the creation of the EIBA Fellows to the establishment of *IBR* as the EIBA journal, going through the digitalisation of several activities and the preparation for important governance changes. In this process, EIBA became more diverse, consolidating the changes in women membership share (went up to 23%, from 20% in the previous period) and assigning women an increasing role in EIBA's governance. However, the dark clouds had not gone away. In spite of the surpluses for most years, these were not enough to solve the debt towards EIASM.

With hindsight, it becomes evident that EIBA's problems in this period were the seeds for future growth. The initiatives taken, including the link with *IBR*, were geared to enable a more sustainable EIBA, less dependent on the annual conference, and capable of enticing a host of younger people to join the organisation. While recognising their importance as moments for knowledge sharing and socialisation and their role in showcasing Europe's multifariousness, it was recognised that the challenge of ensuring a more consistent academic quality standard of EIBA conferences had to be addressed. The missteps taken made clear that a structured conference template was needed. Meanwhile, a younger, more diverse, cohort was preparing to further transform EIBA's governance.

6.4.2. Initiatives to Increase Membership

The evolution of both conference participation and EIBA membership over the period has left much to be desired, after a promising start. EIBA reached new heights in conference attendance at the beginning of this period: 250 in Stockholm, and 320 in Stuttgart. But in the following years, there was a decline, with Jerusalem, Manchester, and Paris recording less than 200 participants. In spite of this, the average attendance was slightly over 220 participants per conference, 10% above the records for the previous period (slightly below 200). Expectations were not met also on what concerns EIBA membership evolution: as a Board member put it at the 1996 Stockholm interim Board meeting, 'the Academy has some difficulty in going beyond the 300 mark' (more on this on Section 6.4.7). No wonder then that the concern with the need to attract more members had been a common thread along this period. However, this was increasingly focused on individual scholars, and no longer on company membership.

At the September 1996 interim Board meeting, Gunnar Hedlund suggested that there was a need to rethink the strategic positioning of the EIBA conference. The underlying argument was that other conferences, in functional disciplinary fields, were adding an international dimension to their programmes. Fortunately, Klaus decided to commit himself to entice increased participation at EIBA Stuttgart. He made a significant and successful effort to attract scholars from the German-speaking countries. This was the main reason why about 320 people have shown up at EIBA Stuttgart. In 2000, it was unanimously agreed by the Board that future presidents should take similar initiatives effort. However, this did not work properly in the years to come. Another initiative by Gunnar Hedlund and Örjan Sölvell was the design a new EIBA logo, also approved at the same meeting. Interestingly, this logo has survived until 2013.

Another idea pioneered by Klaus Macharzina and intended to increase EIBA's visibility was to establish, in the wake of AIB, the International Executive of the Year Prize. It was decided to leave its implementation to the discretion of the conference organiser. Eugene Jaffe decided to go ahead with it in the 1998 Jerusalem conference. However, things did not go as expected, and the prize was not assigned. Eugene later commented that the experience had been disappointing. In view of this, Fred Burton did not implement it in Manchester. As a result, the theme was folded, until the creation of the EIBA Fellows enable to frame it in a different way, not limited to company executives: the establishment of the EIBA Honorary Fellow of the Year.

The need to increase membership was voiced time and again at EIBA Board meetings. Several ideas were suggested, usually involving an increased commitment from the Presidents and/or from NRs, but no sound solutions were found. Problems increased in 2001 for two main reasons: the 11th September 2001 events, leading to a decline in conference attendance, and therefore membership, from the US; and the change stemming from the inclusion of the *IBR* subscription in EIBA membership package, entailing increased membership fees. However, from a medium- to longer-term perspective, the latter proved to be a blessing, since it enabled to set up a stronger and lasting linkage between the Academy and its members, besides the ebb-and-flow of annual conferences. Its effects were still to be felt, since they would only materialise in the next period.

6.4.3. Relationships with Other Organisations

The main relationship, albeit a bit more distanced, continued to be with AIB. A relatively peaceful *modus vivendi* was established along this period, but the pattern of conflict–cooperation was pursued. AIB continued to be envisaged as a role model, as shown below in the process of establishing the EIBA Fellows. It was also a partner, as it happened with the organisation, by Danny Van Den Bulcke, of a joint Doctoral Tutorial at the AIB conference in Vienna (1998). Such a partnership took however strange features, as expressed in the fact that EIBA assumed the representation of the Western Europe AIB (AIB-WE) chapter. For a long time, this role was taken by Danny Van Den Bulcke; when he was elected VP Administration of AIB for 2001–2002, it was assigned to Juán Durán, another former EIBA President. In 1999, when Danny was still the representative of AIB-WE he was invited to a meeting on the future of AIB. There, proposals were presented to increase the role of regional chapters. According to Danny it would be 'extremely important' for EIBA to keep 'close links with AIB in order to make sure that EIBA continues to be recognized as being responsible for Europe' (EIBA Board, 1998a, p. 3). This enmeshing between EIBA and the AIB-WE would give rise to serious problems later, leading to the so-called 'Buckley compromise' (see Chapter 7).

But other voices advocated a more independent position by EIBA. Klaus Macharzina, in his above-mentioned letter from the President, stated that EIBA should position itself 'against other oganizations such as AIB or the [i]nternational [s]ection of the Academy of Management', as EIBA enjoyed 'a competitive edge in our "Europeanness", and this edge might become even sharper with the development towards a European Union', so that 'we can consider ourselves as academic forerunners of a unified Europe' (Macharzina, 1997, p. 3). The desire to keep independence is also expressed in the decision of avoiding to team up with AIB UK in the joint organisation of events. Perhaps the best example of this independent approach was the resolution to venture outside European geographic boundaries, organising the 1998 EIBA conference in Jerusalem.

These apparently contradictory behaviours are an expression of the inherent tensions pervading EIBA–AIB relationships. AIB is a role model: the older and bigger 'brother', whose European membership was by the time larger than EIBA's. There was a need to live together, which might involve some collaboration. But getting too close presented a danger for EIBA's entrenched sense of independence. One may recall the debate reported in the first chapter, when a few participants at EIBA's founding meeting were fiercely advocating that creating a new IB organisation, out of AIB, made no sense. And for some people at AIB this reasoning was still held in the new century.

6.4.4. The Digitalisation of EIBA

For the digital natives it may seem a bit strange to talk about the digitalisation of EIBA. At a time of digital platforms and internet immersion this does not appear to be a problem. However, that was not the case in the 1990s. The older generation, like two of the authors of this book, still remembers the complicated and time-consuming process of paper selection and publishing the proceedings of an international conference, like EIBA, in the first half of the 1990s. Papers were received via fax or even traditional 'snail' mail, without any recourse to digital supports. The review process required the channelling of such papers to the referees via fax. It was extremely difficult to have a common paper format, since different standards applied in distinct countries.

The 1997 conference in Stuttgart marks EIBA's first digital inroad, although it was still far from a digital immersion. In fact, a homepage was created for EIBA, in connection with the conference: http://www.uni-hohenheim.de/~eiba. This website is historical and marks EIBA's entry into a new age. The June 1997 *EIBA Newsletter* was uploaded here as well as the conference's call for papers and advertisements. However, this digital experience was only partial: most contacts, including paper submissions, were undertaken by other carriers, and the proceedings were still published in paper volumes.

That is why Jerusalem 1998 may really be considered as the first EIBA digital conference. Most participants were surprised to find that paper proceedings were no longer available. Instead they would take home a CD-ROM with all the papers. At the December 1998 Board meeting, the idea of building a 'virtual library' with the proceedings of EIBA conferences at the EIBA website was presented (EIBA Board, 1998b). Unfortunately, it has never materialised. If so, writing this history of EIBA would have been much easier.

However, there were still some voices claiming that the traditional printed paper proceedings should be kept along with the CD-ROM. For the eldest EIBAians, the transition was not easy. The movement in favour of paper proceedings gradually dried up, and in 2002 an agreement was reached at the Board that the conference programme would still be printed, a feature that still holds nowadays. Due to cost considerations, only competitive papers were included on the CD-ROM. Simultaneously, all papers were made available at the conference website. The forces of innovation were inexorable: 'Evidence from around the conference circuit suggests that the days of bound volumes of proceedings are rapidly becoming a thing of the past' (Burton, 1999, p. 1). In 2002, Marina Papanastassiou could emphasise the importance of the web culture, making all the relevant information available on the web (EIBA Board, 2002b). By the same token, there was a need to set up a standard digital system to handle the paper submission and revision process, escaping the trap of individual solutions for each conference. These were the challenges to be addressed soon.

6.4.5. EIBA Publications: IBR as the EIBA Journal

The publication of the *EIBA Newsletter* was pursued. From 1997 onwards, it got another look, anchored on the new EIBA logo, and a new editor, Marion

Habbelink, who replaced Gerry Van Dyck, who had taken office as director of EIASM. But the structure and contents did not undergo significant changes. The difficulty to get contents from the EIBA community continued to be a problem, discussed time and again at the EIBA Board.

However, a major change occurred in 2001: *IBR* became the EIBA journal. This was envisaged as a major step towards making EIBA less dependent on annual conferences and ensuring more stability in the Academy's membership.

It is important to recall here that, since its creation, the establishment of a link with a journal had been a goal for EIBA. The issue surfaced again, in 1997, when Klaus Macharzina was simultaneously the President of EIBA and the editor of *MIR*. It was discussed at the intermediary Board meeting in Stuttgart. The two original options of creating a new journal or linking to an existing one were presented. The first option was eschewed, since it was difficult and too risky. Then, Klaus suggested that *MIR* might become the EIBA journal, and volunteered to negotiate with the publishers a 'special rate for EIBA members' (EIBA Board, 1997, p. 2). Two camps emerged: a group of Board members were in favour of a link between EIBA and *MIR*, and another argued for allowing also other journals to present their proposals. No decision was taken. The issue was revisited at the interim Board meeting in Jerusalem. Klaus mentioned the initial proposal regarding the optional fee for EIBA members but pointed out that there was no indication from the publishers if they will keep the offer should *MIR* become the EIBA journal. Danny Van Den Bulcke, who was at the time Associate Editor of *IBR*, and Gabriel Benito argued that the Board should take a neutral position and consider other offers.

At the interim Board meeting held in Maastricht in April 2000, a shortlist of two journals (*MIR* and *IBR*) was identified, since other journals were already linked to 'official bodies'. The committee contacted Klaus Macharzina, who informed that *MIR* 'was not considering being associated with EIBA'. John Hagedoorn contacted then the editor of *IBR*, Pervez Ghauri. Elsevier, the publisher of *IBR*, reacted positively and a draft agreement was sent to John Hagedoorn. Shortly thereafter, John Hagedoorn signed, as President of EIBA, an agreement with Elsevier, scheduled to enter into force on January 2001.

6.4.6. EIBA Accounts

This period is characterised by contradictory tensions. On the one hand, EIBA was on a positive track, generating surpluses for almost all years, except 2001. This exception was a result of the membership break in connection with the inclusion of the *IBR* subscription in the EIBA membership fee, mentioned above. Against the usual procedure, membership fees for that year were not included in the conference registration lump sum and had to be collected directly from EIBA members. On the other hand, it became evident that EIASM would put more pressure on EIBA to pay the outstanding debt, accumulated until 1994, as EIBA's financial situation was clearly improving.

In fact, EIASM thought that it was the right time to claim the payment of the accumulated debt. After several informal approaches, EIBA nominated a committee to respond the issue. More formal conversations were started. In 1991, as a sign of good-will, John Hagedoorn volunteered to transfer to EIASM a surplus of €2,000 from the Maastricht-2000 conference. The issue was only to be solved, in a satisfactory way, in 2003.

6.4.7. EIBA Membership

As mentioned above, the evolution of EIBA membership in the 1996–2002 period was a bit disappointing. After a very good start, in 1996 and 1997, when membership raised to 340, a string of factors (conferences in less attractive places, the change in membership fees, competition from AIB, and the effects of the 11th September 2001 events) led to a significant drop. EIBA membership got its nadir in 2001, to a large extent as a result of a changed approach to collect membership fees due to the teaming up with *IBR*. However, if the picture for this period is bleak, a brighter pattern emerges if a longer-term view is taken. Also, from a gender diversity perspective, this period heralded positive changes, as it will be shown later in this chapter.

Fig. 6 provides information about the countries' average membership and shares for 1996–2002. The number of countries with shares above 2% increased to 17, while it was 15 in the previous period; in contrast, the weight of the top-five countries is similar to the previous period (49%). The top-five includes the following countries: the UK (12% of total), Germany (10%), the US (10%), Sweden (9%) and Finland (7%). The UK has taken the lead from the US, confirming the trend observed for 1992–1995; the gap between both countries has increased along the period. Germany reached the top-five again. The host of Nordic countries continued to be significant, in spite of the decline of Norway.

Membership from Central and Eastern European countries (CEE) was concentrated in Poland and Slovenia, the latter exceeding the former (average of five versus four members per year). Average figures for Estonia, the Czech Republic,

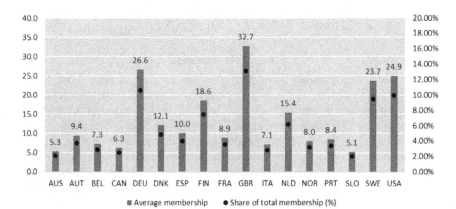

Fig. 6. EIBA Membership per Country (1996–2002). *Source*: EIBA archives.
Note: The figure includes those countries with at least 2% of total average membership in the period concerned.

Hungary, Romania and Bulgaria were not exceeding one member. This indicates that the efforts made in 1989–1995 for attract membership from CEE countries have not been fully successful and have not spread in geographic terms.

Summing up, EIBA membership has experienced significant variation in the 1996–2002 period, reaching a maximum of 340 for 1997 and a minimum of 172 for 2001. The decline was in part due to the already alluded change in membership fee conditions as a result of the link with *IBR*, and was partially redressed in 2002, with a successful Athens conference. The recovery would be further strengthened and sustained from 2003 onwards, when EIBA ventured towards the Baltic countries and became a magnet to attract scholars from South America, especially Brazil.

6.4.8. The EIBA Board

The evolution of the composition of the EIBA Board is provided in Table 4. The Board composition continued to be stable for the period under analysis, but not to the same extent than before: four new chapters were created (Austria, Greece, Israel and Slovenia); and changes occurred in ten, while five remained constant. Stability contributed to strengthen EIBA's memory and cohesion at the top, but simultaneously hindered change and diversity while enticing complacency. One of the main arguments behind Reijo Luostarinen's drive in favour of establishing the EIBA Fellows, was to foster the entry of younger people with new ideas and appetite for action. From a gender perspective, the leadership of EIBA continued to be dominated by men: only two NRs were women, both at the start and at the end of the period.

Unfortunately, two of the replacements in 1996–2002 were due to the passing away of the NRs: Gunnar Hedlund for Sweden, and Roland Schuit for the Netherlands. Their substitutes were, respectively, Örjan Sölvell and John Hagedoorn, both introduced earlier.

There were two further replacements that go unnoticed when reading Table 4 alone, as they occurred between 1995 and 1996, that is, between the two time-windows considered in our account of the history of EIBA. One was already mentioned: Gerry Van Dyck, who had performed that role since the late 1970s, was nominated Director of EIASM. It is fair to say that Gerry's commitment, savoir-faire, kindness and efficiency have been deeply missed by the Board members. The other change had to do with the German representative. Hans-Günther Meissner had served EIBA in a very committed way in hard times (he had organised two EIBA conferences, the last of them in Berlin in very difficult conditions). He was replaced by Klaus Macharzina, who shortly after taking office started the preparation of the memorable Stuttgart conference.

By 2002, the Board included NRs from 19 countries, including the temporarily void US position. It was about to comprise 20, as Philippe Gugler had been nominated as NR of Switzerland at the December Board meeting in Athens. Between 1996 and 2002, the correspondents for Belgium, Italy, Poland, Portugal and Spain had remained unchanged. Board rotation clearly increased as against 1989–1995. Things were moving ... slower than many would have liked, but faster than others wished.

Table 4. Composition of the EIBA Board (1996–2002).

Officers	1996	1997	1998	1999	2000	2001	2002
President	Gunnar Hedlund (+ Ö. Sölvell)	K. Macharzina	Eugene Jaffe	Fred Burton	John Hagedoorn	Alain Chevalier	M. Papanastassiou
President Elect	K. Macharzina	Eugene Jaffe	Fred Burton	John Hagedoorn	Alain Chevalier	M. Papanastassiou	Torben Pedersen
Secret. General	M. Habbelynck	M. Habbelynck	M. Habbelynck	M. Habbelynck	M. Habbelynck	M. Habbelynck	M. Habbelynck
National Representatives							
Austria					Lars Håkansson	Lars Håkansson	Christian Bellak
Belgium	D. V. D. Bulcke	D. V. D. Bulcke	D. V. D. Bulcke	D. V. D. Bulcke	D. V. D. Bulcke	D. V. D. Bulcke	D. V. D. Bulcke
Canada	Rolf Mirus	Rolf Mirus	Rolf Mirus	Rolf Mirus			Alain Verbeke
Denmark	Laurids Hedaa	Laurids Hedaa	Poul Schultz	Poul Schultz	TorbenPedersen	Torben Pedersen	Torben Pedersen
Finland	R. Luostarinen	R. Luostarinen	R. Luostarinen	Jorma Larimo	Jorma Larimo	Jorma Larimo	Jorma Larimo
France	Sabine Urban	Sabine Urban	Sabine Urban	Sabine Urban	Alain Chevalier	Alain Chevalier	Alain Chevalier
Germany	K. Macharzina	K. Macharzina	K. Macharzina	K. Macharzina	K. Macharzina	K. Macharzina	K. Macharzina
Greece				M. Papanastassiou	M. Papanastassiou	M. Papanastassiou	M. Papanastassiou
Israel		Eugene Jaffe	Eugene Jaffe	Eugene Jaffe	Eugene Jaffe	Eugene Jaffe	Eugene Jaffe
Italy	F. Sanna-Randaccio	F. Sanna-Randaccio	F. Sanna-Randaccio	F. Sanna-Randaccio	F. Sanna-Randaccio	F. Sanna-Randaccio	F. Sanna-Randaccio
Netherlands	Roland Schuit	Roland Schuit†	JohnHagedoorn	John Hagedoorn	John Hagedoorn	John Hagedoorn	John Hagedoorn

Country							
Norway	Pat Joynt	Gabriel Benito	Gabriel Benito	Gabriel Benito	Gabriel Benito	Gabriel Benito	Gabriel Benito
Poland	Krzysztof Obloj	K. Obloj	K. Obloj	K. Obloj	K. Obloj	K. Obloj	K. Obloj
Portugal	V. C. Simões	V. C. Simões	V. C. Simões	V. C. Simões	V. C. Simões	V. C. Simões	V. C. Simões
Slovenia					Marjan Svetlicic	Marjan Svetlicic	Marjan Svetlicic
Spain	Juán Durán	Juán Durán	Juán Durán	Juán Durán	Juán Durán	Juán Durán	Juán Durán
Sweden	G. Hedlund	Örjan Sölvell	Örjan Sölvell	Örjan Sölvell	Örjan Sölvell	Örjan Sölvell	Örjan Sölvell
UK	Fred Burton	Fred Burton	Fred Burton	Fred Burton	Fred Burton	Fred Burton	Fred Burton
US	J.-F. Hennart	J.-F. Hennart	J.-F. Hennart	J.-F. Hennart	J.-F. Hennart		

Source: Analysis of EIBA archives.

6.4.9. Gender Diversity in EIBA: Eppur si muove...

EIBA was created by men and has remained for about two and a half decades dominated by men. In the previous chapters we have provided a brief perspective about the evolution of the participation of women in both EIBA's activities and management in the different time windows considered in this account of EIBA history. Between 1996 and 2002, men were still at the helm. However, several important and ground-breaking changes were taking place, sometimes behind the scenes. Hence, the title of this section.

The results of our research regarding the share of women in EIBA membership between 1977 and 2002 are presented in Fig. 7. There was just one woman among the 45 people whose participation at the first EIBA, in 1975, is documented: Monique Lejeune, from France. In the 1976 conference, all attendants were men: not a single woman has shown up. Between 1977 and 1981, the average female share was 3.8%. The highest female contingent at a conference was 8, both in Dortmund (1978) and Antwerp (1980).

Not surprisingly, female participation at EIBA increased in the 1982–1988 period, reaching a 6.3% share. The highest number of female EIBA members occurred in 1984, but the maximum share was recorded for 1986 (slightly above 8%). The 'star' in this period was Edith Penrose, who participated at the 1982 conference, by invitation of José de la Torre, and kept as EIBA member until 1984.

From 1989 onwards, the EIBA membership's female share experienced a quantum leap. In 1989–1995 period, such share reached an average of almost 20%, with a maximum of 26% for 1995. The female host at EIBA conferences and membership roster was no longer limited to two hand's fingers. It kept steadily growing to exceed the 70-mark in 1994. Although the Board was still dominated by men, the role of women was becoming increasingly important. As mentioned in Chapter 5, in 1989–1995, a string of colleagues, who would later become EIBA Fellows, joined our Academy: Francesca Sanna-Randaccio, Rebecca Piekkari, Tamar Almor, Marina Papanastassiou, Lucia Piscitello and Sarianna Lundán. This paved the way for further change in the 1996–2002 period, gradually leading to a much more balanced organisation.

Interestingly, such a change did not happen so much from a quantitative perspective: the female membership share increased just slightly, from 20% to 23%, and the number of women at the EIBA Board declined in absolute and relative terms (from 3% to 2%, and from 19% to 10%, respectively). 1996–2002 also witnessed the arrival of a few female newcomers, who would later hold key positions in EIBA joined our Academy: Ana Teresa Tavares-Lehman, Grazia Santangelo and Rian Drogendijk. In fact, the change was chiefly qualitative: the participation of women in both conference organisation and decision-making tasks significantly upgraded. There are clear temporal milestones in this process. In 1995, EIBA had her first woman President ever (Francesca Sanna-Randaccio). In 2000, Sarianna Lundan was the first woman to organise an EIBA conference, even though she did not wear the President's *chapeau*. And, in 2002, Marina Papanastassiou combined both responsibilities. With hindsight, this was a key change. And it was not an easy one: one of the authors who served in the Board at the time remembers

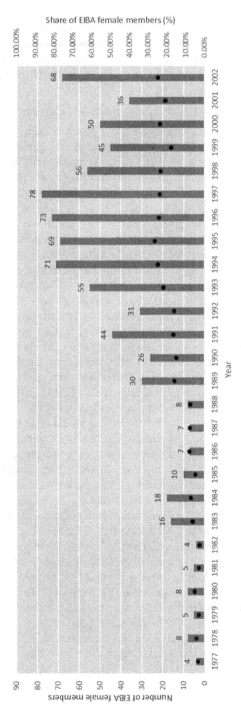

Fig. 7. Evolution of EIBA Membership by Gender (1975–2002). *Source:* EIBA archives.

the faces of several men at the December meeting in Paris, when Marina did not show up, due to maternity. Though their share was still limited, the influence of women at the Board significantly increased, very much due to the committed effort by Francesca Sanna-Randaccio. In 1999, she was the first woman to chair an EIBA Board committee, regarding the creation of the EIBA Fellows.[10]

6.4.10. Preparing Organisational Change

The original statutes of EIBA provided for a governance approach based on a revolving *troika*, including the President (in charge of organising the conference on that year) and the organisers of the two next conferences, as Vice-Presidents. The 1982 review of EIBA statutes, led by José de la Torre, was intended to establish a closer link between EIBA management and membership, with the setting up of both the General Assembly and the Board. It also encompassed the creation of the Executive Committee, composed by the President, the two Vice-presidents, the immediate past president and the secretary general. This governance model was kept unchanged in the 1995 revision, when the former Association was transformed into Academy. It was to a significant extent the expression of an organisation based on the one-conference-a-year model. While it was intended, theoretically, to simultaneously keep EIBA's memory and to enable change in top management, in practice it left much to be desired. The outstanding importance of the annual conferences led the Executive Committee to focus on the short-term, refraining from addressing medium- or longer-term issues. In the deed, the one-year president was really focused on ensuring that 'his' (or 'her') conference would be a success, the past president was tired of organising a demanding event and wanted to rest, and the vice-presidents were still to get acquainted with EIBA's governance, while preparing the conferences they were supposed to chair. For this reason, important decisions as the link with a journal of the establishment of the Fellows have been assigned to committees that were not engaged enough (and encompassed sometimes conflicting views), taking, therefore, a long time to materialise.

However, from 1996/1997 onwards, when financial and organisational sustainability were attained, the need for change was increasingly felt. If EIBA really aimed at getting larger, efforts had to be carried out to ensure more consistency, thereby demanding improved governance. It is not surprising, therefore, that the final item in the agenda of the 2002 Spring Board meeting in Athens was entitled 'EIBA's future development and organisation'. John Hagedoorn is to be credited as the one who provided the main drive behind the process. He proposed the creation of a small group to 'look into the organizational history of EIBA and propose measures to improve' the organisation's governance. He further argued that the 'EIBA President only functions for one year [and] is mainly concerned with the conference' (EIBA Board, 2002a, p. 4). The possibility of changing the structure of the Board and the organisation was discussed, including the creation of vice-presidents for functional areas, such as finance or marketing. It was decided that John Hagedoorn and Danny Van Den Bulcke would draft a document on the issue to be discussed at the next Board meeting.

This was presented in December 2002. The proposed reorganisation was intended to meet two objectives: to ensure more continuity in EIBA's management, and to increase membership. It would encompass three elements: (1) to keep the representation at the Board at its current level; (2) to introduce an Executive Committee – consisting of Chairperson, Vice Chairperson and President – to manage EIBA on a more continuous basis; and (3) to reorganise the Secretariat, considering three options: to keep it within EIASM; to move it to the Chair or Vice-chair's university; or to move it to a particular university which will work in cooperation with EIASM (then the exact 'division of labour' had to be defined). The ensuing discussion led to the decision of mandating the organisers of the 2003 conference in Copenhagen (Lars Håkansson and Torben Pedersen) to prepare a new proposal based on John Hagedoorn and Danny Van Den Bulcke's text, to be discussed at the Spring 2003 Board meeting.

Therefore, nothing was decided in this period. As usual, the decision took long to be made. But the seeds were sown for a major change in EIBA's governance. One that, with hindsight, has proved to be badly needed for EIBA to get more sustainable, to increase consistency, and to achieve further growth. Lars and Torben took the baton to design a new governance model that, after a new round of internal discussion, became operational in 2004, when it was enshrined in the statutes of EIBA.

6.5. THE EIBA FELLOWS

As mentioned earlier, Reijo Luostarinen presented two proposals at the 1992 December Board meeting in Reading, which were discussed at the 1993 Spring Board meeting in Lisboa (see Section 5.7.1): to change EIBA's A, to Academy instead of Association, that was implemented in 1995; and to set up the EIBA Fellows. The latter would take much longer, almost 10 years, to turn into reality. At the end of a bumpy process, the EIBA Fellows were formally created in 2002. This was a major step towards a sounder EIBA governance, enabling a better balance between different age cohorts and retaining organisational memory.

This section includes two parts. The first provides a brief account of the long process leading to the establishment of the EIBA Fellows, spanning between 1992 and 2002. The second is focused on the presentation of a summary of the headlines of the 2002 version of the EIBA Fellows Constitution.

6.5.1. The Process of Creating the EIBA Fellows

In the original version of Reijo's memorandum in favour of the creation of the EIBA Fellows, three main, intertwined arguments were advanced: (i) to allow a faster circulation of EIBA Board members; (ii) to provide a way to make accumulated experience/knowledge more easily available to the Board; and (iii) to stimulate the motivation for older members to devote their time and energy to EIBA. The idea was to have an approach similar to AIB and to offer EIBA a better and more balanced position to start the negotiations with AIB regarding the setting up of the World Academy of International Business (WAIB), an idea then cherished by Reijo.[11]

At the 1998 December Board meeting in Jerusalem, a three-step procedure was agreed: first, the Board and the General Assembly should decide to establish the Fellows, and the EIBA statutes should be revised accordingly; then, the same bodies should nominate the charter members of the EIBA Fellows; and, finally, these would draw up the constitution of the Fellows (EIBA Board, 1998b, p. 3). This procedure was confirmed by the 1998 General Assembly.

At the April 2000 Board meeting in Maastrich, Francesca Sanna-Randaccio addressed the Board, on behalf of the committee in charge of this topic. She suggested a two-step approach: first, to revise EIBA statutes, to include an article on the Fellows; and, then, to draft the constitution of the Fellows. An agreement was reached about the 'Founding Fellows': John Cantwell, John Dunning, Seev Hirsch and Reijo Luostarinen. This way it was possible to head towards the setting up of the EIBA Fellows. Under the leadership of John Dunning, drawing from the statutes of the AIB Fellows, the Fellows completed the initial draft of their Constitution, and submitted it to the Board in the fall of 2002. After an analysis of the draft, the Board approved it while suggesting two changes, regarding the maximum number of Fellows: to set to a limit of 20, not to establish an age limit. The final text, incorporating these changes, was finally approved by the General Assembly in December 2002.

6.5.2. The 2002 Constitution of the EIBA Fellows

Formally designated as The Fellows of the European International Business Academy, the Fellows are an autonomous, self-governing body with four objectives (article II.A): to recognise outstanding contributions to the scholarship and practice of IB; to play a leadership role in education and scholarship in the field, especially in Europe; to support the development of EIBA; and to provide a forum for the dissemination of knowledge in the IB field. The Fellows take the responsibility for one plenary session at each annual conference of EIBA.

The title of Fellow, once conferred, is irrevocable (article IV.C). There are three categories of Fellows (article IV.A): Participating, Inactive and Honorary members.[12] Participating Fellows are those who have been nominated as Founding Fellows (Reijo Luostarinen, John Cantwell, John Dunning and Seev Hirsch) and those who are later elected by the Fellows, and continue to fulfil the requirements regarding dues (both for EIBA and a very small amount for the Fellows themselves) and attending meetings (at least one out of the three preceding meetings of the Fellows). Eligible to be elected as Fellows are scholars, teachers or administrators who have made significant contributions to the field and[13] to EIBA. Originally, due to the change made by the EIBA Board, the maximum number of Participating members was set at 20.[14] Exceptionally, in the first year the founding members might nominate up to eight new Participating members (in fact, they have nominated five). When the Founding Fellows drew up the constitution they had the intention to distinguish the EIBA Fellows from the AIB

Fellows with respect to the concept of a Participating Fellow. It was decided that a Participating Fellow should be an active participant in the Fellows' meetings, still actively engaged in EIBA, and not a remote member. Given that it was understood that not everyone can make every meeting, after discussion it was felt that a rule that a Fellow should attend the annual EIBA conference at least once in any three-year window fairly captured the spirit of this idea. Inactive members are those who, for different reasons, have failed to meet the requirements regarding dues or attendance. Honorary members are inducted as Fellows to honour the actions or contributions to IB of individuals who are not members of EIBA. This idea was substantially further developed in John Dunning's term as Dean, to look at business leaders, practitioners, and academics who make IB contributions in related fields.

There are two officers of the Fellows: the Dean and the Secretary-Treasurer. The Dean is elected for a three-year mandate, and may not serve two full consecutive terms. The Secretary-Treasurer is appointed by the Dean to assist in conducting the affairs of the Fellows. John Dunning was elected as the first Dean of the fellows, while John Cantwell was the first Secretary-Treasurer.

With hindsight, it is fair to say that the original version of the constitution of the EIBA Fellows was prepared to last, providing an excellent base to regulate its life for about two decades. In fact, it has not generated major management problems, except for what concerns the mandatory upper limit of 20 Participating members, for which a slight twist was introduced in 2013, as mentioned in endnote 31 (see further information in the next chapter). Interestingly, this change addressed precisely a combination of the two points that the Board had changed in December 2002.

6.6. SUMMARY

Put in a nutshell, the 1996–2002 period marks the transition between an old-time, male EIBA and a younger, digital, more confident and more gender-balanced EIBA, ready to address the challenges of the 21st century.

It was a time pervaded by contradictions. Some memorable EIBA conferences took place in this period: Stockholm and Stuttgart reached new attendance records; Jerusalem heralded the beginning of a digital EIBA; and Athens introduced innovations that were to last, namely the poster sessions. Yet, at the end of the period, EIBA was much less dependent on the ebb-and-flow of annual conferences. EIBA membership experienced significant declines for 2000 and especially 2001, due to the change in membership fees stemming from *IBR* subscription. Yet, this was the prelude for a steady growth trend in the years to come. Our account has suggested how much time was needed to take important decisions, such as the link with a journal or the creation of the EIBA Fellows. Another field in which significant changes were in the making concerned the core of EIBA's governance. EIBA was therefore preparing to respond to the challenges of the

21st century and to attract younger scholars in a field whose importance was bound to grow. EIBA was already digitalised.

NOTES

1. The initial version of the concept dates back to 1994 (Teece & Pisano, 1994).

2. It is relevant to remark that the theme of the 1998 EIBA conference in Stuttgart was 'Global business in the information age'. A first version of Petersen, Welch and Liesch (2002) was presented at the EIBA 2000 in Maastricht.

3. Some of the initial versions of a few papers mentioned in this paragraph were presented at EIBA conferences; that was the case for Andersson and Forsgren (1996), Birkinshaw (1996) and Fratocchi and Holm (1998).

4. It is interesting to remark that the first version of this article was presented at the 1996 EIBA conference in Stockholm.

5. Meanwhile, the Award was relabeled as the SSE Gunnar Hedlund Award, each award covering a three year period. Due to space constraints, no information is provided here about the subsequent Award winners. The list of winners is available at https://www.hhs.se/hedlund-award.

6. Unfortunately, Pavlos untimely passed away in January 2021.

7. Both John Hagedoorn and Sariana Lundan later became EIBA Fellows.

8. The minutes of the December 2001 Board meeting indicate 215 participants. The difference may be due to the inclusion of non-paying conference staff and to late registration participants. EIBA Paris was the first conference for several well-known EIBA members, namely Arjen Slangen, who became co-chair of the John H. Dunning Doctoral Tutorial, Constantina Kottaridi, who later served at the EIBA Board as representative of Greece, and Niina Nummela (now an EIBA Fellow).

9. Stephen J. Kobrin, who until his death in 2022 was William H. Wurster Emeritus Professor of Multinational Management at Wharton. After retirement he had remained very active in the field of international business relationships, as shown by his later articles (Kobrin, 2020, 2021).

10. For more details, see Section 6.5.1.

11. And also, with a slight twist, by John Dunning. See Section 5.4.5 on this.

12. A new category was introduced by the 2017 constitutional revision: Emeritus Fellow. This will be covered in Chapter 8.

13. The text of the constitution is 'or'. However, the interpretation has increasingly lent towards requiring both types of contributions.

14. This was changed in 2013 by an amendment to the constitution, aimed at enabling the rejuvenation of the Fellows. Still kept at 20, this only applies to members that are less than 66-years-old.

CHAPTER 7

STABILISING THE ORGANISATION TO LAUNCH FURTHER GROWTH (2003–2012)

This chapter addresses the period between 2003 and 2012. Building on the developments achieved earlier (the creation of the EIBA Fellows, and the adoption of *IBR* as the EIBA journal), it was possible to start to overcome the limitations of the one-conference-a-year syndrome, while significantly improving organisational governance and achieving financial stability. The new governance model, establishing an Executive Committee led by the EIBA Chairperson elected for three years, ensured the distinction between the structure of the EIBA leadership and the responsibility for annual conference organisation, and enabled the development of a more stable and medium-term strategic outlook. A sustained increase in membership allowed for the generation of surpluses, paving the way to eliminate the burden of an inherited and persistent debt to EIASM. The role played by women in EIBA made major strides forward, with further women becoming EIBA Presidents and conference organisers: Grazia Santangelo, in 2007 (Catania), and Ana Teresa Tavares-Lehman, in 2010 (Porto).

The geographic scope of EIBA was expanded again. Besides moving North and South, from Oslo to Catania, EIBA headed eastwards towards Central and Eastern Europe, holding conferences in countries involved in the European Union's 2004 and 2007 enlargements: Slovenia, in 2004, Estonia, in 2008, and Romania, in 2011. For the first time, EIBA could boast that its conferences had been held in more than 20 European countries and beyond (Israel).

The much-desired financial stability was attained. EIBA was no longer so much constrained by the difficult balance required to sustain itself and its distinctive European identity, while still pursuing its objectives of stimulating the academic dialogue between IB scholars in Europe and worldwide. The older

The History of EIBA: A Tale of The Co-Evolution Between International Business
Issues and a Scholarly Community, 93–134
Copyright © 2025 by Vítor Corado Simões, John Cantwell and Philippe Gugler
Published under exclusive licence by Emerald Publishing Limited
doi:10.1108/978-1-83608-664-220241008

generation remained at the helm, with Danny Van Den Bulcke and Peter Buckley serving as EIBA Chairpersons, but the engagement of the younger cohorts was successfully achieved. In contrast, this period is marked by the passing away of John Dunning, a founding father of the field who had been for decades the key reference for IB scholars in Europe and worldwide, and who for so long had been at the heart of EIBA's activities.

Like the previous one, this chapter is structured in six parts. The first provides a brief overview of the main political and economic environmental changes with implications for IB activities. The second focuses on the main contributions to the enhancement of IB thinking in the period concerned. Then, a review of the main features of the nine conferences held in this period is offered, which took us all over Europe, from Copenhagen (2003) to Brighton (2012), through Ljubljana, Oslo, Fribourg, Catania, Tallinn, Valencia, Porto and Bucharest. Section four provides a detailed account of the organisational developments. The main changes regarding the membership and activities of the EIBA Fellows are presented next. The chapter closes with a summary of the key features of EIBA in this blossoming phase of its life.

7.1. THE CONTEXT: ATTITUDES TOWARDS FDI

The 2003–2012 period was full of changes and contradictions on the political, environmental and economic dimensions. On the political front, the continuation of the war in Afghanistan and the launching of the war in Iraq in 2003 ironically resulted in a demonstration of the limitations of American power.[1] Instead of contributing to a more secure world, it gave rise, directly and indirectly, to a period of turmoil in the Middle East and North Africa. With respect to the natural environment, the Kyoto Protocol, adopted in 1997 entered into force on 2005, the same year when the United Nations Climate Change conference was held in Montreal (Canada). In 2007, the Intergovernmental Panel on Climate Change (IPCC) published its fourth assessment report, concluding that global climate change is 'very likely' to have a predominantly human cause. On the economy side, the entry of China into the WTO in 2001 did not bring the effects that many commentators in the Western countries had anticipated, in the misplaced belief that economic liberalisation would give rise to democratic reform and a more open society. Another landmark, in the wake of the subprime mortgage crisis, was the fall of *Lehman Brothers* and a crisis in the world finance and banking system, leading to the Great Recession in late 2008.

Against this general backdrop, the main developments observed in this period may be described along four axes: the developments in the EU, with the establishment of the Lisbon Treaty and the 2004 and 2007 enlargements; the expansion of GVCs with an increasing involvement by Chinese players in the process; technological developments, namely the launch of the smartphone and the iPad, fostering the expansion of platform business models (*Facebook, YouTube, Twitter, Spotify, Instagram*); and, last but not least, the Great Recession, in the wake of the financial crisis.

EU membership increased sharply, from 15 to 27 members, as a result of the 2004 and 2007 enlargements. In 2004, 10 new members, from Central and Eastern Europe, joined the Union: Czech Republic, Estonia, Cyprus, Latvia, Lithuania, Hungary, Malta, Poland, Slovenia and Slovakia.[2] The 2007 enlargement led EU borders further East, by expanding to Bulgaria and Romania.[3] Still on the European integration front, three further developments deserve recognition. The first was the failed intent to establish a European Constitution. The failure of the Constitution led to the rethinking of European governance, giving rise in 2009 to the Treaty of Lisbon. This was intended to 'lead to greater efficiency in the decision-making process, increased democratic accountability by associating the European Parliament and national parliaments and increased coherence externally' (European Commission, 2009). However, as a result of the financial crisis and the subsequent 2008–2012 sovereign debt crisis, starting with Iceland and then affecting primarily Greece, Ireland, Italy, Portugal and Spain, there were strong tensions inside the EU, endangering the Euro's sustainability. The speech by Mario Draghi, then President of the European Central Bank (ECB), in July 2012, voicing his commitment to save the Euro 'whatever it takes', marked a turning point in the process. However, the countries subject to rescue packages felt very severe consequences that remained for several years.

The period under analysis is also marked by the spread of GVCs. As companies in information- and knowledge-intensive industries (IKIIs) needed protection on a global scale, the WTO *cum* the Agreement on Trade-Related Aspects of Intellectual Property Rights (TRIPS) enabled an increased harmonisation in international trading conditions, particularly with respect to the dominant industrial property rights (IPR) regime (Athreye, Piscitello & Shadlen, 2020). China's entry into the WTO was envisaged as a trigger for this. Mostly managed by MNCs, GVCs led to growing cross-border trade in inputs and outputs (UNCTAD, 2013), especially between the US and China. By the same token, an increasing geographic spread of innovative activities took shape, leading to new competitiveness patterns and governance structures (Alcácer, Cantwell & Piscitello, 2016; Kano, Tsang & Yeung, 2020; UNCTAD, 2005). Under the WTO *cum* TRIPS discipline it became possible to profit from the opportunities offered by technological developments for the international segmentation of production, and also some services, to a level never observed before. As shown by Degain, Meng and Wang (2017), the degree of integration between China and US trading hubs was especially strong.

2011 may be envisaged at the apex of a decade of GVC growth and swelling international integration. As shown in Chapter 8, since then a trend towards a detachment between China and the US hubs has emerged. Some believed that, according to the HOS framework, the creation of the WTO *cum* TRIPS would enable labour-intensive manufacturing activities to further move to low-wage developing countries, whereas the developed world would lead in higher value-added products and services, supported by IPRs (Godinho & Simões, 2023). This rationale was flawed for two reasons. First, it did not anticipate the emergence and spread of the World Wide Web. Second, it assumed that the relative evolution of technological capabilities and learning would remain unchanged, underestimating Asian countries and firms upgrading strategies, especially in China

(Anand, McDermott, Mudambi & Narula, 2021; Buckley, Strange, Timmer & de Vries, 2020; Luo & Tung, 2007, 2018; Petricevic & Teece, 2019).

The Great Recession further contributed to the erosion of Western countries' positions. Linking these two factors were the third axis of change mentioned earlier, namely developments in the technological field. Enabled by the World Wide Web, a string of technological innovations led to the emergence of a digital economy, characterised by enhanced mobile inter-connectivity (Cirillo, Fanti, Mina & Ricci, 2023). The launch of the iPhone, in 2007, and the iPad, in 2010, and the release of the Android operating system, in 2008, were milestones in this process. Relatedly, the development of cloud storage provided the conditions for the storage of huge volumes of data. The combination of these vectors of change has lent further impetus to the emergence and growth of platform business models, such as *Facebook* (2004), *Alipay* (2004), *YouTube* (2005), *Twitter* (2006), *Spotify* (2008), *Instagram* (2010) or *Meituan* (2010).[4] The business model of such platforms has five key features: direct engagement with stakeholders, automation, network effects, flexibility and scalability (Monaghan, Tippman & Coviello, 2020). The reliance on powerful software engines allows them to internalise the transaction space, while externalising the transactions themselves (Simões, 2018). According to Marc Andreesen's (2011) article in the *Wall Street Journal*, 'Software is eating the World'.

The fourth axis of change mentioned above has to do with the Great Recession. The spread of the crisis is an expression of the level of globalisation reached, insofar as it hurt most of the World. Bernanke (2010) distinguished between latent vulnerabilities and the triggers of the crisis. There were vulnerabilities in both the private (dependence on unstable short-term funding, deficiencies in risk management, leverage and derivatives) and public (statutory gaps and conflicts, ineffective use of existing authorities, insufficient crisis management capabilities and the 'too-big-to-fail' syndrome) sectors.

Another important implication of the Great Recession was a significant decline in global investment flows. After four years of sustained increase since the 2001–2002 fall, FDI flows tumbled again in 2007–2009 before recovering in 2010–2011, though without reaching the pre-crisis levels, just to experience another decline in 2012. The changes in the breakdown by groups of countries are no less relevant. While until 2007 developed economies attracted about two-thirds of total flows, since 2008 the weight of developing economies has significantly increased, surpassing developed as FDI recipients (UNCTAD, 2013). This was mostly due to the attractiveness of Asian economies and, to a much lesser extent, Latin American.

The changes stemming from the financial crisis were even more of a disruptor to the structure of FDI outflows. In fact, the share of developed countries in total outflows declined from above 90% to 65%, between 2003 and 2012, while developing countries' stake increased from 6 to 30%. Two important features in shaping a new structure of the origins of FDI outflows were the growth of investments by sovereign funds, some of them contributing to feed the speculative bubble, and the emergence of China (plus Hong Kong) as a key FDI source, accounting for 9 to 11% of total outflows between 2009 and 2011, becoming the third largest investor abroad in 2012, after the US and Japan (UNCTAD, 2013). This suggests that

Chinese firms profited from the Great Recession to undertake acquisitions in the US and Europe, which were envisaged simultaneously as wedges into developed countries' markets and opportunities for managerial and technological learning (Piscitello, Rabellotti & Scalera, 2015).

The account provided above shows how the overall economic and social setting changed in the time period under analysis as well as the evolution observed in trade and FDI patterns. This had obvious implications for IB research. These will be addressed in the following section.

7.2. THE CONTEXT: IB LITERATURE

The trend towards an increased relevance of journal articles vis-á-vis books was sustained and intensified in 2003–2012. The main book on IB published in this period was the second, revised and updated edition of John Dunning's *Multinational Enterprises and the Global Economy*, now in cooperation with Sarianna Lundan (Dunning & Lundan, 2008). While other interesting contributions had been collected in edited books – for instance, Cantwell and Narula (2003) and Gray (2003), both on the eclectic paradigm – the mood strongly tilted towards the publication of articles. This period experienced an increasing drive towards publishing in reputable journals. Also noticeable was the emergence of a significant cohort of scholars of Chinese origin publishing in the top IB journals.

A comparison between the analysis of Dunning (1993) and Dunning and Lundan (2008) shows that, besides the updating of developments in the IB literature and MNCs' behaviour, the main change between the two editions was the introduction of an institutional perspective and its integration with the eclectic paradigm.[5] This is the result of two intertwined factors. First, John Dunning's intellectual journey to absorb the ideas of Douglass North, namely North (1985, 1990, 2005), and previous IB literature on the subject. Second, Sarianna Lundan's own research on institutions and environmental issues (Lundan, 2003, 2004). Building on a conversation between John Dunning and John Cantwell, a parallel collaborative process led to Cantwell et al. (2010), providing a remarkable theoretical approach to the co-evolution of MNC activity and the institutional environment.

Institutional approaches gained, in fact, further traction in IB literature in the period under analysis. Relevant contributions dealt with IB in transition economies, namely Meyer and Peng (2005), discussing how research on Central and Eastern Europe has furthered theoretical developments, and Peng, Wang and Jiang (2008), who developed an institution-based approach to international strategy, combined with industry- and resource-based views. Santangelo and Meyer (2011) found that the internationalisation processes of learning, opportunity creation and trust building, triggered by commitment decisions, are moderated by institutional influences.[6] Additional avenues for applying institutional approaches to IB concerned corruption (Cuervo-Cazurra, 2006, 2008; Jensen, Li & Rahman, 2010; Kwok & Tadesse, 2006), the analysis of cross-national distance (Berry, Guillén & Zhou, 2010) and local isomorphism (Salomon & Wu, 2012).[7] This is related to both the literature on culture and on national governance and business systems (Jackson & Deeg, 2008; Redding, 2005; Witt & Redding, 2009).

Coming back to IB theory, a key contribution was made by Hennart (2009). Criticising what he perceived as an excessive focus on MNEs, he advanced another line of inquiry, based on the bundling of assets between local and foreign business partners. This approach seems to be especially suited to address the deals between companies based in large developing countries, especially China, and foreign-owned MNEs. Martin and Salomon (2003) undertook a theoretical exploration of the effects of tacit knowledge on market entry modes. This period has also witnessed the diffusion of Rugman and Verbeke's (1992) concepts of FSAs and CSAs, which may be envisaged as a more MNE strategy-driven perspective on Dunning's ownership (O) and location (L) advantages, respectively, which O and L constructs were instead rooted in a more holistic analysis of a wider IB system. A further theoretical contribution was made by Forsgren (2008), with his systematisation of the main theoretical views on MNEs. The concept of a global factory, introduced by Buckley and Ghauri (2004) and further developed in Buckley (2009), is another relevant contribution. Rooted in Buckley and Casson's (1976), it intends to reflect a global network of flexible factories to flexibly respond differentiated customer requirements.

Related to IB theory, another issue that attracted significant contributions concerned the framing of the key IB research issues. The provocative title of Buckley's (2002) article ('Is the International Business research agenda running out of steam?') and his argument that IB research was 'stalled', lacking a big, guiding question, generated a vivid debate about the key tenets of a future IB research agenda, that spread throughout the decade. Peng (2004) argued that the big question was, and would continue to be, the determinants of firms' international success and failure, while Shenkar (2004) suggested that IB's competitive advantage rests on the 'synergetic combination of global and local knowledge'. Buckley and Lessard (2005) re-visited the theme, highlighting the existence of a 'missing middle' of IB theoretical concepts that might appropriately connect current issues with discipline-based theoretical frames. This may be seen as an invitation to an increased inter-disciplinarily perspective, a point earlier made by Dunning (1989), to which Cheng, Henisz, Roth and Swaminathan (2009) have returned. Taking a distinct approach, Jones and Khanna (2006) issued a plea for further research on the role of history in IB research, a challenge taken up by Makino and Tsang (2011).

Two further themes discussed in the 2003–2012 period were the globalisation versus regionalisation debate and the welfare issues stemming from globalisation. As to the first, two diverging views emerged: a majority perspective, led by John Dunning, posited that the world was experiencing a globalisation drive (Dunning, Fujita & Yakova, 2007; Osegowitsch & Sammartino, 2008); and another, maintaining that the prevailing situation might be better characterised as semiglobalisation (Ghemawat, 2003, 2007) or regionalisation (Rugman & Verbeke, 2004, 2007). On the second theme, the key references are the contributions by John Dunning and Joseph Stiglitz on the effects of globalisation on welfare and development.[8]

GVCs experienced an exponential growth over this period (Degain et al., 2017). IB literature showed an increasing interest in the subject, while entry and operation modes became less popular, in spite of a few relevant contributions (Slangen & Hennart, 2008; Welch, Benito & Petersen, 2007). Literature in the field included contributions on offshoring strategies (Roza, Van den Bosch & Volberda, 2011), R&D offshoring (Martínez-Noya & García-Canal, 2011), learning processes (Kotabe, Martin & Domoto, 2003) and performance implications (Bertrand, 2011; Griffith & Myers, 2005; Martínez-Noya & García-Canal, 2011). Mol, van Tulder and Beije (2005, p. 599) argued that 'international outsourcing is a balancing act between lower production costs abroad and lower transaction costs locally'.

The view of the MNE as an internationally distributed network, largely based on intangible assets, gained further relevance in IB thinking and research. One part of the literature has drawn on evolutionary perspectives (Nelson, 2004), helping to improve our understanding of how firm-based capabilities interact with country-based innovation systems (Cantwell et al., 2010), and the features of overseas R&D operations and co-practice processes (Frost & Zhou, 2005; Song & Chin, 2008). Another stream has focused on the firm, addressing the conditions for enhancing successful knowledge sharing. These included knowledge characteristics (Dhanaraj, Lyles, Steensma & Tihanyi, 2004), social interaction (Carlile, 2004; Noorderhaven & Harzing, 2009), networking capabilities (Dyer & Hatch, 2006; Ritter & Gemünden, 2003) or some combination thereof (Argote, McEvily & Reagans, 2003; Martin & Salomon, 2003; Pedersen, Petersen & Sharma, 2003). Jensen and Szulanski (2004) called attention to 'knowledge stickiness' and analysed how the adaptation of organisational practices affects the stickiness of cross-border knowledge sharing.

Related to this, the concern with subsidiary capabilities, and their role in MNE strategies and in knowledge-sharing processes has maintained steam. Two main contributions were Mudambi and Navarra (2004), arguing that subsidiary managers can exploit the power stemming from subsidiary's place in intra-MNE knowledge flows to pursue their own goals, and Cantwell and Mudambi (2005), who found that subsidiary's R&D performance depends on the combination of three distinct elements: MNE structure, subsidiary characteristics, and locational factors. Another influential article was Minbaeva, Pedersen, Björkman, Fey and Park (2003), on the relationships among subsidiary human resource management (HRM) practices, absorptive capacity, and knowledge sharing. Further contributions have addressed the role of subsidiary embeddedness (Andersson, Björkman & Forsgren, 2005; Andersson, Forsgren & Holm, 2007; Santangelo, 2012; Yamin & Andersson, 2011), the structure of subsidiary network (Dellestrand & Kappen, 2012), subsidiary innovative initiatives and learning processes (Ambos, "Andersson & Birkinshaw, 2010; Phene & Almeida, 2008; Schmid & Schurig, 2003; Venaik, Midgley & Devinney, 2005), 'reverse' knowledge transfer (Ambos, Ambos & Schlegelmilch, 2006; Govindarajan & Ramamurti, 2011) and subsidiary political influence in MNEs (Hillman & Wan, 2005).

Learning and knowledge-sharing issues have also been addressed in the context of inter-firm alliances. Relevant contributions include the articles by Grant and Baden-Fuller (2004), on a knowledge-accessing theory of strategic alliances, by Rothaermel and Deeds (2004), on exploration and exploitation in biotechnology alliances, and by Nielsen and Nielsen (2009), on learning in strategic alliances. Learning in IJVs has also generated a significant stream of work (Beamish & Berdrow, 2003; Dhanaraj et al., 2004; Park, 2011). Inkpen and Currall (2004) analysed the co-evolution of trust, control and learning in JVs. Reuer and Ariño (2007) addressed the factors of contractual complexity. Verbeke and Greidanus (2009) introduced the concept of bounded reliability. Yadong Luo's contributions were also relevant, leading to his proposal of 'an integrated anti-opportunism system in international exchange' (Luo, 2007).

While a few contributions have considered acquired subsidiaries (e.g. Cantwell & Mudambi, 2005; Nadolska & Barkema, 2007; Uhlenbruck, 2004), once again IB literature specifically on cross-border M&As has been relatively scarce. It is likely that many issues dealing with M&As have been addressed either by general management or financial management journals. Relevant contributions in the IB field concerned the completion of acquisitions (Dikova, Sahib & van Witteloostuijn, 2010; Zhang, Zhou & Ebbers, 2011), equity preferences (Chari & Chang, 2009), risk mitigation (Reuer, Shenkar & Ragozzino, 2004), and the influence of cultural and institutional factors in the management and success of M&As (Barmeyer & Mayrhofer, 2008; Brannen & Peterson, 2009; Chakrabarti, Gupta-Mukherjee & Jayaraman, 2009; Reus & Lamont, 2009).

In contrast, the period under review witnessed an upsurge in the literature on inward and outward FDI by transition and Asian countries, especially China. The perception of distinctive institutional features, stemming from such increased international involvement, has been one of the reasons behind the heightened focus on institutional aspects (Peng et al., 2008), including institutional voids (Miller, Lee, Chang & Le Breton-Miller, 2009). Two main strands may be identified in this literature: European transition countries, many of which became EU members in this decade; and China.

The first strand has been led by the contributions of Klaus Meyer and colleagues (Bevan, Estrin & Meyer, 2004; Meyer & Gelbuda, 2006; Santangelo & Meyer, 2011). Further references address mode choice (Dikova & van Witteloostuijn, 2007) and the behaviour of foreign subsidiaries in such countries (Filatotchev, Stephan & Jindra, 2008; Steensma, Tihanyi, Lyles & Dhanaraj, 2005). A relevant analysis of the theoretical implications of IB features in transition economies was developed by Meyer and Peng (2005).

Fetscherin, Voss and Gugler (2009) provided a good summary of 30 years of FDI in China. Here we will restrain to a few references to such literature. These concern alliance and JV formation, management and change (Chen, Paik & Park, 2010; Child & Yan, 2003; Dong & Glaister, 2006; Murray, Kotabe & Zhou, 2005; Puck, Holtbrügge & Mohr, 2009), the shaping of parent-subsidiary linkages (Luo, 2003), export propensity (Gao, Murray, Kotabe & Lu, 2010), knowledge and productivity spillovers (Buckley, Wang & Clegg, 2007; Tian, 2007; Wei & Liu, 2006), and innovation performance (Dai & Liu, 2009; Wang & Kafouros, 2009). Since the second half of the decade, the outward internationalisation of Chinese, Indian and Taiwanese firms emerged as a relevant issue (Elango & Pattnaik, 2007; Filatotchev, Strange, Piesse & Lien, 2007; Lu, Zhou, Bruton & Li 2010; Wang, Hong, Kafouros & Wright, 2012). Buckley et al. (2007) identified multiple factors explaining the evolution of Chinese FDI patterns, namely cultural proximity, market seeking, resource seeking and political risk, a feature that is also at the core of the work of Cuervo-Cazurra and Genc (2008). Luo and Tung (2007) advanced a springboard perspective to explain developing-country companies venturing abroad, and especially those from China.

International entrepreneurship, especially fast internationalisation moves by young firms (born globals [BGs] and international new ventures) has been another theme that fuelled research along this period. This is expressed in the influence of the seminal article by Oviatt and McDougall (1994) and the first main quantitative analysis of BGs (Knight & Cavusgil, 2004). Other landmark contributions to frame the research in the field were provided by Oviatt and McDougall (2005), Jones and Coviello (2005) and Coviello (2006). Gabrielsson, Kirpalani, Dimitratos, Solberg and Zucchella (2008) formulated a set of propositions to advance theory in the field and identified three main phases in BGs internationalisation. Exploring a single case, Matthews and Zander (2007) suggested the existence of three organising principles (the discovery of opportunities, the deployment of resources in the exploitation of these opportunities, and the engagement with international competitors) and revisited the eclectic paradigm at the light of accelerated internationalisation. Sarasvathy (2008) introduced the concept of effectuation. Meta-analyses of early literature included Rialp, Rialp and Knight (2005), Keupp and Gassmann (2009) and Jones, Coviello and Tang (2011). To better frame the analysis of this literature one should look at the developments in the traditional literature on internationalisation processes. It may be argued that we have witnessed a co-evolutionary process through which both strands have played reciprocal influences.

The role of the Uppsala model (Johanson & Vahlne, 1977) in shaping the literature on internationalisation is well known. However, the authors' research has led them to gradually infuse a business network perspective (Johanson & Vahlne, 2003, 2006), leading to a revision of the model (Johanson & Vahlne, 2009). While keeping the same structure, with elements of state and change, and the relevance of experiential knowledge, the new version of the model is rooted on business networks as the *locus* for framing international opportunities. The processes of trust and commitment building in a network context are key for the perception of international opportunities. The focus shifted from markets to networks, highlighting the role of liabilities of outsidership instead of liabilities of foreignness (Zaheer, 1995) as the main hindrance to internationalisation. The revision of the Uppsala model is also a response to the criticisms, sometimes unfounded, by much of the literature on accelerated internationalisation.

In contrast to the blossoming of interest in accelerated internationalisation, the research on international management and strategy has not shown signs of recovery from its decline. More than the quality, the number of new contributions was limited, and Bartlett and Ghoshal's (1989) views, though being challenged, still kept a strong influence. The most relevant was Ghemawat's book *Redefining Global Strategy - Crossing Borders in a World Where Differences Still Matter* (Ghemawat, 2007).[9] This is the result of a journey including the concept of semi-globalisation (Ghemawat, 2001, 2003) and the combination of location and IB strategy (Ricart,

Enright, Ghemawat, Hart & Khanna, 2004, p. 175). Another research stream addressed the implications of managerial cognition (Levy, Beechler, Taylor & Boyacigiller, 2007), power relations (Moore, 2012), global/local pressures (Grøgaard, 2012), corporate culture (Welch & Welch, 2006) and language (Luo & Shenkar, 2006; Welch, Welch & Piekkari, 2005) for international management. A network-based view of cross-border management, underlining the role of MNEs' multiple embeddedness, was provided in an edited book by Forsgren, Holm and Johansson (2005). In the wake of Ocasio (1997), a new, promising line of research focused on managerial attention, that is, the time and effort invested by MNEs' executives in understanding the global marketplace (Birkinshaw, Bouquet & Ambos, 2007; Bouquet & Birkinshaw, 2008, 2011; Bouquet, Morrison & Birkinshaw, 2009).

Prefiguring what became the UN Sustainable Development Goals (SDGs), set up in 2015, an increasing share of IB literature has addressed MNEs' corporate social responsibility (CSR) and sustainability. Besides London and Hart (2004), relevant contributions on this regard included the following: the concepts of sustainable value (Hart & Milstein, 2003) and shared value (Porter & Kramer, 2006, 2011); the assessment of how institutional pressures shape MNEs' corporate social responsibility decisions (Husted & Allen, 2006); the claim by Doh, Husted, Matten and Santoro (2010) for an increased synergy between IB and business ethics; and Kolk and Pinkse's (2008) analysis of the conditions for MNEs to develop 'green' FSAs. Scherer and Palazzo (2011, p. 922) concluded that 'the primacy of property rights, the belief in self-regulative markets, and the assumption that the pursuit of private interests automatically promotes the common good are premises that need to be reconsidered' in a globalisation setting.

While being traditionally a key IB research theme, culture witnessed a revival in the early 2000s. This was due to the combination of two factors: the perception that increased globalisation did not erase cultural differences, making them instead more evident; and the publication of the long-awaited findings from the GLOBE (Global Leadership and Organisational Behaviour Effectiveness Research programme) project, envisaged as providing an alternative to the dominant Hofstede's dimensions (House et al., 2004; Waldman et al., 2006). A set of nine attributes was developed to characterise cultural traits in 62 societies around the World. A stream of research emerged, reviewing or updating Hofstede's dimensions (Kirkman, Lowe & Gibson, 2006; Tang & Koveos, 2008), confronting their explanatory power of Hofstede *vis-à-vis* alternatives (Drogendijk & Slangen, 2006), especially GLOBE (Brewer & Venaik, 2010; Venaik & Brewer, 2010). Drawing on Shenkar (2001), Tung and Verbeke (2010) discussed ten limitations or weaknesses in cross-cultural research. Related issues concerned the meaning and measurement of cultural distance (Chapman, Gajewska-De Mattos, Clegg & Buckley, 2008), psychic distance (Dow & Karunaratna, 2006) and cultural friction (Luo & Shenkar, 2011) A very influential article, on the effects of cultural diversity on international team working, was Stahl, Maznevski, Voigt and Jonsen (2010). A related issue concerns international HRM. Besides Minbaeva et al. (2003), mentioned above, the literature addressed knowledge sharing and the development of inter-unit intellectual capital (Minbaeva, 2008; Reiche, Harzing & Kraimer, 2009) as well as expatriate assignment (Bolino, 2007;

Brock, Shenkar, Shoham & Siscovick, 2008; Mezias & Scandura, 2005), return (Lazarova & Cerdin, 2007) and retention (Reiche, Kraimer & Harzing, 2011).

The last observation concerns the revival and the recognition of qualitative research as a relevant epistemological approach to IB research. The roots for this may be found in Yair Aharoni's PhD thesis (Aharoni, 1966) as well as in Johanson and Vahlne (1977) and Bartlett and Ghoshal's (1989) influential contributions. The work by Birkinshaw on subsidiary initiatives (Birkinshaw, 1995, 1997, 1999; Birkinshaw & Hood, 2001), by Yves Doz (1996), and the research on BGs have provided additional fuel for the approach. Rebecca Piekkari and Catherine Welch *Handbook of Qualitative Research Methods for International Business* (Piekkari & Welch, 2004) and their 2011 *Rethinking* (Piekkari & Welch, 2011) provided an important reference for many young qualitative researchers. The article by Mary Yoko Brannen (Brannen, 2011) on generalisation from multiple case studies provided an important contribution. Also influential were Hurmerinta-Peltomäki and Nummela (2006) and Sinkovics, Penz and Ghauri (2008). Remarkable is the *JIBS* special issue on qualitative research in IB, edited by Rosalie L. Tung, Julian Birkinshaw and Mary Yoko Brannen, featuring key qualitative authors (Burgelman, 2011; Doz, 2011; Westney & Van Maanen, 2011); in the last article, Welch, Piekkari, Plakoyiannaki and Paavilainen-Mäntymäki (2011) made a plea for more pluralistic IB approaches in using methods for theorising from case studies.

7.3. EIBA: THE CONFERENCES

The significant developments regarding both the attitudes and behaviour towards FDI and the evolution of IB literature provide the background against which we may address the main features of IB developments in the period under review.

The 10 conferences held over the 2003–2012 period were spread from West to East, from Porto or Brighton to Bucharest, as well as from North to South, from Oslo or Tallinn to Catania. With the exceptions of Oslo and Copenhagen, all locations hosted EIBA for the first time (Ljubljana, Fribourg, Catania, Valencia, Porto Tallinn, Bucharest and Brighton). More importantly, EIBA made its debut in four countries (Slovenia, Switzerland, Estonia and Romania), three of them corresponding to new entrants to the EU. Again, EIBA had the concern to welcome and support the development of IB scholarly communities in East European countries.

This was a time of stabilisation of EIBA on both financial and organisational grounds. On the first, a way was found to close the long-lasting debt to EIASM. On the second, two initiatives championed by Torben Pedersen and Lars Håkansson were essential. First, the revision of EIBA statutes, with the separation between the roles of EIBA Chairman, in charge of the Academy's strategy and management, and EIBA President, focused on the conference organisation. Second, the drafting of the first EIBA Annual Conference Guidelines (EIBA, 2003). EIBA conferences became more attractive, with an increased gender balance, while two more women served as conference convenors (Grazia Santangelo and Ana Teresa Tavares-Lehmann). In spite of a cumbersome dialogue, contractual issues

and *Elsevier*'s low commitment to the marketing of *IBR*, this journal was also
an asset to strengthen EIBA image and to entice new members. Another positive factor was AIB's decision to move its annual conference from November to
July, significantly reducing the conflict between both conferences. As a result of
all the above developments, and despite the ups-and-downs related to conference
location appeal, EIBA membership has shown a remarkable growth, reaching a
record of 424 members in 2010, from 295 in 2003.

Twelve years after the very successful conference in 1991, convened by Harald
Vestergaard, EIBA came back to CBS, in Copenhagen. The conference theme
was 'The MNC as a knowing organisation'. This was in line with the increasing
trend towards the research on knowledge management in MNEs. The conference attracted a very high number of participants (411), a third of which corresponding to doctoral students. This highlights EIBA's capacity to attract young
scholars and to rejuvenate itself. Among those who made their EIBA debut in
Copenhagen, one may find several colleagues who later played important roles
in the Academy, including a Vice-chair of EIBA's Executive Committee (Jonas
Puck), three conference chairs (Birgitte Grøgaard, Isabel Álvarez and again Jonas
Puck), colleagues who served at the EIBA Board (Evis Sinani, Susana Costa e
Silva and Tina Ambos), and still others who generously contributed to EIBA
conference training seminars (Emmanuella Plakoiyannaki).

Lars Håkansson and Torben Pedersen put a strong emphasis on the academic
side of the conference. Two important innovations were introduced. The first was
the setting up of a new track chair system, including eight tracks. This innovation
turned to be a key feature of EIBA conference programmes in the future, ensuring
a consistent process of paper selection. The second regarded the establishment of
a new award: the CBS Award, to recognise the best paper written by young scholars (i.e. authors under 40). Meanwhile re-labelled as SMG Copenhagen Prize, this
award is still today an enticing feature of EIBA conferences for young, promising
scholars. The first prize was granted to Dorothee Feils (University of Alberta,
Canada) for a paper entitled 'The impact of NAFTA on foreign direct investment
in Canada, Mexico and the US'.[10] The poster sessions, launched in Athens, were
pursued and improved. Another feature of the conference was an increased use of
information and communication technologies, which played a key role in the process of registration, paper submission, and payments. The software specifically
developed for this was kept for several years as the backbone of such processes in
future EIBA conferences.

The opening panel featured Peter Buckley and Nicolai Foss, who shared relevant insights about 'The Future Research Agenda in International Business'.
Following the path started in Athens, Danny Van Den Bulcke organised a panel
on the occasion of the 20th anniversary of Jean-François Hennart's *Theory
of the Multinational Enterprise*. The closing plenary addressed the conference
theme. The welcome reception took place at the Design Museum. For those who
praise the strong aesthetical tradition of stylised Danish design and its application to distinct types of everyday objects, it was an amazing experience. The
main social event was the Gala Dinner at the front hall of the National Museum
of Denmark.

As usual, the Doctoral Tutorial was chaired by Danny Van Den Bulcke. The faculty also included Peter Buckley, John Cantwell, Yves Doz, Robert Grosse, Jean-François Hennart and Lars Håkansson. This time there were two winners: Chelsea Freer, from Monash University (Australia), with a project on 'Before and after the ink dries! The implications of resources, structure and relations on alliance outcomes', and Sabina Tacheva, from the University of St. Gallen (Switzerland), addressing the process implications of international top management teams.

From Copenhagen, EIBA moved South, almost following the same meridian, to Ljubljana. This was also a very enjoyable conference, at a time when Slovenia had just joined the European Union. The theme of the conference was 'Enlarged European Union: Challenges to the International Business and Management'. In spite of Marjan Svetlicic's committed effort to attract scholars from Central and Eastern Europe, attendance declined to 283. Nonetheless, EIBA was able to sow the seeds of an increased interest for IB. Among those who had their first EIBA experience in Ljubljana, a reference is due to Jorge Carneiro, who would later become to organise EIBA Rio-2015, two Slovenians who served at the EIBA Board (Andrea Jaklic and Anze Burger) and an EIBA-committed Nordic host (Olli Kuivalainen, Peter Gabrielsson, Randi Lunnan and Sami Saarenketo). 'Competitiveness of the Enlarged EU' was the topic of the opening plenary, chaired by Marjan Svetlicic. Participants included Milan Cvikl (minister for European affairs), Janez Potocnik (EU Commissioner for Science and Research), John Stopford (this was his last attendance of an EIBA conference) and John H. Dunning. The other plenary corresponded to the EIBA Fellows Panel, organised by Seev Hirsch and chaired by John H. Dunning, about 'Can Europe grow more global leaders [like Nokia]?'.

A key feature of this conference was the granting of the EIBA LAA to John Dunning. After two introductory addresses by two well-known former students of Dunning (John Cantwell and Rajneesh Narula), full of humour, sharing episodes of their interaction with their supervisor and showing how he had contributed to shaping their careers, Danny Van Den Bulcke handled the LAA plaque[11] to John Dunning. It was the first time that this Award was granted, and it was otherwise only awarded to Klaus Macharzina, 19 years later. This shows how important has been the stature, example and legacy of John H. Dunning for EIBA!

The fact that the LAA plaque was presented by Danny Van Den Bulcke did not happen by chance, or due to the long friendship between them or the fact that Danny was increasingly seen as Mr. EIBA. It happened for institutional reasons in his capacity as EIBA Chair. In fact, the Ljubljana conference was the first in which the new model of EIBA governance became visible to the ordinary EIBAian.

2004 was the last time that Danny Van Den Bulcke chaired the Doctoral Tutorial, due to his duties as EIBA Chair. The Tutorial was co-chaired with John Cantwell, who took the baton for future editions. The winner was Nejc Martin Jakopin, from the University of Duisburg-Essen (Germany), with a project on 'International Strategy of Mobile Network Operators – Entry Modes,

Management and Success'. The faculty was exactly the same as in Copenhagen: besides the above-mentioned Danny and John Cantwell, it also comprised Yves Doz, Robert Grosse, Jean-François Hennart and Lars Håkansson.

From lovely Ljubljana EIBA moved to Oslo. Another charming little city, facing the Atlantic. It was EIBA's second turn in Oslo. Gabriel Benito was strongly committed to make the 2005 Oslo conference a landmark in EIBA's history – and his goals were achieved. Convened under the *motto* of 'Landscapes and Mindscapes in a Globalised World', most of the conference was held at the brand new BI Norwegian School of Management building, located in Nydalen, at the outskirts of Oslo. The number of participants reached 342, which is a feat for a meeting in December at 60 degrees North. Oslo-2005 was the first EIBA experience for some colleagues who are now frequent attendants of EIBA conferences, such as Axéle Giroud or Hinrich Voss.

The opening plenary focused on research programmes in IB. The closing session corresponded to the first EIBA Fellows Panel, which was to become a key feature of EIBA conferences. Chaired by John H. Dunning, the Panel addressed 'The internationalization of R&D – Implications for countries and firms'. Speakers included three well-known EIBA Fellows (John Cantwell, John Hagedoorn and Francesca Sanna-Randaccio) together with two Norwegian experts: Jan Fagerberg, an outstanding researcher on the economics of innovation; and Knut Haanæs, then at the Research Council of Norway. A commemorative session was dedicated to the 30 years of internationalisation research by Lawrence Welch.[12] Danny chaired a panel on 'The 'new' Triad: China, India and the US? And what about Europe?'. Now that the World is fragmented, with a growing divide between China and the US and a weakened Europe, one is bound to recognise how prescient Danny has been in convening this panel. The EIBA Honorary Fellow Award was awarded to Jorma Olilla, the CEO of Nokia at its golden days, by John H. Dunning, then Dean of the Fellows.

It was a strange feeling that Danny had not chaired the Doctoral Tutorial that he had launched at the 1987 Antwerp Conference. It was however in good hands under the co-chairmanship of John Cantwell and Udo Zander. But it was not so easy for Danny to leave his beloved 'child'. He has still been part of the faculty, which also included Peter Buckley, Jean-François Hennart, Marina Papanastassiou and Torben Pedersen. The winner was Katharina Kretschmer (ESCP-EAP European School of Management Berlin, Germany) for her doctoral project on 'Performance Evaluation of Foreign Subsidiaries'.

South, again... Almost 1500 kms SW. Destination: Fribourg. The EIBA community was landing in Switzerland for the first time. Not in a leading business centre, such as Zurich or Basle, not in the UN hub of Geneva. EIBAians were to discover how charming Fribourg is. They would easily agree with Philippe Gugler, the super-diplomatic and efficient conference organiser, that Fribourg is a lovely place to live. Conference attendance was very close to Oslo (336 people), confirming that the recovery to levels of participation of about 340 was to become a consistent feature. Fribourg has marked the EIBA debut for committed EIBA members, such as Birgit Hagen, Erikka Paavilainen-Mäntymäki, Phillip Kappen, Tiia Vissak, and Harun Emre Yildiz. Philippe was happy to get the EIBA community together at his University and specially to welcome his PhD supervisor, John H. Dunning. This was a very special conference; many EIBAians still remember Fribourg as the location where John H. Dunning has shown his crystal ball for the first time ever!

That happened in the opening plenary, dedicated to discuss the conference theme: Regional and national drivers of business location and competitiveness. John H. Dunning relied on his crystal ball to identify 10 issues likely to shape the IB scene 20 years later, in 2027. We are still not arrived to 2027. However, some of his predictions are not far from reality, namely the suggestions that *movement(s) towards protectionism* could *reverse* the globalisation trend, that there would be a *(relative) rise in efficiency and asset augmenting FDI*, and that a *rising importance of business/society management and relational assets* might emerge in connection with an increasing relevance of institutional considerations. The last point highlighted by John H. Dunning is a very important caveat for present times: 'a rise in non-ergodic uncertainty means that predictions are more difficult to make'. The conference included two further plenary sessions, besides the Gunnar Hedlund Award session. One addressed 'Outstanding issues regarding International Business Competitiveness', a subject dear to Philippe Gugler. The closing plenary corresponded to the Fellows Panel. Dealing with 'Multinationals, Technology and Development', it was held in honour of Sanjaya Lall, founder of the journal *Oxford Development Studies*. Organised by Francesca Sanna-Randaccio, the panel was chaired by John H. Dunning and also included John Cantwell (Rutgers University), Anne Miroux (Chief of the Investment Issues Analysis Branch, UNCTAD) and Karl Sauvant (former director of the UNCTAD Investment Division, awarded the EIBA Honorary Fellowship in 2006).

The top social event was the Gala Dinner. Eleven years after Urbino, a jazz band entertained the EIBA crowd during the dinner. This was followed by the increasing numbers of awards, including the Gunnar Hedlund Award and the CBS Prize, to Christian Schwens and Rüdiger Kabst, both from the University of Giessen (Germany). A new award was launched this year: the *IBR* Best Journal Paper of the Year, assigned to Michael Mol (University of Reading), Rob van Tulder and Paul Beije (Erasmus University Rotterdam), for their article 'Antecedents and performance consequences of international outsourcing'.[13]

The 20th Doctoral Tutorial was chaired by John Cantwell and Udo Zander, who would serve until 2009; the faculty also included Jean-François Hennart, Torben Pedersen, Lucia Piscitello and Francesca Sanna-Randaccio. Twelve students were selected from 50 applications. The size of the demand clearly pointed out for the need to launch another tutorial for students less advanced in their doctoral research process, but it was found that the approach needed further thinking. The winner was Roger Smeets, from Radboud University Nijmegen (Netherlands), with a proposal focused on Multinationals and knowledge spillovers.

In 2007, EIBA went further South, to Catania, in the historical and beautiful Mediterranean island of Sicily. Grazia Santangelo was very committed to take the EIBA community to her home town. The conference theme was 'International

Fig. 8.   John H. Dunning Receiving the EIBA Lifetime Achievement Award
in Ljubljana (2004). *Source*: EIBA website.

Business, Local development and Science-technology Relationships', a subject
that was fully in line with Grazia's research concerns. The number of participants
was 290, recording a fall with regard to the couple of previous EIBA conferences,
though slightly above Ljubljana-2004. Catania marked EIBA's debut of people
who served either as NRs (Dirk Morschett, Ronaldo Parente), organised tutorials (Elizabeth Yi Wang) or played important roles in supporting the organisation
of future conferences (Joaquin Alegre and Stefano Elia). In contrast, it was the
last time that John H. Dunning –the main reference for European IB scholars, the
first Dean of the EIBA Fellows, and long since a committed EIBAian and special
adviser to the Doctoral Tutorial– attended an EIBA conference.[14] His memory
will always remain with us, especially the old-timers (see Fig. 8).

The closing session was the EIBA Fellows Panel, dedicated to International
Corporate Governance organised and chaired by Klaus Macharzina. Danny
Van Den Bulcke of chaired a panel on 'The Eclectic Theory, the Multinational
Enterprise and the Global Economy – John Dunning's *magnum opus*'. It was
an excellent initiative of Danny Van Den Bulcke, who, being aware the health
problems affecting John H. Dunning, has chosen a perfect timing to honour his
outstanding influence over generations of IB scholars. The social part of the conference was marked by the Gala Dinner at Palazzo Biscari, a monumental private
palace, facing the seaside and with magnificent interior decorations, built after
the 1693 earthquake.

The Doctoral Tutorial had two winners: Sergey Filippov (University of
Maastricht, Netherlands), with a project on 'Multinational Subsidiary Evolution
and Regional Economic Integration' and Nikolaos Papageorgiadis (Leeds

University, UK), for his project on 'The effect of International Intellectual Property Rights protection and enforcement on International Business: The case of licensing'. The Tutorial was once again chaired by John Cantwell and Udo Zander, and the faculty was similar to Fribourg, with the replacement of Torben Pedersen by Peter J. Buckley.

When leaving Catania EIBA was heading North again, to Tallinn, on the Baltic Sea shores. The conference was hosted by the Tallinn School of Economics and Business Administration (Tallinn University) and the Tartu University, and was organised by Enn Listra, Professor at the Tallinn University of Technology, with the scientific support of Jorma Larimo. The theme of the conference was 'International Business and Catching-up Economies: Challenges and opportunities'. The idea was to put the focus on catching-up to assess how IB operations could contribute to that endeavour. Estonian welcome was warm and the sun was shining. Ishii Shinish (Osaka Metropolitan University, Japan) and Bernard Swoboda (Trier University, Germany) are among those for whom Tallinn was the first EIBA conference.

There were two plenary sessions. The opening plenary addressed the conference theme, with a focus on IB developments in Estonia. The Fellows plenary was organised and chaired by Seev Hirsch and featured the new EIBA Distinguished Honorary fellow, Eli Hurwitz, then the CEO of *Teva*, the Israeli pharmaceutical MNE specialised in generic drugs. The theme was 'The Nation State and the Global Corporation', an issue that Seev Hirsch was concerned with. The other panel members were Anders Sutt (deputy governor of the Bank of Estonia), Francesca Sanna-Randaccio (University of Rome, Italy) and Louis T. Wells (Herbert F. Johnson Professor of International Management, Harvard Business School, US). The Tallinn conference will also be remembered by the availability for sale at the Edward Elgar stand of *Seasons of a Scholar*, John H. Dunning's memories. The Gala dinner was held at the Estonia Concert Hall, a 1913 neoclassical building, reconstructed in 1947. There was a nice music performance by a small chamber group; some EIBAians may still remind the bell's sound.

The Doctoral Tutorial was again co-chaired by John Cantwell and Udo Zander. There was little change in the faculty: Ulf Andersson (who replaced Peter Buckley), Jean-François Hennart, Lucia Piscitello and Francesca Sanna-Randaccio. The winner was Pooja Thakur (Rutgers University, USA), whose project concerned 'Externalisation of core activities and their geographical coverage: In-house versus offshoring versus outsourcing of clinical trials'.

From the Baltic, EIBA moved to the Mediterranean again. From the cold winter in Tallinn to the mild weather, though with light rain, in Valencia. José Plà-Barber was fully committed to make EIBA Valencia an unforgettable event. He managed to organise a very successful conference, combining an excellent academic programme with plenty of opportunities for socialisation. The conference's theme was 'Reshaping the boundaries of the firm in an era of global interdependence'. Attendance reached 392, the highest since Copenhagen. It was the first EIBA conference for Cristina Villar, who later became the NR for Spain, and other well-known EIBAians, such as Beata Stępień, Francisco Figueira de Lemos, Mario Kafouros and Florian Zapkau.

In Valencia, Danny Van Den Bulcke, the first EIBA Chair, passed the baton to Peter Buckley to serve for three years. The programme included two plenary sessions. The first corresponded to the opening plenary, organised by the EIBA Fellows to discuss 'John Dunning's International Business legacy: Back to the future'. Chaired by Klaus Macharzina and Danny Van Den Bulcke (outgoing and incoming Deans of the Fellows), the panel also included John Cantwell, Sarianna Lundan, Peter Buckley and Seev Hirsch The other plenary session, chaired by Danny Van Den Bulcke, was focused on the work of another influential IB scholar, Yves Doz.

Following a proposal presented to the EIBA Board, the Doctoral Tutorial was renamed as *John H. Dunning (JHD) Doctoral Tutorial in IB*. Danny Van Den Bulcke was nominated Honorary Chair. It was the last time that the Tutorial was co-chaired by John Cantwell and Udo Zander, since John had to resign in view of his incoming commitment as editor of *JIBS*. This year there were two winners: Alessandra Perri, from LUISS Guido Carli University (Italy), with a proposal on 'Firm-level heterogeneity and FDI-mediated knowledge spillovers: Some insights on the role of MNCs' and subsidiaries' characteristics'; and Harun Emre Yildiz, from Stockholm School of Economics (Sweden), whose doctoral project focused on 'Fostering successful transfer of organisational practices in cross-border M&As'. The faculty included Ulf Andersson, Jean-François Hennart, Lucia Piscitello and Alan Rugman, besides the co-chairs. The social programme was excellent, and many people would still remember the guided tour and their dancing experience in Valencia.

The 2010 conference was also held in the Iberian Peninsula, though moving from the Mediterranean to the Atlantic. Superbly organised by Ana Teresa Tavares-Lehman, it was held in Porto that proudly labels itself as the *Cidade Invicta* (undefeated city); this was the second EIBA conference ever in Portugal. The conference's theme was 'IB's role in building a better and stronger global economy'. The conference attracted 320 participants. Among those EIBAians who made their debut in Porto, a reference is due to Chang Hoon Oh, Chie Iguchi and Erzsébet Czakó, who later served at the EIBA Board, as well as to now well-known IB scholars, such as Andrei Panibratov, Noemi Sinkovics, Nuno Reis, Sui Sui and Miguel Torres. This conference also marks the debut of a new EIBA Secretary (Ene Kannel), who would serve at the EIBA Board for almost 15 years.

Three plenary sessions were held. The opening plenary provided room for Portuguese firms to share their internationalisation strategies. The Fellows Plenary addressed the financial and economic crisis and its challenges for IB, and featured Danny Van Den Bulcke (chair), Lars Oxelheim, Marina Papanastassiou, Karl Sauvant (Honorary Fellow) and Marjan Svetlicic. The third plenary, held under the *motto* of 'Network organisation and subsidiary entrepreneurship in Multinational Enterprises' was focused on the work of Julian Birkinshaw. Besides Julian, the panel included Daniel Van Den Bulcke, Björn Ambos, William Egelhoff and Alain Verbeke. It was an excellent opportunity to discuss the work of one of the most influential IB thinkers at the time. Besides the academic programme, Porto provided two memorable socialisation experiences. The first was the visit to Casa Ferreirinha cellars. The second was the Gala Dinner, held at Palácio da Bolsa (Stock Exchange Palace), built in the 19th century by the city's Commercial Association in neoclassical style.

The JHD Doctoral Tutorial was co-chaired by Udo Zander and Jean-François Hennart. The faculty included well-known scholars and EIBAians: Francesca Sanna-Randaccio, Grazia Santangelo and Ulf Andersson. Ten PhD students were selected from 41 applications. The winner was a Slovenian studying in Italy: Andreja Bandelj, from Bocconi University. The research theme was: 'Should Banks be diversified geographically? Evidence from Europe'.

It was mentioned above that the increasing number of applicants highlighted the need for another tutorial, aimed at those students who were less advanced in their PhD research. With his entrepreneurial drive, Danny Van Den Bulcke negotiated with Louis Brennan, then chair of the European Cooperation in Science and Technology (COST), a four-year partnership between EIBA and COST to launch the COST-EIBA/EIASM Doctoral Think Tank (DTT). The first DTT was held in Porto, under the label of 'Emerging Markets and its corporate players: Significance and impact'. Besides Danny, the faculty included Lucia Piscitello and Jeremy Clegg (who would later take charge of the future tutorial). This initiative enabled the setting up of another forum to discuss PhD projects, making a significant contribution from EIBA to stimulate IB research in Europe by attracting younger generations to the Academy.

A long trip of above 2,800 km awaited EIBAians, from Porto to Bucharest, from the Atlantic to near the Black Sea shores. The distance was about the same travelled two years before between Tallinn and Valencia. EIBA was again aiming at sowing the IB seeds in a newcomer to the EU. The host was Liviu Voinea, a very dynamic and entrepreneurial colleague, professor at the Academy of Economic Studies (AES), Faculty of International Business and Economics, Bucharest, who had been EIBA member since 2004.

The conference took place at the ASE. Addressing the theme of 'Taking IB to the next level – Emerging issues, strategies and economies', it was well organised. Liviu Voinea made a significant effort to reduce the conference fees, by attracting company sponsors, including the National Bank of Romania. The Gala Dinner took place at the Crystal Palace Ballroom in Bucharest. It provided another excellent opportunity for the EIBA community to meet and socialise as well as to handle the main conference awards, always under the lead of Mr EIBA, Danny Van Den Bulcke. Among those who made their debut in Bucharest, a reference is due to three colleagues that became EIBA Board members: Barbara Jankowska, Erica Kovacs and Sara Melén Hånell, who served as NRs for Poland, Brasil and Sweden. Barbara was EIBA President in 2018, when she organised EIBA Poznan; she is now co-editor of *EIBAzine*. EIBA Bucharest-2011 was also the first EIBA experience for Ari Van Assche, now the Editor-in-Chief of the *Journal of International Business Policy*.

The conference included in fact only one plenary session: the Opening Plenary. This was very politically orientated. Though led by Peter Buckley as EIBA Chair, the main speakers were the US Ambassador to Romania and the governor of the National Bank of Romania. Three other plenary sessions were advertised in the programme, but in fact they were not plenaries, since they were run together with other sessions. These included the following sessions: '50 years of research on the multinational enterprise', featuring the vice-rector of IES, Alan Rugman (keynote speaker), Klaus Meyer, Rajneesh Narula, Christian Asmussen and Alain Verbeke; Yair Aharoni's contributions to the IB field, organised and chaired by Danny Van Den Bulcke, including an address by Yair Aharoni himself and presentations by Ravi Ramamurti, Niron Hashai and Alain Verbeke; and the EIBA Fellows session, under the *motto* of 'A multipolar global economy: Challenges for investors and governments in transition and advanced economies', chaired again by Danny Van Den Bulcke, the speakers being Peter Buckley, Marjan Svetlicic, Lars Oxelheim and Wilfried Vanhonecker.

The JHD Doctoral Tutorial was co-chaired by Jean-François Hennart and Rebecca Piekkari. The faculty also included Gabriel Benito, Ingmar Björkman and Timothy Devinney. The winner was Sebastian Schrapp (Georg August University, Göttingen, Germany), with a reseach project on 'R&D Spending during the Financial Crisis: The Impact of Country-Specific Mechanisms and Financial Incentives'.

In 2012, EIBA was back in Great Britain, 13 years after Manchester and 20 after Reading. This time the destination was Brighton, where Roger Strange and Pervez Ghauri were waiting for us. With hindsight, it may be said that EIBA Brighton was a landmark in EIBA's history: it was the last EIBA conference attended by Danny Van Den Bulcke. Neither he nor those who have seen him, active as usual, fully involved in EIBA's life, taking his photos and enjoying a very well-managed conference, could not anticipate that we would not meet him the following year in Bremen.

The Conference theme was 'International Business and Sustainable Development'. Attendance reached a new peak, with about 500 participants, significantly above the previous maximum got in Copenhagen in 2003. Almost one-fourth of the attendants came from the UK, testifying its key role as an IB powerhouse in Europe. Many people attended EIBA for the first time, including Vittoria Scalera, who became the Netherlands NR at the EIBA Board, and Jakob Müllner, who was to be one of the co-winners of the Danny Van Den Bulcke Best Paper Prize in 2020.

A relevant feature of EIBA Brighton was the coexistence of three doctoral events. The JHD Doctoral Tutorial and the COST-EIBA/EIASM DTT were joined by a new initiative, the EIBA Doctoral Symposium, chaired by Jeremy Clegg (University of Leeds) and Ödül Bozkurt (University of Sussex). This corresponded to a 'compressed version of the Doctoral Tutorial' and was aimed at responding to an increasing demand, while attracting more students to EIBA conferences. It was specially welcome since the Doctoral Think Tank with COST had a limited time scope, and was already entering its third year. In this opening year, 10 students had the opportunity to present their projects. With hindsight, it is now clear that the Doctoral Symposium was a timely initiative and became another enticing feature of EIBA conferences for PhD students. The JHD Doctoral Tutorial kept its prominence as the lead EIBA doctoral event. In Brighton it was chaired again by Jean-François Hennart and Rebecca Piekkari.

The faculty included old-timers (Gabriel Benito, Timothy Devinney) and one newcomer (Suzana Rodrigues, from Rotterdam School of Management). Again, ten students were selected to present their doctoral projects. The winner was Wolfgang Gleich (Universität Augsburg, Germany), whose theme reminded Frederick Knickerbocker's ideas on oligopolistic reaction: 'Retaliatory Foothold Expansion in Attackers Home Markets'.

The Opening Plenary, addressing the theme of the conference, was chaired by Rob van Tulder, a long-time EIBAian. Another plenary, organised by Danny Van Den Bulcke, honoured the multiple contributions by Paul Beamish, from the Ivey School of Business (Canada). Following a proposal by Seev Hirsch, the Fellows elected Martin Wolf, *Financial Times*' Chief Economics Commentator, as Honorary Fellow. Martin Wolf delivered an outstanding presentation on 'Limits to Growth in the 21st Century'. His address was commented by Sarianna Lundan, Francesca Sanna-Randaccio and James Zhan (UNCTAD). The Panel was chaired by Danny Van Den Bulcke.

Although the distance from Brighton to Bremen is a mere 660 kms,[15] these meetings seemed to us much further apart once we learned that Danny would not be with us. Danny was not in Bremen with his smile and his camera cheering us at the beginning of another EIBA. It was a shock for all EIBAians to find that he was not there. When told about the health reasons, the shock deepened, as we feared we may meet him ever again. EIBA has an immense debt towards Danny for all the services he kindly rendered to our Academy. But he would be extremely pleased to find that, without him, EIBA was able to forge its own path, and to become increasingly sustainable.

7.4. EIBA: ORGANISATIONAL DEVELOPMENTS

If the last period (1996–2002) corresponded to EIBA's adulthood, 2003 witnessed a key organisational decision that has proved essential to stabilise EIBA, making it a sounder organisation, less dependent on the ebb-and-flow of annual conferences. The creation of the elected positions of EIBA Chair and Vice-Chair, serving for three years, renewable for the same period, was key to foster EIBA's stability and further growth. The Chairs came to play a central role in EIBA's management and longer-term strategy, which is quite distinct from the one-year rotating EIBA President, in charge of convening the annual conference. Another important move taken in 2003 was the drafting of the Annual Conference Guidelines (EIBA, 2003), providing an experience-based template that significantly helps the process of conference organisation. There were however still thorny issues to solve, namely the debt towards EIASM and the relationship with the AIB.

To entice membership and to nurture future IB scholars, two further initiatives were taken: the launch of the annual series of PIBR, collecting some of the best conference papers presented; and the setting up of another doctoral tutorial session, started under a COST project, thanks to the effort of Danny Van Den Bulcke. Taking the path recorded in the previous period, the weight of women in EIBA increased, not just in terms of membership, but also – and this is a new feature – with regard to Board positions. In the period under analysis, the EIBA Presidency was taken by two female EIBAians, who had been committed long-term members: Grazia Santangelo, in 2007, and Ana Teresa Tavares-Lehman, in 2010.

The main organisational developments recorded in the 2003–2012 period are briefly presented below. Such presentation is arranged in ten sections: the EIBA governance developments; EIBA's governing bodies; EIBA membership; gender balance in EIBA membership; EIBA accounts and the debt to EIASM; the *EIBA Conference Guidelines*; relationships with other organisations, especially with AIB; further digitalisation of EIBA; the *IBR*; and new EIBA publications. Again, the activities of the EIBA Fellows will be presented in a distinct section.

7.4.1. EIBA Governance and the Revisions of the EIBA Statutes

As mentioned in the previous chapter (see Section 6.4.10), a discussion was held at the Spring Board meeting in Athens (April 2002) on EIBA's future development and organisation, led by John Hagedoorn and Danny Van Den Bulcke. They were mandated to draft a proposal on the reorganisation of EIBA. This was presented at the December Board meeting in Athens, and encompassed three main vectors: keeping the representation at the Board; introducing an Executive Committee (Chairperson, Vice Chairperson and President-Elect) to manage EIBA's affairs; and to reorganise the Secretariat. The discussion held was not conclusive, and the incoming President and Vice-President (Torben Pedersen and Lars Håkansson) were charged of drafting a revised proposal on the reorganisation of EIBA.

Building upon Hagedoorn and Van Den Bulcke's work and earlier discussions, Torben and Lars wrote a very important, five-page document entitled 'The future of EIBA' (Håkansson & Pedersen, 2003). It addressed several key issues regarding the relevance and stability of EIBA, membership drive and future organisational arrangements. They shared Hagedoorn and Van Den Bulcke's view that 'EIBA lacks continuity', and argued that there was potential for a considerable increase in membership (Håkansson & Pedersen, 2003, p. 2). They also stressed that the 'immediate priority should be to implement a set of organisational changes whose primary aim is to maintain and improve the academic quality and general attractiveness of the annual conference' (p. 4). This was translated in two vectors: one corresponded to the Annual Conference Guidelines (EIBA, 2003) (more on this below) and another led to the revision of EIBA governance. The document was circulated at the EIBA Board, and was subject to several comments from Board members. This process led Lars Håkansson and Torben Pedersen to draft a decision proposal to be discussed at the EIBA Board, and to be later submitted to EIBA's General Assembly. It included six points that may be summarised in three key ideas: creation of an Executive Committee, consisting of four members (Chair, Vice-Chair, President and past President), led by the EIBA Chair; election of the Chair and Vice-Chair, each elected for a three-year period, but in different years; and the President is the organiser of the year's annual conference. A discussion on this was held at the Spring 2003 Board meeting. The proposal became the blueprint for the subsequent revision of EIBA's statutes.

A new version of EIBA's statutes was developed, and extensively discussed at the Spring 2004 Board meeting in Ljubljana. The result was submitted to the Belgian authorities, and approved on 17 September 2005. The General Assembly (GA) kept its role as the ultimate governing body, most decisions requiring GA's clearance. With regard to the 1982 statutes, championed by José de la Torre, the objective of EIBA was slightly changed, stressing the purpose to 'promote, disseminate and stimulate high quality research and education in the field in and outside Europe' (EIBA, 2005, art. 2.1). The figure of NRs was kept, though the conditions were slightly different. In the 1982 statutes, it was just required that a country had five or more members (EIBA, 1982b). In 2005, the condition was more stringent, since 'a minimum membership of five members over a consecutive three-year period' (EIBA, 2005, art. 5.2) was required; exceptions to this rule were, however, considered for Central and Eastern Europe or other under-represented areas, as agreed by the Board and General Assembly (EIBA, 2005, art. 5.2). The possibility of having Regional representatives was also provided in 2005 statutes, although it has not been implemented so far.[16]

The main changes concerned, however, the governance of EIBA. With hindsight, the revision of the statutes proved to be essential to enhance EIBA's management stability, making it less dependent on conference organisation.

7.4.2 The EIBA Board

The revision of the statutes led to significant changes in the EIBA Board, although the role of the NRs was kept, as key nodes between EIBA and country members. The evolution of the Board composition in the 2003–2012 period is presented at Tables 5A and 5B. As the change was only implemented in 2004, the 2003 structure is the old one.

Danny Van Den Bulcke, Mr EIBA, was naturally elected as the first EIBA Chair, together with Lars Håkansson as a recognition of the paramount role he had played in the process of statutory change. Since inception it was agreed that Lars would serve for two years only. In 2006, he was replaced by Marjan Svetlicic, organiser of the successful 2004 Ljubljana conference, who also served for two years, handling his position to Torben Pedersen in 2008. This means that during his six years mandate, from 2004 to 2009,[17] Danny Van Den Bulcke worked with three distinct Vice-chairs. In December 2009, Danny was replaced by Peter Buckley, who served as EIBA Chair between 2010 and 2012. Again, he cooperated with more than one Vice-Chair: first, Torben Pedersen, and then Philippe Gugler, who later became the third EIBA Chair. In his opening speech, Peter Buckley put the emphasis on two issues: to increase the quality of research in EIBA and, therefore, the standard of EIBA conferences; and to improve EIBA's commitment to IB education.

The rotation of EIBA Presidents, past Presidents and President elects was marked by the yearly rhythm of EIBA conferences. There was just an exception, in 2012, when, faced with the absence of Liviu Voinea, Peter Buckley asked Ana Teresa Tavares-Lehman, the previous past President, to replace Liviu at the Executive Committee. A look at the Presidents along these ten years shows that, while some

Table 5A. Composition of the EIBA Board (2003–2007).

Officers	2003	2004	2005	2006	2007
Chair	—	Danny Van Den Bulcke	Danny Van Den Bulcke	Danny Van Den Bulcke	Danny Van Den Bulcke
Vice–Chair	—	Lars Håkansson	Lars Håkansson	Marjan Svetlicic	Marjan Svetlicic
President	Torben Pedersen	Marjan Svetlicic	Gabriel Benito	Philippe Gugler	Grazia Santangelo
Past President	M. Papanastassiou	Torben Pedersen	Marjan Svetlicic	Gabriel Benito	Philippe Gugler
President Elect	Marjan Svetlicic	Gabriel Benito	Philippe Gugler	Grazia Santangelo	Enn Listra
Executive Secretary	Nicole Coopman	Nicole Coopman	Nicole Coopman	Nicole Coopman	Nicole Coopman
Austria	Arnold Schuh	Arnold Schuh	Arnold Schuh	Arnold Schuh	Arnold Schuh
Belgium	D. Van Den Bulcke	D. Van Den Bulcke	Filip De Beule	Filip De Beule	Filip De Beule
Canada	Alain Verbeke	Alain Verbeke	Alain Verbeke	Alain Verbeke	Alain Verbeke
Denmark	Torben Pedersen	Torben Pedersen	Torben Pedersen	Torben Pedersen	Torben Pedersen
Estonia				Enn Listra	Enn Listra
Finland	Jorma Larimo	Jorma Larimo	Jorma Larimo	Jorma Larimo	Jorma Larimo
France	Alain Chevalier	Alain Chevalier	Alain Chevalier	Alain Chevalier	Alain Chevalier
Germany	Klaus Macharzina	Klaus Macharzina	Martin Welge	Martin Welge	Martin Welge
Greece	M. Papanastassiou	M. Papanastassiou	M. Papanastassiou	M. Papanastassiou	M. Papanastassiou
Ireland					Camilla Noonan
Israel	Eugene Jaffe	Eugene Jaffe	Tamar Almor	Tamar Almor	Tamar Almor

	Francesca Sanna-Randaccio	Francesca Sanna-Randaccio	Grazia Santangelo	Grazia Santangelo	Grazia Santangelo	Grazia Santangelo
Italy	Francesca Sanna-Randaccio	Francesca Sanna-Randaccio	Grazia Santangelo	Grazia Santangelo	Grazia Santangelo	Grazia Santangelo
Netherlands	John Hagedoorn	John Hagedoorn	Ans Kolk	Ans Kolk	Ans Kolk	Ans Kolk
Norway	Gabriel Benito	Gabriel Benito	Gabriel Benito	Gabriel Benito	Gabriel Benito	Gabriel Benito
Poland	Krzysztof Obloj	Krzysztof Obloj	Krzysztof Obloj	Krzysztof Obloj	Krzysztof Obloj	Krzysztof Obloj
Portugal	Vitor C. Simões	Vitor C. Simões	Vitor C. Simões	Ana Teresa T. Lehman	Ana Teresa T. Lehman	Ana Teresa T. Lehman
Slovenia	Marjan Svetlicic	Marjan Svetlicic	Marjan Svetlicic	Matija Rojec	Matija Rojec	Matija Rojec
Spain	Juan José Durán	Juan José Durán	Juan José Durán	Juan José Durán	Juan José Durán	Juan José Durán
Sweden	Örjan Sölvell	Ulf Andersson	Ulf Andersson	Ulf Andersson	Ulf Andersson	Ulf Andersson
Switzerland	Philippe Gugler	Philippe Gugler	Philippe Gugler	Philippe Gugler	Philippe Gugler	Philippe Gugler
UK	Adam Cross	Adam Cross	Adam Cross	Adam Cross	Adam Cross	Adam Cross
US	Terutomo Ozawa	Tom Brewer	Tom Brewer	Tom Brewer	Tom Brewer	Tom Brewer
Ex-Officio						
EIBA Fellows Dean	John H. Dunning	John H. Dunning	John H. Dunning	John H. Dunning	John H. Dunning	Klaus Macharzina
Editor *IBR*	Pervez Ghauri	Pervez Ghauri	Pervez Ghauri	Pervez Ghauri	Pervez Ghauri	Pervez Ghauri
EIASM Director	Gerry Van Dyck	Gerry Van Dyck	Gerry Van Dyck	Gerry Van Dyck	Gerry Van Dyck	Gerry Van Dyck

Note: New officers are elected in December of a given year. Although we know they may immediately start their functions, we assume here that their service as EIBA Chair, EIBA Vice-Chair or as NRs starts in the next year, to avoid overlaps and make easier for the reader to follow the sequence of officers and the time of their duties.

Table 5B. Composition of the EIBA Board (2008–2012).

	2008	2009	2010	2011	2012
Chair	Danny Van Den Bulcke	Danny Van Den Bulcke	Peter Buckley	Peter Buckley	Peter Buckley
Vice-Chair	Torben Pedersen	Torben Pedersen	Torben Pedersen	Philippe Gugler	Philippe Gugler
President	Enn Listra	José Plà-Barber	Ana Teresa T.-Lehman	Liviu Voinea	Roger Strange
Past President	Grazia Santangelo	Enn Listra	José Plà-Barber	Ana Teresa T.-Lehman	Liviu Voinea[b]
President Elect	José Plà-Barber	Ana Teresa T.-Lehman	Liviu Voinea	Roger Strange	Sarianna Lundan
Executive Secretary	Nicole Coopman	Nicole Coopman	Ene Kannel	Ene Kannel	Ene Kannel
Australia				Catherine Welch	Catherine Welch
Austria	Björn Ambos	Björn Ambos	Björn Ambos	Björn Ambos	Björn Ambos
Belgium	Filip De Beule	Filip De Beule	Filip De Beule	Filip De Beule	Filip De Beule
Brazil				Jorge Carneiro	Jorge Carneiro
Canada	Alain Verbeke	Alain Verbeke	Alain Verbeke	Alain Verbeke	Chang Hoon Ho
Denmark	Torben Pedersen	Torben Pedersen	Jens Gammelgaard	Jens Gammelgaard	Jens Gammelgaard
Estonia	Enn Listra	Enn Listra	Enn Listra	Enn Listra	Enn Listra
Finland	Jorma Larimo	Jorma Larimo	Jorma Larimo	Niina Nummela	Niina Nummela
France	Alain Chevalier	Alain Chevalier	Claude Obadia	Claude Obadia	Claude Obadia
Germany	Martin Welge	Martin Welge	Martin Welge	Andreas Al-Laham	Stefan Schmid
Greece	Pavlos Dimitratos	Pavlos Dimitratos	Pavlos Dimitratos	Pavlos Dimitratos	Pavlos Dimitratos

Ireland	Camilla Noonan	Camilla Noonan	Camilla Noonan	Camilla Noonan	Dorotha Piaskowska
Israel	Tamar Almor	Tamar Almor	Orly Yeheskel	Orly Yeheskel	Orly Yeheskel
Italy	Grazia Santangelo	Grazia Santangelo	Grazia Santangelo	Grazia Santangelo	Grazia Santangelo
Netherlands	Rob Van Tulder[a]	Rob Van Tulder	Rob Van Tulder	Rob Van Tulder	Rob Van Tulder
Norway	Trond Randoy	Trond Randoy	Trond Randoy	Trond Randoy	Trond Randoy
Poland	Marian Gorynia	Marian Gorynia	Marian Gorynia	Marian Gorynia	Marian Gorynia
Portugal	Ana Teresa T.-Lehman	Ana Teresa T.-Lehman	Ana Teresa T.-Lehman	Ana Teresa T.-Lehman	Ana Teresa T.-Lehman
Romania		Liviu Voinea	Liviu Voinea	Liviu Voinea	Liviu Voinea
Slovenia	Matija Rojec	Matija Rojec	Andreja Jaklic	Andreja Jaklic	Andreja Jaklic
Spain	José Plà-Barber	José Plà-Barber	José Plà-Barber	José Plà-Barber	José Plà-Barber
Sweden	Ulf Andersson	Ulf Andersson	Rian Drogendijk	Rian Drogendijk	Rian Drogendijk
Switzerland	Philippe Gugler	Philippe Gugler	Philippe Gugler	Philippe Gugler	Philippe Gugler
UK	Adam Cross	Adam Cross	Roger Strange	Roger Strange	Roger Strange
US	Tom Brewer	John Cantwell	John Cantwell	Ronaldo Parente	Ronaldo Parente
Ex-Officio					
EIBA Fellows Dean	Klaus Macharzina	Klaus Macharzina	D. Van Den Bulcke	D. Van Den Bulcke	D. Van Den Bulcke
Editor *IBR*	Pervez Ghauri	Pervez Ghauri	Pervez Ghauri	Pervez Ghauri	Pervez Ghauri

[a]Replacing Ans Kolk.
[b]Replaced by Ana Teresa Tavares-Lehman, at the December 2012 Board meeting in Brighton.

left little mark (as Enn Listra and Liviu Voinea), all the others have kept their strong commitment to EIBA, by serving at top Board posts of Chair (Philippe Gugler) and Vice-Chair (Lars Håkansson, Marjan Svetlicic, Torben Pedersen, José Plà-Barber), as *IBR* editor (Roger Strange), as editor of the *EIBAzine* (Ana Teresa Tavares-Lehman) or as Doctoral Tutorial faculty (Gabriel Benito, Grazia Santangelo). With hindsight, it may be said that, ironically, the organisers of conferences in countries in which EIBA ventured to foster the interest in IB were those who did not stay attached to the Academy.

Looking at Tables 5A and 5B, it is possible to see that, together Switzerland (already mentioned in Chapter 6), six new chapters have been established or revitalised in this period – Australia (re-started in 2011), Brazil (2011), Estonia (2006), Ireland (2007) and the short-lived Romania (2009). Three out of the new NRs became relevant players in the EIBA landscape, namely Philippe Gugler, Catherine Welch and Jorge Carneiro. Another positive development was the increased dynamics of the US chapter, thanks to the efforts of Tom Brewer, John Cantwell (who had to leave due to a new job as *JIBS* editor) and Ronaldo Parente. By 2012, EIBA could boast to have 25 national chapters.

By establishing a maximum mandate term, the new statutes generated a significant rotation of the Board. This was the time when EIBA old-timers, some of them with significant contributions to EIBA, gave up their NR positions. That happened with Danny Van Den Bulcke (replaced by Filip de Beule as Belgium NR), Alain Verbeke (Chang Hoon Ho, Canada), Torben Pedersen (Jens Gammelgaard, Denmark), Jorma Larimo (Niina Nummela, Finland), Alain Chevalier (Claude Obadia, France), Klaus Macharzina (Martin Welge, and later Andreas Al-Laham, Germany), Marina Papanastassiou (Pavlos Dimitratos, Greece), Eugene Jaffe (Tamar Almor, then Orly Yeheskel, Israel), Francesca Sanna-Randaccio (Grazia Santangelo, Italy), John Hagedoorn (Ans Kolk, and later Rob van Tulder, Netherlands), Gabriel Benito (Trond Randoy, Norway), Krzysztof Obloj (Marian Gorynia, Poland), Vítor Corado Simões (Ana Teresa Tavares-Lehman, Portugal), Marjan Svetlicic (Matija Rojec, then Andreja Jaklic, Slovenia), Juán José Durán (José Plà-Barber, Spain), Ulf Andersson (Rian Drogendijk, Sweden) and Adam Cross (Roger Strange, UK). Many of the EIBA old-timers mentioned above had meanwhile became EIBA Fellows.

The only ill-fated note was the passing away, in December 2011, of Andreas Al-Laham, the relatively young (49 years old) NR for Germany, who had taken charge the organisation of the EIBA 2013 conference in Mannheim (Germany). Fortunately, with his characteristic commitment, Sarianna Lundan who had been behind the 2000 Maastricht conference and had recently moved to Bremen, solved the problem, by expressing her availability to keep EIBA in German soil and convening the 2013 conference, five years after Tallinn, in another Hanseatic city – Bremen.

Another relevant feature of this period was the very significant change in the Board's gender structure. While in 2002, 4 out of the 22 Board positions, including the Executive Secretary (18%) were held by women, the corresponding share for 2012 was 30% (10 out of 33). This is a very significant change in a Board that originally was a men's club. This is also an expression of the increasing change in EIBA's gender balance that will be reported below. Even more important, among the women sitting at the Board in December 2012, two had already served as EIBA Presidents (Grazia Santangelo and Ana Teresa Tavares-Lehman), and other two were in the line to head future conferences (Sarianna Lundan and Rian Drogendijk, who convened EIBA 2013 and 2014, respectively).

7.4.3. EIBA Membership

In the previous chapters an erratic evolution of EIBA membership had been noticed. In the early 1990s, total membership exceeded 300, for 1991 and 1994, to reach an all-time maximum of 340 for 1997. However, since then there has been a sharp decline towards 172, due to several factors identified in the previous chapter, especially the break point in the procedure of collecting membership fees, as a result of the access to *IBR* issues. However, in the period under analysis (2003–2012), this started to bear fruits, and a consistent, though not continuous, trend in increasing membership clearly emerged, heralding new maxima above 400 for the first time ever: 401 (2006), 417 (2007), 424 (2010) and 466 (2012). After many discussions on how to entice membership, EIBA was found to be in the right track, as a result of the joint effect of internal (governance changes ena-bling improved stratdegy and better conference organisation, new doctoral tuto-rial initiatives, new publications including the teaming up with *IBR*) and external (increasing attractiveness of IB research).

Fig. 9 provides information on membership per country for 2003–2012. By ascending order, the top-6 countries are the following: Spain (average of 20 mem-bers), the US (also 20), Sweden (23), Germany (31), Finland (38) and the UK (47). The top-three accounted for almost 30% of EIBA membership along this period, their share having slightly declined between 2003–2007 and 2008–2012.[18] Eleven countries exhibited mid-level cohorts, between 2% and 5% of average total membership: Belgium, Canada, Switzerland, France, Portugal, Australia, Austria, the Netherlands, Denmark, Italy and Norway. This period witnessed a

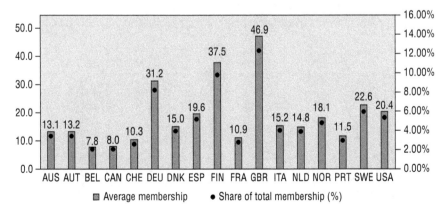

Fig. 9. EIBA Membership per Country (2003–2012). *Source*: EIBA archives.
Note: The figure includes those countries with at least 2% of total average membership in the period concerned.

significant increase in two countries outside Europe: Australia (13 members, from 5 in the previous period; more on this later) and Brazil (that has shown a consistent growth: from an average membership below 1 for 1995–2002, through 4 for 2003–2007 to 9 for 2008–2012).

7.4.4. Gender Diversity

As shown in the previous chapter, in 1996–2002 there was a significant change in the participation and the role played by women in EIBA, female membership share reaching an average of almost 23%, with a maximum close to 25% in 2002. This trend was pursued and strengthened in the period under analysis.

Some indicators of such change have already been presented earlier. First, the fact that two of the ten conferences held in this period were organised by women (Grazia Santangelo and Catania 2007; and Ana Teresa Tavares-Lehman and Porto 2010), with two further ready to convene the 2013 (Sarianna Lundan in Bremen) and 2014 (Ryan Drogendijk in Uppsala). Second, the substantial increase in female participation at the EIBA Board, from 18 to 30%. Below, we will delve into the evolution of gender diversity in EIBA conferences over this period, based on the figures displayed at Fig. 10.

This shows a sustained increase in EIBA's female membership share. As may be seen there, female membership share attained almost 29% for 2003 to increase to levels consistently above 30%, reaching a 38.1% maximum for 2012.

7.4.5. The Deficit Issue and EIBA Accounts

The positive evolution regarding EIBA governance and membership was joined by no less important developments in another front: the improvement in balance sheets and the solution of the debt towards EIASM that had menaced EIBA since the early 1980s.

A meeting was held between EIASM and EIBA in March 2001 on this issue. As mentioned in the previous chapter, it led to the transfer to EIASM of €2,000 of the excedent from the Maastricht conference, by initiative of John Hagedoorn.

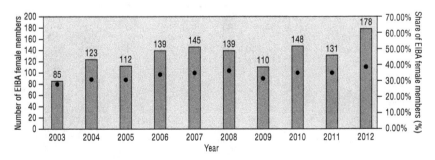

Fig. 10.   Evolution of EIBA Membership by Gender (2003–2012).
Source: EIBA archives.

Being aware that EIBA was getting on the right track, recording moderate financial surpluses, the EIBA Board thought that the time had come to discuss with EIASM both the debt and the future of the partnership. This way, the EIBA Board would take the first step, to avoid being pressed by EIASM again. The chances for a positive settlement were increased by the fact that the Direction of EIASM was held by Gerry Van Dyck, who had followed the earlier years of EIBA and had performed a superb job as EIBA Secretary.

Following a long dialogue, Gerry Van Dyck sent a mail to the EIBA Board on November 2003 with the following proposals: (1) a 25% reduction of the debt, to slightly below €8,000; (2) half of this would be settled within two months after an agreement, and the payment of the remaining half would be spread over three year, i.e., until 2006; and (3) EIBA's contribution to EIASM would increase from €5,600 to €8,500, but this increase will be gradual along three years (EIASM, 2003). This proposal was accepted by the EIBA Board at its December meeting in Copenhagen. The agreement was mutually perceived as beneficial. It enabled a renewed cooperation with EIASM, put an end to EIBA's long-term debt and, together with the organisational changes and the previous launching of the journal, provided the basis for building a sounder, more consistent and self-confident EIBA.

These developments were translated into the evolution of EIBA accounts between 2003 and 2012. Over this period EIBA was able to reach consistent surpluses, except for 2009 and 2010. For the first time ever surpluses above €5,000 were recorded (in four years out of ten). Many of these were used to pay the debt, as it happened with the surpluses of 2003 thru 2006. Meanwhile, the burden of the payments to EIASM, in fact, increased, as a result of the item (3) of the agreement, from €5,600 (2003) to €15,730 (2012); again, this rise has been financed by the successive conference organisations. In spite of a difficult process, EIBA had been able to solve the debt while achieving financial stability!

7.4.6. The Annual Conference Guidelines

Since the late 1990s, several Board members, especially Fred Burton, the organiser of EIBA Manchester-1999, voiced the need to establish a template for managing future conferences. The frustration with Paris-2001 further convinced the Board about the urgency to do so. In the wake of the successful Athens-2002, Marina Papanastassiou wrote a first draft, distilling her own experience. This was taken by Lars Håkansson to develop a first draft of the Annual Conference Guidelines (EIBA, 2003), swiftly followed by a revised version (EIBA, 2004). This document became the conference organisation template. It was subject to several updates, the last of this period being carried out by Ana Teresa Tavares-Lehman as a result of the 2010 Porto conference. The *Guidelines* aimed at compiling and updating the experience of EIBA Presidents and their teams and especially at guiding future Presidents in their endeavours to organise a perfect EIBA conference. They are now what may be called an *EIBAian acquis*, highlighting the key issues and ensuring consistency in conference organisation, while still giving room for diversity and for the introduction of local favour.

7.4.7. Relationships with Other Organisations

EIBA pursued its policy of openness to cooperate with other organisations. Besides the partnerships with EIASM and with COST, further relationships have been developed, with distinct tones. EIBA was approached by EURAM, the European Academy of Management, to cooperate more closely. The objective of EURAM seemed to be to expand the IB field in EURAM. In face of this, the Board 'concluded that cooperation with EURAM should not be excluded per se, but it [was] not an issue for the moment' (EIBA Board, 2011, p. 11).

The key issue concerned the relationships with AIB, on which significant developments emerged in 2004–2005. In earlier chapters, the existence of a 'love–hate' relationship with AIB had been reported. AIB had been for many years a reference for EIBA initiatives, having in mind the differences in terms of maturation, resources and membership size. Formal and informal ways of cooperation with AIB had been established. However, the instances when EIBA partnered with AIB to hold its annual conference (Barcelona-1981, and London-1986) were perceived by EIBA as failures. For many years, there has been a gentlemen's agreement that EIBA worked as the Western Europe region chapter of AIB (AIB-WER), and a member of the EIBA Board performed that linkage role.

However, in the second half of 2004 signs of change emerged. Juán Durán, then the EIBA representative at the AIB Board and chairman of AIB-WER, informed that AIB was intending to revise its constitution, including the role of its chapters. In this vein, there was a stream within AIB arguing that EIBA should become a full fledged and formal AIB chapter, thereby losing its independence. At its December 2004 meeting, the EIBA Board decided that 'EIBA should remain an independent European association [, thereby rejecting] the option of subordination to AIB' (EIBA Board, 2004, p. 9). In the aftermath of the EIBA 2004 conference, a meeting was held between Danny Van Den Bulcke, EIBA Chair, Alan Rugman, President of AIB, and Peter Buckley, immediate past President of AIB, to discuss the issue. Having in mind the damaging effects of this conflict for the IB field, Peter Buckley drafted a compromise text that was accepted by both Danny Van Den Bulcke and Alan Rugman, subject to approval by the Boards of both AIB and EIBA. The text became known as the *Buckley compromise* (EIBA-AIB, 2004).

It proved to be a key instrument to reduce the tensions that emerged in the early 2000s between AIB and EIBA. It enabled to find a mutually satisfactory solution that was accepted by both sides, clarifying the relationships and enhancing EIBA's self-confidence. Furthermore, it paved the way for more balanced and fair relationships between both Academies, in spite of distinct sizes, as well as to develop new forms of cooperation for mutual benefit.

7.4.8. Further Digitalisation of EIBA

Following the step taken in Jerusalem-1998, most proceedings in the 2003–2012 period have been published digitally, via pen-drives. However, as a result of the decision taken by the EIBA Board, conference programmes were still made available on paper. The argument was that this was more user-friendly for older EIBAians, although the younger generations were relying on digital formats.

A key digitalisation move was taken in Copenhagen 2003, through the setting up of a system that enabled the digital handling of most operations required for conference management. This was designed by Casper Pedersen, and became, with annual upgradings, the EIBA standard system between 2003 and 2011. Confronted with the lower interest of the designer in providing annual updates, due to a turn in his career path, Roger Strange decided to use the AIB system to manage the EIBA Brighton-2012. The result was deceiving, as the system faltered on several dimensions, from paper submission to the refereeing process (EIBA Board, 2012). A new solution had to be found for future conferences.

Another digitalisation vector concerned the regular contacts between the EIBA Secretariat and EIBA members. Paper communication was eliminated altogether and all interactions became digital, including the circulation of the *EIBAzine* newsletter, launched in 2004. In 2003 there was a general agreement about the need to upgrade and modernise the EIBA website; EIASM offered to perform the task under the general support package, i.e. at no additional cost, the more so as such efforts were being carried out for other associations under the EIASM umbrella. As a result of the efforts of Nicole Coopman (then the EIBA Secretary) and Torben Pedersen, the new website became operational in 2004. In early 2007 there was a further improvement of the website, intended to make it more user-friendly, but several criticisms were raised, namely the need to improve the homepage and the inclusion of a photo gallery. This led to the setting up of a feature enabling the retrieval of photos from the successive EIBA conferences, since Ljubljana 2004 (see https://www.eiba.org/r/home).

Meanwhile, in 2012, the need was felt to promote EIBA (and EIBA membership) in social media. Thanks to the initiative of Dorota Piaskowska, who was the NR of Ireland at the EIBA Board, a proposal was developed on this regard. It included inter alia the following issues: suggested media for EIBA (Linkedin, Facebook, Twitter, YouTube...); and cross-linking of EIBA's social media pages with the EIBA website. An agreement emerged about the need to reshuffle the EIBA website to enable a social media presence. Under Dorota's drive, this was done still in 2012, and an EIBA LinkedIn group was launched. This was EIBA's entry in the social media world, a feature that was to become increasingly important in the years to come...

7.4.9. International Business Review

The initial relationship with Elsevier had not been easy. Since the very beginning, EIBA felt a lack of ownership regarding *IBR*: contrary to the initial expectations, EIBA had very little influence on *IBR*'s editorial policy. This was illustrated by the time taken to insert the connection with EIBA at *IBR*'s cover page. The perception that Elsevier was very tough and inflexible and that *IBR*'s editor was to a large extent the 'owner' of the journal became clear to the EIBA Board, and especially to Danny Van Den Bulcke.

In 2003, in a move to improve the connections, the EIBA Board decided to invite Pervez Ghauri, then the editor of *IBR*, to become a full member of the EIBA Board. This was intended to make him more aware of, and sensitive to, EIBA's interests. In a positive gesture, *IBR* offered to sponsor an annual award to the best paper published in the journal, to be granted at the EIBA conference; a committee including Torben Pedersen, Ulf Andersen and Alain Verbeke was nominated by the EIBA Board to select the best paper to be awarded the IBR Prize; this award was handed out for the first time at Fribourg 2006. In spite of this, *IBR* was negligent to include in the journal a page on EIBA, an issue raised by Danny Van Den Bulcke at the December 2004 Board meeting in Ljubljana and formally conveyed to both the editor of *IBR* and Elsevier.

Another point of friction happened in 2009, when Elsevier's made a proposal to increase *IBR* subscription rates for 2010 onwards, disregarding the fact that this would entail an increase in EIBA fees. While such increase was acceptable (subscription rates had been flat since 2001), the EIBA Board mandated the new EIBA Chair (Peter Buckley) to conduct the negotiation. This led to an agreement with Elsevier for an 8% increase in *IBR* subscription rate every five years, starting in 2011. However, the wording of Elsevier's contract proposal substantially differed from the previous one, when there was no need for that. EIBA's perception of lack of ownership increased. The issue was discussed at the December 2010 Board meeting, in which criticisms were raised to Elsevier's behaviour as well as to the contract. This was really a thorny issue. As no satisfactory agreement had been reached, the EIBA Board came to it again in the Spring Board meeting, stressing the same points. The Board decided that the draft contract should be analysed by legal experts before taking a decision. At last, the new agreement was signed in January 2012, with a 5-year term, renewable for the same period, unless each party expresses the wish to alter or cancel it. Over 2012, there were signs of an increased commitment by Elsevier to promote *IBR*, including the attendance of EIBA Brighton-2012 with a stand.

To sum up, there are no doubts that the adoption of *IBR* as the EIBA journal became an important asset for the Academy. It enticed more scholars to become EIBA members and enhanced EIBA's standing and attractiveness. However, the dozen years that have elapsed since the start of the linkage with Elsevier have generated a sense of insufficient ownership from the EIBA side. This was not the idea at the outset. In spite of the benefits for EIBA, the linkage was not among equals: Elsevier and the editor of EIBA were in fact the 'owners', and EIBA's voice was too soft. Exit was not an option, but the process of contract renewal, while getting to an acceptable agreement, made EIBA's lack of ownership of *IBR* more evident.

7.4.10. *New EIBA Publications:* EIBAzine *and* PIBR

This time of strengthening of EIBA on distinct grounds was also characterised by significant changes with regard to EIBA publications. The *EIBA Newsletter* was discontinued, and replaced by a fresher approach, the *EIBAzine*, championed by Danny Van Den Bulcke. A volume encompassing selected papers from each

EIBA conference was launched with contributions to the Oslo 2005 conferences; this book series became known as *Progress in International Business Research (PIBR)*, being published on a yearly basis.

It has been noted in the previous chapters that along the 1990s and early 2000s, the publication of the *EIBA Newsletter* was somewhat intermittent. In the context of the 2003 renegotiation of EIBA's debt to EIASM it was agreed to assign *EIBA Newsletter*'s editorial tasks to Danny Van Den Bulcke and Tamar Almor, instead of Marion Hebbelink, the former EIBA secretary. This was a way to reduce the yearly contribution to EIASM. There was since the beginning the idea to refresh the newsletter, and to adjust it to the internet age, profiting from the new EIBA website, and thereby avoiding printing and distribution costs. The first issue, relatively short,[19] became available on November 2004. Gradually, however, the contents of *EIBAzine* increased and improved, starting with the second issue (December 2005), featuring an interesting article by James Leontiades, the first President of EIBA, entitled *The Birth of an Association* (Leontiades, 2005). Up to 2009, *EIBAzine* was published on an annual basis, the exception being the special issue *A Tribute to John H. Dunning*, on the occasion of John Dunning's passing away (https://www.eiasm.org/associations/eiba/chronicle.asp?chronicle_id=22&item_id=132), with contributions from several EIBAians.

In 2010, Danny and Tamar passed the baton to Filip De Beule, who became the *EIBAzine* editor. This corresponded to a significant reshuffling of the publication that became semestral and started to feature short articles on IB issues by older and younger EIBAians. With the difficulties inherent to attract contributions and to ensure their delivery on time, Filip De Beule pursued his work as *EIBAzine* editor until May 2013 (issue number 12), when Ana Teresa Tavares-Lehman replaced him. As a result of the effort and commitment of these EIBAians (together with Philippe Gugler, Barbara Jankowska and John Cantwell who became editors later; see next chapter), it was possible to keep the *EIBAzine* alive, and to make it a tool to foster communication among the EIBA community as well as to reflect about relevant IB research issues.

The idea of publishing a book with the best papers of each EIBA conference had been voiced time and again, as another tool to foster EIBA's brand and to enhance commitment to EIBA. In late 2003, Pervez Ghauri, Gabriel Benito and Torben Pedersen discussed the possible approaches to launch an annual book series. The issue was approached at the December 2003 Board meeting in Copenhagen, the decision being to mandate Gabriel and Torben to further develop a proposal to be presented to the Board. Contacts were established with Elsevier, and a revised proposal was presented to the Spring Board meeting in Ljubljana, Torben Pedersen and Ulf Andersen serving as co-editors of the series. An agreement was signed with Elsevier.

The first *PIBR* was launched in 2006, edited by Gabriel Benito and Heinrich Greve, and published by *J.A.I. Press*, an imprint of *Elsevier*, featuring a set of selected papers from the 2005 Oslo conference. The second volume, with papers from the 2006 Fribourg conference was edited by Philippe Gugler and John H. Dunning under the title of *Foreign Direct Investment, Location and*

Competitiveness. Since then, *PIBR* consistently became an outcome of EIBA conferences, edited by EIBA conference organisers and selected colleagues. However,
there have been some difficulties in the process: first, *Elsevier*'s marketing of the
series was 'disastrous'; second, *Elsevier* sold, in 2007, part of their social sciences
publication series to *Emerald*, that changed the pricing policy and put in danger
the diffusion of the book series. These facts led to the resignation of the editors
of the series (Torben Pedersen and Ulf Andersen), and obliged the Board to reas-
sess the continuation of the series (EIBA Board, 2008). However, the negotiations
with *Emerald* enabled to get discounted rates for EIBA members. Two new series
editors were nominated (Alain Verbeke and Rob Van Tulder), replacing Torben
and Ulf. The last volume related to this time window featured selected contributions from EIBA Brighton 2012, and was published in January 2014, under the
title *International Business and Sustainable Development*; with Alain Verbeke, Rob
Van Tulder and Roger Strange as editors.[20]

7.5. THE EIBA FELLOWS

The process of creating the EIBA Fellows and the drafting of their constitution,
presented in the previous chapter, were concluded in 2002. The following pages
will provide an account of the first ten years of activity of the EIBA Fellows. It is
organised in four parts. The first provides information about the Fellows' officers
and process of nominating new Fellows. The second regards the interpretation of
the Fellows constitution. The third deals with two initiatives taken by the Fellows
since the beginning: the convening of the EIBA Fellows plenary, and the nomination of Honorary Fellows. The section closes with a brief conclusion.

7.5.1. Officers and Nomination of New Fellows

The four 'founding fathers' (John Cantwell, John H. Dunning, Seev Hirsch and
Reijo Luostarinen) decided to nominate John H. Dunning as Dean, and John
Cantwell as Secretary-Treasurer. In accordance with article X.A of the EIBA
Fellows statutes ('the Dean of the Fellows serves for a three-year term of office,
and may not serve two full consecutive three-year terms'), John H. Dunning
stepped down at the end of 2006. The Fellows elected Klaus Macharzina as
the Dean for 2007–2009. John Cantwell served as Secretary-Treasurer until
the end of 2007, being replaced by Vítor Corado Simões. This procedure enabled a smooth transition between EIBA Fellows officials, avoiding the potential disruption associated to a joint replacement of both officials. In December
2009, Danny Van Den Bulcke took office as the new Dean of the Fellows.
Having in mind the previous experience and the impossibility to apply the letter of the Fellows constitution (article X.B), John Cantwell and Vítor Corado
Simões, the first two Secretary-Treasurers, drafted a document proposing the
guidelines for the future elections of Deans (*'Procedure for the Election of the
Dean of the EIBA Fellows'*) (EIBA Fellows, 2009), with a view to establish a
clear procedure on that regard; this proposal was unanimously accepted at the
2009-Valencia Fellows meeting. In 2010, Vítor stepped down, Sarianna Lundan

being nominated as Secretary-Treasurer. The last change in this time window took place on December 2012, in Brighton, when Danny Van Den Bulcke was replaced by Francesca Sanna-Randaccio as Dean of the Fellows. Ten years after the start of EIBA Fellows, both officers were women: Francesca serving as Dean and Sarianna, as Secretary-Treasurer. However, by that time, the EIBA Fellows' female share was still relatively low (15%, i.e. 3 out of 20 Fellows).

Every Fellows Dean has made a significant contribution to foster the Fellows relevance for both EIBA and the IB field. John H. Dunning used his reputation and commitment to nurture internal collaborative relationships as well as to launch initiatives to connect the Fellows with the outside world, namely through the setting up of the EIBA Fellows plenaries, aimed at discussing relevant IB issues, and championing the nomination of the first Honorary EIBA Fellows, Jorma Ollila, the former Chairman and CEO of Nokia, when it was a flourishing Finnish company. Klaus Macharzina used his diplomatic skills to build upon Dunning's achievements as well as to introduce important improvements, namely by convincing the Wandel & Goltermann Foundation to sponsor for a few years the EIBA Fellows Award to a Promising Young Researcher, the first awardee being Jonas Puck, now an outstanding IB scholar and, at the time of writing, EIBA's Vice-Chair. Danny Van Den Bulcke took to the Fellows the spirit of initiative and the commitment he had shown for many years in pushing EIBA forward. He forged stronger linkages between the Fellows and EIBA and launched the process, still pending, of designing a Code of Ethics for the EIBA Fellows. He was also responsible for making his last event as Fellows Dean a memorable one: chairing the EIBA Fellows Plenary with Martin Wolf, the 2012 Honorary Fellow.

The new Fellows elected in 2003 were the following (in alphabetical order): Juán Durán, Klaus Macharzina, Lars-Günnar Mattsson, Francesca Sanna-Randaccio and Danny Van Den Bulcke. A procedure was set up in 2004 regarding the election of new Fellows, on the basis of a proposal prepared by John Cantwell, to avoid the possibility 'that fewer candidates are elected than allowed for in any given year, if enough good nominees share the votes between them such that it becomes very difficult for any one individual to achieve the 60% support that is required' (EIBA Fellows, 2004). This was based on two key considerations: (1) nominees should have a significant track record of contribution to EIBA as well as to the IB field; and (2) to earn at least 60% of the votes. In the following years, more scholars were elected, although in smaller contingents, having in mind the 20 Fellows limit sat up by the Fellows constitution.

By the end of 2012, the maximum of 20 Fellows had been already reached, three of them being women. Francesca Sanna-Randaccio tried to convince the fellow Fellows to increase the women's contingent. It is noticeable that until 2010 Francesca was the only female Fellow. Table 6 provides a summary of EIBA officers' terms as well as the names of the Fellows elected in each year.

7.5.2. Interpretations of the Constitution

The EIBA Fellows constitution was adapted, with several changes, from that of AIB Fellows. It provided general rules that needed to be adjusted to the requirements perceived by the EIBA Fellows. Such a need was perceived since the

Table 6. EIBA Fellows 2002–2012 – Officers, New Fellows and
Honorary Fellows

Year	Dean	Secretary-Treasurer	New Fellows	Honorary Fellows
2002			'Founding Fathers': John Cantwell, John H. Dunning, Reijo Luostarinen and Seev Hirsch	
2003	John H. Dunning	John Cantwell	Danny Van Den Bulcke, Francesca Sanna-Randaccio, Juán Durán, Klaus Macharzina and Lars-Günnar Mattsson	
2004	John H. Dunning	John Cantwell	John Hagedoorn	
2005	John H. Dunning	John Cantwell	Peter J. Buckley and Vítor Corado Simões	Jorma Ollila
2006	John H. Dunning	John Cantwell	Krzysztof Obloj and Mats Forsgren	Karl Sauvant
2007	Klaus Macharzina	John Cantwell	Jean-François Hennart and Marjan Svetlicic	DeAnne Julius
2008	Klaus Macharzina	Vítor Corado Simões	Örjan Sölvell and Pervez Ghauri	Eli Hurwitz
2009	Klaus Macharzina	Vítor Corado Simões	None	
2010	Danny Van Den Bulcke	Vítor Corado Simões	Lars Oxelheim	
2011	Danny Van Den Bulcke	Sarianna Lundan	Marina Papanastassiou	Wilfried Wanhonacker
2012	Danny Van Den Bulcke	Sarianna Lundan (to continue in 2013)	Rebecca Piekkari	Martin Wolf

Source: Built by the authors, on the basis of EIBA Fellows minutes.
Note: New officers are elected in December of a given year. Although we know they may immediately start their functions, we assume here that their service as Dean or as Secretary-Treasurer starts in the next year, to avoid overlaps and make easier for the reader to follow the sequence of officers and the time of their duties.

beginning, and expressed in the following way: 'The Fellows, when acting in consensus, are also the arbiters of how the constitution is to be interpreted or applied' (EIBA Fellows, 2003, p. 1). In 2003, it was decided that, in the spirit of the constitution, clause XIV should be interpreted as meaning that eight new Fellows could be elected during the first two years after the establishment of the EIBA Fellows (and not just during the first year alone).

7.5.3. Relevant Initiatives: Honorary Fellows and the EIBA Fellows Plenary

By the initiative of John H. Dunning and Reijo Luostarinen, the first EIBA Honorary Fellowship was assigned at the Oslo 2005 conference to Jorma Ollila, then Chairman and CEO of the Finnish company *Nokia*. This was an achievement: to start the Honorary Fellowships with the top executive of a company that was considered, by that time, a star in the mobile phone business.

Every year until 2008 an Honorary Fellowship was assigned: Karl Sauvant, who created the *World Investment Report* and had been until 2005 the Director of the United Nations Conference on Trade and Development's (UNCTAD's) Investment Division, focused on FDI matters[21] (https://www.aib.world/about/aib-fellows/karl-sauvant/); DeAnne Julius, an American-British economist, who had been a founder member of the Monetary Policy Committee of the Bank of England and was Chairman of Chatham House in London; and Eli Hurwitz, a businessmen, founder of *Teva*, a well-known Israeli generic pharma company. However, there was a two-year gap, partly due to the impossibility to fit the agenda of Neelie Kroes, who served for two mandates as European Commissioner, first in charge of Competition (2004–2009) and then as Vice-President, with the Digital Agenda portfolio (2010–2014). The two last Honorary Fellows in this period were Wilfried Wanhonacker (2011) and Martin Wolf (2012). The first was a former professor at INSEAD and was then the Dean of the Skolkovo Management School (Russia).[22] The second was (and still is) Associate Editor and Chief Economics Commentator of *Financial Times* having been awarded the CBE (Commander of the Order of the British Empire). As mentioned above, his address at the EIBA Fellows Plenary in 2012 was one of the most impressive presentations to the EIBA conferences.

This reference to the EIBA Fellows Plenary provides the link to another initiative of the EIBA Fellows. The relevance of the themes addressed and the quality of the participants (often including the current year's Honorary Fellow) made the Fellows Plenary an outstanding feature of EIBA conferences. They have also played a bridge role between the Fellows and EIBA's younger audience. Since summaries of the headlines of all the Fellows Panels have been provided in Section 7.3.1, there is no need to come back to them again.

7.5.4. Conclusion

In 2002 the 'Founding Fathers' of the EIBA Fellows were nominated and its constitution was drafted. This paved the way for the EIBA Fellows to formally launch their activities in 2003. Led by John H. Dunning, the first Dean, a programme was started to ensure the relevance of the Fellows for both EIBA and the IB field as a whole. Such a programme unfolded into four main vectors: election of new Fellows; clarification of the procedures regarding the election of the Fellows' officers and new Fellows, based on consensuses regarding the interpretation and application of the constitution; election of EIBA Honorary Fellows; and the setting up of the EIBA Fellows plenaries, intended to discuss important IB issues and to provide guidance for younger EIBAians interested in researching about such issues. Additionally, the Fellows have followed the developments of EIBA activities, being always ready to cooperate when needed. With hindsight, it is possible to observe that the above-mentioned programme has consistently guided the EIBA Fellows activities in the years to come.

7.6. SUMMARY

The period addressed in this chapter (2003–2012) was one of the brightest in EIBA history. A set of changes that were in the making by the end of the 1990s turned into reality, from the redesign of EIBA governance to the launching of activity of the EIBA Fellows. No less important was the capacity to solve the debt towards EIASM, finding a sound solution to ensure that EIBA could make a 'fresh start', unencumbered by a long-term accumulated debt.

The new governance model enabled to disconnect the Academy's general and strategic management from conference organisation. This ensured management continuity, the more so as the Chair and Vice-Chair could be reelected for another three-year mandate, essential to escape the zigzags of a yearly change in the top management official (in spite of Danny Van Den Bulcke's *surveillance*). EIBA turned to be a more consistent and well-run organisation. The changes in organisational governance enabled to square the circle regarding EIBA conferences. The consequence was an increase in the average quality of EIBA conferences, though without losing the local flavour, and a significant reduction in the variance of conference quality.

The launching of EIBA Fellows activities was another important sign of EIBA's dynamics. The setting up of the EIBA Fellows enabled EIBA to benefit from the experience and wisdom of older EIBAians while opening room for new blood to emerge in the EIBA Board. There has clearly been a mutually beneficial cooperation between EIBA and the EIBA Fellows, expressed namely in the institutionalisation of the EIBA Fellows plenaries.

In spite of EIBA's perception of insufficient 'ownership' and unfair behaviour by Elsevier, *IBR* continued to be EIBA's journal. But it was joined by two further publications: the relaunching of the EIBA newsletter, now called *EIBAzine*, and the *PIBR*, encompassing some of the best papers of each EIBA conference. These publications are further links in the disciplinary and emotional chain connecting EIBA and its members.

The main dark cloud was the passing away of John H. Dunning. His last conference was Catania-2007. He was fighting the disease, but his optimism still led him to imagine a future after winning it. Unfortunately, it did not happen that way and in January 2008 he left us. We missed him so much, especially in Tallinn, the first EIBA conference he had missed in years. Some of us could not believe he was not there. We just could buy *Seasons of a Scholar*, his wonderful book of memories. The special issue of the *EIBAzine* dedicated to John Dunning was a way for the EIBA community to pay a tribute to one of its most outstanding figures.

More fortunate was Danny Van Den Bulcke, Mr EIBA, who also bought the book (featuring a photo of him) and has been able to follow EIBA until 2012 (see Fig. 11). For sure, in 2012 he would have felt rewarded for his efforts to foster the development of EIBA. The Academy to which he devoted so much time and effort had been able to get strength and to become a key player in the IB scene. Even Mr. EIBA, for whom delegating power was not an easy decision, would be glad to find that EIBA was already prepared to have a new generation at the helm.

Fig. 11.   Danny Van Den Bulcke's Last Address at an EIBA Plenary
(Brighton, 2012). *Source*: EIBA website.

NOTES

1. Please note that we are not arguing the decline of American power began in 2003, but rather that its limitations were made clear by the events.

2. As on previous occasions, EIBA was involved in further encounters with the path of history. In fact, more than a dozen of EIBA Board members had occasion to join the crowd greeting Slovenia's accession, since the interim Board meeting was held in Ljubljana on 1st May, the day when the enlargement took place. Besides Ljubljana, in 2004, another EIBA conference was held shortly thereafter in an enlargement country (Tallinn, Estonia, in 2008).

3. Once again, EIBA moved fast, holding its annual conference in Bucharest in 2011.

4. However, some of the biggest platform businesses at the end of 2021 had already been founded in the 20th century, such as *Microsoft* (1975), *Apple* (1976), *Amazon* (1994), *Google* (1998) and *Alibaba* (1999).

5. In his address to the plenary session in EIBA Ljubljana 2004, John Dunning had made clear his espousing of such views, namely when he used his 'crystal ball' to forecast IB developments up to 2027.

6. Interestingly, an earlier draft of this article was presented at EIBA 2009 in Valencia.

7. Yildiz and Fey (2012) found that, for firms from transition-countries, there may other ways than local isomorphism for achieving legitimacy abroad.

8. It is interesting to remark that an important step in John Dunning's journey in this regard was taken at the 1998 EIBA conference in Jerusalem, when he participated in an outstanding plenary session on 'Religion and Global Capitalism', as mentioned in the previous chapter.

9. Pankaj Ghemawat gave a keynote address to the 2013 EIBA conference in Bremen.

10. As we have previously done with the Gunnar Hedlund Award, we will not mention the subsequent winners of the CBS Prize due to space constraints. We suggest the interested reader access the winners list at the EIBA website (https://www.eiba.org/r/cbs-prize)

11. The photos of the ceremony are available on the EIBA website (https://www.eiba.org/r/photos-eiba2004-ljubljana). For further information about the award, see https://www.eiba.org/r/lifetime-award.

12. A photo of the event may be found at https://www.eiba.org/r/photos-eiba2005-oslo.

13. We invite the reader to get information about the subsequent winners at https://www.eiba.org/r/ibr-award.

14. The last conference he attended was AIB 2008 in Milan. In Catania, he was already suffering from the illness that led to his death. He was aware of that, but always kept a positive spirit. When discussing the assignment of the status of Inactive Members of the EIBA Fellows, he raised a question about the need for some flexibility in interpretation if a Fellow happened to return, after missing three consecutive conferences.

15. Originally, it was intended to hold the 2013 conference in Mannheim (Germany). However, the untimely death of Andreas Al-Laham made this impossible. Sarianna Lundan took the responsibility to organise this conference at her university (Bremen). For more on this, see Section 7.4.2 as well as Chapter 8.

16. To be fair, it should be remarked that the EIBA Board has not been strict in the application of the rule of five representatives over a three-year period.

17. We count the years of office in a way slightly different from the one considered on the EIBA website. While formally empowered by EIBA's General Assembly in December 2003, Danny Van Den Bulcke in fact started his job as EIBA Chair in 2004. By the same token, while Peter Buckley took over from Danny Van Den Bulcke in December 2009, we count his mandate as 2010–2012.

18. It is interesting that the relevance of the top-three countries was not influenced by the holding of conferences in these countries. Even though the 2012 EIBA conference was held in Brighton, its membership effects were recorded in 2013 only, that is, already in the next time period.

19. Danny and Tamar expressed their disappointment about the insufficient support from the other members of the Editorial Board, and Danny threatened to put an end to the initiative (EIBA Board, 2004).

20. The whole *PIBR* series may be accessed at https://www.eiba.org/r/book-series-pibr.

21. Karl Sauvant also became AIB Fellow in 2011.

22. See endnote 16.

CHAPTER 8

A NEW GENERATION AT THE HELM (2013–2020)

This period, from 2013 to 2020, was characterised for significant changes in EIBA leadership and gender balance, while keeping financial stability and the governance model that enabled the Academy to get a longer-term perspective and to become less dependent on the annual conferences. Due to the COVID-19 pandemic this period ended in an awkward fashion, with the convening of the first EIBA online conference, in 2020, organised by the EIBA Chairs, with the key support from the WU Vienna team. A key feature of this period is the absence of Danny Van Den Bulcke, who had been the EIBA's soul for decades. In Bremen-2013, when Filip De Beule informed us about Danny's illness we felt that a very important page in EIBA's life was about to turn...

In fact, Danny's passing away epitomises the generational change in EIBA's top management as well as in the Board. In December 2012, Peter Buckley had given the baton to Philippe Gugler, who had served as Vice-Chair. A new generation was taking the helm of EIBA's destiny. The new Chair team (Philippe Gugler and José Plà-Barber) was to be in charge for six years (2013–2018), being able to further EIBA's standing, attractiveness and financial health. It handed over its duties to Lucia Piscitello and Jonas Puck, in 2019. These had been the organisers of two excellent EIBA conferences: 2017 (Milan) and 2016 (Vienna), respectively. All these changes happened in an orderly way, showing that EIBA had become a sound organisation, and was in a condition to withstand the challenges that the future might bring. An unattended challenge was to emerge in 2020, with the eruption of the COVID-19 pandemic; with hindsight, we may affirm that EIBA was able to successfully respond it; while conference attendance levels in 2021 and 2022 have not matched the heights of Vienna (613) and Milan (606), Lisbon-2023 enabled to get a new participation record (645).

The History of EIBA: A Tale of The Co-Evolution Between International Business Issues and a Scholarly Community, 135–182
Copyright © 2025 by Vítor Corado Simões, John Cantwell and Philippe Gugler
Published under exclusive licence by Emerald Publishing Limited
doi:10.1108/978-1-83608-664-220241009

In 1998, for the first time ever EIBA ventured outside Europe, holding its annual conference in Jerusalem, the 'city of the three religions', at a time of political *détente*. In 2015, EIBA went further, accepting the challenge raised by Jorge Carneiro, then the Brazilian representative at the EIBA Board, to hold the conference in Rio de Janeiro. This move has shown how alive and self-confident EIBA was, ready to venture into South America. It was, in fact, the major EIBA's move in this period. With the exception of Austria (an extremely successful debut), the other conferences were held in already-known countries, with a return to classic Uppsala and experiences in new cities (Bremen, Milan, Poznan, and Leeds). Conference attendance increased significantly in this period, as a consequence of both EIBA's clout, the efforts to attract young PhD students and the development of IB scholarship.

Over this period, women's participation in EIBA affairs increased further. Lucia Piscitello, elected EIBA Chair in December 2018, was the first woman to chair the Academy. Women took the lead in conference organisation in this period: leaving EIBA 2020 aside, since it has been so far the only EIBA conference not to be held in-person, four of the seven conferences in this period were organised by women: Sarianna Lundan in Bremen-2013; Rian Drogendijk in Uppsala-2014; Lucia Piscitello in Milan-2017; and Barbara Jankowska (with Małgorzata Bartosik-Purgat) in Poznan-2018. Furthermore, as it will be shown later, EIBA membership was about to reach a gender balance.

As the previous one, this chapter is organised in six sections. The first provides an overview of the main political and economic environmental changes relevant for IB. Next, the main developments in IB research contributions are addressed. The third section reviews of the highlights of the eight conferences held in this period, including the visit to Rio de Janeiro (2015) and the 2020 online conference. The fourth summarises the main organisational developments. The fifth is dedicated to the EIBA Fellows membership and activities. The chapter concludes with a summary of the key events in this period of change and simultaneously strengthening of EIBA's attractiveness and dynamics.

8.1. THE CONTEXT: ATTITUDES TOWARDS FDI

The period under study (2013–2020) was again a time of change. Taking a chronological perspective, it was characterised by the strengthening of populist and inward-looking approaches and by the increasing tensions between the US and China, with harmful effects on both international trade and investment. These trends have been reinforced by the emergence of the COVID-19 pandemic, that led to the establishment of border controls as well as to envisage the other as a threat, since he/she might carry the virus, significantly dropping the international circulation of people, goods and capital as well as GDP levels; the other side of the coin was the explosion of several types of platform businesses, especially those that enabled online communication.

The second decade of the 21st century witnessed the eruption of populist and nationalistic movements challenging globalisation, throughout the World.

The roots of the anti-globalisation, populist surge may be found in relation to the way how the Great Recession was addressed (Guillén, 2018). While it had emerged in the 2000s or even earlier – as was the case of Vladimir Putin in Russia, the PiS (Law and Justice Party) in Poland, Viktor Orbán in Hungary or Recep Erdogan in Turkey, the elections of Narendra Modi in India (2014), Donald Trump in the US (2017), Jair Bolsonaro in Brazil (2018), and Boris Johnson in the UK (2019) gave it a new impetus. To some extent, the 2013 election of Xi Jinping as President of China, in spite of internationalisation moves, such as the Belt-and-Road Initiative (BRI), may be envisaged as another facet of the same phenomenon. The Brexit (2016) is also a testimony of this wave. The pandemic further strengthened it, leading to what *The Economist* (2020) called 'globalisation under quarantine'. Martin Wolf, an honorary EIBA Fellow and FT's chief economic commentator, later talked about a lasting 'democratic recession' (Wolf, 2023). This is epitomised by Donald Trump's blunt statement at the UN General Assembly in 2019: *The future does not belong to the globalists. The future belongs to patriots* (The Guardian, 2019).

In 2013–2016, globalisation was reaching a high point in formal terms, with the signing of the WTO Bali Package agreement aimed at loosening global trade barriers in 2013 and of the Trans-Pacific Partnership (TPP) in 2016, as well the unlocking of the negotiations regarding the Transatlantic Trade and Investment Partnership (TTIP). While in 2011 there was a close intertwining between the US and China (see Section 7.1), in 2015 trade flows between the two main international trade hubs were waning. Step-by-step, trade connections between the US and China declined, and some GVCs led by US MNEs were looking for alternatives to China or even starting back-shoring moves (Degain et al., 2017). From a different perspective, the analysis carried out by Witt, Lewin, Li and Gaur (2023) confirms that the levels of trade and FDI reached by the end of the first decade of the 2000s have not been matched in the second decade.

In 2013, China launched the Belt-and-Road Initiative (BRI), with two main interrelated aims. The first was to forge a concept of globalisation alternative to the one led by the US and Europe. The second aim was to enhance China's clout and strategic position worldwide. With hindsight, the results of the BRI are mixed (Buckley, 2020a; Enderwick, 2018a; Lall & Lebrand, 2020; Leahy, Kynge & Parkin, 2023; Ma, 2022). Some projects have been put on hold or even abandoned and several recipient countries faced an increased indebtedness. In contrast, new trade routes and infrastructures were opened and training has helped to enhance human resources capabilities (The Economist, 2023). Not surprisingly, the main beneficiary of the initiative has so far been China itself (Enderwick, 2018a).

Since 2017, the international economic scene has been dominated by the conflict between the US and China, when the Trump administration launched a series of tariff measures addressed at several countries, but mainly at China.[1] Meanwhile, China was strongly involved in the promotion of the negotiations towards the establishment of the Asian free-trade agreement called Regional Comprehensive Economic Partnership (RCEP), signed in 2020, encompassing 15 countries, including some of the biggest Asian economies (Australia, China, Indonesia, Japan and South Korea). China was envisaged as a rival that was cheating the US through unfair behaviour, the stealth of industrial property and industrial spy-ing (Petricevic and Teece, 2019); in their words, China was following a tecno-nationalist approach, thereby leading to a 'bifurcated world order'. The conflict has been pursued, and to some extent intensified, from 2020 onwards. American actions have increasingly focused on sophisticated semiconductors, an industry in which the US manufacturing capacity had been declining for years and which was perceived as key to counter China's technological upgrading and independence (Miller, 2022). China has reacted, launching in May 2020 the Dual Circulation Strategy, promoting an increasing reliance on the domestic market, instead of the export-oriented strategy followed since the 1990s (Herrero, 2021; Tang, 2020).

Another tenet of the Trump Administration, consistent with his statement quoted above, was the fight against multilateralism. This was expressed in several decisions, shortly after taking oath. These included inter alia the withdrawal from the Paris Climate Agreement, that the US and China had joined in 2016, and from the TPP. The first was a serious punch against the much-needed action to counter climate change, although it has been reversed by Joe Biden on his first day in office. The second opened the door for China to join the TPP partners, leading to the Comprehensive and Progressive Agreement for Trans-Pacific Partnership (CPTPP), signed in 2018; interestingly, the main differences between the TPP and the CPTPP concern the withdrawal of clauses that the US had previously cham-pioned. Reference is also due to US's deliberate inaction to nominate referees to the WTO arbitration courts and the US blockading of the appointment of a new CEO of WTO. This was a blow to an organisation that had played a key role in promoting globalisation.

In spite of the US withdrawal from the Paris Climate Agreement, the percep-tion of the need to promote sustainability and the circular economy to respond climate change became more widespread. Most international fora accepted that it demanded concerted action by governments, NGOs and private actors, especially MNCs. In this vein, the UN launched in 2015 the 2030 Agenda for Sustainable Development, including a set of 17 inter-connected SDGs. According to the UN, 'they address the global challenges we face, including those related to poverty, inequality, climate change, environmental degradation, peace and justice', setting up the target to achieve them by 2030 (United Nations, 2023a). The initiative was an important call for action, mobilising multiple players worldwide, including MNCs (United Nations, 2019, 2023b; Van Tulder & van Mil, 2022; Van Tulder, Grøgaard & Lunnan, 2023).

On the European front, this period starts with the accession of Croatia, as the 28th EU member state, on 1 July 2013. After a flurry of enlargement decisions in the 2000s, this was the only entry in the 2010s. Latvia and Lithuania joined the Euro, in 2014 and 2015, respectively. However, these developments were over-shadowed by the withdrawal of the UK from the EU. In fact, the UK – in spite of occasional tensions, as it happened during the Thatcher governments, and the decision to join neither the Euro nor the Schengen Area – had been a heavy-weight of the EU since 1973, both internally and externally. Brexit was a serious setback to the cohesion and international stature of the EU. With hindsight, it may be argued that Brexit was painful for the EU, but not less for the UK itself.

The process of negotiating the withdrawal agreement, started in 2017, was very complex and tricky, leading to the removal of two UK Prime Ministers (Theresa May and Boris Johnson). Finally, an agreement was reached, providing that the withdrawal would be effective on 31 January 2020.

Another tough development was the annexation of Crimea by Russia in 2014, following the removal of Ukraine's pro-Russian President Viktor Yanukovych from office, and his replacement by the pro-Western Oleksandr Turchynov. Supported by Russia, the self-proclaimed Donetsk People's Republic declared its independence from Ukraine. This led to a string of sanctions by Western countries against Russia. This process had further developments in 2022, with the invasion of Ukraine by Russia, and the ensuing war.

The attitude of the EU towards China has been influenced by the distinct approaches taken by their member states as well as by the multiple perspectives shaping the relationship. While until 2017, a welcoming posture was dominant, with Italy and Greece deeply involved in the BRI, the concerns with Chinese acquisitions and the pressures of the US on several European countries to ban *Huawei* from 5G systems led to a change in mood. The 2019 'EU-China – A strategic outlook' communication took a multi-faceted perspective on China, stating that it might be, in different policy areas, a cooperation partner, a negotiating partner, 'an economic competitor in the pursuit of technological leadership, and a systemic rival promoting alternative models of governance' (European Commission & High Representative of the Union for Foreign Affairs and Security Policy, 2019, p. 1). In 2020, the White Paper on the foreign subsidies in the Single Market was to a large extent addressed to Chinese investors, whose preferential relationship with the Chinese state entailed biases in the working of the single market (European Commission, 2020).[2] Even more illustrative of both the interplay of different views and the change in mood was the case of the EU-China bilateral investment treaty. Signed in 2020 after seven years of negotiation, its ratification collapsed within three months amid political bitterness and distrust (McMahon & Liu, 2023).

Regarding regulatory matters, the main development was the issuing in 2016 of the General Data Protection Regulation (GDPR). This is aimed at enhancing individuals' control and rights over their personal information as well as simplifying the regulations for IB through the harmonisation of data privacy laws across Europe. In the same vein, come the Digital Services Act and the Digital Market Act, intended

> to create a safer digital space in which the fundamental rights of all users of digital services are protected and to establish a level playing field to foster innovation, growth, and competitiveness, both in the European Single Market and globally. (European Parliament, 2024)

It is remarkable that during the pandemic there have been two parallel movements: the growth of platform companies, particularly of those following fully digital business approaches; and an increased perception of the need to regulate their behaviour, observed not just in Europe but also in the US and elsewhere, including China and India (Simões, 2020).

The increasing nationalism, the trend towards de-globalisation (Witt, 2019) and the COVID-19 pandemic all militated to create a dull environment for FDI, especially in the second half of the period under analysis (Buckley, 2020b). This was furthered by the unethical behaviour of some MNCs, especially the Cambridge Analytica/Facebook influence on the 2016 US elections and the scandal of Volkswagen diesel emissions. The result was a sustained fall in worldwide FDI flows since 2016, the decline being more abrupt for 2020, as a result of the pandemic. A closer look suggests, however, that developing countries' performance of as FDI destinations was relatively steady over the whole period, with amounts between 662 and 730 billion USD. The evolution of developed countries was extremely uneven, exhibiting a peak in 2016 (when they held a 65% share of world FDI inflows) and strong declines in 2017 and 2020, the first partly due to political factors and the second as a result of the pandemic.

The ranking of investors abroad continued to be dominated by the US until 2017 but experienced sharp declines since then, even taking 2020 aside: while in 2017, the US accounted for 20% of total outflows, in 2019 its share was below 8%, being the fourth ranked, after China, Japan and Germany. Therefore, China (plus Hong Kong) became the leading FDI source between 2018 and 2020, although exhibiting variable portions of total outflows (26%, 15% and 33%, respectively, for 2018, 2019 and 2020). This means that China's covid-zero policy did not tame Chinese outward FDI in 2020, although the same did not happen for 2021 and 2022, when the US regained the leadership (United Nations, 2023c). These developments may also be interpreted as a confirmation of the effects of political drive on the evolution of FDI behaviour.

8.2. THE CONTEXT: IB LITERATURE

Taking a general perspective, there are four general trends coming from earlier periods: the relevance of research articles with regard to books; the drive towards more rigorous methodological approaches, including qualitative methods (Beugelsdijk, van Witteloostuijn & Meyer, 2020; Cantwell & Brannen, 2016; Cuervo-Cazurra, Mudambi, Pedersen & Piscitello, 2017; Fainshmidt, Witt, Aguilera & Verbeke, 2020; Nielsen, Welch, Chidlow, Miller, Aguzzoli, Gardner, Karafyllia & Pegoraro, 2020); the diversity of authors' national origins (Cantwell & Brannen, 2016; Cantwell, Piepenbrink & Shukla, 2014), with a growing cohort of Chinese scholars; and the increasing interdisciplinarity of IB research (Cantwell & Brannen, 2016), expressed for instance in the linkages with geography, political science, sociology, psychology and linguistics.

The 2010s witnessed significant research efforts to enhance the understanding of IB issues by combining insights from the IB field contributory disciplines (Cantwell & Brannen, 2016), somewhat echoing an earlier plea by John Dunning (1989). The advantages of interdisciplinarity were underlined inter alia by Cheng, Birkinshaw, Lessard and Thomas (2014), Buckley, Doh and Benischke (2017), Aichhorn and Puck (2017), Beugelsdijk and Mudambi (2013) and Mudambi, Li, Ma, Makino, Qian and Boschma (2018). The close links between IB and economic geography have been highlighted (Iammarino & McCann, 2013), in spite of some claims that digitalisation would seriously undermine the role of geography for IB.

The view of the MNE as a network, the perception of the advantages of diversity for worldwide innovation, and the geographical dispersion of GVCs softened the perspective of nation-states as the key geographical reference (Qian, Li & Rugman, 2013). The MNE was envisaged as a 'border-crossing multi-location enterprise' (Beugelsdijk & Mudambi, 2013), thereby fostering research on other, often sub-national, territorial agglomerations such as clusters (Li & Bathelt, 2020; Liao, 2015; Turkina & Van Assche, 2018) and cities (Buchholz, Bathelt & Cantwell 2020; Goerzen, Asmussen & Nielsen, 2013; McDonald, Buckley, Voss, Cross & Chen, 2018). While having a territorial scope, these are often internationally linked to similar agglomerations (Bathelt, Cantwell & Mudambi, 2018; Cantwell & Zaman, 2018[3]; Florida, 2008; McDermott, Mudambi & Parente, 2013; Scalera, Perri & Hannigan, 2018), giving rise to the co-existence between international connectedness and local disconnectedness (Lorenzen, Mudambi & Schotter, 2020). Such connectedness plays a critical role in fostering innovation (Alcácer et al., 2016; Cano-Kollmann, Cantwell, Hannigan, Mudambi & Song, 2016).

The view of globalisation as uniformisation of business practices has generated reactions, highlighting the diversity of contexts, cultures, behaviours, languages and world visions, thereby calling for contributions from various disciplines. In 2014, two salient contributions about language emerged: the book *Language in International Business: The multilingual reality of global business expansion* (Piekkari, Welch & Welch, 2014) and the article on the multifaceted role of language in IB (Brannen, Piekkari & Tietze, 2014). The risks entailed by language differences were studied inter alia in the context of multiple IB operations and issues (Aichhorn & Puck, 2017; Khedia & Reddy, 2016; Li, Zhao & Han, 2020; Peltokorpi & Vaara, 2014; Tenzer, Pudelko & Harzing, 2014; Piekkari, Welch, Welch, Peltonen & Vesa, 2013).

The microfoundations of international management behaviour was another study field that gained relevance over this period. Research has focused on the understanding of managers' cognitive traits (Maitland & Sammartino, 2015; Niittymies & Pajunen, 2020), and risk and return perceptions (Ambos, Cesinger, Eggers & Kraus, 2020), at either the EMN (Contractor, Foss, Kundu & Lahiri, 2019; Foss & Pedersen, 2019; Kano & Verbeke, 2019) or the subsidiary (Nuruzzaman, Gaur & Sambharya, 2018; O'Brien, Scott, Andersson, Ambos & Fu, 2018) levels.

Interdisciplinarity has also pervaded the growing literature on the challenges to globalisation, as exemplified by Witt's (2019) landmark contribution. His point was that a tip of globalisation had been achieved,[4] being bound to decline as a result of the working of political and economic factors. Anti-globalisation moves gained strength in the aftermath of the economic crisis, when distinct strands of populism emerged (Devinney & Hartwell, 2020; Hoekman & Nelson, 2018; Mudambi, 2018; Rodrik, 2018) and the scepticism about globalisation started to rise (Evenett, 2019; Kobrin, 2017; Sinkovics, Yusuf & Sinkovics, 2018). The emergence of the pandemic (Kobrin, 2020) and the heightening of the US–China conflict raised new challenges for globalisation. Buckley and Hashai (2020) addressed a theme that was to become central later due to the Chips and Science Act and US export controls: the negative consequences of anti-globalisation policies on the international sharing of technological knowledge.

Some articles about populism and the globalisation backlash mentioned above were published in a novel journal, the *Journal of International Business Policy* (*JIBP*), whose first editor was Sarianna Lundan, a long-standing EIBA member and Dear of the EIBA Fellows. In her opening editorial address, she positioned *JIBP* as 'intended to build a leading outlet for research that demonstrates how a greater understanding of MNE strategies, organizational structures and systems can yield better public policy' (Lundan, 2018, p. 12). *JIBP* contributed to stimulate research in IB policy and to foster interdisciplinarity, while addressing key societal issues that may be alleviated or aggravated by MNE behaviour.

IB theory kept its central role for improved research and policy. Teece (2014) presented a 'dynamic capabilities-based theory of the multinational enterprise', envisaged as alternative to the internalisation/transaction costs perspective. In its successive shapes (Lessard et al., 2016; Teece, 2007; Teece, 2014; Teece, Pisano & Shuen, 1997), the concept has significantly influenced three streams of IB research: internationalisation (Villar, Alegre & Plà-Barber, 2014); organisational evolution (Riviere, Bass & Andersson, 2021; Vahlne & Jonsson, 2017; Zollo, Bettinazzi, Neumann & Snoeren, 2016); and the behaviour of emerging countries firms (Gölgeci, Assadinia, Kuivalainen & Larimo, 2019; Williamson, 2016). Luo and Tung (2018) elaborated on their earlier springboard perspective (Luo & Tung, 2007), intended to capture the international investment moves by emerging countries' forms, specially from China.

Most of the research on IB theory has, however, been dedicated to revisit extant theories as well as to apply them either to reinterpret historical developments (da Silva Lopes, Casson & Jones, 2019) or to current issues. This was the case of the application of internalisation to new IB issues – such as digitalisation (Banalieva & Dhanaraj, 2019) and value chains (Benito, Petersen & Welch, 2019; Strange & Humphrey, 2019) – or at combining it with other perspectives: corporate governance (Grøgaard, Rygh & Benito, 2019), behavioural approaches (Elia, Larsen & Piscitello, 2019), and decision-making theories (Buckley & Casson, 2019). Peter Buckley and Mark Casson applied internalisation to the study of emerging market multinationals (Buckley & Tian, 2017; Casson & Wadeson, 2018) and, combined with the institutional approach, to the analysis of host country risk and ownership decisions (Tang & Buckley, 2020). For Casson, Porter and Wadeson (2016), the internalisation agenda is still 'unfinished', in the sense that it is ready for application to new issues.

Jan-Erik Vahlne and Jan Johanson introduced further revisions to their Uppsala model with a view to adapt it to new challenges (Vahlne & Johanson, 2017, 2020). The first contribution, influenced by Vahlne and Ivarsson (2014), was intended to develop 'a general model of the evolution of the multinational business enterprise (MBE), from early steps abroad to being a global firm', a theme revisited by Vahlne (2020). Drawing on microfoundations, he revised the model to address managers' psychological traits. Among the articles revisiting the Uppsala approach, a reference is due to Clarke and Liesch (2017), Coviello, Kano and Liesch (2017), Forsgren (2016) and Santangelo and Meyer (2017). Also interesting is the revival of Luostarinen's (1979) concept of lateral rigidity to address SMEs' export decisions (Tan, Brewer & Liesch, 2018).

Institutional views have increased their relevance over this period, leading to develop or improve related concepts, such as institutional advantage (Martin, 2013), institutional distance (Kostova, Beugelsdijk, Scott, Kunst, Chua & van Essen, 2020; van Hoorn & Maseland, 2016) and institutional voids (Doh, Rodrigues, Saka-Helmhout & Makhija, 2017). Institution-based views were used to developing countries firms' internationalisation, giving rise to two contrasting approaches: one, coined 'escapism', leads to investments in developed economies, with more stable and predictable institutional environments, in order to escape home-country institutional voids (James, Sawant & Bendickson, 2020; Cuervo-Cazurra & Ramamurti, 2015; Kottaridi, Giakoulas & Manolopoulos, 2019; Stoian & Mohr, 2016); the other argues that firms' capabilities to navigate institutional voids at home may provide them with an advantage when investing in similar countries (Buckley et al., 2020; Wang, Luo, Lu, Sun & Maksimov, 2014). Aguilera and Grøgaard (2019) called for the need to better understand the effects of institutions. Another line of reasoning recognises the advantages of adjusting to and learning from institutional diversity (Lundan & Li, 2019) and points out the opportunities for co-evolution between firms and governments (Lundan & Cantwell, 2020).

Research on internationalisation processes and decisions continued to attract significant attention. Challenging contributions addressed the role of heuristic decision-making (Niittymies, 2020), the dual dimension of foreignness as liability and asset (Edman, 2016; Stahl, Tung, Kostova & Zellmer-Bruhn, 2016; Taussig, 2017) and the concept of internationalisation footprint as the location-mode combinations the firm is active in (Békés, Benito, Castellani & Muraközy, 2021).

International entrepreneurship, including research on international new ventures and born globals, gained further steam (Almor, Tarba & Margalit, 2014; Cannone & Ughetto, 2014; Choquette, Rask, Sala & Schroder, 2017; Coviello, 2015; Hagen & Zucchella, 2014; Vanninen, Kuivalainen & Ciravegna, 2017; Zander, McDougall-Covin & Rose, 2015), also including firms from emerging economies (Dimitratos, Buck, Fletcher & Li, 2016; McCormick & Somaya, 2020). International opportunity identification emerged as an interesting research topic (Dimitratos, Johnson, Plakoyiannaki & Young, 2016; Zaefarian, Eng & Tasavori, 2016), also in connection with born globals (Chandra 2017; Reuber, Dimitratos & Kuivalainen, 2017; Reuber, Knight, Liesch & Zhou, 2018). Hennart (2014) posited that fast internationalisation is rooted on the business model. Increased attention was assigned to the process of learning as internationalisation unfolds (Casillas, Barbero & Sapienza, 2015; Choquette, 2019; Hohenthal, Johanson & Johanson, 2014; Hutzschenreuter & Matt, 2017; Schwens, Zapkau, Brouthers & Hollender, 2018; Vahlne, 2020).

A new internationalisation stream, intended to capture changes in the IB landscape, namely the growth of digitalisation, addressed ibusiness and platform companies. Relevant contributions included K. Brouthers, Geisser and Rothlauf (2016), on the relevance of networks, and Chen, Shaheer, Yi and Li (2019), on the role of country clout. A related issue concerned the suitability of extant IB theory to analyse such businesses. Banalieva and Dhanaraj (2019) argued that networks were a new mode of governance. In contrast, Hennart (2019) took the opposite position, stating that no further theoretical tools were needed, as the behaviour of such firms might be well explained by extant theory. Another controversy, already mentioned above, concerned the scope of digitalisation. Monaghan, Tippmann and Coviello (2020) introduced the concept of 'born digitals', very much based on firms' technological capabilities that enable them to quickly 'access insights from many users across many country markets' (p. 15), while Stallkamp and Schotter (2019) stressed the existence of restrictions regarding the international scope of network externalities.

More conventional approaches to internationalisation have also developed. These included inter alia entry modes (Brouthers, 2013; Hollender, Zapkau & Schwens, 2017; Ji & Dimitratos, 2013; Slangen, 2013)[5] and their changes (Putzhammer, Puck & Lindner, 2020),[6] location decisions (Magnani, Zucchella & Floriani, 2018; Rasciute & Downward, 2017), psychic distance (Dow, Baack & Parente, 2020; Rovira-Nordman & Tolstoy, 2014; Safari & Chetty, 2019), and managerial cognition including the role of CEOs and top management teams (Chittoor, Aulakh & Ray, 2018; Maitland & Sammartino, 2015). There was a boost on family firms' internationalisation literature (Boellis, Mariotti, Minichilli & Piscitello, 2016; Denicolai, Hagen, Zucchella & Dudinskaya, 2019; Hennart, Majocchi & Forlani, 2019; Kano & Verbeke, 2018; Lahiri, Mukherjee & Peng, 2020; Metsola, Leppäaho, Paavilainen-Mäntymäki & Plakoyiannaki, 2020).

The research on the involvement by emerging countries in the world economy mushroomed. While in the earlier periods most research dealt with investing in those economies, now there was a radical change in focus: research on investments abroad, especially by Chinese firms, took the lead. This somehow reflects IB scholars' adaptation to a changing international context, as shown in the earlier section. In contrast, research on European transition countries (Gorynia, Nowak, Trąpczyński & Wolniak, 2019; Musteen, Datta & Francis, 2014) lost weight. The literature has also shown the complex inter-relationships between firms' international moves and their home country competitiveness and catching-up (Buckley, Munjal, Enderwick & Forsans, 2016; Chen, Zhan, Tong & Kumar, 2020; Liu, Gao, Lu & Lioliou, 2016). Venturing abroad, especially through acquisitions, was instrumental for accessing technological, managerial and organisational knowledge to combine with domestic capabilities to foster catching-up and competitiveness in the home country market (Luo & Tung, 2018). In fact, several investments abroad, especially acquisitions in Europe, have been led by strategic asset-seeking motivations (Elia & Santangelo, 2017; Giuliani, Gorgoni, Günther & Rabellotti, 2014; Piscitello et al., 2015; Sutherland, Anderson & Hu, 2020); The existence of a co-evolution of MNE subsidiaries and local competitors/partners was highlighted (Brandl, Jensen & Lind, 2018; Kumar, Gaur, Zhan & Luo, 2019; Nuruzzaman, Singh & Pattnaik, 2019; Saranga, Schotter & Mudambi, 2019). Another research stream addressed the behaviour of emerging countries' state-owned multinational enterprises (Bass & Chakrabarty, 2014; Cuervo-Cazurra, 2018; Cuervo-Cazurra, Inkpen, Musacchio & Ramaswamy, 2014; Kalasin, Cuervo-Cazurra & Ramamurti, 2020; Liang, Ren & Sun, 2015).

This stream of research has also called attention for cultural issues. Culture and cultural distance/friction (Ahammad, Tarba, Liu, Glaister & Cooper, 2016; Avloniti & Filippaios, 2014; L. E. Brouthers, Marshall & Keig, 2016; Jain, Pangarkar, Yuan & Kumar, 2019; Joshi & Lahiri, 2015; Koch, Koch, Menon & Shenkar, 2016; Malik & Zhao, 2013) as well as psychic distance (Blomkvist & Drogendijk, 2013; Dow et al., 2020; Magnani et al., 2018; Safari & Chetty, 2019; Yildiz & Fey, 2016) were found to influence internationalisation drives, headquarters–subsidiary relationships, international alliances, M&A, and human resource management. However, a set of criticisms has been raised to the dominant patterns of IB research on culture (Devinney & Hohberger, 2017; Stahl & Tung, 2015), stressing the need to espouse more dynamic views of culture (Tung & Stahl, 2018). Yan, Hu and Liu (2020) argued that 'institutional influence overrides psychic distance' in explaining the international market selection by Chinese SMEs. This view is convergent with the increasing focus on institutional issues to explain IB decisions and outcomes, instead of relying on a culture's 'black-box'.

The literature on innovation and knowledge sharing attracted a large host of articles. The review by Papanastassiou, Pearce and Zanfei (2020, p. 623) highlighted some key trends in this field, namely 'the network-like characteristics of international R&D activities' and the role of location-specific factors. MNEs are envisaged as orchestrators of internationally dispersed knowledge. As Cano-Kollman et al. (2016, p. 260) put it, '[t]he co-evolution of locations and firms increases the volume of horizontal knowledge flows and reduces the hierarchical distance between headquarters and subsidiaries, and between flagship orchestrating firms and GVC partners'. Alcácer et al. (2016) addressed the inter-actions between the environmental changes of the information age and the changing nature of the competitive advantage of places, firms' strategies and the governance of IB networks. In a similar vein, research has focused on the international location and connectivity of R&D activities (Belderbos, Leten & Suzuki, 2013; Castellani, Jimenez & Zanfei, 2013; Castellani & Lavoratori, 2020; Scalera, Perri & Hannigan, 2018). However, Hsu, Lien and Chen (2015) argued that the effect of R&D internationalisation on innovation performance is contingent on firms' capabilities to manage international activities.

Another research stream has to do with knowledge sharing processes within MNEs, in which human resources are protagonists (Caligiuri, 2014; Haas & Cummings, 2015; Minbaeva, Pedersen, Björkman, Fey & Park, 2014). Research has also highlighted the role of subsidiaries in such processes, namely in the sourcing (Asakawa, Park, Song & Kim, 2018; Foss & Pedersen, 2019; Minbaeva & Santangelo, 2018a), internal sharing (Ambos, Nell & Pedersen, 2013; Andersson, Buckley & Dellestrand, 2015; Andersson, Gaur, Mudambi & Persson, 2015) and reverse transfer (Chung, 2014; Nair, Demirbag & Mellahi, 2016) of knowledge. Awate, Larsen and Mudambi (2015) pointed out an interesting contrast between the strategic approaches to internationalisation by advanced and emerging countries' MNEs: while the first international moves are aimed at both competence exploitation and creation, for the latter the main thrust is to catch up with industry leaders. Knowledge-sharing and innovation has also been studied in the context of inter-firm relationships such as alliances (Choi & Contractor, 2016) and joint ventures (Khan, Lew & Sinkovics, 2015). A final issue is the protection of industrial property rights. These are mainly used to support the appropriability of innovations (Bucheli & Kim, 2015; Ivus, Park & Saggi, 2017; Kim, 2013), especially in a context of international fragmentation of business processes (Gooris & Peeters, 2016). However, Contractor (2019) and Inkpen, Minbaeva and Tsang (2019) argue that knowledge leakage is not necessary negative for the firm, converging with the co-evolutionary view of foreign investments and local governments (Lundan & Cantwell, 2020).

Research on GCVs has gained importance in the wake of their expansion in the 2000s and the concept of 'global factory', introduced by Peter Buckley. This led to two interesting review articles, aimed at taking stock of the developments and at suggesting new research paths (De Marchi, Di Maria, Golini & Perri, 2020; Kano et al., 2020). They underline the need for inter-disciplinary approaches. This is expressed by the contributions by Gary Gereffi, a sociologist and one of the pioneers of GVC research, to IB journals (Gereffi, 2019, 2020; Pananond, Gereffi & Pedersen, 2020).[7] Two key themes emerged in IB literature on GVCs over the 2013–2020 period[8]: GVCs and IB theory; and GVCs effects on countries' development and technological upgrading. With regard to the first, two contributions address the applicability of internalisation to GVCs (Benito, Petersen & Welch, 2019; Strange & Humphrey, 2019); they converge on the fact that GVCs are between markets and hierarchies, which constrains a full reliance on internalisation. These views call for governance flexibility and adaptation, as emphasised by Kano (2018) in her relational perspective of GVC governance. She envisages GVCs as asymmetrical networks, in which the lead firm draws on a set of relational mechanisms to foster GVCs efficiency and sustainability. With regard to the second theme, the *World Investment Report* dedicated its 2013 issue to GVCs (UNCTAD, 2013). It addressed the pluses and the minuses of GVCs contribution to recipient countries' development. On the plus side, the effects on income per capita growth in many countries and the opportunities for technological upgrading and skill building are pointed out. However, such effects cannot be taken for granted and there is the risk of developing countries to be locked in low value-added activities. Such problems were identified by Narula (2019) in his research on Bangladesh. Enderwick (2018b) reached similar conclusions, highlighting the multiplicity of factors that influence corporate social responsibility in a GCV context. Using an input–output approach, Buckley et al. (2020) found that the probability for income convergence is higher for fabrication activities than for knowledge-intensive activities. In general, public policies and learning drives are key to foster catching up.

In contrast with the two previous periods, 2013–2020 witnessed an upsurge in research on international management and strategy. This may be related to the increasing recognition of the *Global Strategy Journal* (launched in mid-2011) as an attractive outlet for publishing on those issues. A key contribution, based on the longitudinal in-depth case study of Unilever, was made by Mees-Buss, Welch and Westney (2019). They analysed how strategic levers and organisational structures have changed over time and show how Unilever moved from a transnational organisation to a 'neo-global' one. The need to respond distinct stakeholders' demands was also addressed by Devinney, McGahan and Zollo (2013) and by Henisz (2013), who introduced the concept of 'engineering of consent'. Other research efforts have followed more traditional paths, such as matrix structures (Egelhoff, Wolf & Adzic, 2013) and their potential for conflict (Wolf & Egelhoff, 2013), Prahalad and Doz's (1987) I/R framework application to subsidiaries (Meyer & Estrin, 2014; Wei & Nguyen, 2017) and the spatial location of headquarters (Kunisch, Menz & Birkinshaw, 2019; Meyer & Benito, 2016; Pedersen & Tallman, 2016).

New approaches that generated interesting research efforts concerned modularity and the architecture of the MNE (McDermott et al., 2013) and the microfoundations of strategy (Contractor et al., 2019). Kano and Verbeke (2019) applied the concepts of bounded rationality and bounded reliability to Forsgren's (2008) theoretical views on MNEs. However, most articles focused on CEOs' cognition, behaviour and motivations (Beleska-Spasova & Glaister, 2013; Fung, Qiao, Yau & Zeng, 2020; Li & Tang, 2013; Maitland & Sammartino, 2015; Oesterle, Elosge & Elosge, 2016). Board members international origins and experience (Oxelheim, Gregoric, Randøy & Thomsen, 2013; Schmid & Wurster, 2017) and the board's role (Heyden, Oehmichen, Nichting & Volberda, 2015; Thams, Chacar & Wiersema, 2020) were also addressed.

A reference is due to headquarters-subsidiary relationships. Research topics have addressed agency issues (Hoenen & Kostova, 2015), procedural justice (Asmussen, Foss & Nell, 2019), the role of geographic (Baaij & Slangen, 2013), institutional distance (Li, Jiang & Shen, 2016) and the tensions pervading relationships in specific organisational structures (Ambos, Fuchs & Zimmermann, 2020). This leads to the next theme: subsidiary management and behaviour.

As we have seen in previous chapter, the view of the MNE as an internationally dispersed network has been the main driver to focus on subsidiary behaviour. Over the 2013–2020 period there has been a further increase in research in this field as becomes evident in the review by Meyer, Li and Schotter (2020). A core theme was the analysis of subsidiary contrasting roles as agent of headquarters or as a source of initiatives. This was framed in similar ways in two articles: 'assigned versus assumed' (Cavanagh, Freeman, Kalfadellis & Herbert, 2017) and 'loaned or owned?' (Cuervo-Cazurra et al., 2019). A similar reasoning was applied to subsidiary learning by Dimitratos, Plakoyiannaki, Thanos & Förbom (2014). These ideas call for the role of subsidiary managers in instilling an entrepreneurial drive (O'Brien et al., 2018; Sarabi, Froese, Chng & Meyer, 2020) that was found to be an antecedent or a microfoundation of subsidiary R&D efforts (Nuruzzaman et al., 2018).

Research has also addressed two related issues: subsidiaries' liability of foreignness (Moeller, Harvey, Griffith & Richey, 2013; Wan, Williamson & Pandit, 2020) and dual identity (Durand & Jacqueminet, 2015; Edman, 2016; Smale, Björkman, Ehrnrooth, John, Mäkelä & Sumelius, 2015). The best illustration of the tensions stemming from this duality is provided on longitudinal case study of Unilever India (Pant & Ramachandran, 2017). Zhang, Jiang and Cantwell (2015, p. 224) found that the subsidiary capability to combine knowledge not new to the MNE and knowledge new to the MNE play a key role in reconciling subsidiary and MNE's interests 'by balancing exploration and exploitation' at the MNE-level and 'by balancing exploration and integration at the subsidiary-level'. Subsidiary's absorptive capacity (Peltokorpi, 2017; Schleimer & Pedersen, 2014; Song, 2014) and subsidiary's knowledge flows and learning practices (Ahlvik & Björkman, 2015; Chidlow, Holmström-Lind, Holm & Tallman, 2015; Crespo, Griffith & Lages, 2014; Ha & Giroud, 2015; Parker, Tippmann & Kratochvil, 2019) have also generated a significant research stream. A reference is also due to subsidiary divestment, on which deserve a mention the contributions by Paul Beamish and his team on subsidiary exit from emerging markets (Dai, Eden & Beamish, 2013; Getachew & Beamish, 2017; Sartor & Beamish, 2020) and review article by Schmid and Morschett (2020).

The last theme of this review has to do with cross-border alliances, including joint ventures, and M&A. Over the 2013–2020 period, research on international alliances and joint ventures do not appear to have increased proportionally to overall IB research. This may be related to the emergence of new themes. A look at the literature on international alliances enables the identification of six main vectors: technology and R&D alliances (Lew, Sinkovics, Yamin & Khan, 2016; van Kranenburg, Hagedoorn & Lorenz-Orlean, 2014); governance modes (Billitteri, Lo Nigro & Perrone, 2013; Choi & Contractor, 2016; Contractor & Reuer, 2014); MNEs-SMEs cooperation (Hennart, 2020; Prashantham & Birkinshaw, 2020); the roles of trust and power (Couper, Reuber & Prashantham, 2020; Mohr & Puck, 2013); rivalry and alliance networks (Pesch & Bouncken, 2017); and learning processes (Caner & Tyler, 2015; Howard, Steensma, Lyles & Dhanaraj, 2016). It is worth to remark the reliance on social networks (Cuypers, Ertug, Cantwell, Zaheer & Kilduff, 2020; Iurkov & Benito, 2018) and institutional (Golesorkhi, Mersland, Randøy & Shenkar, 2019) perspectives as foundations for research on strategic alliances. The research on IJVs has also lost steam. A key contribution to research in this field was made by Nippa and Reuer (2019), providing a framework of IJV research topics and advanced suggestions for further research. Another interesting article concerned the use of relational metaphors in improving IJV management (Liu, Adair & Bello, 2015). The main literature published in this period may be aggregated in five streams: IJV formation (Owens, Palmer & Anna Zueva-Owens, 2013; Yeniyurt & Carnovale, 2017); IJV management (Devarakonda, Klijn, Reuer & Duplat, 2021; Merchant, 2014), including control (Nguyen, Larimo & Wang, 2019); relational mechanisms (Ertug, Cuypers, Noorderhaven & Bensaou, 2013; Reuer & Klijn, 2020); knowledge sharing and creation (Khan, Shenkar & Lew, 2015; Park & Harris, 2014; Park, Vertinsky & Becerra, 2015); IJVs longevity (Triki & Mayrhofer, 2016); and termination (Chung, Lee & Lee, 2013; Mata & Portugal, 2015; Nemeth & Nippa, 2013; Perkins, Morck & Yeung, 2014).

With regard to M&A, we will not focus on the literature on M&A by emerging countries firms, since it has been addressed above. A review shows that M&A were analysed from multiple perspectives. The effects of country and/or organisational/cultural (Ahammad et al., 2016; Lee, Kim & Park, 2015; Wang, Hain, Larimo & Dao, 2020), psychic (Yildiz & Fey, 2016), linguistic (Khedia & Reddy, 2016), religious (Dow, Cuypers & Ertug, 2016) and institutional (Alimov, 2015;

Kim & Song, 2017; Dikova, Panibratov & Veselova, 2019) environment and/or differences were the focus of a large host of literature; in this vein, it is important to recognise that partners' perceptions may not be reciprocal (Yildiz & Fey, 2016). Another strand has focused on control mechanisms (Park & Choi, 2014). Post-M&A management and its effects on employees' emotions and behaviour were also addressed (Gunkel, Schlaegel, Rossteutscher & Wolff, 2015; Hassett, Reynolds & Sandberg, 2018; Kroon, Cornelissen & Vaara, 2015), highlighting how difficult is to build post-M&A shared identities (Łupina-Wegener, Schneider & van Dick, 2015).

8.3. EIBA: THE CONFERENCES

In 2013–2020, eight conferences were held. Two of them corresponded to exceptional events: the first EIBA conference outside the Euro-Mediterranean area, in Rio de Janeiro (2015); and the only online conference so far, showing how EIBA was able to withstand the problems raised by the pandemic. In contrast, the other six conferences were held in Central and Northern Europe, four of them over the 50 degrees parallel (Bremen 2013, Uppsala 2014, Poznań 2018 and Leeds 2019), and two about at the foothills of the Alps (Vienna 2016 and Milan 2017). The thrust recorded in the previous period to venture into the East European EU member countries (Ljubljana 2004, Tallinn 2008 and Bucharest 2011) faded, Poznan 2018 being the only conference held in those countries. This may be due to two main factors: the increasing complexity of organising EIBA conferences, and the difficulty in maintaining stable and sizeable chapters there, Poland and Slovenia being the exceptions. Leaving Rio-2015 aside, the geographical spread of EIBA conferences in this period was much lower than in the previous one. In contrast, venturing towards South America looked as a bold move, entering an area that traditionally was under AIB's remit (an AIB conference had taken place in Rio de Janeiro in 2010), when there still was a latent tension between both academies, even though 10 years had elapsed since the 2004 *Buckley's compromise*.

EIBA became stronger, in terms of financial stability, managerial processes, conference attendance and membership, and more balanced, gender-wise. The payment of the debt to EIASM and the renegotiation of the terms of the service package (see Chapter 7) together with EIBA's attractiveness paved the way for a new age, in which successive deficits were replaced by surpluses, and a financial situation enabling the launching of new initiatives. The new governance model, implemented in 2004, enabled the setting up of a core management team (Chair, Vice-chair and the Executive Secretary), leading to sounder and formalised managerial processes. Conference attendance increased from an average of about 350 participants, for 2003–2012, to an average of almost 490, for 2013–2020, with two conferences (Vienna-2016 and Milan-2017) attracting more than 600 people, while only one was (slightly) below 400. These developments are also translated into EIBA membership, that reached its maximum so far in 2017 (664 members), partly as a result of the outstanding attractiveness of the Vienna conference. Significant steps were taken towards increasing gender balance, as shown by the increasing share of women membership, the almost parity of Board members in 2020 (18 women versus 19 men) and EIBA's leadership held by a woman (Lucia Piscitello).

A brief summary of the main features of the eight EIBA conferences held over this period is presented below.

The EIBA 2013 conference was held in Bremen (Germany), organised by Sarianna Lundan, who had already been co-organiser of Maastricht-2000. It was the first EIBA conference in Germany in the 21st century, 16 years after the memorable Stuttgart conference. As explained in the previous chapter, originally the idea was to hold the conference in Mannheim, with Andreas Al-Laham in charge. However, Andreas' illness and death in December 2011 led the Board to invite EIBA members to submit proposals. Bremen was selected, ahead of Aalborg (Denmark) and Linz (Austria), mostly because of Sarianna's reputation and the possibility to keep the event in Germany. It is not easy to organise an EIBA conference in such a short term, but Sarianna, with the support from the University of Bremen, has done a superb job and put together an excellent conference, under the *motto* of *Transnational Firms, Markets and Institutions.* The conference was attended by 438 people. Anna Veselova, Emilia Rovira Nordman, Raquel Meneses, Tilo Halaszowitch and Thomas Lindner were among those who made their debut in Bremen.

The conference was unforgettable for good and bad reasons. The latter were the recent death of Andreas Al-Laham and especially the fact that Danny Van Den Bulcke, Mr EIBA, the first EIBA Chair and former Dean of the EIBA Fellows, was not in Bremen. This was a surprise for most people, but those closest to Danny, such as Filip De Beule, told us that Danny's health was faltering, and eventually he passed away less than one month after the conference. The good reasons were the professionalism and attention to the detail of Sarianna Lundan and her team, the quality of the academic programme, with two outstanding plenary sessions, the doctoral tutorials and the social events.

The conference featured two plenary sessions. The opening one was the EIBA Fellows Plenary, focused on Chinese FDI in the EU, then a hot topic, after a string of acquisitions of relevant European (and German) firms by Chinese competitors, often aimed at getting access to technology and organisational assets, as seen in the previous section. The other, in the context of Danny's initiative of commemorative sessions on influential IB contributions, addressed Pankhaj Ghemawat's article 'Semiglobalisation and IB strategy' (Ghemawat, 2003). It is remarkable how prescient Danny was to introduce a reference to de-globalisation, a concept that was to become fashionable at the end of the decade, especially after Witt's (2019) article. The discussion was very lively, focusing on the extent of globalisation, the regional- or semi-globalisation versus globalisation dispute, and its implications for research and management.

In the wake of Brighton, there were three doctoral events. The fourth and last COST-EIBA/EIASM Doctoral Think Tank, an initiative pioneered by Danny, was chaired by Lucia Piscitello alone. The second edition of the Doctoral Symposium was again led by Jeremy Clegg, this time with the support of Elisabeth Wang, from the University of Leeds. The JHD Doctoral Tutorial was chaired by Jean-François Hennart and Rebecca Piekkari. Faculty also included Timothy Devinney, Dana Minbaeva and Bent Petersen. As usual there were 10 students, some of which became committed EIBA members, such as Vittoria Scalera, who later became the Netherlands' NR. The winner was Liudmyla Svystunova, from Bath University, with a proposal on 'Managing institutional complexity in global professional service firms: Subsidiary responses to conflicting institutional logic'.

A short trip along the North and the Baltic seas led EIBA to its next stop: Uppsala in Sweden. This was the third EIBA conference in Sweden, after Uppsala-1977 and Stockholm-1996. Uppsala was known by IB scholars as the place where the famous Uppsala model (Johanson & Vahlne, 1977) was born. Now EIBA was coming back to Uppsala, with a much larger host that could not be pictured as the small group of 1977: attendance reached an all-time record of 512. Uppsala was the first EIBA conference for well-known scholars as Nicole Coviello and Liena Kano, but also for younger people as Michal Budrik, Dinorá Floriani, Giovanna Magnani and Katarzyna Mroczek-Dabrowska.

Rian Drogendijk made a superb job in arranging a memorable conference on both academic and social grounds. The conference's theme was *The Future of Global Organizing*, aimed at stimulating reflections on the changes with regard 'to the organisation and structure of international firms since the 1970s, resulting in the great variety of organisational and geographic structures in multinational corporations (MNCs) that we see today; [t]hese structures, in turn, reflect the tensions between different organisational principles, such as, the MNC as a hierarchy or a network, internalizing or externalizing core business activities, and the relative importance of headquarters and subsidiaries in the value creation processes' (Rian Drogendijk, 2014, p. 4).

The conference featured three plenaries that have been remembered for many years. Profiting from the fact that Jan Tirole, the year's Nobel Prize winner, was scheduled to deliver a Nobel lecture at Uppsala University on December 13th, it was possible for EIBA participants to follow his broadcast speech. This was fascinating, especially the account he provided about his career and the logic behind the establishment of platform companies, heralding a new paradigm to provide services worldwide, that would later become an important IB research issue. While this was an intellectual lesson, another plenary was emotionally touching, since it was a tribute to Danny Van Den Bulcke's role in the development of the IB field and more specifically his enormous contribution to EIBA. Chaired by John Cantwell, who delivered an excellent summary of Danny as a man, a scholar and Mr EIBA, the session provided a multi-faceted perspective about Danny. EIBA Uppsala has also honoured the memory of Alan Rugman, a major IB scholar, former President of AIB and regular attendant of EIBA conferences, who had passed away in mid-2014. Finally, a reference is due to the EIBA Fellows Plenary, which corresponded to the Opening Plenary of the conference, chaired by Vítor Corado Simões and held at the main University Building. The Fellows thought that it was the right place and time to discuss 'The role of Uppsala in IB research'. We had the pleasure to have Jan Johanson and Jan-Erik Vahlne in the audience, participating actively in the session as shown in Fig. 12.

Fig. 12.   Mats Forsgren, Reijo Luostarinen, Peter Buckley and Jan Johansson After the
Opening Plenary in Uppsala (2014). *Source*: EIBA website.

There were two doctoral sessions: the 28th JHD Doctoral Tutorial, chaired
again by Jean-François Hennart and Rebecca Pikkari, with the help of top-
level faculty (Gabriel Benito, Univ. Oslo; Timothy Devinney, Univ. Leeds, and
D. Eleanor Westney, York University, Canada); and the 3rd EIBA Doctoral
Symposium, co-chaired by Jeremy Clegg and Elisabeth Yi Wang, both from the
University of Leeds, with 30 plus faculty members, who discussed the presentations by 30 PhD students. The winner of the JHD Tutorial was Ziad Elsahn,
coming from antipodes (University of Auckland Business School, New Zealand),
with a dissertation project entitled 'Making Sense of Foreign Direct Investment:
Towards a Process Model of MNE Decision-Making'.

The Uppsala conference introduced a new award, the Danny Van Den Bulcke
Best Paper Prize, to recognise the best paper presented to the Conference. This
was a way to honour the contribution from Danny Van Den Bulcke, and would
become a key feature of EIBA conferences. The first winner was the paper 'BRIC
companies seeking legitimacy through corporate social responsibility', authored
by Elisa Giuliani, Davide Fiaschi and Federica Nieri (University of Pisa, Italy).
Besides the JIBS Paper Development Workshop (PDW), launched in Bremen and
now co-chaired by Ulf Andersson and José Plà-Barber, there was the first *IBR*
PDW, led by Roger Strange and Pervez Ghauri, and thanks to the initiative of the
EIBA Early Career Network, led by Tilo Halaszowithch, a paper development
workshop focused on providing advice to young scholars was launched. Another
innovation was the post-conference Qualitative Methods Workshop, directed
by Catherine Welch, that was to become a further attraction of future of EIBA
conferences. Besides the welcome reception at the magnificent main University

Building, the social programme included an unforgettable Gala Dinner at the imposing Uppsala castle, located at the top of a hill overseeing the city.

From the cold of Uppsala, EIBAians were expecting to move to the warmth of the samba in 2015, when EIBA was held in Rio de Janeiro. The EIBA decision to go out of bounds, leaving Europe for the second time (after Jerusalem-1998) to cross the Atlantic, had raised some concerns, regarding distance and the risk of being perceived by AIB as a challenge. With hindsight, it may be argued that the decision was based on a range of factors: Jorge Carneiro's reputation, the existence of a large Brazilian host membership, the lack of competing locations in which to hold the conference in 2015, and the appeal of Rio de Janeiro in December. The main drawback discussed at the Board was distance. The actions taken to counter the negative effects of distance were related to the design of some kind of sponsorship for students and the venue of the 2015 Spring Board meeting. Jorge Carneiro took several actions to address these issues. However, contrary to our expectations, it was not possible to fully profit from the 'marvellous city's' jewels: it rained continuously during the time of the conference (1-3 December)!

The conference was held at the Pontifical Catholic University of Rio de Janeiro, under the theme of 'International Business after the BRIC's rush'. It was attended by almost 400 people (398, in fact), a figure below previous conferences, but still a feat, having in mind the distance issue. Rio was the first EIBA experience for Becky Reuber, but also for young scholars such as Ludivine Chalençon, Tanja Leppäaho, and Federica Nieri. The conference included two main plenary sessions. The first corresponded to the opening Fellows plenary, addressing MNEs–Government interaction, in the wake of an idea proposed by Seev Hirsch. It featured four panellists: Seev Hirsch, Pervez Ghauri, Ana Teresa Tavares-Lehman and the 2015 EIBA Honorary Fellow, Mr José Rubens de la Rosa, the CEO of *Marcopolo*, a bus manufacturing multinational, based in Caxias do Sul, in Southern Brazil. The closing plenary was about 'Internalisation Theory and Emerging Market Multinationals'. The chair was Jorge Carneiro, and the speakers were two of the most outstanding proponents on internalisation theory, Peter Buckley and Jean-François Hennart. The main conclusion was that, according to the speakers, internalisation is robust enough to be expanded to explain emerging market multinationals' behaviour. The Danny Van Den Bulcke Best Paper Prize was given to the paper 'Taking the long way: How international work experience affects managers' time to the top', authored by Stefan Schmid, a committed EIBA member, and Dennis Wurster (ESCP Europe, Germany).

The innovations introduced by Jorge Carneiro included the five 'Practitioner-academia panels' aimed at stimulating the interaction between academics and business managers, the increased visibility assigned to the poster session and the Quantitative Research Methods Workshop, conducted by Adamantios Diamantopoulos, from the University of Vienna, Austria. This was an addition to the Qualitative Research Methods Workshop, led by Catherine Welch, launched in Uppsala.

EIBA's doctoral initiatives in Rio included the JHD Doctoral Tutorial and the Doctoral Symposium, now labelled Danny Van Den Bulcke Doctoral

Symposium, in honour of Danny's efforts to promote EIBA's activities to support doctoral students. The latter was managed by Jeremy Clegg and Elizabeth Yi Wang, and attracted a large number of students, including many from Brazil and Latin America. The 29th Doctoral Tutorial was co-chaired by Jean François Hennart and Gabriel Benito, analysing the selected doctoral projects of nine students. Faculty included Timothy Devinney, Suzana Rodrigues and Udo Zander. The winner was Rilana Riikkinen (Aalto University School of Business, Finland), with a dissertation project on an increasingly relevant theme: Sustainability ('What Drives Sustainability in Multinational Corporations? An Examination of the Purchasing Function').

After going out-of-bounds, in 2016 EIBA was coming to classical heart Europe. After the samba, what a contrast to go to Vienna to enjoy opera and classical music. It was EIBA's first conference in Austria, after two lost opportunities in Linz. However, EIBA's desire to visit Austria was to materialise shortly afterwards, due to the initiative of Jonas Puck. EIBA Vienna-2016 was superbly organised, under the *motto* of 'Liabilities of foreignness versus the value of diversity', reaching a new maximum attendance level (613 participants), that was to become a record for almost one decade. Jonas took the decision to move to ConfTool platform, which was to become the norm for future EIBA conferences. The conference combined a high academic standing and an outstanding social programme. This started with an innovation that was to become a must for future conferences: the 'Meet & Greet' session. It provided an opportunity for newcomers to meet older EIBAians, including EIBA Fellows. A large set of scholars made their EIBA debut in Vienna, namely Francisco J. Acedo, Luciano Ciravegna, Iris Koleša, Vera Kunczer, Miguel Preto, Harald Puhr, Khadija Van Der Straeten and Božidar Vlačić.

The opening plenary commemorated the 40th anniversary of one of the most influential IB books ever: 'The future of "The future of the Multinational Enterprise"'. Peter Buckley and Mark Casson were part of the panel; this also included Niron Hashai, Davide Castellani and Liena Kano. The plenary was very insightful, combining the presentation of the internalisation tenets with suggestions for their updating, considering new IB developments and challenges. The conference included another plenary, aimed at addressing the conference's theme. The new EIBA Honorary Fellow Matti Alahuta, former CEO and President of Kone Corporation (Finland) participated in this session.

The conference programme also included three paper development workshops, three faculty development workshops and two doctoral events (the 5th Danny Van Den Bulcke [DVDB] Doctoral Symposium, chaired by Elisabeth Yi Wang, Igor Kalinic and Jeremy Clegg and the JHD Doctoral Tutorial). The latter was again chaired by Jean-François Hennart and Gabriel Benito. Faculty also included Timothy Devinney, Lars Håkansson and Elisabeth Rose. Ten doctoral projects were presented, the award being granted to one of the WU Vienna's PhD students: Renate Kratochvil, with a project entitled 'Managers in MNCs Receiving Knowledge from Geographically Distant Individuals: The Moderating Effects of Cognitive, Social and Organizational Proximity'. The winner of the Danny Van Den Bulcke Best Paper Prize was very much in line with the conference's theme: 'Institutional Distance and Subsidiary Performance: Climbing up vs. Climbing down the Institutional Ladder', authored by Palitha Konara (University of Huddersfield, UK) and Vikrant Shirodkar (University of Sussex, UK).

Lucia Piscitello was waiting the EIBA family at Politecnico di Milano for another excellent conference. After taking almost 20 years to visit Italy for the first time, in less than 25 years three EIBA conferences were held in Italy: first in Marche (Urbino-1994), then in Sicily (Catania-2007), and now in Lombardy, close to the Po river. Lucia was able to attract many relevant scholars to participate in EIBA Milan as well as to entice younger colleagues to enable a wonderful mix of experience and youth to address key IB issues.

The conference's theme was 'International Business and the Information Age'. It was the first EIBA conference to deeply reflect about the implications of the EU GDPR, to discuss the growth of platform businesses and to figure out how information and knowledge impinges upon international management behaviour and organisation. It was also the first EIBA conference to provide participants with a dual approach to follow the conference and to take their decisions about what sessions to follow on the spot: besides the well-organised paper programme, an app was available for EIBAians to access the programme on their phones. The number of participants was slightly below Vienna but still above 600. Milan was the EIBA debut for Radek Cajka, Simone Guercini, Hara Yoritoshi, Katiuscia Lavoratori, Jong-Min Lee and Linda Rademaker. The winner of the Danny Van Den Bulcke's Best Paper Prize addressed an issue that was not common in IB research: 'Back so fast? Empirical evidence on the speed of foreign market re-entry after initial entry and exit'. The trio of awardees was from the UK: Irina Surdu (University of Reading), Kamel Mellahi and Keith Glaister (University of Warwick).

The opening plenary was chaired by Lucia Piscitello, addressing 'Internationalisation in the Information Age'. The speakers were Salvatore Annelo (Managing director of Accenture Italy), John Cantwell (Rutgers University, US), Silvia Massini (University of Manchester, UK) and Roberta Rabellotti (University of Pavia, Italy, and Aalborg University, Denmark). After taking a minute of silence in memory of Reijo Luostarinen, a set of interesting presentations ensued. The Fellows Plenary was held in the last day of the conference to reflect about 'Digitalisation, business and policies: Confronting challenges in Europe today (and tomorrow)'. Chaired by John Cantwell, the panel included Francesca Sanna Randaccio, Andrea Goldstein (Managing Director of Nomisma, after working at OECD, UNESCAP and the World Bank Group)[9] and Reinhilde Veugelers (KU Leuven), the 2017 Honorary EIBA Fellow. The discussion revolved around two main issues: the lights and shadows of the contribution of digital businesses, especially platform companies, towards development, and the role of policy to ensure more positive outcomes.

Even though key figures of EIBA, such as Danny Van Den Bulcke and Reijo Luostarinen, had passed away, EIBA had shown to be able to attract younger research cohorts, while keeping its distinctive nature of combining friendship and high-quality academic work. This was shown in the Poster papers plenary (envisaged as a way to support promising research lines), in the three paper development workshops (IBR, JIBS and the EIBA Early Career Network), and in the doctoral sessions (6th DVDB Doctoral Symposium and the 31st JHD Doctoral Tutorial). This was chaired again by Jean-François Hennart and Gabriel Benito, and the faculty was the same (Timothy Devinney, Lars Håkansson and Elisabeth Rose). Ten students presented their doctoral projects. For the second consecutive year, the award for the best project went to a WU Vienna student: this time was Florian Klein, with his research project on 'Institutional Dynamism in International Business: Conceptualization, Measurement, and Firm Strategies'.

In 2018, EIBA was to cross the Alps again to visit Poznań, the city of Wieslaw Otta, one of the Polish EIBA pioneers in the 1980s, that had already left us. This was the second EIBA conference in Poland, after the memorable Warsaw-1994. Poznań was not an unknown place for EIBA scholars: the two last Polish NR at the EIBA Board, Marian Gorynia and Barbara Jankowska, were both from its university; and Marlena Dzikowska, winner of the 2014 CBS Prize, was also from Poznań. The organisation was once again assigned to women: Barbara Jankowska, with the support of Małgorzata Bartosik-Purgat as co-chair.

The conference's theme was 'International Business in a Transforming World – the Changing Role of States and Firms'. The conference attendance was 420, not very far from Bremen-2013 and above Rio 2015. Among the EIBA first-timers in Poznań, a reference goes to Kristin Brandl, who was to play a key role in dynamising the 2020 online EIBA, as well as to Johannes Kleinhempel, Eva Křenková and Richard Afriyie Owusu.

The main innovation introduced in Poznań was the Pedagogy Workshop, dealing with 'Incorporating Video Clips: An Engaging and Accessible Pedagogical Tool for International Business Teaching' and a Mentoring Event for Women in EIBA. The three paper development workshops (IBR, JIBS and the EIBA Early Career Network) were joined by a new one, concerning the JIBP, organised by Ari Van Assche. The JHD Tutorial and the Danny Van Den Bulcke Doctoral Symposium reached their 32nd and 7th editions, respectively. Regarding the first, it is interesting to remark that both the chairs and the faculty were the same as in Vienna and Milan: Jean-François Hennart, Gabriel Benito, Timothy Devinney, Lars Håkansson and Elisabeth Rose. It seemed to be a case of application of the sports' maxima of 'never change a winning team'. The students' cohort, however, was a different one: 10 new students were presenting their projects. The awardee was Johannes Kleinhempel (University of Groningen, Netherlands) with a project on comparative entrepreneurship research.

The conference included three plenaries. The opening plenary was entitled 'Transformation facilitating transformation: from a local player to a multinational company'. It presented the internationalisation processes of three Polish firms. Another plenary discussed the 'Backlash of Globalization – Cyclical and structural phenomena. How can IB respond to and investigate them?'. The panel was led by Erszbet Czakó (Corvinus University of Budapest, Hungary), then the Hungarian NR at the EIBA Board. The traditional Fellows Plenary was the last one, focusing on 'Addressing Processes of Change and the Emergence of New Phenomena in the International Business Environment'. It was chaired by John Cantwell, then Dean of the Fellows, and included as a special guest Jan Švejnar (Director of the Center on Global Economic Governance and Professor of International and Public Affairs at Columbia University, USA), the 2018 Honorary EIBA Fellow. Once again, EIBA was addressing an issue that later would become relevant for IB mainstream, especially in the wake of Witt's (2019) influential article in JIBS.

The EIBA community was already well acquainted to the quality of the Leeds University IB team, mostly due to the reputation of Peter Buckley and Jeremy Clegg. However, none of them was directly involved in the organisation of EIBA Leeds. This was taken by an Aussie and a Kiwi. In fact, the team in charge of the conference was Timothy Devinney, an Australian, and Elisabeth Rose, a New Zealander. Both were already known for their contributions to the profession and especially for their service to the JHD Doctoral Tutorial. The conference itself was organised in a very professional way, and included several very interesting events and sessions, including the visit to the Business Confucius Institute, founded and then led by Peter Buckley.

The conference's theme was again intended to express the conflictual and challenging times we were experiencing: 'What Now? International Business in a Confused World Order'. This title fully expressed the perplexities that IB had to address to understand a changing business climate, in which nationalistic and conflictual forces were challenging globalisation. The conference was attended by 509 participants. This was the first EIBA conference for Christos Pitelis, as well as for members of the younger generation, like Aleksi Eerola Amy Linh Thuy Nguyen, Diletta Pegoraro, Helene Tenzer and Priit Vahter. The 6th DVDB Best Paper Prize was awarded to Sarah Edris and John Cantwell, both from Rutgers University (USA), for their paper 'Organizational and Geographic Sources of MNE Networks in the Pharmaceutical Industry'.

The conference featured the already traditional Paper Development Workshops (IBR, JIBS, JIBP and EIBA Early Career Network), joined this time by the *Journal of World Business/Journal of Management Studies* PDW. There were four post-conference workshops: two focused on research methods (structural equations modelling and qualitative methods), the pedagogy workshop initiated in Poznań and another on research in culture. The DVDB Doctoral Symposium and the JHD Doctoral Tutorial attracted an increasing number of students. The first was led by Rebecca Piekkari, Elisabeth Yi Wang and Igor Kalinic. The second was once again chaired by Jean-François Hennart and Gabriel Benito. Elisabeth Rose and Lars Håkansson kept their chairs and were joined by Eleanor Westney. The winner was Michael Juergen Müller (Rotterdam School of Management, Erasmus University, Netherlands), with a dissertation project entitled 'Strangers in a Strange Land: Essays on Migration in Management'.

The conference included two plenary sessions. The opening plenary (International Business in a Confused World Order) addressed the conference's theme. Chaired by Elisabeth Rose, the session was mainly focused at the identification of the main threats that globalisation was facing, envisaged from an historical perspective, as well as on the challenges for IB. The EIBA Fellows Plenary was chaired by John Cantwell and discussed a theme at the intersection between geography and IB ('From Regional Convergence to Divergence: The Changing Economic Geography of International Business Activities and Connections'), profiting from the contribution from Michael Storper (UCLA, Luskin School of Public Affairs, USA), the 2019 EIBA Honorary Fellow. To some extent this session, while recognising the challenges to globalisation, was a counterpoint to the opening Plenary, since it underlined the relevance of international connectivity in a digitalised world, a theme emphasised two years ago at Milan, and the changing configuration of the main connecting hubs, China and SE Asia clearly gaining importance vis-à-vis Europe.

At the EIBA General Assembly in Leeds, the calendar for the forthcoming EIBA conferences, both led by women, were presented. EIBA 2020 would be held in Madrid, hosted by Isabel Álvarez (ICEI, Complutense University, Madrid). Similarly to what had happened 30 years ago, when John H. Dunning was granted an *honoris causa* doctorate by the Autonomous University of Madrid, John Cantwell would be given another *honoris causa* doctorate, this time by the Complutense University. In 2021, EIBA would go northeast to meet for the third time in Oslo, under the leadership of Birgitte Grøgaard (BI Oslo), together with Alan Ilon (University of Agder, Norway). The future looked pretty clear for EIBA...

However, reality was to turn otherwise. Nobody could anticipate that shortly thereafter the World would be confronted with the COVID-19 pandemic. In the early months of 2020, the COVID-19 outbreak was strong. The setting up of sanitary restrictions by most countries, especially in Europe, followed suit, with significant implications for international travel and business. This impinged upon EIBA's conference calendar.

The hypothesis of changing the format to an online conference was voiced, following the AIB decision to hold its annual conference online. Isabel Álvarez was approached regarding her availability to organise the event online. However, she was firmly committed to an in-person conference, and declined to go online, while accepting to postpone the Madrid conference for December 2021. This led the EIBA Chairs to address the issue, launching the preparations for an on-line event, organised by WU Vienna, Politecnico di Milano, and Henley Business School. The idea was that 'EIBA 2020 will be a very special annual conference – a 'regular' annual event plus special digital features' (Piscitello & Puck, 2020a, p. 2). Lucia Piscitello and Jonas Puck were to serve as Conference Chairs, Thomas Lindner as Program Chair, and Kristin Brandl as Social Chair.

The theme of the conference was 'obviously', as Lucia and Jonas put it (Piscitello & Puck, 2020b, p. 16), 'International Business in the Pandemic and Post-Pandemic Era'. It has held online between 10th and 12th December 2020. The basic structure of EIBA conferences was kept, but some new features were introduced. The first day of the conference closely followed the traditional format, with the doctoral events (the 34th JHD Doctoral Tutorial and the 9th Danny Van Den Bulcke Doctoral Symposium) and the PDWs (IBR, JIBS, JIBP and EIBA Early career network) taking place along the day, before the Opening Plenary. The second day was almost fully dedicated to the presentation of the papers selected for Competitive and Interactive sessions and a few panels; the day closed with the online General Assembly. The third day corresponded to workshops and social events. The workshops covered a wide set of issues, from research methods (qualitative and qualitative) to societally engaged IB and women in IB, through online teaching, leadership, patent policy harmonisation, theory development on IB and measuring and conceptualising internationalisation. Having in mind the online nature of the conference, attendance was relatively high (416 registrations). While some regular conference participants might not have felt comfortable with an online event, the possibility of bridging distance through digitalisation might have enticed other scholars to attend. Some of those who made their debut online were to come back later to in-person conferences, as was the case of Alexandre Bohas, Vanessa Bretas, Louise Curran, Anna Dimitrova, Qiuling Gao and Bart Postma.

The students presenting their doctoral projects at the 34th JHD Doctoral Tutorial came from three continents, spreading from Japan to Brazil. The faculty was the same of Leeds-2019: Jean-François Hennart and Gabriel Benito as co-chairs, together with Lars Håkansson, Elisabeth Rose and Eleanor Westney. The winner was Rico Kremer (University of Erfurt, Germany), with a project on a socio-cognitive perspective of the effect of geographical distance on multinational downsizing decisions.

The EIBA Fellows Opening Plenary, entitled 'Implications of COVID-19 for International Business', was led by Alain Verbeke. The panellists were four Fellows: Timothy Devinney, Grazia Santangelo, Vítor Corado Simões and Ana Teresa Tavares-Lehman. In his introduction, Alain Verbeke forcefully argued that the pandemic does not demand a change to extant IB theory while calling for refocusing our attention towards issues such as the most relevant types of FSAs, the changing importance of country level dimensions or the pattern of subsidiary integration in MNEs' networks. The speakers introduced further issues, including the change in investment risk perception, the adaptation and management of GVCs, the acceleration of digitally based internationalisation strategies and the differentiated behaviour of distinct types of platform companies during and after the pandemic, having in mind the locus (inside versus outside platform) of the interactions to carry out the business transaction.

Besides the above plenary, the EIBA Fellows have been deeply involved in two panels. One was the session in honour of Seev Hirsch's memory. Chaired by Peter Buckley, it featured contributions from Tamar Almor, John Cantwell, Niron Hashai and Jonas Puck. Seev Hirsch had been one of the most fruitful, inquisitive and challenging members of EIBA. In particular, he played a very important role in the dynamisation of EIBA Fellows activities. At this juncture, it is important to mention the passing away of two other IB scholars whose work has been a source of inspiration for future generations of IB researchers: Yair Aharoni and Lawrence Welch. The other panel, entitled 'The early years of EIBA: Views from the founding fathers', came in the wake of a series of panels on the EIBA history launched by Vítor Corado Simões in Rio de Janeiro. Transforming a challenge into an opportunity, he was able to use the EIBA conference online to collect the live contributions of five colleagues who had been EIBA presidents between 1975 and 1982. James Leontiades (first President of EIBA, 1975), Michel Ghertman (EIBA President, 1976), Lars-Gunnar Mattsson (EIBA President, 1977), Sylvain Plasschaert (EIBA President, 1980) and José de la Torre (EIBA President, 1982) presented their remembrances about the teething years of EIBA, the challenges faced, and their perspectives about the future of our Academy.

EIBA Madrid was to happen in 2021, at a time when the pandemic was still threatening. Isabel Álvarez and her team were brave enough to organise EIBA-2021, keeping her commitment even though the pandemic had postponed the event that she had carefully prepared. She had to start anew to attract the EIBA community to join EIBA Madrid, under harsh conditions in terms of health conditions and travel restrictions. Fortunately, in spite of the hindrances faced, she was able to arrange a very good conference that many of us will remember forever. Going into EIBA Madrid-2021 details is out of the scope of this book, but Isabel Álvarez's efforts deserve a mention here. As a result of the joint efforts of a number of EIBAians – namely Lucia Piscitello, Jonas Puck, Thomas Lindner, Kristin Brandl and Isabel Álvarez – EIBA was able to respond the challenges raised by the COVID-19 pandemic, and to enter 2022 with further confidence towards a new stage of consolidation and venturing into new initiatives that would foster its relevance and attractiveness for different vintages of IB scholars.

8.4. EIBA: ORGANISATIONAL DEVELOPMENTS

The period under analysis (2013–2020) was marked by a generational change. While some of those who had witnessed or even participated in the creation of EIBA passed away, a new host of committed EIBAians was taking the lead positions in our Academy. In the same vein, the fruitful dialogue between the Board and the Fellows enabled to inject new blood while keeping the lessons from the past. The most pressing issues of the past had been solved, especially the debt problem, and EIBA entered a time in which, while careful financial management was still needed, profits became the standard. This provided room for systematising procedures (with regard to the election of the Chairs and NRs, for instance) and fostering new strategic approaches. These were translated into new initiatives, including the improvement of tutorial initiatives, further PDWs, the launching of the EIBA Workshops (EIBA-W) and the espousing of new challenges, particularly in the fields of digitalisation, gender balance and sustainability.

This section encompasses 11 parts: EIBA governance; EIBA strategy; new initiatives to increase EIBA's attractiveness, consistency and research quality as well as to foster membership; progress in improving the standard of EIBA conferences; the EIBA Board; EIBA membership; gender balance; EIBA financial situation; the relationships with other organisations; further progress regarding the digitalisation of EIBA; and EIBA publications.

8.4.1. EIBA Governance

No major changes were introduced in the EIBA governance model, since it proved to be sound and adaptable. In fact, the distinction between the EIBA Chairs (meaning Chair and Vice-Chair), elected for three years, and the EIBA President, a rotating job assigned to future (and past) conference organisers, was essential to keep an appropriate balance between continuity and change. The annual conferences are still a key trait of **EIBA**. As Jonas Puck put it, they should be 'localized but consistent' (Puck, 2019): localised, in the sense that each location should have specific assets to ensure its attractiveness in winter; consistent, as each conference should abide to a set of guidelines, ensuring its high quality in academic and social terms.Therefore, the main developments regarding EIBA governance were observed in two fronts: the change of EIBA Chairs[10]; and a set of decisions aimed at developing transparent, standardised procedures regarding the election of the EIBA Chairs and the nomination/election of Board members.

The changes in EIBA Chairs were already briefly mentioned in the introduction to this chapter. They deserve, however, to be recalled here. In Brighton 2012, Philippe Gugler replaced Peter Buckley as EIBA Chair, after serving for two years as Vice-Chair. This provided him the insider knowledge about the organisation to enable a steady transition. He served for the triennium 2013–2015, being re-elected for 2016–2018, always with the support from José Plà-Barber as Vice-Chair. In Poznan 2018, the Chairs were replaced by a new team: Lucia Piscitello as Chair, and Jonas Puck, as Vice-Chair. Their first three-year term run between 2019 and 2021.[11] The new Chair team includes two long-standing and committed EIBA members. They had organised two very successful conferences that reached record participation: Milan-2017 and Vienna-2016, respectively. EIBA was keeping on the right track…

While no significant changes were introduced in the statutes, important decisions were taken to set up clear guidelines for the election or nomination of the Chair team and the Board members. With regard to the first, related to the re-election of Philippe Gugler and José Plà-Barber for another term, a set of procedures were established. These were summarised in a document entitled *Procedure regarding the nomination/election of the Chair and Vice-Chair of EIBA* (EIBA Board, 2017b).

Guidelines regarding the nomination of NRs were also clarified. The basic procedure is the outgoing NR to consult with the members of his/her country chapter on this regard, to identify and propose to the Board a suitable candidate. Only if there is more than one suitable candidate will a vote by secret ballot be deemed necessary. In this case, the EIBA Chair should be informed and, together with the Executive Secretary, will take charge of the process.

8.4.2. EIBA Strategy

The significant improvements achieved in the previous period, especially in the governance field and the solution of the debt problem, created conditions for a new strategic thrust. Less concerned with the ebb-and-flow of the EIBA conferences, EIBA Chair teams had more time and attention to devote to the longer-term issues regarding the development of the Academy.

In 2015 and 2016, a strategic reflection exercise was promoted by the EIBA Chairs on the basis of two documents: the *EIBA Chair Strategic Paper* (Gugler & Plà-Barber, 2015); and the PowerPoint presentation on EIBA strategy (Gugler & Plà-Barber, 2016). Recognising that 'EIBA's competitiveness has significantly increased over the past few years' (Gugler & Plà-Barber, 2015, p. 1), a set of actions was suggested to enhance the organisation. This included inter alia the promotion of young scholars and the strengthening of the Chair governance of EIBA. The strategy statement was anchored on the provision of the EIBA statutes that 'The aim of EIBA is to serve as the core communication network for disseminating information and promoting international exchange in the field of International Business' (Gugler & Plà-Barber, 2015, p. 4).

The programme presented in 2018 by the incoming Chair team (Lucia Piscitello and Jonas Puck) was built upon the above strategy headlines while including new strategic approaches and actions (Piscitello & Puck, 2018).

8.4.3. New Initiatives

Profiting from a brighter financial situation and in line with the strategic orientations mentioned above, a set of initiatives were taken to enhance EIBA's image, attractiveness, membership, internal communication, research quality and, in broad terms, EIBA's footprint in the IB landscape. Such initiatives may be clustered around six main axes: attracting new blood, namely PhD students and junior faculty; expanding EIBA's geographical scope; improving internal and external communication; launching smaller EIBA events; developing a sounder award policy; and addressing gender, diversity and sustainability issues.[12]

8.4.3.1. Attracting Younger Scholars

Since inception, EIBA has followed an open and welcoming attitude, aimed at attracting younger scholars, from different places. The decisions regarding the location of EIBA conferences were guided by this perspective of expanding the EIBA community, by venturing into less-tracked countries and by providing a gentle smile to newcomers. With this background into account, it is not surprising that an initiative was launched to positioning EIBA as the junior scholar-friendly academy, following a proposal presented in 2013 by Claude Obadia and Dorota Piaskowska.

8.4.3.2. Expanding EIBA's Geographical Scope

Since the late 1980s, EIBA has followed a committed policy to attract members from CEE countries. This has been a sustained endeavour throughout the most recent periods of EIBA history. The convening of EIBA conferences in these countries (Warsaw-1994, Ljubljana-2004, Tallinn-2008 and Bucharest-2011), though with distinct results in terms of chapter size and longevity.

In 2013–2020, only one conference (Poznan-2018) was held in CEE countries. In spite of this, the commitment towards such countries continued to be envisaged as a key objective for EIBA. A taskforce on membership enlargement, chaired by Andrea Jaklic, then the NR for Slovenia and one of the enthusiasts to promote IB in those countries, was created. Later, an explicit 'EIBA goes East strategy' was adopted in 2016, which included inter alia the EIBA-Workshops. These were intended 'to offer the opportunity to IB scholars located in these countries or regions to gather and form geographical communities within the greater EIBA family' (EIBA Board, 2017a, p. 21). The first EIBA-W was held in October 2016 in Budapest, under the *motto* 'MNEs in the CEE region – Factors of competitiveness'. The second, dealing with 'Competitiveness of firms and locations in the digital age', was also in Budapest in March 2018. The third was held in Prague in May 2019. In the same vein, it was decided to create new EIBA chapters in the Czech Republic, Hungary and Russia. However, except for Russia, their membership never exceeded five members. In contrast, membership in Poland significantly increased. Furthermore, as it will be reported in detail in the membership sub-section, EIBA membership also expanded in several large countries outside Europe, such as Brazil and Japan.

8.4.3.3. Improving Internal and External Communication
In the previous period, thanks to the initiative of Dorota Piaskowska, EIBA started to be promoted through social media, namely through LinkedIn. However, activity on this field has been limited. There was a perception that more needed to be done with regard to internal and external communication. Therefore, in line with the strategic thrust of strengthening EIBA Board members' roles, Kristin Brandl (NR for Canada) and Ulrike Mayhofer (NR for France) were nominated responsible for Internal and External relations, respectively.

A final reference is due to the change of the EIBA logo. As mentioned in Chapter 6, the existing logo was almost 20 years old, dating back to 1996. Therefore, a decision was taken to redesign the EIBA logo to make it more adapted to 2010s. The green colour was obviously kept, as the colour of EIBA. The new logo is presented on Fig. 13.

8.4.3.4. Launching Smaller EIBA Events
Besides the EIBA-Ws, mostly aimed at promoting EIBA at the IB academic communities in CEE countries, and the PDWs, other initiatives were taken, in furtherance of the strategic programme presented by the new EIBA Chairs. At the Spring Board meeting in Leeds, a task force was established, with the mandate to develop 'a holistic strategy that covers and structures all relevant EIBA events' (EIBA Board, 2019a, p. 10). The first proposal for a Summer School and a potential partnership with EIASM to grant ECTS credits were discussed. On the basis of the report of the taskforce, a first proposal regarding the 'EIBA event

Fig. 13. The New EIBA Logo. *Source*: EIBA website.

portfolio' was presented by Jonas Puch, EIBA's Vice-Chair, at the December Board meeting in Leeds.

In 2019, an EIBA Summer School task force was established with the mandate of preparing a detailed business model to be presented to the Spring Board meeting of 2020. The emergence of the COVID-19 pandemic led to the postponing of the initiative. But the idea was still being developed and improved. Therefore, the first Summer School was to be held in Lake of Como, organised by Politecnico di Milano, in 25–29 July 2022, under the leadership of Lucia Piscitello. The theme was 'Research methods for traditional and emerging themes in IB: Navigating the complexities of the digital age' and the faculty included several EIBA members, such as John Cantwell, Bo Nielsen, Torben Peddersen and Catherine Welch. After this, another Summer School was held in Santander (Spain) in 2023.

8.4.3.5. Developing a Sounder Award Policy

EIBA awards have emerged on an ad hoc basis, very much influenced by the emergence of funding for highlighting the best papers in specific fields, often sponsored by IB journals. The need to set up a coherent policy on this regard became clearer after the decision, taken in 2014, to honour Danny Van Den Bulcke's memory with the homonym award, assigned to the best paper of each EIBA conference. After a first report on the issue, prepared by Niina Nummela, that included an e-consultation of the Board, a committee was nominated to further develop the awards policy.

8.4.3.6. Addressing Gender, Diversity and Sustainability Issues

The aspects related to gender balance and diversity have been on the EIBA agenda since the early 2000s, though mostly in a tacit form. The gender issue was explicitly addressed in point 3.4 of the *EIBA Chair Strategic Paper*). This suggested the nomination of a head of 'EIBA gender initiatives', with the mandate to be 'responsible for the whole spectrum of EIBA policy and action having an impact on this issue' (Gugler & Plà-Barber, 2015, p. 10). The theme was highlighted again in the programme presented by the incoming Chairs in 2018 (Piscitello & Puck, 2018), stressing the need to nominate a coordinator for the actions to be taken in this field. This turned into reality, and Dana Minbaeva was nominated. A document entitled *EIBA Inclusion Guidelines*, written by Dana Minbaeva and Grazia Santangelo, established a set of eight points to be addressed by the organisers of future EIBA conferences, 'in order to make them more inclusive and balanced in terms of social group diversity' (Minbaeva & Santangelo, 2018b).

EIBA had already addressed sustainability issues. In fact, the theme of EIBA Brighton-2012 was 'International Business and Sustainable Development'. However, this was not really translated into organisational practice. When Valentina De Marchi became a Board member (as NR for Italy), in 2019, she expressed her surprise to find 'that EIBA had no institutional approach for making its events greener and more sustainable' (EIBA Board, 2019a, p. 13). This led to the setting up of a task force on this theme. The report of this task force, entitled *'Greening EIBA' – Proposal for Discussion*, was presented and discussed at the December Board meeting in Leeds (De Marchi, Muller & Alon, 2019). The recommendations were approved in 2020 by the Board and included in the *EIBA Conference Guidelines*. They were strictly followed especially in the EIBA 2022 conference, held in Oslo and organised by Birgitte Grøgaard. Interestingly, its theme was sustainability: *Walking the talk? Transitioning towards a sustainable world.*

8.4.4. Enhancing EIBA Conferences' Attractiveness and Quality Standards

While EIBA has endeavoured to promote shorter IB events to reduce the dependency on the annual conferences, efforts have been pursued to increase the overall EIBA conferences' standards. As mentioned above, the *motto* 'localized but consistent', suggested by Jonas Puck, nicely captures the increasing need to combine location attractiveness, in the wider context of Europe's diversity, with high-quality standards. This has been done through three interrelated approaches. These will be addressed in chronological order, although they are clearly intertwined.

There has been a continuous updating and upgrading of *EIBA Conference Guidelines*. In 2014, at the light of his experience with the EIBA Brighton Conference, Roger Strange wrote a new version of the *Guidelines*. Since 2014, every EIBA President, without exception, has updated the *Guidelines*, on the basis of his/her experience. They cover all the relevant aspects related to EIBA conference organisation and management, throughout the various phases of pre-conference issues (budgeting, promotion, conference design, paper selection and structuring the programme), running the conference, and post-conference activities and duties. They also provide a longitudinal perspective of relevant information regarding previous initiatives and conference attendance, for instance.

As pointed out above, one of the main thrusts of EIBA Chairs over the period under analysis has been to promote the design of consistent, standardised procedures for key aspects of EIBA management. This was already exemplified in the case of inclusion and sustainability, as mentioned in the previous section. The guidelines approved by the Board on these issues were set out in the *Guidelines* for both the sake of consistency and helping future conference organisers.

Another example concerns the decision regarding an important issue in paper selection and programme design: the 'rule of three'. This was discussed at the 2015 Spring Board meeting due to the initiative of Rian Drogendijk, who had organised EIBA Uppsala-2014. A decision was taken to adopt the 'rule of three': 3 is the maximum number of paper submissions/presentations per author. It was also decided to document this policy in the Guidelines (EIBA Board, 2015a).

The launching of calls for proposals regarding future EIBA conferences was another important step in two directions: first, the formalisation of EIBA procedures; and, second, to enable sounder decisions regarding conference location, by assessing location attractiveness and organising team's credibility and capabilities.

8.4.5. The EIBA Board

In spite of the very successful changes introduced in EIBA governance structures, mentioned in 8.4.1 above, the EIBA Board has kept its role as EIBA's key decision-making body. The rules established for EIBA Board members' tenure (three-years renewable for another term) were essential to ensure a continuous circulation of new ideas. As we have done in earlier chapters, information about the Board membership for 2013–2020 is provided in Tables 7A and 7B.

Lucia Piscitello, who had been responsible for the very successful EIBA Milan-2017, replaced Philippe Gugler as EIBA Chair. With the support of Jonas Puck, convenor of another excellent EIBA conference, she was to manage EIBA for two 3-year terms, in which the Academy achieved further growth, in spite of the challenges raised by the COVID-19 pandemic.

A look at the tables shows how the procedures regarding the terms of the Chair and Vice-Chair and of most NRs as well as the rotation of EIBA Presidents, in charge of conference organisation, have been tightly followed. The majority of NRs have been re-elected for another three-year term. As mentioned above, this steady procedure was subject to an exceptional and unanticipated change in 2020–2021, due to the emergence of the COVID-19 pandemic.

The 2020 EIBA President, Isabel Álvarez, kept her position for two years, as she has been in charge of the 2021 conference in Madrid that was still influenced by international health restrictions and the fear of contagion. By the same token, Birgitte Grøgaard has also served as President-Elect for two years, before organising EIBA Oslo-2022.

A longitudinal analysis of both tables shows how the country scope changed in 2013–2020. The number of countries with NRs in the Board increased from 25 for 2012 to 28 for 2020. As mentioned above, four additional countries became represented at the EIBA Board: the Czech Republic, Hungary, Japan and Russia.[13] In contrast, Romania has left the Board. These developments show that EIBA has continued to its expansion, with new chapters in Europe, while expanding its chapters in large countries elsewhere, such as the US, Canada, Brazil, Japan and Australia.

A final reference concerns the increase in the *ex-officio* members of the Board, to include the editor(s) of the *EIBAzine*, the EIBA newsletter launched by Danny Van Den Bulcke in 2004. This was envisaged as a way to foster the coordination between *EIBAzine* editorial policy and the Board general orientations. Recognising the need for a single, coordinated EIBA communication policy, especially with regard to social media, a Communications officer was nominated, becoming also a Board member.

8.4.6. EIBA Membership

Our readers are already acquainted with the references to the ups-and-downs in the evolution of EIBA membership. The period under analysis was no exception to this. In contrast to 1996–2002, when the time series was influenced by a path-breaking event – the change in the collection of membership fees as a result of the teaming-up with *IBR*– this time the path-breaking event was exogenous: the COVID-19 pandemic. Its effects were felt in 2020 and 2021.

Table 7A. Composition of the EIBA Board (2013–2016).

Officers	2013	2014	2015	2016
Chair	Philippe Gugler	Philippe Gugler	Philippe Gugler	Philippe Gugler
Vice-Chair	José Plá_Barber	José Plá_Barber	José Plá_Barber	José Plá_Barber
President	Sarianna Lundan	Rian Drogendijk	Jorge Carneiro	Jonas Puck
Past President	Roger Strange	Sarianna Lundan	Rian Drogendijk	Jorge Carneiro
President Elect	Rian Drogendijk	Jorge Carneiro	Jonas Puck	Lucia Piscitello
Executive Secret.	Enne Kannel	Enne Kannel	Enne Kannel	Enne Kannel
Australia	Catherine Welch	Catherine Welch	Catherine Welch	Catherine Welch
Austria	Tina Ambos	Jonas Puck	Jonas Puck	Jonas Puck
Belgium	Filip De Beule	Leo Sleuwaegen	Leo Sleuwaegen	Leo Sleuwaegen
Brazil	Jorge Carneiro	Jorge Carneiro	Jorge Carneiro	Jorge Carneiro
Canada	Chang Hoon Oh	Chang Hoon Oh	Chang Hoon Oh	Chang Hoon Oh
Denmark	Jens Gammelgaard	Jens Gammelgaard	Jens Gammelgaard	Jens Gammelgaard
Estonia	Enn Listra	Tiia Vissak	Tiia Vissak	Tiia Vissak
Finland	Niina Nummela	Niina Nummela	Niina Nummela	Niina Nummela
France	Claude Obadia	Claude Obadia	Claude Obadia	Claude Obadia
Germany	Stefan Schmid	Stefan Schmid	Stefan Schmid	Stefan Schmid
Greece	Pavlos Dimitratos	Pavlos Dimitratos	Pavlos Dimitratos	Constantina Kottaridi
Ireland	Dorota Piaskowska	Dorota Piaskowska	Dorota Piaskowska	Dorota Piaskowska

Table 7A. *(Continued)*

Officers	2013	2014	2015	2016
Israel	Orly Yeheskel	Orly Yeheskel	Orly Yeheskel	Orly Yeheskel
Italy	Grazia Santangelo	Grazia Santangelo	Lucia Piscitello	Lucia Piscitello
Japan		Chie Iguchi	Chie Iguchi	Chie Iguchi
Netherlands	Rob van Tulder	Rob van Tulder	Rob van Tulder	Rob van Tulder
Norway	Trond Randoy	Trond Randoy	Trond Randoy	Ilan Alon
Poland	Marian Gorynia	Marian Gorynia	Marian Gorynia	Barbara Jankowska
Portugal	Ana Teresa T.-Lehman	Susana Costa e Silva	Susana Costa e Silva	Susana Costa e Silva
Romania	Liviu Voinea	—	—	—
Slovenia	Andreja Jaklic	Andreja Jaklic	Andreja Jaklic	Andreja Jaklic
Spain	José Plà-Barber	José Plà-Barber	José Plà-Barber	Joaquin Alegre
Sweden	Rian Drogendijk	Rian Drogendijk	Lena Zander	Lena Zander
Switzerland	Björn Ambos	Björn Ambos	Björn Ambos	Dirk Morschett
UK	Roger Strange	Roger Strange	Roger Strange	Roger Strange
US	Ronaldo Parente	Ronaldo Parente	Ronaldo Parente	Ronaldo Parente
Ex-Officio				
EIBA Fellows Dean	Francesca S. Randaccio	Francesca S. Randaccio	Francesca S. Randaccio	John Cantwell
Editor *IBR*	Pervez Ghauri	Pervez Ghauri	Pervez Ghauri	Pervez Ghauri
Editor *EIBAzine*		Ana Teresa T.-Lehman	Ana Teresa T.-Lehman	Ana Teresa T.-Lehman

Table 7B. Composition of the EIBA Board (2017–2020).

Officers	2017	2018	2019	2020
Chair	Philippe Gugler	Philippe Gugler	Lucia Piscitello	Lucia Piscitello
Vice-Chair	José Plà_Barber	José Plà_Barber	Jonas Puck	Jonas Puck
President	Lucia Piscitello	Barbara Jankowska	Timothy Devinney	Isabel Álvarez
Past President	Jonas Puck	Lucia Piscitello	Barbara Jankowska	Timothy Devinney
President Elect	Barbara Jankowska	Timothy Devinney	Isabel Álvarez	Birgitte Grogaard
Executive Secret.	Enne Kannel	Enne Kannel	Enne Kannel	Enne Kannel
Australia	Catherine Welch	—	Bo Nielsen	Bo Nielsen
Austria	Jonas Puck	Jonas Puck	Desislava Dikova	Desislava Dikova
Belgium	Leo Sleuwaegen	Leo Sleuwaegen	Leo Sleuwaegen	Leo Sleuwaegen
Brazil	Erika Kovacs	Erika Kovacs	Erika Kovacs	Erika Kovacs
Canada	Chang Hoon Oh	Kristin Brandl	Kristin Brandl	Kristin Brandl
Czech Republic	Radek Čajka	Radek Čajka	Radek Čajka	Radek Čajka
Denmark	Jens Gammelgaard	Dana Minbaeva	Dana Minbaeva	Dana Minbaeva
Estonia	Tiia Vissak	Tiia Vissak	Tiia Vissak	Priit Vahter
Finland	Sami Saarenketo	Sami Saarenketo	Sami Saarenketo	Sami Saarenketo
France	Ulrike Mayrhofer	Ulrike Mayrhofer	Ulrike Mayrhofer	Ulrike Mayrhofer
Germany	Stefan Schmid	Stefan Schmid	Joachim Wolf	Joachim Wolf
Greece	Constantina Kottaridi	Constantina Kottaridi	Constantina Kottaridi	Constantina Kottaridi
Hungary	Erzsébet Czakó	Erzsébet Czakó	Erzsébet Czakó	Erzsébet Czakó
Ireland	Dorota Piaskowska	Josephine Igoe	Josephine Igoe	Josephine Igoe

Table 7B. (*Continued*)

Officers	2017	2018	2019	2020
Israel	Orly Yeheskel	Tamar Almor	Tamar Almor	Tamar Almor
Italy	Lucia Piscitello	Lucia Piscitello	Valentina De Marchi	Valentina De Marchi
Japan	Chie Iguchi	Chie Iguchi	Chie Iguchi	Chitose Furukawa
Netherlands	Alan Muller	Alan Muller	Alan Muller	Alan Muller
Norway	Ilan Alon	Ilan Alon	Ilan Alon	Ilan Alon
Poland	Barbara Jankowska	Barbara Jankowska	Barbara Jankowska	Barbara Jankowska
Portugal	Susana Costa e Silva	Susana Costa e Silva	Susana Costa e Silva	Vitor Corado Simões
Russia	Andrei Panibratov	Andrei Panibratov	Andrei Panibratov	Andrei Panibratov
Slovenia	Anze Burger	Anze Burger	Anze Burger	Anze Burger
Spain	Joaquin Alegre	Joaquin Alegre	Cristina Villar	Cristina Villar
Sweden	Lena Zander	Lena Zander	Lena Zander	Lena Zander
Switzerland	Dirk Morschett	Dirk Morschett	Dirk Morschett	Dirk Morschett
UK	Roger Strange	Timothy Devinney	Timothy Devinney	Timothy Devinney
US	Sumit Kundu	Sumit Kundu	Sumit Kundu	Sumit Kundu
Ex-Officio				
EIBA Fellows Dean	John Cantwell	John Cantwell	Juán José Durán	Juán José Durán
Editor *IBR*	Pervez Ghauri	Pervez Ghauri	Pervez Ghauri	Pervez Ghauri
Editor *EIBAzine*	Ana Teresa T.-Lehman	(Philippe Gugler)	J.Cantwell/B.Jankowska	J.Cantwell/B.Jankowska
Commun. Officer	Tilo Halaszovich	Tilo Halaszovich	Tilo Halaszovich	Tilo Halaszovich

Taking the pandemic aside and adopting a general perspective, it is important to remind that EIBA membership changes are to a large extent due to the combination of two factors, both related to the location of the EIBA conference: its attractiveness per se; and the size of the IB research groups in the country concerned or in nearby places. This happened again over 2013–2020. EIBA membership varied from a minimum of 456 (for 2019) and a maximum of 664 (for 2017). A closer look at the figures along the 2013–2020 period shows that membership dropped below 500 for two years (2016 and 2019), but exceeded 600 for three years (2013,[14] 2017 and 2018).

Taking a longer-term perspective, the trend towards increasing membership kept its momentum. This is confirmed by the analysis of the average membership figures for the last three periods of the history of EIBA: around 250 for 1996–2002; 400 for 2003–2012; and above 550 for 2013–2020. The message is that EIBA has achieved a consistent increase in membership. Should the focus be put on the period under analysis, the conclusion is similar, since average membership grew from 533, for the first quadrennium (2013–2016), to 573, for the second (2017–2020). Such figures confirm that EIBA is increasingly stable and attractive for IB scholars.

We now turn to a country-wise analysis, based on Fig. 14. The top-five includes, by descending order, the following countries: UK, as undisputed leader, Germany, Finland, Sweden and Brazil. It is interesting to remark that, to a large extent due to Rio de Janeiro-2015, Brasil reached the top-five, while the US dropped from there.

A close analysis of EIBA membership in 2013–2020 leads to eight main conclusions. First: there has been an increasing membership trend, due to a large extent to EIBA conferences' attractiveness and the initiatives taken to stimulate the participation of doctoral students. Second: non-European countries – especially Brazil, Australia and Japan – have experienced consistent membership increases; there are signs that the decline of US membership might be witnessing a reversal. Third: there is a significant number of EU countries with steady and committed EIBA teams. Fourth: Poland is a very good example of the development of a consistent EIBA chapter, although the same has not happened for other Central and Eastern European countries, such as the Czech Republic and Hungary. Fifth: the Nordic countries, especially Sweden and Finland, continue to show a significant attachment to EIBA, expressed in increases in both membership and percentage shares. Sixth: German membership experienced a noticeable growth in 2013–2020, although it has been powered by the convening of EIBA conferences in two German-speaking countries. Seventh: the UK keeps the undisputed lead as the main contributor to the EIBA community, increasing its share in total membership to more than 14%, though this figure is influenced by recent EIBA conferences held in Brighton and Leeds. Eight: statistical evidence shows that location attractiveness continues to play an important role in contributing to increase EIBA membership, a feature that demands further efforts to launch initiatives, other than the annual conference, that might stimulate IB communities as well as doctoral students worldwide to join EIBA.

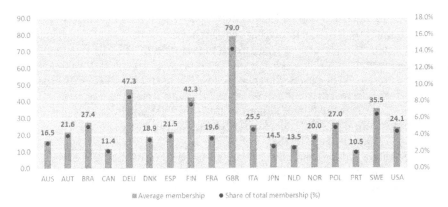

Fig. 14. EIBA Membership per Country (2013–2020). *Source*: EIBA website.
Note: The figure includes those countries with at least 2% of total average
membership in the period concerned.

8.4.7. Gender Diversity

The number and the role of women in EIBA has continued to increase in 2013–
2020, both in terms of membership share and on what concerns the roles played
in the Academy. Over this period, women have participated as conference organisers or co-organisers in six events out of eight. More importantly, Lucia Piscitello
served as EIBA Chair and Francesca Sanna-Randaccio as Dean of the Fellows.[15]
A look at Fig. 15 shows how the share of female membership experienced a sound
increase to reach about 45% of total in 2019 and 2020.

The conclusion from this information is that a gender balance is about to
be achieved in EIBA. In less than 50 years, EIBA was able to change from a
men's club to an organisation in which women play key roles, contributing to our
Academy on an equal footing. Many women have played key roles in the transformation of EIBA into the sound, open and inclusive body it is today.

8.4.8. EIBA Financial Situation

In the previous chapter it was shown that, as a result of the negotiation of the
debt towards EIASM and the ensuing payment, EIBA has been able to get rid of
its liabilities. In the context of a steady positive financial performance that goes
back to the late 1990s and the increasing membership trend, this period is characterised by financial stability and successive surpluses.

A closer look at the income and expenses accounts for 2013–2020 enables the
identification of drivers of continuity together with some factors of change, related
to both specific aspects related to the EIBA conferences and to EIBA initiatives.
Obviously, the main item on the income part corresponds to membership fees.
With regard to expenditures, the two main items were, as in the previous period,
the contributions to Elsevier, in connection with *IBR* (54% of total expenditures,
below the 60% recorded for the 2003–2012) and EIASM (26%). With regard to
the later, following an agreement between both organisations, it increased from

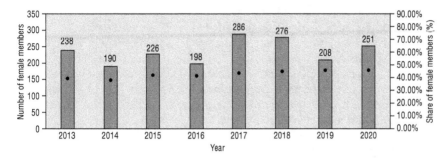

Fig. 15.   Evolution of EIBA Membership by Gender (2013–2020).

€13,000 to €15,000 for 2014–2016, to record a very moderate average growth since then (around 2% per year). Together, the share of these two items decreased from around 88% for 2002–2013 to 80% for 2013–2020. This means that it was possible to manage a wider budget to launch initiatives considered to be relevant to EIBA, from the Workshops or the launch of the DVDB Best Paper Prize[16] to the project on the history of EIBA. Combining sound risk management approaches with initiatives to forge ahead, the top managers of EIBA, with the support from the Board and all the EIBA community, have been able to make EIBA an increasingly relevant orgainisation for IB scholars worldwide.

8.4.9. Relationships with Other Organisations

Over this period, relationships with other organisations were much less tense than they have been in the early 2000s, when a solution had to be found to solve the long-term accumulated debt to EIASM, and the *Buckley compromise* was achieved to reach a solution for the conflict with AIB (see Chapter 7). The presentation will be structured in three axes, regarding AIB, EURAM and UNCTAD. Cooperation was also established with Australia and New Zealand International Business Academy (ANZIBA).

With regard to the AIB, two aspects deserve a mention. First, the EIBA Board has been kept informed about the developments of the recently established Central and Eastern Europe chapter (AIB-CEE); this was launched by the initiative of EIBA members, namely Andreja Jaklic. AIB-CEE conferences were held from 2014 onwards, the first taking place in Budapest (Hungary), addressing the theme 'Competitiveness of the CEE Region in the Global Economy'. Second, and more importantly, EIBA pursued its responsibility for hosting the annual meetings of AIB-Western Europe (AIB-WE). There were no major troubles on this regard. This positive mood was promoted by the fact that José Plà-Barber, the President of AIB-WE, was simultaneously the Vice-Chair of EIBA between 2013 and 2018. In this period, JIBS PDWs and later JIBP PDWs were held at EIBA conferences, and a set of AIB-WE Summer Schools took place in Valencia. The situation changed when José Plà-Barber stepped down from the Presidency of AIB-WE at the end of 2018. The EIBA Board was informed about AIB's plans to rejuvenate and change its AIB-WE chapter as distinct from EIBA. A transition team, including several long-term EIBA members, was established to further the above objective.

Relationships with EURAM have been pursued in a friendly mood. EIBA Chair representatives have participated in EURAM conferences. Dorota Piaskowska was involved, as EIBA representative, in the development, under EURAM, of a vision of responsible science (Vision 2030). The positive relationships between the organisations led to a draft of a Memorandum of Understanding, involving a reciprocal joint membership scheme for EURAM and EIBA members, at a reduced rate. However, this did not go further up to 2020, since the discussion at the EIBA Board has not been conclusive.

Another cooperation vector, cherished by both EIBA Chair teams, was with international organisations, especially UNCTAD. EIBA acted as organisational partner of the World Investment Forum. EIBA was involved in a session entitled 'Shaping a new policy research agenda', in cooperation with the Graduate Institute, Geneva, AIB and the Society of International Economy and Law (SIEL). Cooperation with UNCTAD was pursued along the whole period, with several UNCTAD high executives, namely James Zhan, often actively participating at EIBA conferences.

8.4.10. Further Digitalisation of EIBA

The digitalisation of EIBA was pursued, along four main axes: acquisition of the domain *eiba.org*; renewal of the EIBA website; promotion of EIBA through social media; and the increased digitalisation of EIBA conferences.

In 2015, the opportunity emerged for EIBA to purchase the domain *eiba.org*. As a result of this, it was decided to move to the domain *eiba.org* only and allow the (old) domain *eiba-online.org* to lapse in 2016. In the same vein, it was agreed that future EIBA conferences URLs will be consolidated into the new domain (EIBA Board, 2015a).

The EIBA website was renewed to become more user-friendly. In this process the information available was revised, adopting the new EIBA logo and further information was made available. This included an easier access structure, facilitating search and the identification of relevant information. The *EIBAzine* issues, since 2004, may also be accessed at the website. Two relevant additions were the sets of photos from all EIBA conferences, since 2004, and the access to the EIBA History project website, in which photos from older conferences are stored as well as the record of the 2020 online EIBA History session featuring the EIBA 'founding fathers' still alive at the time.

EIBA conferences became increasingly digitalised. The decision to move to the ConfTool platform, taken by Jonas Puck for the Vienna-2016 conference, proved to be very successful. While a proper exploration of the multiple ConfTool facilities demands a significant investment in time, it provided an excellent tool to manage a significant part of the main conference organisation tasks, from paper selection and programme design to the management of conference registration (with the exception of payments). Since Milan-2017, a conference app was made available, facilitating the life of conference participants, namely the process of session selection and room location. In Poznan-2018, a dedicated mobile app (Conference4me) was used to communicate with participants and promote specific events, as it has been done with the EIBA History quizes.

8.4.11. EIBA Publications

In this period, EIBA publication portfolio continued to be anchored in three main publications: *IBR, EIBAzine* and *PIBR*.[17] For distinct reasons, all have faced challenges, but the final outcome is positive, with an overall improvement of publications policy, and better conditions for EIBA members to have access to the publications' contents.

8.4.11.1. International Business Review

The troubled relationship with Elsevier regarding *IBR* continued over this period. The feeling of lack of EIBA's ownership regarding *IBR* pursued, and Elsevier's arrogance towards EIBA made such feeling more poignant. EIBA's perception was that Elsevier was not committed enough to the Academy and its membership, and envisaged the relationship as a pure financial deal. However, EIBA had already made sunk investments that were to a large extent irreversible, not being amenable to an alternative course of action, viz., moving to another publisher.

A closer look shows that three stages may be identified. By 2012–2013 relationships improved, following the agreement signed in 2012 (see Chapter 7). Then, a deterioration came after Elsevier's proposals regarding IBR's online access for EIBA members and an 8% increase in the fee for 2016–2020. In 2014, the EIBA Board decided to continue with the print option in the conditions foreseen in the present contract. Over 2016, Elsevier did not react to EIBA's approaches. In view of this, the Board decided to mandate the EIBA Chair (Philippe Gugler) and the editor of *IBR* (Pervez Ghauri) 'to contact Elsevier with a formal list of discussion points to lobby for more and better options for the next contract' (EIBA Board, 2017a, p. 10). Such meeting was inconclusive, as Elsevier had not been flexible to move to an online version without extra costs. The third stage started with the nomination of a new Elsevier representative that was more sympathetic to EIBA's concerns. This led to a renewal of the agreement for 2021–2022 under changed conditions: EIBA eschewed the delivery of printed copies,[18] EIBA members having online access to *IBR*. This became available at the price suggested by EIBA: €10,000 per year for 500 members with a small additional for 100 additional members, enabling EIBA to save about €80,000 per year.

8.4.11.2. EIBAzine

Over this period, the two-yearly issues of *EIBAzine* (Spring and Fall) continued to be published uninterruptedly, in spite of the changes in the editorial team. This was mostly due to the efforts of the editors and the proficient editorial support from EIBA's Executive Secretary. Filip De Beule carried on as editor until the Spring 2013 issue. He was replaced by Ana Teresa Tavares-Lehman. Her term was shorter than expected, because she was appointed Secretary of State for Industry in Portugal in July 2017. As a result of this, Philippe Gugler, then EIBA Chair, stepped up as *ad interim* Editor for three issues. With the new EIBA Chairs team, Barbara Jankowska and John Cantwell were nominated editors, from issue n° 24 onwards. The new editors slightly changed the title to *EIBAzine – International Business Perspectives* (*EIBAzine-IBP*) to better convey their thrust. They raised three key questions for positioning the publication with regard to potential competitors:

(i) How to develop EIBazine-ibp for the future? (ii) How to encourage authors to contribute? (iii) How to position it relative to *AIB Insights*?

8.4.11.3. PIBR

The relationships with Emerald, the publisher of *PIBR*, were much less troubled. As a result of the inter-actions held, EIBA members started, as of 2017, to have online access to the *PIBR* series. This entailed an additional cost of around €20 per EIBA member. According to the Board decision taken at the December meeting in 2015, such additional amount was translated into a similar increase in membership fees (EIBA Board, 2015b). Later, in 2020, it was agreed that EIBA members would have access to four journals published by Emerald (*European Business Review, Competitiveness Review, International Marketing Review*, and *International Journal of Emerging Markets*).

As mentioned in Chapter 7, Alain Verbeke and Rob Van Tulder were the editors of PIBR. From 2013 onwards, most PIBR volumes were dedicated to outstanding IB scholars. The full list of PIBR volumes, with a reference to their respective EIBA conferences, is provided in Table 8.

Table 8.   Summary of *PIBR* Volumes.

Year of Conference	PIBR Volume Title	Editors	Year of Publication
2013	Multinational Enterprises, Markets and Institutional Diversity (in honour of Danny Vasn Den Bulcke)	Alain Verbeke, Rob Van Tulder and Sarianna Lundan	2014
2014	The Future of Global Organizing	Alain Verbeke, Rob Van Tulder and Rian Drogendijk	2015
2015	The Challenge of BRIC Multinationals	Alain Verbeke, Rob Van Tulder, Jorge Carneiro and Maria Alejandra Gonzalez-Perez	2016
2016	Distance in International Business: Concept, Cost and Value (in honour of Rosalie Tung)	Alain Verbeke, Rob Van Tulder and Jonas Puck	2017
2017	International Business in the Information and Digital Age (in honour of Lorraine Eden)	Alain Verbeke, Rob Van Tulder and Lucia Piscitello	2018
2018	International Business in a VUCA World: The Changing Role of States and Firms (in honour of Peter Buckley)	Alain Verbeke, Rob Van Tulder and Barbara Jankowska	2019
2019	The Multiple Dimensions of Institutional Complexity in International Business Research (in honour of Eleanor Westney)	Alain Verbeke, Rob Van Tulder, Elisabeth Rose and Yingqi Wei	2021
2020	International Business in Times of Crisis (in honour of Geoffrey Jones)	Alain Verbeke, Rob Van Tulder Lucia Piscitello and Jonas Puck	2022

Source: Developed by the authors, based on https://books.emeraldinsight.com/page/series-detail/progress-in-international-business-research/

8.5. THE EIBA FELLOWS

The EIBA Fellows have kept and expanded their activities, always with a view to enhance the contribution of EIBA to IB research and scholarship. In this section we will present a summary of the main activities carried out by the Fellows, structured in a way similar to the one followed in the previous chapter: officers and nomination of Fellows; changes to the constitution; and relevant initiatives, followed by a brief conclusion.

8.5.1. Officers and Nomination of New Fellows

Before delving into the presentation of the officers and the new Fellows, a deeply emotional reference is due to three outstanding EIBA Fellows who passed away over the period under analysis: Danny Van Den Bulcke, Reijo Luostarinen and Seev Hirsch.[19] The two latter were, together with John Dunning and John Cantwell, among the four founding Fellows.

It was a shock for all of us to learn, in Bremen-2013, that Danny was seriously ill. He had been for many years the 'soul' of EIBA. He has dedicated a significant part of his life to EIBA, always aiming at strengthening our Academy. With his warmth, friendship, strange stories, Gala Dinner speeches and, of course, his camera, he was known as Mr EIBA. Danny had completed his three-year term as Dean of the Fellows in 2012.

Less flamboyant, but no less important for EIBA was Reijo Luostarinen. He made relevant research contributions to firm internationalisation processes (see, for instance, Forsgren & Piekkari, 2018). EIBA's debt to him is very significant, as he was the organisational master, always aiming at finding new ways to make EIBA more agile and efficient. Reijo was also the 'dynamo' behind the change from Association to Academy and the establishment of the EIBA Fellows.

Seev Hirsch was the third Fellow to leave us in this period. He was the eldest Fellow, but he had always kept his mind active. Permanently in quest of relevant IB issues and conundrums, he has suggested several themes for discussion that became topics for EIBA Fellows Panels. As Buckley and Hashai (2020) underlined, his article 'An International Trade and Investment Theory of the Firm' was a seminal contribution to the development of IB theory. He also believed in the potential for economic cooperation between Israel and its Arab neighbours, especially with regard to distance-sensitive goods (Buckley & Hashai, 2020).

Turning now to the EIBA Fellows officers, it is important to recall that in 2013 the two EIBA Fellows officers were women: Francesca Sanna-Randaccio and Sarianna Lundan. Three Fellows have served as Dean of the EIBA Fellows over this period. The fist was Francesca Sanna-Randaccio, who was also the first woman to hold this role. John Cantwell, who was one of the founding Fellows, was the next Dean, serving between 2016 and 2018. He was replaced by Juán Durán, who was to keep the post until 2021. A summary of the main EIBA Fellows developments is provided in Table 9.

Table 9.   EIBA Fellows 2013–2020 – Officers, New
Fellows and Honorary Fellows

Year	Dean	Secretary-Treasurer	New Fellows	Honorary Fellows
2013	Francesca Sanna-Randaccio	Sarianna Lundan	None	None
2014	Francesca Sanna-Randaccio	Pervez Ghauri	Jorma Larimo and Philippe Gugler	None
2015	Francesca Sanna-Randaccio	Pervez Ghauri	Lucia Piscitello	José Rubens de la Rosa
2016	John Cantwell	Lucia Piscitello	Ana Teresa T.-Lehman and Torben Pedersen	Matti Alahuhta
2017	John Cantwell	Lucia Piscitello	Gabriel Benito and Grazia Santangelo	Reinhilde Veugelers
2018	John Cantwell	Lucia Piscitello	Ram Mudambi and Udo Zander	Jan Švejnar
2019	Juán Durán	Grazia Santangelo	Alain Verbeke and José Plà-Barber	Michael Storper
2020	Juán Durán (term to be completed in 2021)	Grazia Santangelo (term to be completed in 2021)	Tamar Almor and Timothy Devinney	None

Source: Built by the authors, on the basis of EIBA Fellows minutes
Note: New officers are elected in December of a given year. Although we know they may immediately start their functions, we assume here that their service as Dean or as Secretary-Treasurer starts in the next year, to avoid overlaps and make easier for the reader to follow the sequence of officers and the time of their duties.

As explained in Chapter 7, the upper limit of 20 Fellows provided by the constitution had been reached by 2012. For this reason, no new Fellows were elected in 2013. Only in 2014, after the constitutional change (see below), more Fellows joined the group. As shown in the table, between 2014 and 2020, 13 new Fellows were elected. They were the following (by chronological order): Jorma Larimo and Philippe Gugler, in 2014; Lucia Piscitello, in 2015; Ana Teresa Tavares-Lehman and Torben Pedersen, in 2016; Gabriel Benito and Grazia Santangelo, in 2017; Ram Mudambi and Udo Zander, in 2018; Alain Verbeke and José Plà-Barber, in 2019; and Tamar Almor and Timothy Devinney, in 2020. In contrast, three Fellows became inactive, since either they have not met the conditions provided by the constitution (payment of dues and attendance of at least one of the three last EIBA conferences) or have expressed their will to become inactive: John Hagedoorn, Lars-Gunnar Mattsson and Örjan Sölvell.

The nomination of Honorary Fellows was pursued. Every year, between 2015 and 2019, an Honorary Fellow was elected; in 2020, the intention was to nominate Manuel Conthe, former Chairman of the Spanish Stock Exchange Commission, but this was postponed for 2021, since the EIBA Madrid conference was not held in 2020. The names of the new Honorary Fellows are also provided in Table 9. In 2015 and 2016, they were businessmen: José Rubens de la Rosa, then CEO of *Marcopolo*, a Brazilian MNE in the bus transport industry; and Matti Alahuhta, former President and CEO of *Kone* (2005–2014), the Finnish elevator MNE, and former member of *Nokia*'s executive board (1993–2004). The latter three were academics: Reinhilde Veugelers is a full professor at KU Leuven, a senior fellow at the Bruegel think-tank, a CEPR Research Fellow, and a member of the Royal Flemish Academy of Belgium for Sciences; Jan Švejnar, full professor at the School of International and Public Affairs, Columbia University (New York, USA), who had also a relevant civic intervention, when he ran for election as President of the Czech Republic, in 2008; and Michael Storper, an expert on the relationship between globalisation and the growth and decline of regions throughout the World, who held several chairs in both the US and Europe (Centennial professor of Economic Geography at the London School of Economics [UK], professor of Regional and International Development in Urban Planning in the University of California at Los Angeles [USA], and affiliated with the *Centre de Sociologie des Organisations* at Sciences-Po [Paris, France]). All have delivered insightful and challenging presentation at EIBA Fellows Plenary sessions.

8.5.2. Changes to the Constitution and Internal Procedures

As a result of its work, the Commission on Constitutional Change suggested a solution to solve the bottleneck raised by constitutional provision to have a maximum of 20 Fellows that has been approved by the Fellows in secret ballot in 2013. The approach was similar to the one previously adopted by AIB: to establish an age ceiling for counting the 20 Fellows limit. Such ceiling was defined as 66 years. Later, in 2017, another change was introduced in the Fellows constitution, due to the initiative of Seev Hirsch – the introduction of the Emeritus member category.

While with no bearing on the constitution, another relevant procedural change introduced in this period concerned the regulation regarding the assignment of the previous EIBA LAA. At the Fellows' meeting in Milan in December 2017, it was acknowledged that it would be desirable to revisit and decide on a statement of criteria for this award, which was previously awarded only to John Dunning in Ljubljana in 2004. A clear set of rules were defined and accepted by the Fellows. It was made clear that the ELAA is given only in a truly exceptional case. For this reason, and in spite of the revised rules, the EIBA LAA was not awarded. It was only to be given later, in Lisbon-2023, to Klaus Macharzina, the second Dean of the EIBA Fellows (2007–2009) for his outstanding contributions to scholarship and European-based teaching and research in IB as well as to EIBA.

8.5.3. Relevant Initiatives

Over 2013–2020, the Fellows have continued and/or launched important initiatives to strengthen EIBA as well as to reinforcing the bonds between the EIBA Board and EIBA Fellows. The cooperation between both has been furthered, and the EIBA Fellows Plenary became a key event in the context of EIBA conferences.

Another initiative, taken in 2015 and warmly supported since inception by the EIBA Board, was the project on the History of EIBA. At the Fellows meeting in Rio de Janeiro an EIBA History Committee (Vítor Corado Simões, John Cantwell and Philippe Gugler) was nominated to carry out research aimed at collecting and diffusing relevant materials as well at writing a history of EIBA. This was envisaged as a collective endeavour, intended to mobilise the EIBA community. The first main task carried out was the interviews with the still alive EIBA 'founding fathers' (James Leontiades, Michel Ghertman, Lars-Gunnar Mattsson, Sylvain Plasschaert, José de la Torre and Pål Korsvold), available at the EIBA History website (https://history.eiba.org/). Several contributions about relevant EIBAians as well as EIBA's activities and awards were contributed by many EIBA members, and are also available at the website. This book is a result of such project. However, it does not encapsulate all the relevant information regarding the almost 50 years of EIBA's history. More information will be diffused through the EIBA History website, as a result of both of this project and the contributions from dedicated EIBAians. Even though the EIBA History project closes with this book, we do hope that it will still be kept alive as a result of multiple contributions from the EIBA community.

8.5.4. Conclusion

EIBA Fellows activities continued and strengthened over 2013–2020. Although three of the four 'founding fathers' have passed away (John Dunning, in 2009, Reijo Luostarinen, in 2017, and Seev Hirsch, in 2020), and Danny Van Den Bulcke is also no longer with us, the Fellows are increasingly active and contributing with new ideas for the strengthening of EIBA. As it happened before with EIBA itself, a younger generation of Fellows, mostly nominated in the 2010s is taking the lead and contributing to launch new initiatives and to forge ahead in cooperation with the EIBA Chairs and the whole EIBA community.

8.6. SUMMARY

This period is marked by a generational change at the top of EIBA. The organisational changes that took place in the previous period paved the way for a smooth transition from those who had been among EIBA pioneers or had joined the organisation in the early 1980s to a new cohort of younger scholars who became engaged with EIBA along the 1990s. As a result of such changes, the management of EIBA became more medium- to long-term-orientated, and less dependent on the successive annual conferences. Additional initiatives to entice membership, besides the conferences and *IBR*, were taken, namely the EIBA Workshops, especially addressed to young scholars, particularly from Central and Eastern Europe. EIBA strengthened its appeal as providing the best environment for PhD students and young IB researchers to socialise and deliver their papers. Additionally, EIBA has ventured in two ways that would not have been imagined at the turn of the 2010 decade: one by choice – holding an EIBA conference in Rio de Janeiro (Brazil); another by need – an online conference to respond the constraints raised by the COVID-19 pandemic. In contrast, all the other conferences, except one (Vienna-2016), were held in countries that were not new for EIBA (Germany, Sweden – a return to Uppsala – Italy, Poland and the UK).

Over this period several outstanding members of EIBA have left us. The passing away of Danny Van Den Bulcke, who had been EIBA's soul for many years, serving as EIBA chair and later as Dean of the Fellows, was an emotional blow for EIBA and for all those who had got accustomed to Danny's energy, speeches and camera. But, thanks to a sound governance system, EIBA was able to withstand this loss. Besides Danny, also Reijo Luostarinen and Seev Hirsch – both of whom were among the four founding EIBA Fellows – passed over. While they will no longer join us in EIBA conferences, they will be in our hearts forever.

The EIBA Fellows's membership experienced a significant growth, leading to a constitutional revision to provide a new meaning to the 20-member limit. Cooperation between the Fellows and the EIBA Board was pursued in a very constructive way. The Fellows Plenary became a key feature of EIBA conferences, addressing relevant present and future issues for IB research. For the first time ever, this period started and ended with women as Deans of the Fellows: Francesca Sanna-Randaccio and Sarianna Lundan, respectively.

In fact, women's participation in EIBA affairs increased further. Lucia Piscitello, elected EIBA Chair in December 2018, was the first woman to chair the Academy. Together with this, women took the lead in conference organisation in this period: leaving EIBA 2020 aside, since it has been so far the only EIBA not to be held in-person, four of the seven conferences in this period were organised by women: Sarianna Lundan in Bremen 2013; Rian Drogendijk in Uppsala 2014; Lucia Piscitello in Milan 2017; and Barbara Jankowska (with Małgorzata Bartosik-Purgat) in Poznan 2018. Simultanously, the trend towards gender balance in EIBA membership was pursued.

By December 2020, after providing an excellent response to the challenges raised by the COVID-19 pandemic, EIBA was confident about the future. It was prepared to address further challenges, from the launching of more initiatives, such as the Summer Schools, to sustainability and the 'greening' of EIBA.

NOTES

1. For a convergent, though slightly different view, see Tung, Zander and Fang (2023).
2. After public consultation, this led to the Regulation 2022/2560, of 14 December 2022 (European Commission, 2022).
3. A further follow-up study was published in 2024 (Cantwell & Zaman, 2024).
4. Also on this Rosa, Gugler and Verbeke (2020) updated Rugman and Verbeke (2004) for 2017, and confirmed that many large firms are still home-region oriented, although to a lesser extent than in the early 2000s.
5. An interesting discussion in this regard concerned the need for entry mode research, with Shaver (2013) questioning such a need, while Hennart and Slangen (2015) argued in the opposite direction.
6. This issue had been previously introduced by Benito et al. (2009) and Benito, Petersen and Welch (2012).
7. In the same vein, Gary Gereffi will be honoured as EIBA Honorary Fellow at the 2024 Helsinki Conference, commemorating EIBA's 50th anniversary.

8. Another theme, not mentioned here because most contributions emerged after 2020, concerns the effects of the pandemic on GVCs. In 2020, two contributions deserve a mention: Gereffi (2020) and Verbeke (2020).

9. When he was at the OECD Development Centre, Andrea Goldstein co-authored, with Lucia Piscitello, *Le multinazionale* (Goldstein & Piscitello, 2007), a book that analyses the multifaceted effects of multinationals on development.

10. The change in the composition of the Board and the decision to set up new chapters is also a governance feature but much less important than the election of the Chairs. Therefore, this is addressed in the present sub-section, while the former will be considered in Section 8.4.3, dealing with the EIBA Board.

11. They were re-elected for a second term, between 2022 and 2024, already beyond of the scope of this book.

12. Other initiatives, such as the EIBA History project that is at the inception of this book, are not considered.

13. The Russian chapter was short lived, as a result of the Russian invasion of Ukraine. Andrei Panibratov, the first NR for Russia, is now working in France.

14. This was due to the high level of participation at the EIBA 2012 in Brighton.

15. In the early 2020s, Lucia Piscitello and Sarianna Lundan served simultaneously for several years as EIBA Chair and Dean of the Fellows, respectively.

16. The Workshops will be addressed in the next section. The DVDB Best Paper Prize was mentioned previously. In Section 8.4.3.5 we also made reference to it in the context of the EIBA awards policy.

17. In April 2023 EIBA was to launch the *EIBA Bulletin*, mainly envisaged as a news-feed for EIBA members.

18. Individual EIBA members who wish to still receive printed copies can pay for this service under special conditions.

19. Besides them, another EIBA Fellow passed away more recently in 2022: Jorma Larimo.

CHAPTER 9

1974–2020 AND BEYOND: AN ASSESSMENT OF EIBA EVOLUTION AND AN AGENDA FOR THE FUTURE

This book has been intended to provide a history of EIBA by addressing the co-evolution between the development of the Academy, both as an organisation and a research community, and the IB context and the key features of IB research. EIBA is now a sound organisation, widely recognised by the IB community in Europe and elsewhere in the world. EIBA has come a long way since its inception, in the early 1970s, to the confident Academy it is today. EIBA's trajectory was to a large extent shaped by the commitment and effort of a dedicated set of people, men and women, but also by its relationships with other organisations and by its evolving context. This development of EIBA may be envisaged along two key inter-related vectors: the first embraces geopolitics, international economics and managerial decisions of MNEs and smaller players; the second corresponds to IB research issues and methods.

Our presentation of such co-evolution has taken a chronological approach, using time windows that basically corresponded to the various stages of EIBA's evolution. This final chapter provides an overall perspective on the path taken by EIBA and suggests an agenda for the future. It is structured in three sections. The first is intended to give the reader an overall assessment of EIBA evolution over the course of 45 years, in which we summarise the turning points and the chief tenets in EIBA's evolution. The second section revisits the paradox between a need to improve the structure of the annual conferences while overcoming the constraint imposed by having one-conference-a-year, which pervaded the history of EIBA; solving this contradiction required changes to the governance of EIBA.

The History of EIBA: A Tale of The Co-Evolution Between International Business
Issues and a Scholarly Community, 183–192
Copyright © 2025 by Vítor Corado Simões, John Cantwell and Philippe Gugler
Published under exclusive licence by Emerald Publishing Limited
doi:10.1108/978-1-83608-664-220241010

The third section identifies the key challenges ahead for EIBA as well as for IB research, and proposes an agenda to address them.

9.1. THE EVOLUTION OF EIBA (1974–2020)

EIBA's life has been marked by paradoxes and contradictions that emerged since inception. Anchored at EIASM, which had been established in 1971 with the support of Ford Foundation, EIBA was aimed at developing a European way of addressing IB issues, as distinct from the American one, that had provided the standard approach at the time. Yet, many of its founders had studied and researched in America. The discussion held in 1974, leading to the establishment of EIBA, was pervaded by this contradiction, with a small group contending that it should become the Continental Europe chapter of AIB, while the majority was in favour of a 'European way', while maintaining a continuous dialogue with AIB. Therefore, EIBA was created as a pan-European association, encompassing scholars from some specific European countries – especially France and Sweden, but also Belgium, Germany, Netherlands, Norway, Spain, Switzerland and the UK – but also from the US and Canada. Interestingly, in some of the early years the US had the biggest number of participants in EIBA. The first EIBA officers were Jim Leontiades (President), Michel Ghertman (organiser of the 1975 conference) and Lars-Gunnar Mattsson, organiser of the 1977 conference.

At a time when there was no internet, communication and information sharing were among the main objectives of EIBA. The need was felt to overcome national, inward-looking approaches and to identify common research interests; the fact that many scholars had got their PhDs on the other side of the Atlantic and the presence of colleagues from Canada and the US working in Europe, namely at INSEAD and EIASM, was highly relevant for cross-pollination. The launching of the *EIBA Newsletter*, together with a roster of EIBA members, in 1978, shortly after inception, illustrates the concern with the circulation of information. This concern persisted throughout EIBA's life, in various guises, from the *EIBA Newsletter* to the present *EIBAzine*. Of course, innovations in ICT have changed the format and the media used to diffuse information. Simultaneously, the increasing stability of EIBA as well as the growth of the IB community and its evolving interests have contributed to gradually change the contents of the information circulated.

EIBA was born at a time in which nationalistic attitudes prevailed, national borders were often difficult to overcome, and a confrontational logic between States and MNEs remained strong. This was expressed in the distinct, often contradictory, views underlying the papers presented to EIBA conferences. However, it proved possible to create a tolerant atmosphere, enabling the sharing and discussion of often conflicting ideas. With hindsight, it may be said that the bonds that united EIBA members were stronger than the differences that pulled them apart. This spirit of tolerance, together with the welcoming of new members, is still one of the hallmarks of EIBA today. These features were critical to the way in which EIBA anticipated and responded the contextual changes stemming from the fall of the Berlin Wall. Since the early 1980s, EIBA has made efforts to attract scholars from Eastern Europe, in particular from Poland. The decisions to hold conferences in Poland (Warsaw-1994 and Poznan-2018), Slovenia (Ljubljana-2004), Estonia (Tallinn-2008), and Romania (Bucharest-2011) are expressions of this commitment.

The evolution of EIBA was not without its troubles. The most significant occurred in 1981 and 1986, in each case following conferences in which EIBA had teamed up with AIB. The presence of the then senior partner reduced local involvement and the conference attendance by EIBA members. However, in both cases, it was possible to move EIBA back on to the right track once more. In 1982, profiting from INSEAD's capacities and clout, José de la Torre convened a memorable conference in Fontainebleau, whose structure became a reference point for future conferences, and brought the revision of the EIBA statutes to ensure a better balance between stability and change, by making the Board the key ultimate governance body while allowing for a process of new initiatives and defining the responsibilities of Executive Committee members. In 1986 and 1987, for the first time since 1977, EIBA membership fell below 100.[1] Two committed EIBAians – Danny van Den Bulcke and Hans-Günther Meissner – volunteered to organise the 1987 and 1988 conferences. The role of Danny was especially important, as he introduced an innovation that still is today one of the core EIBA events: the Doctoral Tutorial, later renamed John H. Dunning Doctoral Tutorial. However, it was only in 1989, with the Helsinki conference, under Reijo Luostarinen's energetic leadership, that the turnaround was fully accomplished; in 1990, membership reached 204, heralding a phase of growth leading to figures above 300 by 1991 and 1994 (see Fig. 16).

Two other troubled moments arose in the first half of the 2000s, both in connection with relationships with other organisations. In 2001, being aware of the consistent improvement in EIBA's accounts, EIASM reclaimed the payment of the accumulated debt, that exceeded €10,000. This was somewhat expected, but nonetheless it was an issue for EIBA at a time when it had agreed with Elsevier to make *IBR* the official journal of EIBA. After a lengthy and constructive dialogue, it was possible to arrange a settlement, through which EIBA was relieved of its debt burden. This faciliated EIBA being better able or prepare for a renewed spurt of growth in 2003–2012, in which membership figures reached the 400 or 400 plus mark in five years.

The second issue concerned relationships with the AIB. In fact, in 2004 the AIB decided to revise its constitution, including the role of its chapters. A group inside AIB held the view that EIBA should be an AIB chapter; this would put EIBA's independence at stake. The EIBA Board took a firm position against this. A meeting was held between Danny Van Den Bulcke, EIBA Chair, Alan Rugman, President of AIB, and Peter Buckley, immediate past President of AIB, to reach a solution. This was achieved through a proposal of Peter Buckley, later labelled as the *Buckley compromise*. Contrary to expectations, this compromise passed the test of time, proving to be sustainable and heralding a new phase, marked by cooperation instead of conflict, in EIBA-AIB relationships.

From the early 2000s, EIBA entered a phase of increasing confidence and growth. This was to a large extent the result of the 2004 changes in EIBA statutes.

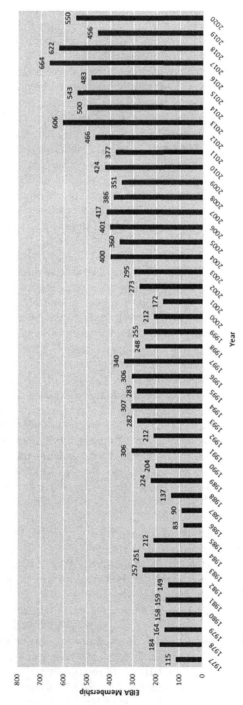

Fig. 16. Overall Perspective of the Evolution of EIBA Membership (1977–2020). *Source:* EIBA archives.

In fact, the revision of the statutes was key to improve the management of EIBA, making it less dependent on the ebb-and-flow of conference organisation, while ensuring a more strategic and longer-term stance by the EIBA Board. There has been an increasing trend both in conference attendance and EIBA membership. Between 2003 and 2012 EIBA membership averaged almost 400; it rose to 553 in 2013–2020. This is a real achievement and confirms the sustainability of EIBA, in spite of the ups-and-downs due to the varying attractiveness of conference locations.

This positive outlook has also been associated with two other important factors: the increasing role of women in EIBA; and the Academy's attractiveness for young scholars. The first has to do with the significant increase in female membership. It is interesting to remind ourselves how far we have come in this respect. In the late 1970s EIBA was essentially a male terrain: the list of participants at the first EIBA conference included just one woman. Until 1988 EIBA's female membership did not exceed 10, with the exception of 1983 and 1984. During the 1990s it averaged 55, corresponding to 22% of total; these figures rose in the 2000s to 98% and 26%, respectively. The most significant change, however, took place during the 2010s, when EIBA came close to achieving gender balance, with an average female membership reaching 208, corresponding to an overall share exceeding 40%. Besides this, the preeminence of women as conference organisers, as EIBA Chair and as Dean of the EIBA Fellows reached new heights.

EIBA's welcoming attitude towards newcomers has already been mentioned with regard to colleagues from Eastern Europe, and earlier from Southern Europe. Another dimension was the attraction of junior researchers. The John H. Dunning Doctoral Tutorial played a spearhead role in this, bringing in new blood. The idea of making EIBA an increasingly junior scholar-friendly academy has been behind many of the initiatives taken, such as the launching of the Danny Van Den Bulcke Doctoral Symposium, the multiple PDWs and the pre-and post-conference courses on specific methodological issues. In the same vein have been the 'Meet & Greet' initiative and the EIBA Early Career Network.

As a result of all these moves, EIBA is now widely regarded as an Academy that fosters diversity, welcomes new people and new ideas and promotes interdisciplinarity by fostering the links between the IB field and specific cognate disciplines to better make sense of a changing international context, posing new challenges for IB research.

9.2. ESCAPING THE ONE-CONFERENCE-A-YEAR SYNDROME: GOVERNANCE CHALLENGES

EIBA's evolution has been marked by another trade-off. On the one hand, a need was felt to respond to the one-conference-a-year syndrome. On the other, it was essential to raise the standards of the annual conference, first to ensure survival, and later to enhance EIBA's visibility, attractiveness and status in the IB scholarly community.

In the beginning, annual conferences were a vital instrument to enable the creation of an interactive IB research community in Europe. At a time when communications were difficult and based on snail mail and telephone, the conference was the key opportunity for socialisation. While it was felt that other tools, besides the conference needed to be used to build the community, its destiny was very much dependent on conference quality and attractiveness. A conference failure or a series of not-so-good conferences might create an existential threat to the young organisation. The Executive Committee was made up of scholars whose main duty was to convene a successful conference, profiting from the diversity offered by the European locations. The multiple attempts to foster corporate membership, over the first 20 years of EIBA were motivated by two considerations: to better understand the behaviour and demands of businesses, and to ensure a stable, medium-term source of funding, to enable financial stability as well as a hedge against less successful conferences. While the problems stemming from teaming up with companies, in terms of both ethics and independence, have been raised, the initiatives all collapsed for a single reason: the lack of interest on the business side. By the turn of the century, it became clear that company membership was not a viable approach. Shortly thereafter, there has been a contextual change that came to provide an important alternative source of linkages to mitigate EIBA's problems: the increasing recognition by policymakers in Europe and elsewhere of the benefits of investing in research, including in the social sciences. This significantly contributed to increase the size of the IB research community and, consequently, the demand for IB conferences. This has been translated into increasing conference attendance as well as in conference financial surpluses.

EIBA conferences had to be attractive and meet consistent quality standards. Our research on the history of EIBA shows how some conferences have played especially important roles in the pursuit of such higher standards. This may be epitomised in four conferences over the two first decades of EIBA's life: Uppsala-1977 contributed towards the standardisation of paper submissions; Fontainebleau-1982 introduced a set of core themes, that became a template for future conferences and were the seeds of today's tracks; Helsinki-1989 was an example of mobilisation of a domestic IB community to leverage international connections; and Copenhagen-1991 introduced a reliable blind-review paper selection procedure. These moves have been key steps in EIBA's pursuit for increased conference quality. It is interesting to notice how there has been a co-evolution between the features, contents and themes of EIBA conferences and contextual conditions. In particular, it is noteworthy that the concerns with sound methodological approaches, both qualitative and quantitative, have gained relevance.[2] Another step, no less relevant, was the initiative taken by the Copenhagen-2003 organising committee (Lars Håkansson and Torben Pedersen) to write the first draft of the *EIBA Conference Guidelines*. This formalised an element of organisational memory which had previously been passed between conference organisers only more informally, and less consistently. With successive revisions, distilling the experience of subsequent conference organisers, this became an essential tool for anyone intending to convene an EIBA conference as well as putting into practice the 'localized but consistent' idea of Jonas Puck for EIBA conferences (Puck, 2019). In the same vein was the decision to launch a call for proposals to organise future EIBA conferences.

Paradoxically, escaping the one-conference-a-year syndrome demanded improving conference quality standards and reducing its variance. In fact, high-quality conferences increase the sense of identification with the Academy and, therefore, its image. However, to ensure inter-temporal learning and its accumulation, a division of labour is essential. Those who are in charge of conferences should not be the ones that also design its longer-term strategy and run the organisation. This calls for changes in governance.

The decision, taken in 2000, to make *IBR* the official journal of EIBA was another initiative to make EIBA less dependent on the annual conference. It was expected that this would entice members of the IB community to join EIBA even when they were unable to attend the annual conference. The rationale was that the opportunity to have access to a journal like *IBR* would encourage EIBA membership as well as longer-term attachment. However, for various reasons, partly associated with the shift from hard copy to electronic journals, this did not happen.

Returning to governance, a turning point for EIBA was the revision of the statutes completed in the first half of the 2000s. The revision led by José de la Torre in 1982 was an important step in the right direction to move beyond the 'old-boys' network approach that was common in the early years; however, the size of the IB community and the financial conditions prevented the opportunity from being fully realised. John Hagedoorn's idea, seconded by Danny Van Den Bulcke and further developed by Lars Håkansson and Torben Pedersen, of establishing a separation between EIBA management and conference organisation, was essential to transform EIBA into what it is today. This was also supported by another governance change: the creation of the EIBA Fellows.

The revision of statutes enabled EIBA to rely on a managerial team that could better address medium- to long-term challenges, unencumbered by the duties of organising the annual conference. The two most recent EIBA Chair teams devoted much energy to launching initiatives that have provided further options for IB scholars to become members without attending the annual conference: the EIBA-Ws and the Summer Schools. However, the pandemic was a temporary hindrance to the development and/or earlier launching of these.

The quest to escape the conference-based syndrome is likely to be a never-ending process. EIBA is now much stronger and prepared to tackle it. But the task is not easy, since it demands striking a balance between contradictory tensions. This balance will be contingent on contextual factors, related to the overall IB climate as well as to the developments of the global IB community. This leads us to the concluding section: developing an agenda to address the challenges and opportunities for EIBA and for IB research.

9.3. AN AGENDA FOR EIBA AND IB RESEARCH

The future is based on the past. The history of EIBA has shown how over these almost 50 years the international IB atmosphere and IB research has changed and, with them, the features of IB scholarly organisations, in particular EIBA.

About 20 years have elapsed since the key changes in EIBA, specially the separation between the overall management of the Academy and the convening of annual conferences. EIBA's status, confidence, size and balance have improved a lot. There are, however, three issues to address: promoting multi-year EIBA membership, together with a revision of the relationship with Elsevier/*IBR*; attracting researchers from under-represented countries; and relaunching initiatives aimed at promoting EIBA in social media.

The first, directly stemming from the observations made in the previous section, concerns the evolution of EIBA membership. In spite of the initiatives taken so far, a comparison of EIBA membership and annual conference attendance shows how the latter influences the former. As membership is, for many members, a yearly issue and not a longer-term one, the attractiveness of conference locations and the commitment by conference organisers in promoting the conferences and enticing potential attendees have a significant effect on membership figures. Access to *IBR* no longer plays a role in promoting continuous membership, as researchers usually have free online access through their libraries. From this perspective, *IBR* risks becoming a liability, rather than an asset, for EIBA members. In spite of recent improvements, together with Elsevier's disinterest and the perception of insufficient ownership of *IBR* by EIBA, this demands a reassessment of the relationships between EIBA and Elsevier/*IBR*.

This does not necessarily mean a divorce for several reasons. First, there are sunk costs, whose recovery is very difficult from EIBA's perspective. Second, we think that there are factors that militate towards a common effort towards increasing the perceived value of *IBR* for EIBA's members. These are related to the cost and the status of *IBR*. The cost might be reduced should three-year subscriptions be available at low cost. These might be combined with three-year EIBA membership fees. With regard to the status, a joint effort should be developed to enhance *IBR's`* image and performance indicators, making it more enticing for top IB scholars as a publishing outlet. This might lead to reduce the present gap between *IBR* and *JIBS*. A coordinated set of joint initiatives between EIBA and the *IBR* editors might contribute to enhance the perceived advantages of multi-year subscription of *IBR* and payment of EIBA membership fees. This would be very important to 'flatten the curve', reducing the variability of EIBA membership resulting from distinct conference location attractiveness.

The second issue is related to the need to increase EIBA membership in four groups of countries. These concern Eastern Europe, smaller European countries, the US, and China and India. Multiple initiatives have been taken to encourage Eastern European scholars to join EIBA. However, they have not been successful, except for Poland and, to some extent, Slovenia. It is important to recall at this juncture the words of Erzsébet Czakó, then the NR for Hungary: 'institutional EIBA membership for schools in the CEE countries would increase EIBA membership substantially as most potential members in the CEE are not supported by schools individually' (EIBA Board, 2018, p. 25). This would require a twist in EIBA's approach in this regard. Several smaller EU countries have witnessed declines in average membership during 2013–2020. In connection with NRs, EIBA might think about locating EIBA-Ws and Summer Schools in these countries, engaging local IB researchers. US membership has also declined. It might make sense to approach former members, to entice them to join EIBA again, possibly in connection with invitations to participate in events in Europe. China and India are under-represented in EIBA. These are countries in which IB research communities are growing. Drawing on the cooperation of Chinese and Indian scholars who are EIBA members, directed promotional campaigns should be addressed to younger IB researchers in these countries to join EIBA.

The third concerns the use of social media. The initiatives taken so far in this regard have not proved to be very successful. The Executive Committee together with the Communications officer, the EIBA Early Career Network and other interested Board members should make a 'fresh start' on this issue, targeted at young scholars in particular. The purpose would be for junior scholars to become more aware of, and more involved in, EIBA, to encourage them to participate in EIBA initiatives (not just the annual conference) and to become EIBA members. The EIBA Summer Schools may also play a crucial role in this respect.

The work we carried out also led us to suggest some ideas regarding an agenda for future IB research.

Writing the history of EIBA has shown how the IB context and climate have changed. To some extent, the present context of fragmentation of the world economy represents a return to the environment prevailing when EIBA was born; yet the conditions are different, both in terms of technology and international connectivity. The changes that have taken place over the most recent years have significant implications for IB research as was shown both at EIBA Leeds-2019 and Lisbon-2024, as well as in various articles by EIBA members. They also raise new challenges for future IB research: how will the 'confused world order', to quote the theme of the Leeds conference, unfold? How will it impact upon the behaviour of MNEs and smaller internationalised firms? This is just an example of one strand for a future IB research agenda. It demands an inter-disciplinary approach, combining IB with other perspectives, namely political science, geography, sociology and history. We argue that such an approach is increasingly relevant to better understand the behaviours and motivations of the key players in IB.

Besides political challenges there are also major environmental, health and societal grand challenges, which are a topic increasingly relevant for by IB. In fact, such challenges are inherently international and impinge upon international relationships and actors. IB has a role to play in understanding how such challenges affect the international context and constrain or stimulate companies to engage in partnerships to address them. For instance, while some IB research has focused on COVID-19, this global sanitary challenge needs to be analysed in general terms. In particular, it would be relevant to carry out research on how governments, NGOs and companies are cooperating, on an international basis, to anticipate and respond to new variants of infectious viral diseases as well as other kinds of health contingencies.

Another important strand, that has already been addressed in the past but raises new challenges, concerns the role of technological developments in shaping the strategy, the behaviour, and the connectivity between firms, and their location across space. The hype regarding the opportunities for using artificial intelligence (AI) will for sure have significant implications for our field, especially for concerns over the effects of AI on international strategy. IB research needs to be careful in addressing such cross-cutting technologies. The way in which AI may be applied is likely to be contingent upon countries' cultural and institutional traits. From another perspective, its implications for firms' international strategies are likely to be differentiated, having in mind distinct 'administrative heritages' (Bartlett & Ghoshal, 1989). A further issue concerns international cooperation in AI, as a way to counter data source biases.

Decision-making in international contexts by MNCs is a third strand that has received less attention than it deserves. To fully understand IB, it is essential to appreciate how decisions are taken. Interestingly, this is a theme that has been addressed in the early years of EIBA but has lost impetus in recent years. It is especially relevant in changing contexts like the one we are facing nowadays, forcing companies to adapt (often not as swiftly as they might wish) to new business environment conditions.

Institutional vectors may still open further promising avenues for IB research. Formal and informal institutions shape behaviour and stimulate or constrain the development of new business approaches. Their effects may be envisaged at different levels: supra-national (e.g. the influence of EU membership in changing attitudes and behaviour), country, organisation, team and individual. One interesting issue is how national institutions influence individual behaviour in foreign contexts; this may apply to managerial behaviour as well as to team working.

Our account of EIBA history has also shown how methodological approaches have changed over time. Such issues are increasingly relevant for IB. Over the last 35 years, significant progress has been achieved. But more efforts need to be made in this regard. In particular, the use of mixed methods, combining qualitative and quantitative apprroches, appears to be very promising for IB research.

Finally, policy issues are another theme that figures high on an agenda for future IB research. There are specific IB policy issues that reach much further than FDI regulation. In fact, the perception that international policy cooperation is often the best way to address the deleterious effects of a lack of coordination between worldwide players has grown in recent years. A good example is the OECD-driven efforts towards base erosion and profit shifting (BEPS). Others concern environmental issues or the management of GVCs.

***

EIBA has come a long way to become the strong and well-recognised Academy it is today. Our account of about 45 years of EIBA's life shows how it was possible to transform an idea into reality. EIBA is increasingly dynamic, with new initiatives, and attractive, for both senior and junior scholars. The generational transition of the 2010s was very successful and the commitment of the new generation to EIBA will, for sure, hold an auspicious future for our Academy.

NOTES

1. Recall that membership in year x is usually related to conference attendance in year $x-1$.
2. See the research on the topics of EIBA conference papers between 1975 and 2020 carried out in the context of the EIBA History project (Simões, Rocha, Piepenbrink, Cantwell & Gugler, 2023).

REFERENCES

To make reading easier, abbreviations of the most relevant journals were used. Please see the List of Abbreviations.

Aguilera, R. V., & Grøgaard, B. (2019). The dubious role of institutions in international business: A road forward'. *JIBS*, 50(1), 20–35.

Ahammad, M. F., Tarba, S. Y., Liu, Y., Glaister, K. W., & Cooper, C. L. (2016). Exploring the factors influencing the negotiation process in cross-border M&A. *IBR*, 25(2), 445–457.

Aharoni, Y. (1966). *The foreign investment decision process*. Harvard Graduate school of Business Administration.

Ahuja, G., & Katila, R. (2001). Technology acquisitions and the innovation performance of acquiring firms: A longitudinal study. *SMJ*, 22(3), 197–220.

Aichhorn, N., & Puck, J. (2017). "I just don't feel comfortable speaking English": Foreign language anxiety as a catalyst for spoken-language barriers in MNCs. *IBR*, 26(4), 749–763.

Alcácer, J., Cantwell, J., & Piscitello, L. (2016). Internationalization in the information age: A new era for places, firms, and international business networks. *JIBS*, 47(5), 499–512.

Aliber, R. Z. (1971). The multinational enterprise in a multiple currency world. In J. H. Dunning (Ed.), *The multinational enterprise* (pp. 49–56). Allen & Unwin.

Alimov, A. (2015). Labor market regulations and cross-border mergers and acquisitions. *JIBS*, 46, 984–1009.

Almor, T., Tarba, S. Y., & Margalit, A. (2014). Maturing, technology-based, born-global companies: surviving through mergers and acquisitions. *MIR*, 54, 421–444.

Alonso, J. A., & Donoso, V. (1989). *Características y estratégias de la empresa exportadora española*. ICEX.

Ambos, B., & Schlegelmilch, B. B. (2007). Innovation and control in the multinational firm: A comparison of political and contingency approaches. *SMJ*, 28(5), 473–486.

Ambos, T. C., Ambos, B., & Schlegelmilch, B. B. (2006). Learning from foreign subsidiaries: An empirical investigation of headquarters' benefits from reverse knowledge transfers. *IBR*, 15(3), 294–312.

Ambos, T. C., Andersson, U., & Birkinshaw, J. (2010). What are the consequences of initiative-taking in multinational subsidiaries? *JIBS*, 41(7), 1099–1118.

Ambos, T. C., Cesinger, B., Eggers, F., & Kraus, S. (2020). How does de-globalization affect location decisions? A study of managerial perceptions of risk and return. *GSJ*, 10(1), 210–236.

Ambos, T. C., Fuchs, S. H., & Zimmermann, A. (2020). Managing interrelated tensions in headquarters–subsidiary relationships: The case of a multinational hybrid organization. *JIBS*, 51, 906–932.

Ambos, T. C., Nell, P. C., & Pedersen, T. (2013). Combining stocks and flows of knowledge: The effects of intra-functional and cross-functional complementarity. *GSJ*, 3(4), 283–299.

Anand, J., McDermott, G., Mudambi, R., & Narula, R. (2021). Innovation in and from emerging economies: New insights and lessons for international business research. *JIBS*, 52(4), 545–559.

Anderson, E., & Gatignon, H. (1986). Modes of foreign entry: A transaction cost analysis and propositions. *JIBS*, 17(3), 1–26.

Andersson, U., Björkman, I., & Forsgren, M. (2005). Managing subsidiary knowledge creation: The effect of control mechanisms on subsidiary local embeddedness. *IBR*, 14(5), 521–538.

Andersson, U., Bjorkman, I., & Furu, P. (2002). Subsidiary absorptive capacity, MNC headquarters' control strategies and transfer of subsidiary competences. In S. Lundan (Ed.), *Network knowledge in international business* (pp. 115–136). Edward Elgar.

Andersson, U., Buckley, P. J., & Dellestrand, H. (2015). In the right place at the right time!: The influence of knowledge governance tools on knowledge transfer and utilization in MNEs. *GSJ*, *5*(1), 27–47.

Andersson, U., & Forsgren, M. (1996). Subsidiary embeddedness and control in the multinational corporation. *IBR*, *5*(5), 487–508.

Andersson, U., & Forsgren, M. (2000). In search of centre of excellence: Network embeddedness and subsidiary roles in multinational corporations. *MIR*, *40*(4), 329–350.

Andersson, U., Forsgren, M., & Holm, U. (2001). Subsidiary embeddedness and competence development in MNCs – A multi-level analysis. *Organization Studies*, *22*(6), 1013–1034.

Andersson, U., Forsgren, M., & Holm, U. (2002). The strategic impact of external networks: Subsidiary performance and competence development in the multinational corporation. *SMJ*, *23*(11), 979–996.

Andersson, U., Forsgren, M., & Holm, U. (2007). Balancing subsidiary influence in the federative MNC: A business network view. *JIBS*, *38*(5), 802–818.

Andersson, U., Gaur, A., Mudambi, R., & Persson, M. (2015). Unpacking interunit knowledge transfer in multinational enterprises. *GSJ*, *5*(3), 241–255.

Andreesen, M. (2011). Software is eating the World. *Wall Street Journal*, August 2020. Retrieved 16 February from https://www.wsj.com/articles/SB10001424053111903480904576512250915629460

Archibugi, D., & Iammarino, S. (1999). The policy implications of the globalisation of innovation. *RP*, *28*(2–3), 317–336.

Archibugi, D., & Michie, J. (Eds.). (1997). *Technology, globalisation and economic performance*, Cambridge University Press.

Argote, L., McEvily, B., & Reagans, R. (2003). Managing knowledge in organizations: An integrative framework and review of emerging themes. *MS*, *49*(4), 571–582.

Ariño, A., de la Torre, J., & Ring, P. S. (2001). Relational quality: Managing trust in corporate alliances. *CMR*, *44*(1), 109–131.

Arora, A., Fosfuri, A., & Gambardella, A. (2001). *Markets for technology: The economies of innovation and corporate strategy*. MIT Press.

Artisien, P. F. R., & Buckley, P. J. (1985). Joint ventures in Yugoslavia: opportunities and constraints. *JIBS*, *16*, 111–135.

Asakawa, K., Park, Y., Song, J., & Kim, S.-J. (2018). Internal embeddedness, geographic distance, and global knowledge sourcing by overseas subsidiaries. *JIBS*, *49*(6), 743–752.

Asmussen, C. G., Foss, N. J., & Nell, P. C. (2019). The role of procedural justice for global strategy and subsidiary initiatives. *GSJ*, *9*(4), 527–554.

Athreye, S., Piscitello, L., & Shadlen, K. C. (2020). Twenty-five years since TRIPS: Patent policy and international business. *JIBP*, *3*(4), 315–328.

Avloniti, A., & Filippaios, F. (2014). Unbundling the differences between psychic and cultural distance: An empirical examination of the existing measures. *IBR*, *23*(3), 660–674.

Awate, S., Larsen, M., & Mudambi, R. (2015). Accessing vs sourcing knowledge: A comparative study of R&D internationalization between emerging and advanced economy firms. *JIBS*, *46*(1), 63–86.

Baaij, M., & Slangen, A. (2013). The role of headquarters–subsidiary geographic distance in strategic decisions by spatially disaggregated headquarters. *JIBS*, *44*(9), 941–952.

Baldwin, R. (2012). *Global supply chains: Why they emerged, why they matter, and where they are going?* (CEPR Discussion Paper No. 9103).

Banalieva, E., & Dhanaraj, C. (2019). Internalization theory for the digital economy. *JIBS*, *50*(8), 1372–1387.

Baranson, J. (1978). *Technology and the multinationals: Corporate strategies in a changing world economy*. Lexington Books.

Barmeyer, C., & Mayrhofer, U. (2008). The contribution of intercultural management to the success of international mergers and acquisitions: An analysis of the EADS group. *IBR*, *17*(1), 28–38.

Barney, J., & Hansen, M. H. (1994). Trustworthiness as a source of competitive advantage. *SMJ*, *15* (Winter), 175–190.

Barney, J. (1991). Firm resources and sustained competitive advantage. *JoM*, *17*(1), 99–120.

Barney, J. (1999). How firm capabilities affect boundary decisions. *SMR*, *40*(1), 19–32.

Bartlett, C. A., Doz, Y. L., & Hedlund, G. (Eds.). (1990). *Managing the global firm*. London: Routledge.

Bartlett, C. A., & Ghoshal, S. (1987). Managing across borders: New strategic requirements. *SMR*, *27* (Summer), 7–17.

Bartlett, C. A., & Ghoshal, S. (1989). *Managing across borders – The transnational solution*. Harvard Business School Press.

Bartlett, C. A., & Ghoshal, S. (1990). Managing innovations in the transnational corporation. In C. A. Bartlett, Y. Doz, & G. Hedlund (Eds.), *Managing the global firm* (pp. 215–255). Routledge.

Bass, A. E., & Chakrabarty, S. (2014). Resource security: Competition for global resources, strategic intent, and governments as owners. *JIBS*, *45*(8), 961–979.

Bathelt, H., Cantwell, J. A., & Mudambi, R. (2018). Overcoming frictions in transnational knowledge flows: Challenges of connecting, sense-making and integrating. *JEG*, *18*(5), 1001–1022.

Beamish, P. W. (1984). *Joint venture performance in developing countries* (Unpublished Doctoral Dissertation). University of Western Ontario, London, Canada.

Beamish, P. W. (1985). The characteristics of joint ventures in developed and developing countries. *Columbia JWB*, *20*, 13–20.

Beamish, P. W. (1988). *Multinational joint ventures in developing countries*. Routledge.

Beamish, P. W., & Banks, J. C. (1987). Equity joint ventures and the theory of the multinational enterprise. *JIBS*, *18*(2), 1–16.

Beamish, P. W., & Berdrow, I. (2003). Learning from IJVs: The unintended outcome. *LRP*, *36*(3), 285–303.

Beamish, P. W., & Killing, J. P. (Eds.). (1997a). *Cooperative strategies: Asian Pacific perspectives*. New Lexington Press.

Beamish, P. W., & Killing, J. P. (Eds.). (1997b). *Cooperative strategies: North American perspectives*. New Lexington Press.

Beamish, P. W., & Killing, J. P. (Eds.). (1997c). *Cooperative strategies: European perspectives*. New Lexington Press.

Békés, G., Benito, G. R. G., Castellani, D., & Muraközy, B. (2021). Into the unknown: The extent and boldness of firms' international footprint. *GSJ*, *11*(3), 468–493.

Belderbos, R., Leten, B., & Suzuki, S. (2013). How global is R&D? Firm-level determinants of home-country bias in R&D. *JIBS*, *44*(8), 765–786.

Beleska-Spasova, E., & Glaister, K. W. (2013). Intrafirm causal ambiguity in an international context. *IBR*, *22*(1), 32–46.

BenAissa, H. (1993). Foreword. In J. H. Dunning (Ed.), *The theory of transnational corporations, Volume I, The United Nations LIBRary on transnational corporations* (pp. vii, ix). Routledge.

Benito, G. R. G., & Gripsrud, G. (1992). The expansion of foreign direct investments: Discrete rational location choices or a cultural learning process?' *JIBS*, *23*(3), 461–476.

Benito, G. R. G., Pedersen, T., & Petersen, B. (1999). Foreign operation methods and switching costs: conceptual issues and possible effects. *Scandinavian JoM*, *15*(2), 213–229.

Benito, G. R. G., Petersen, B., & Welch, L. S. (2009). Towards more realistic conceptualisations of foreign operation modes. *JIBS*, *40*(9, December), 1455–1470.

Benito, G. R. G., Petersen, B., & Welch, L. S. (2012). Dynamics of foreign operation modes and their combinations: Insights for international strategic management. In A. Verbeke & H. Merchant (Eds.), *Handbook of international strategic management* (pp. 93–115). Edward Elgar.

Benito, G. R. G., Petersen, B., & Welch, L. S. (2019). The global value chain and internalization theory. *JIBS*, *50*(8), 1414–1423.

Bernanke, B. S. (2010). *Causes of the recent financial and economic crisis*, Statement before the Financial Crisis Inquiry Commission. Washington DC, September 2nd. Retrieved February 17, 2002, from https://www.federalreserve.gov/newsevents/testimony/bernanke20100902a.htm

Berry, H., Guillén, M. F., & Zhou, N. (2010). An institutional approach to cross-national distance. *JIBS*, *41*(9), 1460–1480.

Bertrand, O. (2011). What goes around, comes around: Effects of offshore outsourcing on the export performance of firms. *JIBS*, *42*(2), 334–344.

Beugelsdijk, S., & Mudambi, R. (2013). MNEs as border-crossing multi-location enterprises: The role of discontinuities in geographic space. *JIBS*, *44*(5), 413–426.

Beugelsdijk, S., van Witteloostuijn, A., & Meyer, K. E. (2020). A new approach to data access and research transparency (DART). *JIBS*, *51*(6), 887–905.

Bevan, A., Estrin, S., & Meyer, K. (2004). Foreign investment location and institutional development in transition economies. *IBR*, *13*(1), 43–64.

Billitteri, C., Nigro, G. L., & Perrone, G. (2013). How risk influences the choice of governance mode in biopharmaceutical inter-firm relationships. *IBR*, *22*(6), 932–950.

Birkinshaw, J. (1995). *Entrepreneurship in multinational corporations: The initiative process in foreign subsidiaries* (Digitized Theses). https://ir.lib.uwo.ca/digitizedtheses/2523.

Birkinshaw, J. (1996). How multinational subsidiary mandates are gained and lost. *JIBS*, *27*(3), 467–495.

Birkinshaw, J. (1997). Entrepreneurship in multinational corporations: The characteristics of subsidiary initiatives. *SMJ*, *18*(3), 207–229.

Birkinshaw, J. (1999). The determinants and consequences of subsidiary initiative in multinational corporations. *ETP*, *24*(1), 9–36.

Birkinshaw, J. (2000). *Entrepreneurship in the global firm.* Sage.

Birkinshaw, J., Bouquet, C., & Ambos, T. C. (2007). Managing executive attention in the global company. *SMR*, *48*(4), 39–45.

Birkinshaw, J., & Hood, N. (1998). Multinational subsidiary evolution: Capability and charter change in foreign-owned subsidiary companies. *AMR*, *23*(4), 773–795.

Birkinshaw, J., & Hood, N. (2000). Characteristics of foreign subsidiaries in industry clusters. *JIBS*, *31*(1), 141–154.

Birkinshaw, J., & Hood, N. (2001). Unleash innovation in foreign subsidiaries. *HBR*, *79*(3), 131–137.

Birkinshaw, J., Hood, N., & Jonsson, S. (1998). Building firm specific advantages in multinational corporations: The role of subsidiary initiative. *SMJ*, *19*(3), 221–242.

Birkinshaw, J., & Morrison, A. J. (1995). Configurations of Strategy and Structure in Subsidiaries of Multinational Structure. *JIBS*, *26*(4), 729–753.

Blomkvist, K., & Drogendijk, R. (2013). The impact of psychic distance on Chinese outward foreign direct investments. *MIR*, *53*, 659–686.

Boellis, A., Mariotti, S., Minichilli, A., & Piscitello, L. (2016). Family involvement and firms' establishment mode choice in foreign markets. *JIBS*, *47*(8), 929–950.

Bolino, M. C. (2007). Expatriate assignments and intra-organizational career success: Implications for individuals and organizations. *JIBS*, *38*(5), 819–835.

Bouquet, C., & Birkinshaw, J. (2008). Weight versus voice: How foreign subsidiaries gain attention from corporate headquarters. *AMJ*, *51*(3), 577–601.

Bouquet, C., & Birkinshaw, J. (2011). How global strategies emerge: An attention perspective. *GSJ*, *1*(3–4), 243–262.

Bouquet, C., Morrison, A., & Birkinshaw, J. (2009). International attention and multinational enterprise performance. *JIBS*, *40*(1), 108–131.

Brandl, K., Jensen, P. Ø., & Lind, M. J. (2018). Advanced service offshore outsourcing: Exploring the determinants of capability development in emerging market firms. *GSJ*, *8*(2), 324–350.

Brannen, M. Y. (2011). Using multiple case studies to generalize from ethnographic research. In R. Piekkari & C. Welch (Eds.), *Rethinking the case study in international business and management research* (pp. 124–145). Edward Elgar.

Brannen, M. Y., & Peterson, M. F. (2009). Merging without alienating: interventions promoting cross–cultural organizational integration and their limitations. *JIBS*, *40*(3), 468–489.

Brannen, M. Y., Piekkari, R., & Tietze, S. (2014). The multifaceted role of language in international business: Unpacking the forms, functions and features of a critical challenge to MNC theory and performance. *JIBS*, *45*(5), 495–507.

Bresman, H., Birkinshaw, J., & Nobel, R (1999). Knowledge transfer in international acquisitions', *JIBS*, *30*(3), 439–462.

Brewer, P., & Venaik, S. (2010). GLOBE practices and values: A case of diminishing marginal utility?' *JIBS*, *41*(8), 1316–1324.

Brock, D. M., Shenkar, O., Shoham, A., & Siscovick, I. C. (2008). National culture and expatriate deployment. *JIBS, 39*(8), 1293–1309.

Brouthers, K. (2013). Institutional, cultural and transaction cost influences on entry mode choice and performance. *JIBS, 44*(1), 1–13.

Brouthers, K., Brouthers, L. E., & Wilkinson, T. J. (1995). Strategic Alliances: Choose Your Partners. *LRP, 28*(3), 18–25.

Brouthers, K., Geisser, K., & Rothlauf, F. (2016). Explaining the internationalization of ibusiness firms. *JIBS, 47*(5), 513–534.

Brouthers, L. E., Marshall, V., & Keig, D. (2016). Solving the single–country sample problem in cultural distance studies. *JIBS, 47*(4), 471–479.

Bucheli, M., & Kim, M. (2015). Attacked from both sides: A dynamic model of multinational corporations' strategies for protection of their property rights. *GSJ, 5*(1), 1–26.

Buchholz, M., Bathelt, H., & Cantwell, J. A. (2020). Income divergence and global connectivity of U.S. urban regions. *JIBP, 3*(3), 229–248.

Buckley, P. J. (2002). Is the international business research agenda running out of steam?' *JIBS, 33*(2), 365–373.

Buckley, P. J. (2009). The impact of the global factory on economic development. *JWB, 44*(2), 131–143.

Buckley, P. J. (2020a). China's belt and road initiative and the COVID–19 crisis. *JIBP, 3*, 311–314.

Buckley, P. J. (2020b). The theory and empirics of the structural reshaping of globalization. *JIBS, 51*(9), 1580–1592.

Buckley, P. J., & Casson, M. (1976). *The future of the multinational enterprise.* London: Macmillan.

Buckley, P. J., & Casson, M. (1978). A theory of international operations. In : M. Ghertman & J. Leontiades (Eds.), *European research in international business* (pp. 1–8). North–Holland Publishing.

Buckley, P. J., & Casson, M. (1985). *The economic theory of the multinational enterprise: Selected papers.* London: MacMillan.

Buckley, P. J., & Casson, M. (1988). A theory of cooperation in international business. *MIR,* 28(Special Issue), 19–38.

Buckley, P. J., & Casson, M. (Eds.). (1992a). *Multinational enterprises in the world economy – Essays in honour of John Dunning.* Edward Elgar.

Buckley, P. J., & Casson, M. (1992b). Organizing for innovation: The multinational enterprise in the twenty-first century. In P. J. Buckley & M. Casson (Eds.), *Multinational enterprises in the world economy – Essays in honour of John Dunning* (pp. 212–232). Edward Elgar.

Buckley, P. J., & Casson, M. (1996). An economic model of international joint venture strategy. *JIBS, 27*(5), 849–876.

Buckley, P. J., & Casson, M. (1998a). Models of the multinational enterprise. *JIBS, 29*(1), 21–44.

Buckley, P. J., & Casson, M. (1998b). Analyzing foreign market entry strategies: Extending the internalization approach. *JIBS, 29*(3), 539–561.

Buckley, P. J., & Casson, M. (2003). The future of the multinational enterprise in retrospect and in prospect. *JIBS, 34*(2), 219–222.

Buckley, P., & Casson, M. (2019). Decision–making in international business. *JIBS,* 5088, 1424–1439.

Buckley, P. J., Doh, J. P., & Benischke, M. H. (2017). Towards a renaissance in international business research? Big questions, grand challenges, and the future of IB scholarship. *JIBS, 48*(9), 1045–1064.

Buckley, P. J., & Ghauri, P. (Eds.). (1993). *The internationalization of the firm – A reader.* Academic Press.

Buckley, P. J., & Ghauri, P. (2004). Globalisation, economic geography and the strategy of multinational enterprises. *JIBS,* 35(2), 81–98.

Buckley, P. J., & Hashai, N. (2020). Skepticism toward globalization, technological knowledge flows, and the emergence of a new global system. *GSJ, 10*(1), 94–122.

Buckley, P. J., & Lessard, D. R. (2005). Regaining the edge for international business research. *JIBS, 36*(6), 595–599.

Buckley, P. J., Munjal, S., Enderwick, P., & Forsans, N. (2016). Do foreign resources assist or impede internationalisation? Evidence from internationalisation of Indian multinational enterprises. *IBR, 25*(1), 130–140.

Buckley, P. J., & Strange, R. (2015). The governance of the global factory: Location and control of world economic activity. *AMP*, *29*(2). 237–249.

Buckley, P. J., Strange, R., Timmer, M. P., & de Vries, G. J. (2020). Catching-up in the global factory: Analysis and policy implications. *JIBP*, *3*(2), 79–106.

Buckley, P. J., & Tian, X. (2017). Internalization theory and the performance of emerging-market multinational enterprises. *IBR*, *26*(5), 976–990.

Buckley, P. J., Wang, C., & Clegg, J. (2007). The impact of foreign ownership, local ownership and industry characteristics on spillover benefits from foreign direct investment in China. *IBR*, *16*(2), 142–158.

Burgelman, R. A. (2011). Bridging history and reductionism: A key role for longitudinal qualitative research. *JIBS*, *42*(5), 591–601.

Burton, F. (1999). Letter from the president. *EIBA Newsletter*, May.

Caligiuri, P. (2014). Many moving parts: Factors influencing the effectiveness of HRM practices designed to improve knowledge transfer within MNCs. *JIBS*, *45*(1), 63–72.

Caner, T., & Tyler, B. B. (2015). The effects of knowledge depth and scope on the relationship between R&D alliances and new product development. *JPIM*, *32*, 808–824.

Cannone, G., & Ughetto, E. (2014). Born globals: A cross-country survey on high-tech start-ups. *IBR*, *23*(1), 272–283.

Cano-Kollmann, M., Cantwell, J., Hannigan, T. J., Mudambi, R., & Song, J. (2016). Knowledge connectivity: An agenda for innovation research in international business. *JIBS*, *47*(3), 255–262.

Cantwell, J. (1987). The reorganisation of European industries after integration: Selected evidence on the role of multinational enterprise activities. *Journal of Common Market Studies*, *26*(2), 127–151.

Cantwell, J. (1989a). *Technological innovation and multinational corporations*. Basil Blackwell.

Cantwell, J. (1989b). *Letter to Gerry van Dyck*. Reading, October 10th.

Cantwell, J. (Ed.). (1992). *Multinational investment in modern Europe: Strategic interaction in the integrated community*. Edward Elgar.

Cantwell, J. (1995a). Multinational corporations and innovatory activities: Towards a new, evolutionary approach. In J. Molero (Ed.), *Technological innovation, multinational corporations and new international competitiveness: The case of intermediate countries* (pp. 21–58). Harwood Academic Publishers.

Cantwell, J. (1995b). The globalisation of technology: What remains of the product cycle model? *CJE*, *19*(1), 155–174.

Cantwell, J., & Brannen, M. Y. (2016). The changing nature of the international business field, and the progress of JIBS. *JIBS*, *47*(9), 1023–1031.

Cantwell, J., & Dunning, J. H. (1982). *American inward investment and Europe's technological competitiveness*. Paper delivered at the 8th EIBA conference, Fontainebleau.

Cantwell, J., Dunning, J. H., & Lundan, S. M. (2010). An evolutionary approach to understanding international business activity: The co-evolution of MNEs and the institutional environment. *JIBS*, *41*(4), 567–586.

Cantwell, J., & Mudambi, R. (2005). MNE competence-creating subsidiary mandates. *SMJ*, *26*(12), 1109–1128.

Cantwell, J., & Narula, R. (2001). The eclectic paradigm in the global economy. *International Journal of the Economics of Business*, *8*(2), 155–172.

Cantwell, J., & Narula, R. (Eds.). (2003). *International business and the eclectic paradigm: Developing the OLI framework*. Routledge.

Cantwell, J., Piepenbrink, A., & Shukla, P. (2014). Assessing the impact of JIBS as an interdisciplinary journal: A network approach. *JIBS*, *45*(7), 787–799.

Cantwell, J., Piepenbrink, A., Shukla, P., & Vo, A. (2016). The changing landscape of *JIBS* authorship. *JIBS*, *47*(7), 749–777.

Cantwell, J., & Zaman, S. (2018). Connecting local and global technological knowledge sourcing. *CR*, *28*(3), 277–294.

Cantwell, J., & Zaman, S. (2024). International knowledge connectivity and the increasing concentration of innovation in major global cities. *JEG*, *24*(3), 421–446.

Cardoso, F. H. (1980). Una critica a las tesis actuals sobre desarrollo y dependencia en América Latina. In V. Donoso, J. Molero, J. Muñoz, & A. Serrano (Eds.), *Transnacionalización y Dependencia* (pp. 27–41). Ediciones Cultura Hispanica, Instituto de Cooperación Iberoamericana.

Carlile, P. R. (2004). Transferring, translating and transforming: An integrative framework for managing knowledge across boundaries. *OS, 15*(5), 555–568.

Carstairs, R. T., & Welch, L. S. (1983). Licensing and the internationalization of smaller companies: Some Australian evidence. *MIR, 22*(3), 33–44.

Casillas, J. C., Barbero, J. L., & Sapienza, H. J. (2015). Knowledge acquisition, learning, and the initial pace of internationalization. *IBR, 25*(1), 102–114.

Casson, M., Porter, L., & Wadeson, N. (2016). Internalization theory: An unfinished agenda. *IBR, 25*(6), 1223–1234.

Casson, M., & Wadeson, N. (2018). Emerging market multinationals and internalisation theory. *IBR, 27*(6), 1150–1160.

Castellani, D., Jimenez, A., & Zanfei, A. (2013). How remote are R&D labs? Distance factors and international innovative activities. *JIBS, 44*(7), 649–675.

Castellani, D., & Lavoratori, K. (2020). The lab and the plant: Offshore R&D and co-location with production activities. *JIBS, 51*, 121–137.

Castells, M. (1996). *The information age: Economy, society and culture, Volume I: The rise of the network society*. Blackwell.

Cavanagh, A., Freeman, S., Kalfadellis, P., & Cavusgil, S. T. (2017). How do subsidiaries assume autonomy? A refined application of agency theory within the subsidiary–headquarters context. *GSJ, 7*(2), 1168–1183.

Caves, R. E. (1971). Industrial corporations: The industrial economics of foreign investment. *Economica, 41*, 176–193.

Caves, R. E. (1974). Causes of direct investment: Foreign firms' shares in Canadian and United Kingdom manufacturing industries. *Review of Economics and Statistics, 56*, 279–293.

Caves, R. E., Crookell, H., & Killing, J. P. (1983). The imperfect market for technology licenses. *OBES, 45*(3), 249–267.

Chakrabarti, R., Gupta-Mukherjee, S., & Jayaraman, N. (2009). Mars–Venus marriages: Culture and cross-border M&A. *JIBS, 40*(2), 216–236.

Chandler, A. D. (1962). *Strategy and structure: Chapters in the history of the American industrial enterprise*. MIT Press.

Chandler, A. D. (1977). *The visible hand: The managerial revolution in American business*. Belknap Press/Harvard University Press.

Chandler, A. D., Jr. (1982). The M-Form: Industrial groups, American style. *European Economic Review, 19*(1), 3–23. Reprinted in G. Hedlund (Ed.), *Organization of transnational corporations, The UN LIBRary on transnational corporations*, Volume 6. Routledge, 1993, pp. 123–142.

Chandra, Y. (2017). A time–based process model of international entrepreneurial opportunity evaluation. *JIBS, 48*, 423–451.

Chapman, M., Gajewska-De Mattos, H., Clegg, J., & Buckley, P. J. (2008). Close neighbours and distant friends — Perceptions of cultural distance. *IBR, 17*(3), 217–234.

Chari, M. D. R., & Chang, K. (2009). Determinants of the share of equity sought in cross-border acquisitions. *JIBS, 40*(8), 1277–1297.

Chen, D., Paik, Y., & Park, S. H. (2010). Host–country policies and MNE management control in IJVs: Evidence from China. *JIBS, 41*(3), 526–537.

Chen, J., Zhan, W., Tong, Z., & Kumar, V. (2020). The effect of inward FDI on outward FDI over time in China: A contingent and dynamic perspective. *IBR, 29*(5), 101734.

Chen, L., Shaheer, N., Yi, J., & Li, S. (2019). The international penetration of ibusiness firms: Network effects, liabilities of outsidership and country clout. *JIBS, 50*(2), 172–192.

Cheng, J. L. C., Birkinshaw, J., Lessard, D. R., & Thomas, D. C. (2014). Advancing interdisciplinary research: Insights from the JIBS special issue. *JIBS, 45*, 643–646.

Cheng, J. L. C., Henisz, W., Roth, K., & Swaminathan, A. (2009). Advancing interdisciplinary research in the field of international business: Prospects, issues and challenges. *JIBS, 40*(7), 1070–1074.

Chi, T. (1994). Trading in strategic resources: Necessary conditions, transaction cost problems, and choice of exchange structure. *SMJ, 15*(4), 271–290.

Chi, T., & McGuire, D. J. (1996). Collaborative ventures and value of learning: Integrating the transaction cost and strategic option perspectives on the choice of market entry modes. *JIBS*, *27*(2), 285–307.

Chidlow, A., Holmström-Lind, C., Holm, U., & Tallman, S. (2015). Do I stay or do I go? Sub-national drivers for post-entry subsidiary development. *IBR*, *24*(2), 266–275.

Child, J., & Yan, Y. (2003). Predicting the performance of international joint ventures: An investigation in China. *JMS*, *40*(2), 283–320.

Chittoor, R., Aulakh, P. S., & Ray, S. (2018). Microfoundations of firm internationalization: The owner CEO effect. *GSJ*, *9*(1), 255–275.

Choi, J., & Contractor, F. J. (2016). Choosing an appropriate alliance governance mode: The role of institutional, cultural and geographical distance in international research & development (R&D) collaborations. *JIBS*, *47*, 210–232.

Choquette, E. (2019). Import-based market experience and firms' exit from export markets. *JIBS*, *50*, 423–449.

Choquette, E., Rask, M., Sala, D., & Schröder, P. (2017). Born globals—Is there fire behind the smoke?. *IBR* 26(3), 448–460.

Chung, C., Lee, S. H., & Lee, J. Y. (2013). Dual-option subsidiaries and exit decisions during times of economic crisis. *MIR*, *53*, 555–577.

Chung, L. (2014). Headquarters' managerial intentionality and reverse transfer of practices. *MIR*, *54*, 225–252.

Ciborra, C. (1991). Alliances as learning experiments. In L. K. Mytelka (Ed.), *Strategic partnerships in the world economy* (pp. 51–77). Frances Pinter.

Cirillo, V., Fanti, L., Mina, A., & Ricci, A. (2023). The adoption of digital technologies: Investment, skills, work organisation. *Structural Change and Economic Dynamics*, *66*, 89–105.

Clarke, J. E., & Liesch, P. W. (2017). Wait-and-see strategy: Risk management in the internationalization process model. *JIBS*, *48*, 923–940.

Coase, R. H. (1937). The nature of the firm. *Economica*, *4*, 386–405.

Contractor, F. J. (1981). *International technology licensing: Compensation, costs, and negotiation*. Lexington Books.

Contractor, F. J. (1985). *Licensing in international strategy: A guide for planning and negotiation*. Quorum Books.

Contractor, F. J. (1990). Contractual and cooperative forms of international business: Towards a unified theory of modal choice. *MIR*, *30*, 31–54.

Contractor, F. J. (2019). Can a firm find the balance between openness and secrecy? Towards a theory of an optimum level of disclosure. *JIBS*, *50*, 261–274.

Contractor, F. J., Foss, N. J., Kundu, S., & Lahiri, S. (2019). Viewing global strategy through a microfoundations lens. *GSJ*, *9*(1), 3–18.

Contractor, F. J., & Lorange, P. (1988a). Why should firms cooperate? In F. J. Contractor & P. Lorange (Eds.), *Cooperative strategy in international business* (pp. 3–28). Lexington Books.

Contractor, F. J., & Lorange, P. (Eds.). (1988b). *Cooperative strategies in international business*. Lexington Books.

Contractor, F. J., & Lorange, P. (Eds.). (2002). *Cooperative strategies and alliances*. Elsevier Science.

Contractor, F. J., & Reuer, J. J (2014). Structuring and governing alliances: New directions for research. *GSJ*, *4*(4), 241–256.

Couper, C., Reuber, A. R., & Prashantham, S. (2020). Lost that lovin' feeling: The erosion of trust between small, high–distance partners. *JIBS*, *51*, 326–352.

Coviello, N. (2006). The network dynamics of international new ventures. *JIBS*, *37*(5), 713–731.

Coviello, N. (2015). Re–thinking research on born globals. *JIBS*, *46*(1), 17–26.

Coviello, N., Kano, L., & Liesch, P. W. (2017). Adapting the Uppsala model to a modern world: Macro–context and microfoundations. *JIBS*, 48(9), 1151–1164.

Coviello, N., & Munro, H. (1997). Network relationships and the internationalisation process of small software firms. *IBR*, *6*(4), 361–386.

Crespo, C. F., Griffith, D. A., & Lages, L. F. (2014). The performance effects of vertical and horizontal subsidiary knowledge outflows in multinational corporations. *IBR*, *23*(5), 993–1007.

Cuervo-Cazurra, A. (2006). Who cares about corruption. *JIBS*, *37*(6), 807–822.

Cuervo-Cazurra, A. (2008). The effectiveness of laws against bribery abroad. *JIBS, 39*(4), 634–651.

Cuervo-Cazurra, A. (2018). Thanks but no thanks: State-owned multinationals from emerging markets and host–country policies. *JIBP, 1*(1), 128–156.

Cuervo-Cazurra, A., Gaur, A., & Singh, D. (2019). Pro–market institutions and global strategy: The pendulum of pro–market reforms and reversals. *JIBS, 50*(4), 598–632.

Cuervo-Cazurra, A., & Genc, M. (2008). Transforming disadvantages into advantages: Developing-country MNEs in the least developed countries. *JIBS, 39*(6), 957–979.

Cuervo-Cazurra, A., Inkpen, A., Musacchio, A., & Ramaswamy, K. (2014). Governments as owners: State-owned multinational companies. *JIBS, 45*, 919–942.

Cuervo-Cazurra, A., Mudambi, R., & Pedersen, T. (2019). Subsidiary power: Loaned or owned? The lenses of agency theory and resource dependence theory. *GSJ, 9*(4), 151–175.

Cuervo-Cazurra, A., Mudambi, R., Pedersen, T., & Piscitello, L. (2017). Research methodology in global strategy research. *GSJ, 7*(3), 233–240.

Cuervo-Cazurra, A., & Ramamurti, R. (2015). *The escape motivation of emerging market multinational enterprises*, Columbia FDI perspectives No. 43. Columbia Center of Sustainable Investment: Columbia University LIBRaries.

Cuervo-Cazurra, A., & Ramamurti, R. (2017). Home country underdevelopment and internationalization: Innovation-based and escape-based internationalization. *CR, 27*(3), 217–230.

Cullen, J. B., Johnson, J., & Sakano, T. (1995). Success through commitment and trust: The soft side of strategic alliance management. *JWB, 35*(3), 223–240.

Cuypers, I. R. P., Ertug, G., Cantwell, J., Zaheer, A., & Kilduff, M. (2020). Making connections: Social networks in international business. *JIBS, 51*(5), 714–736.

da Silva Lopes, T., Casson, M., & Jones, G. (2019). Organizational innovation in the multinational enterprise: Internalization theory and business history. *JIBS, 50*(8), 1338–1358.

da Silva Lopes, T., & Simões, V. C. (2020). Foreign investment in Portugal and knowledge spillovers: From the Methuen treaty to the 21st century. *Business History, 62*(7), 1079–1106.

Dai, L., Eden, L., & Beamish, P. (2013). Place, space, and geographical exposure: Foreign subsidiary survival in conflict zones. *JIBS, 44*(6), 554–578.

Dai, O., & Liu, X. (2009). Returnee entrepreneurs and firm performance in Chinese high-technology industries. *IBR, 18*(4), 373–386.

Davidson, W. H., & McFetridge, D. G. (1984). International technology transactions and the theory of the firm. *The Journal of Industrial Economics, 32*(3), 253–264.

Davidson, W. H., & McFetridge, D. (1985). Key characteristics in the choice of international technology transfer mode. *JIBS, 16*(2), 5–21.

Degain, C., Meng, B., & Wang, Z. (2017). Recent Trends in global trade and global value chains. In IBRD/World Bank (Ed.), *Global value chain development report 2017: Measuring and analyzing the impact of GVCs on economic development* (pp. 37–68). IBRD/World Bank.

de la Torre, J. (1981). Foreign investment and economic development: Conflict and negotiation. *JIBS, 12*(2), 9–32.

de la Torre, J. (1982). President's letter. *EIBA Newsletter, 7*(April), 2–3.

de la Torre, J., & Moxon, R. W. (2001). Introduction to the symposium E–commerce and global business: The impact of information and communication technology revolution on the conduct of international business. *JIBS, 32*(4), 617–639.

Dellestrand, H., & Kappen, P. (2012). The effects of spatial and contextual factors on headquarters resource allocation to MNE subsidiaries. *JIBS, 43*(3), 219–243.

De Marchi, V., Di Maria, E., Golini, R., & Perri, A. (2020). Nurturing international business research through global value chains literature: A review and discussion of future research opportunities. *IBR, 29*(5), Article 101708.

De Marchi, V., Muller, A., & Alon, I. (2019). Greening of EIBA: Proposal for discussion, Leeds, December.

Denicolai, S., Hagen, B., Zucchella, A., & Dudinskaya, E. C. (2019). When less family is more: Trademark acquisition, family ownership, and internationalization. *IBR, 28*(2), 238–251.

Deubner, C. (1981), *Foreign capital in Portuguese industrialization: Past experience, perspectives after EC–entry and the option of Luso–Spanish cooperation*, Paper presented at the Conference on 'Underdevelopment, Immigration and Industrialization in Portugal'. McGill University, Montreal.

Devarakonda, S., Klijn, E., Reuer, J., & Duplat, V. (2021). Institutional differences and arbitration mechanisms in international joint ventures. *GSJ*, *11*(2), 125–155.

Devinney, T. M., & Hartwell, C. A. (2020). Varieties of populism. *GSJ*, *10*(1), 32–66.

Devinney, T. M., & Hohberger, J. (2017). The past is prologue: Moving on from culture's consequences. *JIBS*, *48*, 48–62.

Devinney, T. M., McGahan, A. M., & Zollo, M. (2013). A research agenda for global stakeholder strategy. *GSJ*, *3*(4), 325–337.

Dhanaraj, C., Lyles, M. A., Steensma, H. K., & Tihanyi, L. (2004). Managing tacit and explicit knowledge transfer in IJVs: The role of relational embeddedness and the impact on performance. *JIBS*, *35*(5), 428–442.

Dikova, D., Panibratov, A., & Veselova, A. (2019). Investment motives, ownership advantages and institutional distance: An examination of Russian cross-border acquisitions. *IBR*, *28*(4), 625–637.

Dikova, D., Sahib, P. R., & van Witteloostuijn, A. (2010). Cross-border acquisition abandonment and completion: The effect of institutional differences and organizational learning in the international business service industry, 1981–2001. *JIBS*, *41*(2), 223–245.

Dikova, D., & van Witteloostuijn, A. (2007). Foreign direct investment mode choice: Entry and establishment modes in transition economies. *JIBS*, *38*(6), 1013–1033.

Dimitratos, P., Buck, T., Fletcher, M., & Li, N. (2016). The motivation of international entrepreneurship: The case of Chinese transnational entrepreneurs. *IBR*, *25*(5), 1103–1113.

Dimitratos, P., Johnson, J. E., Plakoyiannaki, E., & Young, S. (2016). SME internationalization: How does the opportunity-based international entrepreneurial culture matter? *IBR*, *25*(6), 1211–1222.

Dimitratos, P., Plakoyiannaki, E., Thanos, I. C., & Förbom, Y. K. (2014). The overlooked distinction of multinational enterprise subsidiary learning: Its managerial and entrepreneurial learning modes. *IBR*, *23*(1), 102–114.

Doh, J., Husted, B. W., Matten, D., & Santoro, M. (2010). Ahoy there! Toward greater congruence and synergy between international business and business ethics theory and research. *Business Ethics Quarterly*, *20*(3), 481–502.

Doh, J., Rodrigues, S., Saka-Helmhout, A., & Makhija, M. (2017). International business responses to institutional voids. *JIBS*, *48*(3), 293–307.

Dong, L., & Glaister, K. W. (2006). Motives and partner selection criteria in international strategic alliances: Perspectives of Chinese firms. *IBR*, *15*(6), 577–600.

Donges, J., Krieger-Boden, C., Langhammer, R. J., Schatz, K-W., & Thoroe, C. S. (1982). *The second enlargement of the European community: ADJUSTMENT requirements and challenges for policy reform*. Kieler Studien No. 171, Kiel.

Douglas, S. P., & Wind, Y. (1987). The myth of globalization. *Columbia JWB*, Winter, 19–29.

Dow, D., Baack, D., & Parente, R. (2020). The role of psychic distance in entry mode decisions: Magnifying the threat of opportunism or increasing the need for local knowledge? *GSJ*, *10*(2), 309–334.

Dow, D., Cuypers, I., & Ertug, G. (2016). The effects of within-country linguistic and religious diversity on foreign acquisitions. *JIBS*, *47*(3), 319–346.

Dow, D., & Karunaratna, A. (2006). Developing a multidimensional instrument to measure psychic distance stimuli. *JIBS*, 37(5), 578–602.

Doz, Y. L. (1986). *Strategic management in multinational corporations*. Pergamon Press.

Doz, Y. L. (1996). The evolution of cooperation in strategic alliances: Initial conditions or learning processes?' *SMJ*, *17*(S1), Special Issue: Evolutionary Perspectives on Strategy, 55–83.

Doz, Y. L. (2011). Qualitative research for international business. *JIBS*, *42*(5), 582–590.

Doz, Y. L., Bartlett, C. A., & Prahalad, C. K. (1981). Global competitive pressures and host country demands managing tensions in MNCs. *CMR*, *23*(3), 63–74.

Doz, Y. L., & Prahalad, C. K. (1980). How MNCs cope with host government intervention. *HBR*, March.

Doz, Y. L., & Prahalad, C. K. (1984). Patterns of strategic control in multinational corporations. *JIBS*, *15*(2), 55–72.

Doz, Y. L., & Prahalad, C. K. (1991). Managing DMNCs: A search for a new paradigm. *SMJ*, *12*(Special Issue 1), 145–164.

Doz, Y. L., Santos, J., & Williamson, P. (2001). *From global to metanational: How companies win in the knowledge economy*. Harvard Business Press.

Drogendijk, R. (2014). Welcome to EIBA 2014 in Uppsala. *EIBAzine, 15*, 4–5.

Drogendijk, R., & Slangen, A. (2006). Hofstede, Schwartz, or managerial perceptions? The effects of different cultural distance measures on establishment mode choices by multinational enterprises. *IBR, 15*(4), 361–380.

Dunning, J. H. (1958). *American investment in British manufacturing industry*. George Allen & Unwin.

Dunning, J. H. (1970), *Studies in international investment*. Allen and Unwin.

Dunning, J. H. (1973). The determinants of international production. *OEP, 25*(3), 289–336.

Dunning, J. H. (1977). Trade location of economic activity and the multinational enterprise: A search for an electic approach. In B. Ohlin, P-O. Hesselborn, & P. M. Wijkman (Eds.), *The international allocation of economic activity*. (pp. 395–418) MacMillan.

Dunning, J. H. (1979). Explaining changing patterns of international production: In defense of the eclectic theory. *OBES, 41*(4), 269–295.

Dunning, J. H. (1980). Towards an eclectic theory of international production: Some empirical tests. *JIBS, 11*(1), 9–31.

Dunning, J. H. (1981). *International production and the multinational enterprise*. Allen & Unwin.

Dunning, J. H. (1982). International business in a changing world climate. *Banca Nazionale del Lavoro Quarterly Review, 143*, 351–374.

Dunning, J. H. (1983a). Changes in the level and structure of international production: The last one hundred years. In M. Casson (Ed.), *The growth of international business* (pp. 84–139). Allen and Unwin.

Dunning, J. H. (1983b). Market power of the firm and international transfer of technology: An historical excursion. In B. Remiche (Ed.), *Transfert de Technologie: Enjeux Économiques et Structures Juridiques* (pp. 77–106). Economica.

Dunning, J. H. (1988a). The eclectic paradigm of international production: A restatement and some possible extensions. *JIBS, 19*(1), 1–31.

Dunning, J. H. (1988b). *Multinationals, technology and competitiveness*. Allen & Unwin.

Dunning, J. H. (1989). The study of international business: A plea for a more interdisciplinary approach. *JIBS, 20*(3), 411–436.

Dunning, J. H. (1993). *Multinational enterprises and the global economy*. Addison–Wesley.

Dunning, J. H. (1995). Reappraising the eclectic paradigm in an age of alliance capitalism. *JIBS, 26*(3), 461–491.

Dunning, J. H. (2000). The eclectic paradigm as an envelope for economic and business theories of MNE activity. *IBR, 9*(2), 163–190.

Dunning, J. H. (2001). The key literature on IB activities, 1960–2000. In A. M. Rugman & T. L. Brewer (Eds.), *The Oxford handbook of international business* (pp. 36–68). Oxford University Press.

Dunning, J. H. (2002). Relational assets, network and international business activity. In F. J. Contractor & P. Lorange (Eds.), *Cooperative strategies and alliances* (pp. 569–594). Elsevier Science.

Dunning, J. H. (2003). *Making globalization good*. Oxford University Press.

Dunning, J. H. (2008), *Seasons of a scholar*. Edward Elgar.

Dunning, J. H., Fujita, M., & Yakova, N. (2007). Some macro-data on the regionalisation/globalisation debate: A comment on the Rugman/Verbeke analysis. *JIBS, 38*(1), 177–199.

Dunning, J. H., & Hamdani, K. A. (Eds.). (1997). *The new globalism and developing countries*. United Nations.

Dunning, J. H., & Lundan, S. (2008). *Multinational enterprises and the global economy* (2nd ed.). Edward Elgar.

Dunning, J. H., & Wymbs, C. (2001). The challenge of electronic markets for international business theory. *Internationmal Journal of the Economics of Business, 8*(2), 273–301.

Durán, J. J. (1992). Cross-direct investment and technological capability of Spanish domestic firms. In J. Cantwell (Ed.), *Multinational investment in modern Europe: Strategic interaction in the integrated community* (pp. 214–255). Edward Elgar.

Durand, R., & Jacqueminet, A. (2015). Peer conformity, attention, and heterogeneous implementation of practices in MNEs. *JIBS, 46*(8), 917–937.

Dyer, J. H., & Hatch, N. W. (2006). Relation-specific capabilities and barriers to knowledge transfers: Creating advantage through network relationships. *SMJ*, *27*, 701–719.

Dyer, J. H., Kale, P., & Singh, H. (2001). How to make strategic alliances work. *SMR*, *42*(4), 37–43.

Dyer, J. H., & Singh, H. (1998). The relational view: Cooperative strategy and sources of interorganizational competitive advantage. *AMR*, *23*(4), 660–679.

Edman, J. (2016). Reconciling the advantages and liabilities of foreignness: Towards an identity-based framework. *JIBS*, *47*(6), 674–694.

Edström, A., & Galbraith, J. R. (1977). Transfer of managers as a coordination and control strategy in multinational organizations. *ASQ*, *22*(2), 248–263.

Egelhoff, W. G. (1982). Strategy and structure in multinational corporations: An information-processing approach. *ASQ*, *27*(3), 435–458.

Egelhoff, W. G. (1984). Patterns of control in U.S., UK and European multinational corporations. *JIBS*, *15*(Fall), 73–84.

Egelhoff, W. G., Wolf, J., & Adzic, M. (2013). Designing matrix structures to fit MNC strategy. *GSJ*, *3*(3), 205–226.

EIASM. (2003). *Letter to the EIBA Board*. Brussels, November 20.

EIBA. (1978). *EIBA Newsletter 1*, May.

EIBA. (1979). *EIBA Newsletter 2*, April.

EIBA. (1982a). *EIBA Newsletter 7*, April.

EIBA. (1982b). Proposed changes in Statutes for the European International Business Association. *EIBA Newsletter 8*, October, 11–16.

EIBA. (1987). EIBA 1987, A new feature: The special session for doctoral students in international business. *EIBA Newsletter*, November, 2.

EIBA. (2003). *Annual conference guidelines*, First draft. Copenhagen.

EIBA. (2004). *Annual conference guidelines*, Revised version. Copenhagen [this has been subject to successive revisions, distilling the experience of most EIBA conference organisers].

EIBA. (2005). *EIBA statutes*. Brussels: EIBA.

EIBA–AIB. (2004). *Buckley compromise*. Ljubljana, December.

EIBA Board. (1985). *Minutes of the EIBA Board meeting*. Brussels, May 31.

EIBA Board. (1989). *Minutes of the EIBA Strategy Board meeting*. Brussels, September.

EIBA Board. (1990). *Minutes of the EIBA Board meeting*, Brussels, September.

EIBA Board. (1995). *Minutes of the EIBA Board meeting*. Urbino, December.

EIBA Board. (1996a). *Minutes of the intermediate EIBA Board meeting*. Stockholm, September.

EIBA Board. (1996b). *Minutes of the EIBA Board meeting*. Stockholm, December.

EIBA Board. (1997). *Minutes of the EIBA Board meeting*. Stuttgart, June.

EIBA Board. (1998a). *Minutes of the intermediate EIBA Board meeting*. Jerusalem, May.

EIBA Board. (1998b). *Minutes of the EIBA Board meeting*. Jerusalem, December.

EIBA Board. (1999). *Minutes of the EIBA Board meeting*. Manchester, December.

EIBA Board. (2002a). *Minutes of the intermediate EIBA Board meeting*, Athens, April.

EIBA Board. (2002b). *Minutes of the EIBA Board meeting*. Athens, December.

EIBA Board. (2003). *Minutes of the EIBA Board meeting*. Copenhagen, December.

EIBA Board. (2004). *Minutes of the Board meeting*. Ljubljana, December.

EIBA Board. (2008). *Minutes of the intermediate Board meeting*. Tallinn, May.

EIBA Board. (2011). *Minutes of the EIBA Board meeting*. Bucharest, December.

EIBA Board. (2012). *Minutes of the Board meeting*. Brighton, December.

EIBA Board. (2015a). *Minutes of the Board meeting*. Paris, May.

Eiba Board. (2015b). *Minutes of the Board meeting*. Rio de Janeiro, December.

EIBA Board. (2017a). *Minutes of the Board meeting*. Milan, May.

EIBA Board. (2017b). *Procedure regarding the nomination/election of the Chair and Vice–Chair of EIBA*. Milan.

EIBA Board. (2018). *Minutes of the Board meeting*. Poznan, April.

EIBA Board. (2019a). *Minutes of the Board meeting*. Leeds, May

EIBA Fellows. (2003). *Minutes of the EIBA Fellows meeting*. Copenhagen, December.

EIBA Fellows. (2004). *Scheme for the Election of EIBA Fellows*. Ljubljana, December.

EIBA Fellows. (2009). *Procedure for the Election of the Dean of the EIBA Fellows*. Valencia, December.

Elango, B., & Pattnaik, C. (2007). Building capabilities for international operations through networks: a study of Indian firms. *JIBS*, *38*(4), 541–555.

Elia, S., Larsen, M. M., & Piscitello, L. (2019). Entry mode deviation: A behavioral approach to internalization theory. *JIBS*, *50*(8), 1359–1371.

Elia, S., & Santangelo, G. D. (2017). The evolution of strategic asset-seeking acquisitions by emerging market multinationals. *IBR*, *26*(5), 855–866.

Emmanuel, A. (1981). *Technologie Appropriée ou Technologie Sous–développée*. IRM-Presses Universitaires de France.

Enderwick, P. (2018a). The economic growth and development effects of China's one belt one road initiative. *Strategic Change*, *27*, 447–454.

Enderwick, P. (2018b). The scope of corporate social responsibility in networked multinational enterprises. *IBR*, *27*(2), 410–417.

Engwall, L., Pahlberg, C., & Persson, O. (2018). The development of IB as a scientific field. *IBR*, *27*(5), 1080–1088.

Ernst, D. (1980). International transfer of technology, technological dependence and development. In D. Ernst (Ed.), *The new international division of labour, technology and underdevelopment* (pp. 15–75). Campus Verlag.

Ertug, G., Cuypers, I. R. P., Noorderhaven, N. G., & Bensaou, B. M. (2013). Trust between international joint venture partners: Effects of home countries. *JIBS*, *44*(3), 263–282.

European Commission. (2009). *Explaining the Treaty of Lisbon*, MEMO/09/531, Brussels: European Commission. Retrieved February 15, 2022, from https://ec.europa.eu/commission/presscorner/detail/en/MEMO_09_531.

European Commission. (2020). *Commission adopts White Paper on foreign subsidies in the Single Market*. Press Release, Brussels, June 17. Retrieved October 10, 2023, from https://ec.europa.eu/commission/presscorner/detail/en/ip_20_1070.

European Commission. (2022). Regulation (EU) 2022/2560 of the European Parliament and of the Council of 14 December 2022 on foreign subsidies distorting the internal market. *Official Journal of the European Union*, December 23, 2022. Retrieved January 11, 2024, from https://eur-lex.europa.eu/legal-content/EN/TXT/PDF/?uri=CELEX:32022R2560

European Commission & High Representative of the Union for Foreign Affairs and Security Policy. (2019). EU–China – A strategic outlook. JOIN(2019) 5 final. Strasbourg, March. Retrieved December 2, 2020, from https://commission.europa.eu/system/files/2019–03/communication-eu–china–a–strategic–outlook.pdf

European Parliament. (2024). *Digital Services and Digital Markets Act*. Retrieved January 11, 2024, from https://multimedia.europarl.europa.eu/en/topic/digital–services–and–digital–markets–act_17701?tab=overview&photoType=25

Evans, J., & Mavondo, F. T. (2002). Psychic distance and organizational performance: An empirical examination of international retailing operations. *JIBS*, *33*(3), 515–532.

Evans, P., & Wurster, T. S. (1997). Strategy and the new economics of information. *HBR*, Sept.–Oct., 71–82.

Evenett, S. J. (2019). Protectionism, state discrimination, and international business since the onset of the global financial crisis. *JIBP*, *2*(1), 9–36.

Fainshmidt, S., Witt, M. A., Aguilera, R. V., & Verbeke, A. (2020). The contributions of qualitative comparative analysis (QCA) to international business research. *JIBS*, *51*(4), 455–466.

Fernández-de-Sevilla, T. (2016). International business in Southern Europe: Renault in Italy, Portugal and Spain (1908–2007). *Journal of Evolutionary Studies in Business*, *2*(1), 129–155.

Fetscherin, M., Voss, H., & Gugler, P. (2009). 30 Years of foreign direct investment to China: An interdisciplinary literature review. *IBR*, *19*(3), 235–246.

Filatotchev, I., Stephan, J., & Jindra, B. (2008). Ownership structure, strategic controls and export intensity of foreign-invested firms in transition economies. *JIBS*, *39*(7), 1133–1148.

Filatotchev, I., Strange, R., Piesse, J., & Lien, Y-C. (2007). FDI by firms from newly industrialized economies in emerging markets: Corporate governance, entry mode and location. *JIBS*, *38*(4), 556–572.

Florida, R. (1997). The globalization of R&D: Results of a survey of foreign-affiliated R&D laboratories in the USA. *RP*, *26*(1), 85–103.

Florida, R. (2008). *Who's your city?* Basic Books.

Forsgren, M. (2008). *Theories of the multinational firm: A multidimensional creature in the global economy.* Edward Elgar.

Forsgren, M. (2016). A note on the revisited Uppsala internationalization process model – The implications of business networks and entrepreneurship. *JIBS, 47*(9), 1135–1144.

Forsgren, M., Holm, U., & Johanson, J. (Eds.). (2005). *Managing the embedded multinational: A business network view.* Edward Elgar.

Forsgren, M., & Pedersen, T. (1998). Centres of excellence in multinational companies: The case of Denmark. In J. Birkinshaw & N. Hood (Eds.), *Multinational corporate evolution and subsidiary development* (pp. 213–238). MacMillan.

Forsgren, M., & Pedersen, T. (2000). Subsidiary influence and corporate learning: Centres of excellence in Danish owned forms. In U. Holm & T. Pedersen (Eds.), *The emergence and impact of MNC centers of excellence: A subsidiary perspective* (pp. 68–78). MacMillan Press.

Forsgren, M., & Piekkari, R. (2018). Reijo's work and the Uppsala model: Similarities and differences. *EIBAzine, 22,* 7–9.

Foss, N. J. (1994). Why transaction cost economics needs. Evolutionary economics. *Revue d'Économie Industrielle, 68*(2), 7–26.

Foss, N. J., & Pedersen, T. (2004). Organizing knowledge processes in the multinational corporation: An introduction. *JIBS, 35*(5), 340–349.

Foss, N. J., & Pedersen, T. (2019). Microfoundations in international management research: The case of knowledge sharing in multinational corporations. *JIBS, 50*(9), 1594–1621.

Franko, L. G. (1976). *The European multinationals.* Harper & Row.

Fratocchi, L., & Holm, U. (1998). Centres of excellence in international firms. In J. Birkinshaw & N. Hood (Eds.), *Multinational corporate evolution and subsidiary development* (pp. 189–209). MacMillan.

Frost, T. S., Birkinshaw, J., & Ensign, P. C. (2002). Centers of excellence in multinational corporations. *SMJ, 23*(11), 997–1018.

Frost, T. S., & Zhou, C. (2005). R&D co-practice and "reverse" knowledge integration in multinational firms. *JIBS, 36*(6), 676–687.

Fung, H-G., Qiao, P., Yau, J., & Zeng, Y. (2020). Leader narcissism and outward foreign direct investment: Evidence from Chinese firms. *IBR, 29*(1), Article 101632.

Gaba, V., Pan, Y., & Ungson, G. R. (2002). Timing of entry in international market: An empirical study of US Fortune 500 firms in China. *JIBS, 33*(1), 39–55.

Gabrielsson, M., Kirpalani, V. H. M., Dimitratos, P., Solberg, C. A., & Zucchella, A. (2008). Born globals: Propositions to help advance the theory. *IBR, 17*(4), 385–401.

Gao, G. Y., Murray, J. Y., Kotabe, M., & Lu, J. (2010). A "strategy tripod" perspective on export behaviors: Evidence from domestic and foreign firms based in an emerging economy. *JIBS, 41*(3), 377–396.

Gassmann, O., & Keupp, M. M. (2007). The competitive advantage of early and rapidly internationalising SMEs in the biotechnology industry: A knowledge-based view. *JWB, 42*(3), 350–366.

Gereffi, G. (1999). International trade and industrial upgrading in the apparel commodity chain. *Journal of International Economics, 48*(1), 37–70.

Gereffi, G. (2014). Global value chains in a post-Washington Consensus world. *Review of International Political Economy, 21*(1), 9–37.

Gereffi, G. (2019). Global value chains and international development policy: Bringing firms, networks and policy-engaged scholars back in. *JIBP, 2*(3), 195–210.

Gereffi, G. (2020). What does the COVID-19 pandemic teach us about global value chains? The case of medical supplies. *JIBP, 3*(3), 287–301.

Gereffi, G., Humphrey, J., Kaplinsky, R., & Sturgeon, T. J. (2001). Introduction: Globalisation, value chains and development. *IDS Bulletin, 32*(3), 1–8.

Geringer, J. M. (1988). *Joint venture partner selection: Strategies for developed countries.* Quorum Books.

Getachew, Y. S., & Beamish, P. W. (2017). Foreign subsidiary exit from Africa: The effects of investment purpose diversity and orientation. *GSJ, 7*(1), 58–82.

Ghemawat, P. (2001). Distance still matters: The hard reality of global expansion. *HBR, 79*(8), 137–147.

Ghemawat, P. (2003). Semiglobalisation and international business strategy. *JIBS, 34*(2), 138–152.

Ghemawat, P. (2007). *Redefining global strategy – Crossing borders in a world where differences still matter*. Harvard Business School Press.

Ghertman, M. (1981). *La prise de décision*. Presses Universitaires de France.

Ghertman, M. (2016). *Interview with Vitor Corado Simões*. Cagnes-sur-Mer, November.

Ghertman, M., & Leontiades, J. (Eds.). (1978). *European research in international business*. North-Holland Publishing.

Ghoshal, S. (1987). Global strategy: An organizing framework. *SMJ, 88*(5), 425–440.

Ghoshal, S., & Westney, D. E. (1993). *Organization theory and the multinational enterprise*. Macmillan.

Giuliani, E., Gorgoni, S., Günther, C., & Rabellotti, R. (2014). Emerging versus advanced country MNEs investing in Europe: A typology of subsidiary global–local connections. *IBR, 23*(4), 680–691.

Godinho, M. M., & Simões, V. C. (2023). "Tech Cold War": What can we learn from the most dynamic patent classes?' *IBR, 32*(6), Article 102140.

Goerzen, A., Asmussen, C., & Nielsen, B. B. (2013). Global cities and multinational enterprise location strategy. *JIBS, 44*(5), 427–450.

Goldstein, A., & Piscitello, L. (2007). *Le Multinazionali*. Il Mulino.

Golesorkhi, S., Mersland, R., Randøy, T., & Shenkar, O. (2019). The performance impact of informal and formal institutional differences in cross-border alliances. *IBR, 28*(1), 104–118.

Gölgeci, I., Assadinia, S., Kuivalainen, O., & Larimo, J. (2019). Emerging-market firms' dynamic capabilities and international performance: The moderating role of institutional development and distance. *IBR, 28*(6), Article 101593.

Gooris, J., & Peeters, C. (2016). Fragmenting global business processes: A protection for proprietary information. *JIBS, 47*(5), 535–562.

Gorynia, M., Nowak, J., Trąpczyński, P., & Wolniak, R. (2019). Friend or Foe? On the role of institutional reforms in the investment development path of Central and East European economies. *IBR, 28*(3), 575–587.

Govindarajan, V., & Ramamurti, R. (2011). Reverse innovation, emerging markets, and global strategy. *GSJ, 1*(3/4), 191–205.

Graham, E. M. (1978). Transatlantic investment by multinational firms: A rivalistic phenomenon. *Journal of Post–Keynesian Economics, 1*, 82–99.

Granovetter, M. (1985). Economic action and social structure: The problem of embeddedness. *American Journal of Sociology, 91*(3), 481–510.

Granstrand, O. (1999). Internationalization of corporate R&D: A study of Japanese and Swedish corporations. *RP, 28*(2), 275–302.

Grant, R. M. (1991). Porter's "competitive advantage of nations": An assessment. *SMJ, 12*(7), 535–548.

Grant, R. M., & C. Baden-Fuller (2004). A knowledge accessing theory of strategic alliances. *JoM Studies, 41*(1), 61–84.

Gray, H. P. (Ed.). (2003). *Extending the eclectic paradigm in international business: Essays in honor of John Dunning*. Edward Elgar.

Griffith, D. A., & Myers, M. B. (2005). The performance implications of strategic fit of relational norm governance strategies in global supply chain relationships. *JIBS, 36*(3), 254–269.

Grøgaard, B. (2012). Alignment of strategy and structure in international firms: An empirical examination. *IBR, 21*(3), 397–407

Grøgaard, B., Rygh, A., & Benito, G. (2019). Bringing corporate governance into internalization theory: State ownership and foreign entry strategies. *JIBS, 50*(8), 1310–1337.

Gugler, P. (1991). *Les Alliances Stratégiques Internationales*. Presses Universitaires de Fribourg.

Gugler, P. (1992). Building transnational alliances to create competitive advantage. *LRP, 25*, 90–99.

Gugler, P., & Plà-Barber, J. (2015). *EIBA chair strategic paper*. Fribourg and Valencia, November.

Gugler, P., & Plà-Barber, J. (2016). *EIBA strategy discussion*. Vienna, April.

Guillén, M. F. (2002). Imitation, inertia, and foreign expansion: South Korean firms and business groups in China, 1987–1999. *AMJ, 45*(3), 509–525.

Guillén, M. (2018). *Rude awakening: threats to the global liberal order*. University of Pennsylvania Press.

Gulati, R. (1995). Does familiarity breed trust? The implications of repeated ties for contractual choice in alliances. *AMJ, 38*(1), 85–112.

Gulati, R. (1998). Alliances and networks. *SMJ*, *19*(4), 293–317.

Gunkel, M., Schlaegel, C., Rossteutscher, T., & Wolff, B. (2015). The human aspect of cross–border acquisition outcomes: The role of management practices, employee emotions, and national culture. *IBR*, *24*(3), 394–408.

Gupta, A. K., & Govindarajan, V. (1991). Knowledge flows and the structure of control within multinational corporations. *AMR*, *16*(4), 768–792.

Gupta, A. K., & Govindarajan, V. (1994). Organizing for knowledge flows within MNCs. *IBR*, *3*(4), 443–457.

Ha, Y. J., & Giroud, A. (2015). Competence-creating subsidiaries and FDI technology spillovers. *IBR*, *24*(4), 605–614.

Haas, M., & Cummings, J. (2015). Barriers to knowledge seeking within MNC teams: Which differences matter most?. *JIBS*, *46*(1), 36–62.

Hagedoorn, J. (1990). Organizational modes of inter–firm co–operation and technology transfer. *Technovation*, *10*(1), 17–30. .

Hagedoorn, J. (1993). Understanding the rationale of strategic technology partnering: Interorganizational modes of cooperation and sectoral differences. *SMJ*, *14*(5), 371–385.

Hagedoorn, J. (2002). Inter-firm R&D partnerships: An overview of major trends and patterns since 1960. *RP*, *31*(4), 477–492.

Hagedoorn, J., & Sadowski, B. (1999). The transition from strategic technology alliances to mergers and acquisitions: an exploratory study. *Journal of Management Studies*, *36*(1), 87–107.

Hagen, B., & Zucchella, A. (2014). Born global or born to run? The long–term growth of born global firms. *MIR*, *54*, 497–525.

Håkansson, L., & Pedersen, T. (2003). The future of EIBA. Cf. EIBA Board (2003). *Minutes of the intermediate Board meeting*. Copenhagen, December.

Håkanson, L., & Zander, U. (1988). International management of R&D: The Swedish experience. *R&D Management*. Retrieved March 2, 2020, from https://doi.org/10.1111/j.1467–9310.1988.tb00588.x.

Hamel, G. (1991). Competition for competence and interpartner learning within international strategic alliances. *SMJ*, *12*, 83–103.

Hamel, G., Doz, Y. L., & Prahalad, C. K. (1989). Collaborate with your competitors – and win. *HBR*, *67*(1), 133–139.

Hamel, G., & Prahalad, C. K. (1985). Do you really have a global strategy?' *Thunderbird IBR*, *27*(3), 13–14.

Harrigan, K. R. (1985). *Strategies for joint venture success*. D.C. Heath.

Hart, S. L., & Milstein, M. B. (2003). Creating sustainable value. *Academy of Management Executive*, *17*(2), 56–67.

Harzing, A-W. (2000). An empirical analysis and extension of the Bartlett and Ghoshal typology of multinational companies. *JIBS*, *31*(1), 101–120.

Hassett, M. E., Reynolds, N-S., & Sandberg, B. (2018). The emotions of top managers and key persons in cross-border M&As: Evidence from a longitudinal case study. *IBR*, *27*(4), 737–754.

Hedlund, G. (1980). The role of foreign subsidiaries in strategic decision-making in Swedish multinational corporations. *SMJ*, *1*(1), 23–36.

Hedlund, G. (1984). Organization in-between: The evolution of the mother–daughter structure of managing foreign subsidiaries in Swedish MNCs. *JIBS*, *15*(Fall), 109–123.

Hedlund, G. (1986). The hypermodern MNC: An heterarchy?' *Human Resource Management*, *25*(1), 9–35.

Hedlund, G., & Rolander, D. (1990). Action in heterarchies: New approaches to managing the MNC. In C. A. Bartlett, Y. L. Doz, & G. Hedlund (Eds.), *Managing the global firm* (pp. 15–46). Routledge.

Helpman, E. (1984). A simple theory of international trade with multinational corporations. *Journal of Political Economy*, *92*(3), 451–471.

Helpman, E. (1985). Multinational corporations and trade structure. *Review of Economic Studies*, *52*(3), 443–457

Helpman, E., & Krugman, P. N. (1985). *Market structure and foreign trade: Increasing returns, imperfect competition, and the international economy*. Wheatsheaf.

Henisz, W. J. (2013). Preferences, structure, and influence: The engineering of consent. *GSJ*, *3*(4), 338–359.

Henisz, W. J., & Delios, A. (2001). Uncertainty, imitation, and plant location: Japanese multinational corporations, 1990–1996. *ASQ*, *46*(3), 443–475.

Hennart, J-F. (1977). *A theory of foreign direct investment*, Doctoral dissertation. Maryland: University of Mariland (published as a book in 1982).

Hennart, J-F. (1986). What is internalisation?. *Weltwirtschaftliches Archiv*, *122*, 791–806.

Hennart, J-F. (1988). A transaction costs theory of equity joint ventures. *SMJ*, *9*, 361–374.

Hennart, J-F. (1991). The transaction costs theory of joint ventures: An empirical study of Japanese subsidiaries in the United States. *MS*, *37*(4), 483–497.

Hennart, J-F. (1993). Explaining the swollen middle: Why most transactions are a mix of "Market" and "Hierarchy". *OS*, *4*(4), 529–547.

Hennart, J-F. (2001). Theories of the multinational enterprise. In A. M. Rugman & T. L. Brewer (Eds.), *The Oxford handbook of international business* (pp. 127–149). Oxford University Press.

Hennart, J-F. (2009). Down with MNE-centric theories! Market entry and expansion as the bundling of MNE and local assets. *JIBS*, *40*(9), 1432–1454.

Hennart, J-F. (2014). The accidental internationalists: A theory of born globals. *ETP*, *38*(1), 117–135.

Hennart, J-F. (2019). Digitalized service multinationals and international business theory. *JIBS*, *50*, 1388–1400.

Hennart, J. F. (2020). More than intent: A bundling model of MNE–SME interactions. *Journal of International Business Studies*, *51*(7), 1176–1194.

Hennart, J-F., & Larimo, J. (1998). The impact of culture on the strategy of multinational enterprises: Does national origin affect ownership decisions?' *JIBS*, *29*(3), 515–538.

Hennart, J-F., Majocchi, A., & Forlani, E. (2019). The myth of the stay-at-home family firm: How family-managed SMEs can overcome their internationalization limitations. *JIBS*, *50*(5), 758–782.

Hennart, J-F., & Slangen, A. (2015). Yes, we really do need more entry mode studies! A commentary on Shaver. *JIBS*, *46*(1), 114–122.

Herrero, A. G. (2021). What is behind China's dual circulation strategy. *China Leadership Monitor*, Fall(69). Retrieved February 11, 2022, from https://www.prcleader.org/herrero.

Heyden, M., Oehmichen, L. M. J., Nichting, S., & Volberda, H. W. (2015). Board background heterogeneity and exploration–exploitation: The role of the institutionally adopted board model. *GSJ*, *5*(2), 154–176.

Hill, C. W. L., Hwang, P., & Kim, W. C. (1990). An eclectic theory of the choice of international entry mode. *SMJ*, *11*(2), 117–128.

Hillman, A. J., & Wan, W. P. (2005). The determinants of MNE subsidiaries' political strategies: evidence of institutional duality. *JIBS*, *36*(3), 322–340.

Hirsch, S. (1967). *Location of industry and international competitiveness*. Oxford University Press.

Hirsch, S. (1976). An international trade and investment theory of the firm. *OEP*, *28*, 258–270.

Hoekman, B., & Nelson, D. R. (2018). Reflecting on populism and the economics of globalization. *JIBP*, *1*(1), 34–43.

Hoenen, A., & T. Kostova (2015). Utilizing the broader agency perspective for studying headquarters – Subsidiary relations in multinational companies. *JIBS*, *46*(1), 104–113.

Hofstede, G. (1980). *Culture's consequences: International differences in work-related attitudes*. Sage.

Hofstede, G. (1997). *Cultures and organizations: Software of the mind*. McGraw Hill.

Hohenthal, J., Johanson, J., & Johanson, M. (2014). Network knowledge and business–relationship value in the foreign market. *IBR*, *23*(1), 4–19.

Hollender, L., Zapkau, F. B., & Schwens, C. (2017). SME foreign market entry mode choice and foreign venture performance: The moderating effect of international experience and product adaptation. *IBR*, *26*(2), 250–263.

Holm, U., & Pedersen, T. (Eds.). (2000). *The emergence and impact of MNC centers of excellence*. Macmillan.

Hood, N., & J-E. Vahlne (Eds.). (1987). *Strategies in Global Competition*. London: Croom Helm,

Horaguchi, H., & Toyne, B. (1990). Setting the record straight: Hymer, internalization theory and transaction cost economics. *JIBS*, *21*(3), 487–494.

House, R. J., Hanges, P. J., Javidan, M., Dorfman, P. W., & Gupta, V. (Eds.). (2004). *Culture, leadership and organizations: The GLOBE study of 62 societies*. Sage Publications.

Howard, M., Steensma, H. K., Lyles, M., & Dhanaraj, C. (2016). Learning to collaborate through collaboration: How allying with expert firms influences collaborative innovation within novice firms. *SMJ, 37*(10), 2092–2103.

Hsu, C-W., Lien, Y-C., & Chen, H. (2015). R&D internationalization and innovation performance. *IBR, 24*(2), 187–195.

Humphrey, J., & Schmitz, H. (2002). How does insertion in global value chains affect upgrading in industrial clusters? *Regional Studies, 36*(9), 1017–1027.

Hurmerinta-Peltomäki, L., & Nummela, N. (2006). Mixed methods in international business research: A value-added perspective. *MIR, 46*(4), 439–459.

Husted, B. W., & Allen, D. B. (2006). Corporate social responsibility in the multinational enterprise: Strategic and institutional approaches. *JIBS, 37*(6), 838–849.

Hutzschenreuter, T., & Matt, T. (2017). MNE internationalization patterns, the roles of knowledge stocks, and the portfolio of MNE subsidiaries. *JIBS, 48*(9), 1131–1150

Hymer. S. H. (1968). La grande "corporation" multinationale: Analyse de certaines raisons qui poussent à l'intégration internationale des affaires. *Revue Économique, 19*(6), 949–973.

Hymer, S. H. (1970). The efficiency (contradictions) of multinational corporations. *American Economic Review, LX*(2), 441–448.

Hymer, S. H. (1972). The multinational corporation and the law of uneven development. In J. Bhagwati (Ed.), *Economics and world order* (pp. 113–140). Macmillan.

Hymer, S. H. (1976/1960), *The international operations of national firms: A study of direct foreign investment.* MIT Press (Ph.D. dissertation, MIT, 1960).

Iammarino, S., & McCann, P. (2013). *Multinationals and economic geography: Location, technology and innovation.* Edward Elgar.

Inkpen, A. C., & Crossan, M. (1995). Believing is seeing: Joint ventures and organization learning. *JMS, 32*(5), 595–618.

Inkpen, A. C., & Currall, S. C. (1997). International joint venture trust: An empirical examination. In P. W. Beamish & J. P. Killing (Eds.), *Cooperative strategies: North American perspectives* (pp.308–334). New Lexington Press.

Inkpen, A. C., & Currall, S. C. (2004). The coevolution of trust, control and learning in joint ventures. *OS, 15*(5), 586–599.

Inkpen, A. C., Minbaeva, D., & Tsang, E. W. K. (2019). Unintentional, unavoidable, and beneficial knowledge leakage from the multinational enterprise. *JIBS, 50*(2), 250–260.

Iurkov, V., & Benito, G. R. G. (2018). Domestic alliance networks and regional strategies of MNEs: A structural embeddedness perspective. *JIBS, 49*(8), 1033–1059.

Ivarsson, I., & Vahlne, J-E. (2002). Technology integration through international acquisitions: The case of foreign manufacturing TNCs in Sweden. *Scandinavian Journal of Management, 18*(1), 1–27.

Ivus, O., Park, W. G., & Saggi, K. (2017). Patent protection and the composition of multinational activity: Evidence from US multinational firms. *JIBS, 48*(7), 808–836.

Jackson, G., & Deeg, R. (2008). Comparing capitalisms: Understanding institutional diversity and its implications for international business. *JIBS, 39*(4), 540–561.

Jain, N. K., Pangarkar, N., Yuan, L., & Kumar, V. (2019). Rapid internationalization of emerging market firms – The role of geographic diversity and added cultural distance. *IBR, 28*(6), Article 101590.

James, B. E., Sawant, R. J., & Bendickson, J. S. (2020). Emerging market multinationals' firm-specific advantages, institutional distance, and foreign acquisition location choice. *IBR, 29*(5), 101702.

Javidan, M., & Dastmalchian, A. (2009). Managerial implications of the GLOBE project: A study of 62 societies. *Asia Pacific Journal of Human Resources, 47*(1), 41–58.

Javidan, M., Dorfman, P. W., de Luque, M. S., & House, R. J. (2006). In the eye of the beholder: Cross–cultural lessons in leadership for project GLOBE. *The AMP, 20*(1), 67–90.

Jensen, N. M., Li, Q., & Rahman, A. (2010). Understanding corruption and firm responses in cross–national firm–level surveys. *JIBS, 41*(9), 1481–1504.

Jensen, R., & Szulanski, G. (2004). Stickiness and the adaptation of organizational practices in cross-border knowledge transfers. *JIBS, 35*(6), 508–523.

Ji, J., & Dimitratos, P. (2013). An empirical investigation into international entry mode decision-making effectiveness. *IBR, 22*(6), 994–1007.

Johanson, J., & Mattson, L-G. (1988). Internationalization in industrial systems – A network approach. In N. Hood & J-E. Vahlne (Eds.), *Strategies in global competition* (pp. 287–314). Croom Helm.

Johanson, J., & Vahlne, J-E. (1977). The internationalization process of the firm – A model of knowledge development and increasing foreign market commitments. *JIBS, 8*(1), 23–32.

Johanson, J., & Vahlne, J-E. (1978). A model for the decision–making process affecting the pattern and pace of the internationalization of the firm. In M. Ghertman & J. Leontiades (Eds.), *European research in international business* (pp. 9–28). North–Holland Publishing.

Johanson, J., & Vahlne, J-E. (1990). The mechanism of internationalization. *IMR, 7*(4), 11–24.

Johanson, J., & Vahlne, J-E. (1992). Management of foreign market entry. *Scandinavian IBR, 1*(3), 9–27.

Johanson, J., & Vahlne, J-E. (2003). Business relationship learning and commitment in the internationalization process. *JIE, 1*, 83–101.

Johanson, J., & Vahlne, J-E. (2006). Commitment and opportunity development in the internationalization process: A note on the Uppsala internationalization process model. *MIR, 46*(2), 165–178.

Johanson, J., & Vahlne, J-E. (2009). The Uppsala internationalization process model revisited: From liability of foreignness to liability of outsidership. *JIBS, 40*(9), 1411–1431.

Johanson, J., & Vahlne, J-E. (2020). The Uppsala model: Networks and micro-foundations. *JIBS, 51*(1), 4–10.

Jones, G. (1984). The growth and performance of British multinational firms before 1939: The case of Dunlop. *Economic History Review*. Retrieved February 27, 2020, from https://doi.org/10.1111/j.1468–0289.1984.tb00315.x

Jones, G. (1985). The gramophone company: An Anglo-American multinational, 1898–1931. *Business History Review, 59*(1), 76–100.

Jones, G. (1988). Foreign multinationals and British industry before 1945. *Economic History Review, 41*, 429–53.

Jones, G., & Khanna, T. (2006). Bringing history (back) into international business. *JIBS, 37*(4), 453–468.

Jones, M. (1999). The internationalisation of small high technology firms. *JIM, 7*(4), 15–41.

Jones, M. V., & Coviello, N. E. (2005). Internationalisation: Conceptualising an entrepreneurial process of behaviour in time. *JIBS, 36*(3), 284–303.

Jones, M. V., Coviello, N. E., & Tang, Y. K. (2011). International entrepreneurship research (1989–2009): A domain ontology and thematic analysis. *Journal of Business Venturing, 26*(6), 632–659.

Joshi, M. A., & Lahiri, N. (2015). Language friction and partner selection in cross-border R&D alliance formation. *JIBS, 46*(2), 123–152.

Kalasin, K., Cuervo-Cazurra, A., & Ramamurti, R. (2020). State ownership and international expansion: The S-curve relationship. *GSJ, 10*(2), 386–418.

Kano, L. (2018). Global value chain governance: A relational perspective. *JIBS, 49*, 684–705.

Kano, L., Tsang, E. W. K., & Yeung, H. W-C. (2020). Global value chains: A review of the multi–disciplinary literature. *JIBS, 51*(4), 577–622.

Kano, L., & Verbeke, A. (2018). Family firm internationalization: Heritage assets and the impact of bifurcation bias. *GSJ, 8*(1), 158–183.

Kano, L., & Verbeke, A. (2019). Theories of the multinational firm: A microfoundational perspective. *GSJ, 9*(1), 117–147.

Kanter, R. M. (1994). Collaborative advantage: The art of alliances. *HBR, 72*(4), 96–108.

Kaplinski, R. (1976). Accumulation and the transfer of technology: Issues of conflict and mechanisms for the exercise of control. *World Development, 4*(3), 197–224.

Katz, J. M. (1976). *Importación de Tecnología, Aprendizaje e Industrialización Dependiente*. Fondo de Cultura Económica.

Keupp, M. M., & O. Gassmann (2009). The past and the future of international entrepreneurship: A review and suggestions for developing the field. *JoM, 35*(3), 600–633.

Khan, K. M. (Ed.). (1987). *Multinationals of the south – New actors in the international economy*. Frances Pinter.

Khan, Z., Lew, Y. K., & Sinkovics, R. R. (2015). International joint ventures as boundary spanners: Technological knowledge transfer in an emerging economy. *GSJ, 5*(1), 48–68.

Khan, Z., Shenkar, O., & Lew, Y. (2015). Knowledge transfer from international joint ventures to local suppliers in a developing economy. *JIBS, 46*(6), 656–675.

Khanna, T., Gulati, R., & Nohria, N. (1998). The dynamics of learning alliances: Competition, cooperation, and relative scope. *SMJ, 19*(3), 193–210.

Khedia, B. L., & Reddy, R. K. (2016). Language and cross-border acquisitions: An exploratory study.
IBR, 25(6), 1321–1332.

Killing, J. P. (1980). Technology acquisition: License agreement or joint venture. *Columbia JWB*, Fall,
38–46.

Killing, J. P. (1983). *Strategies for joint venture success*. Praeger.

Killing, J. P. (1988). Understanding alliances: The role of task and organizational complexity. In
F. Contractor & P. Lorange (Eds.), *Cooperative strategy in international business* (pp. 55–68).
Lexington Books.

Kim, H., & Song, J. (2017). Filling institutional voids in emerging economies: The impact of capital
market development and business groups on M&A deal abandonment. *JIBS, 48*, 308–323.

Kim, M. (2013). Many roads lead to Rome: Implications of geographic scope as a source of isolating
mechanisms. *JIBS, 44*(9), 898–921.

Kim, W. C., & Hwang, P. (1992). Global strategy and multinationals' entry mode choice. *JIBS, 23*(1),
29–53.

Kirkman, B. L., Lowe, K. B., & Gibson, C. B. (2006). A quarter century of culture's consequences:
A review of empirical research incorporating Hofstede's cultural values framework. *JIBS,
37*(3), 285–320.

Knickerbocker, F. T. (1973). *Oligopolistic reaction and the multinational enterprise*. Harvard University
Press.

Knight, G. A., & Cavusgil, S. T. (2004). Innovation, organizational capabilities, and the born–global
firm. *JIBS, 35*(2), 124–141.

Kobrin, S. J. (2017). Bricks and mortar in a borderless world: Globalization, the backlash, and the
multinational enterprise. *GSJ, 7*(2), 159–171.

Kobrin, S. J. (2020). How globalization became a thing that goes bump in the night. *JIBP, 3*, 280–286.

Kobrin, S. J. (2021). Is a networked world economy sustainable?. In A. Verbeke, R. van Tulder, E. Rose,
& Y. Wei (Eds.), *The multiple dimensions of institutional complexity in international business
research*, Progress in International Business Research No. 15 (pp. 63–70). Emerald Publishing.
https://doi.org/10.1108/S1745–886220210000015004.

Koch, P. T., Koch, B., Menon, T., & Shenkar, O. (2016). Cultural friction in leadership beliefs and
foreign-invested enterprise survival. *JIBS, 47*, 453–470.

Kogut, B. (1985). Designing global strategies: Corporate and competitive value added chain. *SMR,
25*, 15–28.

Kogut, B. (1988). Joint ventures: Theoretical and empirical perspectives. *SMJ, 9*, 319–322.

Kogut, B., & Singh, H. (1988). The effect of national culture on the choice of entry mode. *JIBS, 19*(3),
411–432.

Kogut, B., & Zander, U. (1992). Knowledge of the firm, combinative capabilities, and the replication
of technology. *OS, 3*(3), 383–397.

Kogut, B., & Zander, U. (1993). Knowledge of the firm and the evolutionary theory of the multinational corporation. *JIBS, 24*(4), 625–645.

Kogut, B., & Zander, U. (1995). Knowledge, market failure and the multinational enterprise: A reply.
JIBS, 26(2), 417–426.

Kogut, B., & Zander, U. (1996). What firms do? coordination, identity, and learning. *OS, 7*(5), 502–518.

Kojima, K. (1978). *Direct foreign investment: A Japanese model of multinational business operations*.
London.

Kolk, A., & Pinkse, J. (2008). A perspective on multinational enterprises and climate change: Learning
from "an inconvenient truth"? *JIBS, 39*(8), 1359–1378.

Koopmans, T. C., & Montias, J. M. (1971). On the description and comparison of economic systems.
In A. Eckstein (Ed.), *Comparison of economic systems*. University of California Press.

Kostova, T. (1996). *Success of the transnational transfer of organizational practices within multinational
companies*, Ph.D. dissertation. University of Minnesota.

Kostova, T., Beugelsdijk, S., Scott, W. R., Kunst, V. E., Chua, C. H., & van Essen, M. (2020). The con-
struct of institutional distance through the lens of different institutional perspectives: Review,
analysis, and recommendations. *JIBS, 51*(4), 467–497.

Kostova, T., & Zaheer, S. (1999). Organizational legitimacy under conditions of complexity: The case of the multinational enterprise. *AMR*, 24(1), 64–81.

Kotabe, M., Martin, X., & Domoto, H. (2003). Gaining from vertical partnerships: Knowledge transfer, relationship duration, and supplier performance improvement in the U.S. and Japanese automotive industries. *SMJ*, *24*, 293–316.

Kottaridi, C., Giakoulas, D., & Manolopoulos, D. (2019). Escapism FDI from developed economies: The role of regulatory context and corporate taxation. *IBR*, *28*(1), 36–47.

Kroon, D. P., Cornelissen, J. P., & Vaara, E. (2015). Explaining employees' reactions towards a cross-border merger: The role of English language fluency. *MIR*, *55*, 775–800.

Kuemmerle, W. (1997). Building effective R&D capabilities abroad. *HBR*, *75*, 61–72.

Kuemmerle, W. (1999). The drivers of foreign direct investment into research and development: An empirical investigation. *JIBS*, *30*(1), 1–24.

Kumar, V., Gaur, A., Zhan, W., & Luo, Y. (2019). Co–evolution of MNCs and local competitors in emerging markets. *IBR*, *28*(5), Article 101527.

Kunisch, S., Menz, M., & Birkinshaw, J. (2019). Spatially dispersed corporate headquarters: A historical analysis of their prevalence, antecedents, and consequences. *IBR*, *28*(1), 148–161.

Kwok, C. C. Y., & Tadesse, S., (2006). National culture and financial systems. *JIBS*, *37*(2), 227–247.

Lahiri, S., Mukherjee, D., & Peng, M. W. (2020). Behind the internationalization of family SMEs: A strategy tripod synthesis. *GSJ*, *10*(4), 813–838.

Lall, S. (1983). *The new multinationals*. John Wiley.

Lall, S. (1985). *Multinationals, technology and exports*. Macmillan.

Lall, S. (1997). Investment, technology and international competitiveness. In J. H. Dunning & K. A. Hamdani (Eds.), *The new globalism and developing countries* (pp. 232–259). United Nations.

Lall, S., & Streeten, P. (1977). *Foreign Investment, transnationals and developing countries*. Macmillan.

Lall, S. V., & Lebrand, M. (2020). Who wins, who loses? Understanding the spatially differentiated effects of the belt and road initiative. *JDE*, *146*, 102496.

Lane, H. W., & Beamish, P. W. (1990). Cross–cultural cooperative behavior in joint ventures in LDCs. *MIR*, *30*(Special Issue), 87–102.

Lane, P. J., Salk, J. E., & Lyles, M. (2001). Absorptive capacity, learning, and performance in international joint ventures. *SMJ*, *22*(12), 1139–1161.

Lazarova, M. B., & Cerdin, J-L. (2007). Revisiting repatriation concerns: Organizational support versus career and contextual influences. *JIBS*, *38*(3), 409–429.

Leahy, J., Kynge, J., & Parkin, B. (2023). Ten years of China's Belt and Road: what has $1tn achieved?' *Financial Times*, October 22. Retrieved October 22, 2023, from https://www.ft.com/content/83501dd5-fe6d-4169-9d83-28a8cf46e681.

Lee, C., Lee, K., & Pennings, J. M. (2001). Internal capabilities, external networks, and performance: A study on technology-based ventures. *SMJ*, *22*(6–7), 615–640.

Lee, S-J., Kim, J., & Park, B. (2015). Culture clashes in cross–border mergers and acquisitions: A case study of Sweden's Volvo and South Korea's Samsung. *IBR*, *24*(4), 580–593.

Leong, S. M., & Tan, C. T. (1993). Managing across borders: an empirical test of the Bartlett and Ghoshal (1989) organizational typology. *JIBS*, *24*(3), 449–464.

Leontiades, J. (2005). The Birth of an Association. *EIBA Newsletter*, issue #2.

Leontiades, J. (2017). *Personal communication to Vítor Corado Simões*. December.

Lessard, D., Teece, D. J., & Leih, S. (2016). The dynamic capabilities of meta-multinationals. *GSJ*, *6*(3), 211–224.

Levinson, C. (1977). *Vodka-Cola*. Stock.

Levitt, T. (1983). The globalization of markets. *HBR*, May–June, 92–102.

Levy, O., Beechler, S., Taylor, S., & Boyacigiller, N. A. (2007). What we talk about when we talk about "global mindset": Managerial cognition in multinational corporations. *JIBS*, *38*(2), 231–258.

Lew, Y. K., Sinkovics, R. R., Yamin, M., & Khan, Z. (2016). Trans-specialization understanding in international technology alliances: The influence of cultural distance. *JIBS*, *47*(5), 577–594.

Li, J., Jiang, F., & Shen, J. (2016). Institutional distance and the quality of the headquarters–subsidiary relationship: The moderating role of the institutionalization of headquarters' practices in subsidiaries. *IBR*, *25*(2), 589–603.

Li, J., & Tang, Y. (2013). The social influence of executive hubris. *MIR*, *53*, 83–107.

Li, J., Zhao, Y., & Han, X. (2020). Would you work abroad? The effect of English proficiency on Chinese employees' willingness to accept international assignments. *IBR*, *29*(2), Article 101669.

Li, P., & Bathelt, H. (2020). Headquarters-subsidiary knowledge strategies at the cluster level. *GSJ*, *10*(3), 585–618.

Liang, H., Ren, B., & Sun, S. (2015). An anatomy of state control in the globalization of state-owned enterprises. *JIBS*, *46*, 223–240.

Liao, T-J. (2015). Local clusters of SOEs, POEs, and FIEs, international experience, and the performance of foreign firms operating in emerging economies. *IBR*, *24*(1), 66–76.

Lin, H. (2000). Choice of market entry mode in emerging markets: Influences on entry strategy in China. *Journal of Global Marketing*, *14*(1/2), 83–109.

Liu, L., Adair, W., & Bello, D. (2015). Fit, misfit, and beyond fit: Relational metaphors and semantic fit in international joint ventures. *JIBS*, *46*(7), 830–849.

Liu, X., Gao, L., Lu, J., & Lioliou, E. (2016). Does learning at home and from abroad boost the foreign subsidiary performance of emerging economy multinational enterprises? *IBR*, *25*(1), 141–151.

London, T., & Hart, S. L. (2004). Reinventing strategies for emerging markets: Beyond the transnational model. *JIBS*, *35*(5), 350–370.

Lorange, P., & Roos, J. (1992). *Strategic alliances: Formation, implementation and evolution*. Blackwell.

Lorenzen, M., Mudambi, R., & Schotter, A. (2020). International connectedness and local disconnectedness: MNE strategy, city-regions and disruption. *JIBS*, *51*(8), 1199–1222.

Lu, Y., Zhou, L., Bruton, G., & Li, W. (2010). Capabilities as a mediator linking resources and the international performance of entrepreneurial firms in an emerging economy. *JIBS*, *41*(3), 419–436.

Lundan, S. (2003). Institutions, exclusivity and foreign investment. In H. P. Gray (Ed.), *Extending the eclectic paradigm in international business: essays in honor of John Dunning* (pp. 93–106). Edward Elgar.

Lundan, S. (2004). *Multinationals, environment and global competition*. JAI (Elsevier).

Lundan, S. (2018). From the editor: Engaging international business scholars with public policy issues. *JIBP*, *1*(1), 1–11.

Lundan, S., & Cantwell, J. (2020). The local co-evolution of firms and governments in the Information Age. *JIBS*, *51*(9), 1516–1528.

Lundan, S., & Li, J. (2019). Adjusting to and learning from institutional diversity: Toward a capability-building perspective. *JIBS*, *50*(1), 36–47.

Luo, Y. (1998). Timing of investment and international expansion performance in China. *JIBS*, *29*(2), 391–407.

Luo, Y. (2000). Dynamic capabilities in international expansion. *JWB*, *35*(4), 355–378.

Luo, Y. (2003). Market-seeking MNEs in an emerging market: How parent-subsidiary links shape overseas success. *JIBS*, *34*(3), 290–309.

Luo, Y. (2007). An integrated anti-opportunism system in international exchange. *JIBS*, *38*(6), 855–877.

Luo, Y., & Peng, M. W. (1999). Learning to compete in a transition economy: Experience, environment, and performance. *JIBS*, *30*(2), 269–295.

Luo, Y., & Shenkar, O. (2006). The multinational corporation as a multilingual community: Language and organization in a global context. *JIBS*, *37*(3), 321–339.

Luo, Y., & Shenkar, O. (2011). Toward a perspective of cultural friction in international business. *Journal of International Management*, *17*(1), 1–14.

Luo, Y., & Tung, R. L. (2007). International expansion of emerging market enterprises: A springboard perspective. *JIBS*, *38*(4), 481–498.

Luo, Y., & Tung, R. L. (2018). A general theory of springboard MNEs. *JIBS*, *49*(2), 129–152.

Luostarinen, R. (1979). *Internationalization of the firm: An empirical study of the internationalization of firms with small and open domestic markets with special emphasis on lateral rigidity as a behavioral characteristic in strategic decision making* [PhD Dissertation, Helsinki School of Economics].

Luostarinen, R. (1979/1989). *Internationalization of the firm: An empirical study of the internationalization of firms from small and open domestic markets with special emphasis on lateral rigidity as a behavioral characteristic in strategic decision-making*. Acta Academiae Oeconomicae Helsingiensis, Helsinki School of Economics.

Luostarinen, R. (1989). *Membership drive project – Memo to the strategy meeting of EIBA Board.* March 17.

Luostarinen, R. (1990). *EIBA-membership survey.* EIBA, 113 pp.

Luostarinen, R., & Welch, L. S. (1988). Internationalisation: Evolution of a concept. *Journal of General Management, 14*(2), 34–55.

Łupina-Wegener, A., Schneider, S. C., & van Dick, R. (2015). The role of outgroups in constructing a shared identity: A longitudinal study of a subsidiary merger in Mexico. *MIR, 55*, 677–705.

Ma, S. (2022). Growth effects of economic integration: New evidence from the belt and road initiative. *Economic Analysis and Policy, 73.* https://doi.org/10.1016/j.eap.2022.01.004.

Macharzina, K. (1993). Steuerung von Auslandsgesellschaften bei Internationalisierungsstrategien. In M. Haller, K. Bleicher, H-J. Pleitner, R. Wunderer, & A. Zünd (Eds.), *Globalisierung der Wirtschaft – Einwirkungen auf die Betriebswirtschaftslehre* (pp. 177–109). Verlag Paul Haupt.

Macharzina, K. (1997). Letter from the president. *EIBA Newsletter*, June.

Madhok, A. (1995). Revisiting multinational firms' tolerance for joint ventures: A trust-based approach. *JIBS, 26*(1), 117–137.

Madhok, A. (1997). Cost, value and foreign market entry mode: The transaction and the firm. *SMJ, 18*(1), 39–61.

Madhok, A. (2002). Reassessing the fundamentals and beyond: Ronald Coase, the transaction cost and resource-based theories of the firm and the institutional structure of production. *SMJ, 23*(6), 535–550.

Madhok, A., & Osegowitsch, T. (2000). The international biotechnology industry: A dynamic capabilities perspective. *JIBS, 31*(2), 325–335.

Madsen, T. K., & Servais, P. (1997). The internationalisation of born globals: An evolutionary process?' *IBR, 6*(6), 561–593.

Magnani, G., Zucchella, A., & Floriani, D. E. (2018). The logic behind foreign market selection: Objective distance dimensions vs. strategic objectives and psychic distance. *IBR, 27*(1), 1–20.

Maitland, E., & Sammartino, A. (2015). Managerial cognition and internationalization. *JIBS, 46*(7), 733–760.

Makino, S., & Tsang, E. W. K. (2011). Historical ties and foreign direct investment: An exploratory study. *JIBS, 42*(4), 545–557.

Malik, T. H., & Zhao, Y. (2013). Cultural distance and its implication for the duration of the international alliance in a high technology sector. *IBR, 22*(4), 699–712.

Malnight, T. W. (1996). The transition from decentralized to network-based MNC structures: An evolutionary perspective. *JIBS, 27*(1), 43–65.

Marois, B. (2018). *Personal e-mail communication.* February.

Martin, C. (1989). *Spain's foreign trade and industrial structure: The effects of EEC membership and the Single European Market of 1992.* CEPR and European Commission.

Martin, X., & Salomon, R. (2003). Knowledge transfer capacity and its implications for the theory of the multinational corporation. *JIBS, 34*(4), 356–373.

Martinez, J. I., & Jarillo, J. C. (1988). La respuesta de las multinacionales ante el reto de 1992. *Información Comercial Española, 662*(October), 71–82.

Martínez-Noya, A., & García-Canal, E. (2011). Technological capabilities and the decision to out-source/outsource offshore R&D services. *IBR, 20*(3), 264–277.

Mata, J., & Portugal, P. (2015). The termination of international joint ventures: Closure and acquisition by domestic and foreign partners. *IBR, 24*(4), 677–689.

Mathews, J. A., & Zander, I. (2007). The international entrepreneurial dynamics of accelerated internationalization. *JIBS, 38*(3), 387–403.

Mattsson, L-G. (2009). *Uppsala in the world – The world in Uppsala: Half a century of research at the Department of Business Studies at Uppsala University,* Acta Universitatis Upsaliensis No. 50. Uppsala: University of Uppsala.

Mattsson, L-G. (2017). *Personal interview with Vítor Corado Simões.* Stockholm, June 13.

Mattsson, L-G., & Wiedersheim-Paul, F. (Eds.). (1979). *Recent research on the internationalization of business.* Almqvist & Wiksell.

McCormick, M., & Somaya, D. (2020). Born globals from emerging economies: Reconciling early exporting with theories of internationalization. *GSJ, 10*(2), 251–281.

McDermott, G., Mudambi, R., & Parente, R. (2013). Strategic modularity and the architecture of multinational firm. *GSJ*, *3*(1), 1–7.

McDonald, C., Buckley, P. J., Voss, H., Cross, A. R., & Chen, L. (2018). Place, space, and foreign direct investment into peripheral cities. *IBR*, *27*(4), 803–813.

McDougall, P. P., & Oviatt, B. M. (2000). International entrepreneurship: The intersection of two research paths. *AMJ*, *43*(5), 902–906.

McGee, J. E., Dowling, M. J., & Megginson, W. L. (1995). Cooperative strategy and new venture performance: The role of business strategy and management experience. *SMJ*, *16*(7), 565–580.

McMahon, R., & Hongsong, L. (2023). Making sense of the European Union: Chinese representations. *Comparative European Politics*, *21*, 575–589.

McManus, J. C. (1972). The theory of the international firm. In G. Paquet (Ed.), *The multinational firm and the nation state* (pp. 32–59). Collier–MacMillan.

Mees-Buss, J., Welch, C., & Westney, D. E. (2019). What happened to the transnational: The emergence of the neo–global corporation. *JIBS*, *50*(9), 1513–1543.

Merchant, H. (2014). Configurations of governance structure, generic strategy, and firm size: Opening the black box of value creation in international joint venture's. *GSJ*, *4*(4), 292–309.

Metsola, J., Leppäaho, T., Paavilainen-Mäntymäki, E., & Plakoyiannaki, E. (2020). Process in family business internationalisation: The state of the art and ways forward. *IBR*, *29*(2), Article 101665.

Meyer, K., & Benito, G. (2016). Where do MNEs locate their headquarters? at home! *GSJ*, *6*(2), 149–159.

Meyer, K., & Estrin, S. (2014). Local context and global strategy: Extending the integration responsiveness framework to subsidiary strategy. *GSJ*, *4*(1), 1–19.

Meyer, K. E. (2001). Institutions, transaction costs, and entry mode choice in Eastern Europe. *JIBS*, *32*(2), 357–367.

Meyer, K. E., & Gelbuda, M. (2006). Process perspectives in international business research in CEE. *MIR*, *46*(2), 143–164.

Meyer, K. E., Li, C., & Schotter, A. P. J. (2020). Managing the MNE subsidiary: Advancing a multilevel and dynamic research agenda. *JIBS*, *51*(4), 538–576.

Meyer, K. E., & Peng, M. W. (2005). Probing theoretically into Central and Eastern Europe: Transactions, resources, and institutions. *JIBS*, *36*(6), 600–621.

Mezias, J. M., & Scandura, T. A. (2005). A needs-driven approach to expatriate adjustment and career development: A multiple mentoring perspective. *JIBS*, *36*(5), 519–538.

Miller, C. (2022). *Chip war: The fight for the world's most critical technology*. Simon and Schuster.

Miller, D., Lee, J., Chang, S., & Breton-Miller, I. L. (2009). Filling the institutional void: The social behavior and performance of family vs non-family technology firms in emerging markets. *JIBS*, *40*(5), 802–817.

Minbaeva, D. (2007). Knowledge transfer in multinational corporations. *MIR*, *47*(4), 567–593.

Minbaeva, D. (2008). HRM practices affecting extrinsic and intrinsic motivation of knowledge receivers and their effect on intra-MNC knowledge transfer. *IBR*, *17*(6), 703–713.

Minbaeva, D., Pedersen, T., Björkman, I., Fey, C., & Park, H. J. (2003). MNC knowledge transfer, subsidiary absorptive capacity, and HRM. *JIBS*, *34*(6), 586–599.

Minbaeva, D., Pedersen, T., Björkman, I., Fey, C., & Park, H. J. (2014). A retrospective on: MNC knowledge transfer, subsidiary absorptive capacity, and HRM. *JIBS*, *45*(1), 52–62.

Minbaeva, D., & Santangelo, G. D. (2018a). Boundary spanners and intra-MNC knowledge sharing: The roles of controlled motivation and immediate organizational context. *GSJ*, *8*(2), 220–241.

Minbaeva, D., & Santangelo, G. D. (2018b). Gender diversity at EIBA. *EIBAzine*, *23*(November), 12–15.

Moeller, M., Harvey, M., Griffith, D., & Richey, G. (2013). The impact of country-of-origin on the acceptance of foreign subsidiaries in host countries: An examination of the 'liability-of-foreignness. *IBR*, *22*(1), 89–99.

Mohr, A., & Puck, J. (2013). Revisiting the trust–performance link in strategic alliances. *MIR*, *53*, 269–289.

Mol, M. J., van Tulder, R., & Beije, P. R. (2005). Antecedents and performance consequences of international outsourcing. *IBR*, *14*(5), 599–617.

Monaghan, S., Tippmann, E., & Coviello, N. (2020). Born digitals: Thoughts on their internationalization and a research agenda. *JIBS*, *51*(1), 11–22.

Moore, F. (2012). Identity, knowledge and strategy in the UK subsidiary of an Anglo–German automobile manufacturer. *MIR*, *21*(2), 281–292.

Moore, K. J. (2001). A strategy for subsidiaries: Centres of excellence to build subsidiary specific advantages. *MIR, 41*(3), 275–290.

Morosini, P., Shane, S., & Singh, H. (1998). National cultural distance and cross-border acquisition performance. *JIBS, 29*(1), 137–158.

Mort, G. S., & Weerawardena, J. (2006). Networking capability and international entrepreneurship: How networks function in Australian born global firms. *IMR, 23*(5), 549–572.

Motta Veiga, P. (2004). *Foreign direct investment in Brazil: Regulation, flows and contribution to development*, mimeo. Retrieved October 15, 2018, from https://www.iisd.org/pdf/2004/investment_country_report_brazil.pdf.

Mowery, D. C., Oxley, J. E., & Silverman, B. S. (1996). Strategic alliances and interfirm knowledge transfer. *SMJ, 17*(S2), 77–91.

Mowery, D. C., Oxley, J. E., & Silverman, B. S. (1998). Technological overlap and interfirm cooperation: Implications for the resource-based view of the firm. *RP, 27*(5), 507–523.

Mowery, D. C., Oxley, J. E., & Silverman, B. S. (2002). The two faces of partner-specific absorptive capacity: Learning and co-specialization. In F. J. Contractor & P. Lorange (Eds.), *Cooperative strategies and alliances* (pp. 291–320). Elsevier Science.

Mudambi, R. (2018). Knowledge-intensive intangibles, spatial transaction costs, and the rise of populism. *JIBP, 1*(1), 44–52.

Mudambi, R., Li, L., Ma, X., Makino, S., Qian, G., & Boschma, R. (2018). Zoom in, zoom out: Geographic scale and multinational activity. *JIBS, 49*(8), 929–941.

Mudambi, R., & Navarra, P. (2002). Institutions and international business: A theoretical overview. *IBR, 11*(6), 635–646.

Mudambi, R., & Navarra, P. (2004). Is knowledge power? Knowledge flows, subsidiary power and rent-seeking within MNCs. *JIBS, 35*(5), 385–406.

Murray, J. Y., Kotabe, M., & Zhou, J. N. (2005). Strategic alliance-based sourcing and market performance: Evidence from foreign firms operating in China. *JIBS, 36*(2), 187–208.

Musteen, M., Datta, D. K., & Francis, J. (2014). Early internationalization by firms in transition economies into developed markets: The role of international networks. *GSJ, 4*(3), 221–237.

Mytelka, L. K. (1978). Licensing and technology dependence in the Andean Group. *World Development, 6*(4), 447–459.

Nadolska, A., & Barkema, H. G. (2007). Learning to internationalise: The pace and success of foreign acquisitions. *JIBS, 38*(7), 1170–1186.

Nair, S. R., Demirbag, M., & Mellahi, K. (2016). Reverse knowledge transfer in emerging market multinationals: The Indian context. *IBR, 25*(1), 152–164.

Narula, R. (2019). Policy opportunities and challenges from the COVID–19 pandemic for economies with large informal sectors. *JIBP, 3*(3), 302–310.

Narula, R., & Dunning, J. H. (1998). Explaining international R&D alliances and the role of governments. *IBR, 7*(4), 377–397.

Nelson, R., & Winter, S. (1982). *An evolutionary theory of economic change*. Belknap Press/Harvard University Press.

Nelson, R. R. (1995). Recent evolutionary theorizing about economic change. *Journal of Economic Literature, 33*, 48–90.

Nelson, R. R. (2004). The co–evolution of technology, industrial structure, and supporting institutions. *ICC, 3*(1), 47–63.

Nelson, R. R. (2005). *Technology, institutions, and economic growth*. Harvard University Press.

Nemeth, A., & Nippa, M. (2013). Rigor and relevance of IJV exit research. *MIR, 53*, 449–475.

Neumayer, E. (1999). Multilateral agreement on investment: Lessons for the WTO from the failed OECD–negotiations. *Wirtschaftspolitische Blatter, 46*(6), 618–628.

Nguyen, H. L., Larimo, J., & Wang, Y. (2019). Control, innovation and international joint venture performance: The moderating role of internal and external environments. *IBR, 28*(6), Article 101591.

Nielsen, B. B., & Nielsen, S. (2009). Learning and innovation in international strategic alliances: An empirical test of the role of trust and tacitness. *JMS, 46*(6), 1031–1056.

Nielsen, B. B., Welch, C., Chidlow, A., Miller, S. R., Aguzzoli, R., Gardner, E., Karafyllia, M., & Pegoraro, D. (2020). Fifty years of methodological trends in JIBS: Why future IB research needs more triangulation," *JIBS, 51*(9), 1478–1499.

Niittymies, A. (2020). Heuristic decision-making in firm internationalization: The influence of context-specific experience. *IBR*, *29*(6), Article 101752.

Niittymies, A., & Pajunen, K. (2020). Cognitive foundations of firm internationalization: A systematic review and agenda for future research. *IBR*, *29*(4), Article 101654.

Nippa, M., & Reuer, J. J. (2019). On the future of international joint venture research. *JIBS*, *50*(4), 555–597.

Noorderhaven, N., & Harzing, A-W. (2009). Knowledge-sharing and social interaction within MNEs. *JIBS*, *40*(5), 719–741.

North, D. (1985). Transaction costs in history. *Journal of European Economic History*, *42*, 566–576.

North, D. (1990). *Institutions, institutional change, and economic performance.* Cambridge Univ. Press.

North, D. (2005). *Understanding the process of economic change.* Princeton Univ. Press.

Nuruzzaman, N., Gaur, A. S., & Sambharya, R. B. (2018). A microfoundations approach to studying innovation in multinational subsidiaries. *GSJ*, *9*(1), 92–116.

Nuruzzaman, N., Singh, D., & Pattnaik, C. (2019). Competing to be innovative: Foreign competition and imitative innovation of emerging economy firms. *IBR*, *28*(5), Article 101490.

O'Brien, D., Sharkey Scott, P., Andersson, U., Ambos, T., & Fu, N. (2018). The microfoundations of subsidiary initiatives: How subsidiary manager activities unlock entrepreneurship. *GSJ*, *9*(1), 66–91.

Ocasio, W. (1997). Towards an attention-based view of the firm. *SMJ*, *18*, Special Issue: 'Organizational and Competitive Interactions', 187–206.

OECD. (1981). *Investissement International et Entreprises Multinationales: Tendences Recentes des Investissements Directs Internationaux.* OECD.

OECD (2020). *Multilateral agreement on investment: Documentation from the negotiations.* Retrieved July 12, 2020, from https://www.oecd.org/daf/mai/intro.htm.

Oesterle, M-J., Elosge, C., & Elosge, L. (2016). Me, myself and I: The role of CEO narcissism in internationalization decisions. *IBR*, *25*(5), 1114–1123.

Ohmae, K. (1985). *Triad power: The coming shape of global competition.* The Free Press.

Oman, C. (1984). *New forms of international investment in developing countries.* OECD Development Center.

Ordonneau, P. (1975). *Les Multinationales contre les États.* Éditions Économie et Humanisme.

Osborn, R. N., & Christopher Baughn, C. (1990). Forms of interorganizational governance for multinational alliances. *AMJ*, *33*(3), 503–519.

Osegowitsch, T., & Sammartino, A. (2008). Reassessing (home-)regionalization. *JIBS*, *39*(2), 184–196.

Oviatt, B. M., & McDougall, P. P. (1994). Toward a theory of international new ventures. *JIBS*, *25*(1), 45–64.

Oviatt, B. M., & McDougall, P. P. (1997). Challenges for internationalization process theory: The case of international new ventures. *MIR*, *37*(2), 30–44.

Oviatt, B. M., & McDougall, P. P. (2005). The internationalization of entrepreneurship. *JIBS*, *36*(1), 2–8.

Owens, M., Palmer, M., & Zueva-Owens, A. (2013). Institutional forces in adoption of international joint ventures: Empirical evidence from British retail multinationals. *IBR*, *22*(5), 883–893.

Oxelheim, L., Gregoric, A., Randøy, T., & Thomsen, S. (2013). On the internationalization of corporate boards: The case of Nordic firms. *JIBS*, *44*(3), 173–194.

Padmanabhan, P., & Cho, K. R. (1999). Decision specific experience in foreign ownership and establishment strategies: Evidence from Japanese firms. *JIBS*, *30*(1), 25–41.

Pan, Y., & Tse, D. K. (2000). The hierarchical model of market entry modes. *JIBS*, *31*(4), 535–554.

Pananond, P., Gereffi, G., & Pedersen, T. (2020). An integrative typology of global strategy and global value chains: The management and organization of cross-border activities. *GSJ*, *10*(3), 421–443.

Pant, A., & Ramachandran, J. (2017). Navigating identity duality in multinational subsidiaries: A paradox lens on identity claims at Hindustan Unilever 1959–2015. *JIBS*, *48*(6), 664–692.

Papanastassiou, M., Pearce, R., & Zanfei, A. (2020). Changing perspectives on the internationalization of R&D and innovation by multinational enterprises: A review of the literature. *JIBS*, *51*(4), 623–664.

Park, B. I. (2011). Knowledge transfer capacity of multinational enterprises and technology acquisition in international joint ventures. *IBR*, *20*(1), 75–87.

Park, B. I., & Choi, J. (2014). Control mechanisms of MNEs and absorption of foreign technology in cross-border acquisitions. *IBR*, *23*(1), 130–144.

Park, C., Vertinsky, I., & Becerra, M. (2015). Transfers of tacit vs. explicit knowledge and performance in international joint ventures: The role of age. *IBR*, *24*(1), 89–101.

Park, J-Y., & Harris, S. (2014). Microfoundations for learning within international joint ventures. *IBR*, *23*(3), 490–503.

Parker, A., Tippmann, E., & Kratochvil, R. (2019). Accessing diverse knowledge for problem solving in the MNC: A network mobilization perspective. *GSJ*, *9*(3), 423–452.

Parkhe, A. (1993). Strategic alliance structuring: A game theoretic and transaction cost examination of interfirm cooperation. *AMJ*, *36*(4), 794–829.

Pavitt, K. (1988). International patterns of technology accumulation. In N. Hood & J-E. Vahlne (Eds.), *Strategies in global competition* (pp. 126–157). Croom Helm.

Pearce, R., & Tavares, A. T. (2002). On the dynamics and coexistence of multiple subsidiary roles: An investigation of multinational operations in the U.K. In S. Lundan (Ed.), *Network knowledge in international business* (pp. 73–90). Edward Elgar.

Pedersen, T., Petersen, B., & Deo Sharma, D. (2003). Knowledge transfer performance of multinational companies. *MIR*, *3*, 69–90.

Pedersen, T., & Tallman, S. (2016). How we facilitate conversations in global strategy—and the location of MNE HQS. *GSJ*, *6*(2), 124–126.

Peltokorpi, V. (2017). Absorptive capacity in foreign subsidiaries: The effects of language-sensitive recruitment, language training, and interunit knowledge transfer. *IBR*, *26*(1), 119–129.

Peltokorpi, V., & Vaara, E. (2014). Knowledge transfer in multinational corporations: Productive and counterproductive effects of language-sensitive recruitment. *JIBS*, *45*(5), 600–622.

Peng, M. W. (2004). Identifying the big question in international business research. *JIBS*, *35*(2), 99–108.

Peng, M. W., Wang, D. Y. L., & Jiang, Y. (2008). An institution-based view of international business strategy: A focus on emerging economies. *JIBS*, *39*(5), 920–936.

Perkins, S., Morck, R., & Yeung, B. (2014). Innocents abroad: The hazards of international joint ventures with Pyramidal Group firms. *GSJ*, *4*(4), 310–330.

Perlmutter, H., & Sagafi-Nejad, T. (1981). *International technology transfer, guidelines, codes and a muffled quadrilogue*. Pergamon Press.

Pesch, R., & Bouncken, R. B. (2017). How to achieve benefits from diversity in international alliances: Mechanisms and cultural intelligence. *GSJ*, *8*(2), 275–300.

Peteraf, M. A. (1993). The cornerstones of competitive advantage: A resource-based view. *SMJ*, *14*(3), 179–191.

Petersen, B., & Pedersen, T. (1997). Twenty years after – Support and critique of the Uppsala internationalization model. In M. Forsgren & I. Björkman (Eds.), *The nature of the international firm* (pp. 117–134). Copenhagen Business School Press.

Petersen, B., Welch, D., & Welch, L. (2000). Creating meaningful switching options in international operations. *LRP*, *35*(5), 688–705.

Petersen, B., Welch, L. S., & Liesch, P. W. (2002). The Internet and foreign market expansion by firms. *MIR*, *42*(2), 207–221.

Petricevic, O., & Teece, D. J. (2019). The structural reshaping of globalization: Implications for strategic sectors, profiting from innovation, and the multinational enterprise. *JIBS*, *50*(9), 1487–1512.

Phene, A., & Almeida, P. (2008). Innovation in multinational subsidiaries: The role of knowledge assimilation and subsidiary capabilities. *JIBS*, *39*(5), 901–918.

Piekkari, R. (2023). *EIBA Lisbon, 30 years later – Recollections and visions on how the world and EIBA have been changing. Address to the EIBA History Panel*. EIBA: Lisbon, December.

Piekkari, R., & Welch, C. (Eds.). (2004). *Handbook of qualitative research methods for international business*. Edward Elgar.

Piekkari, R., & Welch, C. (Eds.). (2011). *Rethinking the case study in international business and management research*. Edward Elgar.

Piekkari, R., Welch, D. E., & Welch, L. S. (2014). *Language in international business*. Edward Elgar.

Piekkari, R., Welch, D. E., Welch, L. S., Peltonen, J-P., & Vesa, T. (2013). Translation behaviour: An exploratory study within a service multinational. *IBR*, *22*(5), 771–783

Piscitello, L., & Puck, J. (2018). Address to the EIBA Board, Poznan, April.

Piscitello, L., & Puck, J. (2020a). *Digital EIBA 2020 – Proposal*. Vienna, July.

Piscitello, L., & Puck, J. (2020b). Welcome to the EIBA 2020 Online Conference – International Business in the Pandemic and Post–Pandemic Era. *EIBAzine*, 25.

Piscitello, L., Rabellotti, R., & Giada Scalera, V. (2015). Chinese and Indian M&As in Europe: The relationship between motive and ownership choice. In A. Risberg, D. R. King, & O. Meglio (Eds.), *The Routledge companion to mergers and acquisitions* (pp. 114–129). Routledge.

Porter, M. E. (1985). *Competitive advantage*. The Free Press.

Porter, M. E. (1986). Changing patterns of international competition. *CMR*, 28(2), 9–40.

Porter, M. E. (1990). *The competitive advantage of nations*. Free Press.

Porter, M. E., & Fuller, V. (1986). Coalitions and global strategy. In M. E. Porter (Ed.), *Competition in global industries* (pp. 315–344). Harvard Business School Press.

Porter, M. E., & Kramer, M. R. (2006). Strategy and society: The link between competitive advantage and corporate social responsibility. *HBR*, 84(12), 78–92.

Porter, M. E., & Kramer, M. R. (2011). Creating shared value: How to reinvent capitalism—and unleash a wave of innovation and growth. *HBR*. Retrieved February 27, 2022, from https://www.communitylivingbc.ca/wp–content/uploads/2018/05/Creating–Shared–Value.pdf.

Porter, M. E., Sölvell, Ö., & Zander, I. (1991). *Advantage Sweden*. Norstedts Förlag.

Prahalad, C. K., & Oesterveld, J. (1999). Transforming internal governance: The challenge for multinationals. *SMR*, Spring, 31–39.

Prahalad, C. K., & Doz, Y. L. (1987). *The multinational mission: Balancing local demands and global vision*. The Free Press and Collier Macmillan.

Prashantham, S., & Birkinshaw, J. (2020). MNE–SME cooperation: An integrative framework. *JIBS*, 51(7), 1161–1175.

Puck, J. (2019). *Presentation to the EIBA Board*. Leeds.

Puck, J. F., Holtbrügge, D., & Mohr, A. T. (2009). Beyond entry mode choice: Explaining the conversion of joint ventures into wholly owned subsidiaries in the People's Republic of China. *JIBS*, 40(3), 388–404.

Putzhammer, M., Puck, J., & Lindner, T. (2020). Changes in foreign operation modes: A review and research agenda. *IBR*, 29(1), Article 101619.

Qian, G., Li, L., & Rugman, A. (2013). Liability of country foreignness and liability of regional foreignness: Their effects on geographic diversification and firm performance. *JIBS*, 44(6), 635–647.

Rasciute, S., & Downward, P. (2017). Explaining variability in the investment location choices of MNEs: An exploration of country, industry and firm effects. *IBR*, 26(4), 605–613.

Redding, G. (2005). The thick description and comparison of societal systems of capitalism. *JIBS*, 36(2), 123–155.

Regnér, P., & Zander, U. (2011). Knowledge and strategy creation in multinational companies: Social-identity frames and temporary tension in knowledge combination. *MIR*, 51, 821–850.

Reich, R. B., & Mankin, E. D. (1986). Joint ventures give away our future. *HBR*, 86, 78–86.

Reiche, B. S., Harzing, A-W., & Kraimer, M. L. (2009). The role of international assignees' social capital in creating inter-unit intellectual capital: A cross-level model. *JIBS*, 40(3), 509–526.

Reiche, B. S., Kraimer, M. L., & Harzing, A-W. (2011). Why do international assignees stay? An organizational embeddedness perspective. *JIBS*, 42(4), 521–544.

Reuber, A. R., Dimitratos, P., & Kuivalainen, O. (2017). Beyond categorization: New directions for theory development about entrepreneurial internationalization. *JIBS*, 48(4), 411–422.

Reuber, A. R., Knight, G. A., Liesch, P-W., & Zhou, L. (2018). International entrepreneurship: The pursuit of entrepreneurial opportunities across national borders. *JIBS*, 49(4), 395–406.

Reuer, J., & Ariño, A. (2007). Strategic alliance contracts: Dimensions and determinants of contractual complexity. *SMJ*, 28(3), 313–330.

Reuer, J. J., & Klijn, E. (2020). Board leadership structures in international joint ventures. *GSJ*, 10(4), 700–725.

Reuer, J. J., Shenkar, O., & Ragozzino, R. (2004). Mitigating risk in international mergers and acquisitions: the role of contingent payouts. *JIBS*, 35(1), 19–32.

Reus, T. H., & Lamont, B. T. (2009). The double-edged sword of cultural distance in international acquisitions. *JIBS*, 40(8), 1298–1316.

Rialp, A., Rialp, J., & Knight, G. A. (2005). The phenomenon of early internationalizing firms: What do we know after a decade (1993–2003) of scientific inquiry? *IBR*, 14(2), 147–166.

Ricart, J. E., Enright, M. J., Ghemawat, P., Hart, S. L., & Khanna, T. (2004). New frontiers in international strategy. *JIBS, 35*(3), 175–200.

Ritter, T., & Gemünden, H. G. (2003). Network competence: Its impact on innovation success and its antecedents. *JBR, 56*(9), 745–755.

Riviere, M. A., Bass, E., & Andersson, U. (2021). Dynamic capability development in multinational enterprises: Reconciling routine reconfiguration between the headquarters and subsidiaries. *GSJ, 11*(3), 380–401.

Rodrik, D. (2018). Populism and the economics of globalization. *JIBP, 1*(1), 12–33.

Ronen, S. S., & Shenkar, O. (1985). Clustering countries on attitudinal dimensions: A review and synthesis. *AMR, 10*(3), 435–454.

Root, F. R. (1994). *Entry strategies for international markets* (2nd ed.). Lexington Books.

Rothaermel, F. T., & Deeds, D. L. (2004). Exploration and exploitation alliances in biotechnology: A system of new product development. *SMJ, 25*, 201–221.

Rovira-Nordman, E., & Tolstoy, D. (2014). Does relationship psychic distance matter for the learning processes of internationalizing SMEs? *IBR, 23*(1), 30–37.

Rosa, B., Gugler, P., & Verbeke, A. (2020). Regional and global strategies of MNEs: Revisiting Rugman & Verbeke (2004). *Journal of International Business Studies, 51*(7), 1045–1053.

Roza, M., Van den Bosch, F. A. J., & Volberda, H. W. (2011). Offshoring strategy: Motives, functions, locations, and governance modes of small, medium–sized and large firms. *IBR, 20*(3), 314–323.

Rubin, S. J. (1995). Transnational corporations and international codes of conduct: A study of the relationship between international legal cooperation and economic development. *American University International Law Review, 10*(4), 1275–1289. Retrieved November 11, 2018, from https://digitalcommons.wcl.american.edu/cgi/viewcontent.cgi?referer=https://www.google.pt/&httpsredir=1&article=1448&context=auilr.

Rugman, A. M. (1975). Motives for foreign investment: The market imperfections and risk diversification hypotheses. *Journal of World Trade Law, 9*, 567–573.

Rugman, A. M. (1979). *International diversification and the multinational enterprise*. Lexington Books.

Rugman, A. M. (1981). *Inside the multinationals: The economics of internal markets*. Croom Helm.

Rugman, A. M. (Ed.). (1982). *New theories of the multinational enterprise*. Croom Helm.

Rugman, A. M. (1985). Internalization is still a general theory of foreign direct investment. *Weltwirtschaftliches Archiv, 121*(3), 570–575.

Rugman, A. M. (1991). Diamond in the rough. *Business Quarterly, 55*(3), 61–64.

Rugman, A. M. (2009). *The Oxford handbook of international business* (2nd ed.). Oxford University Press.

Rugman, A. M., & Brewer, T. L. (Eds.). (2001). *The Oxford handbook of international business* (1st ed.). Oxford University Press.

Rugman, A. M., & D'Cruz, J. R. (1993). The "double diamond" model of international competitiveness: The Canadian experience. *MIR, 33*(Special Issue), 17–39.

Rugman, A. M., & Verbeke, A. (1992). Multinational enterprise and national economic policy. In P. J. Buckley & M. Casson (Eds.), *Multinational enterprises in the world economy – Essays in honour of John Dunning* (pp. 194–211). Edward Elgar.

Rugman, A. M., & Verbeke, A. (1993). Foreign subsidiaries and multinational strategic management: An extension and correction of Porter's single diamond framework. *MIR, 33*(Special Issue), 71–84.

Rugman, A. M., & Verbeke, A. (2001). Subsidiary-specific advantages in multinational enterprises. *SMJ, 22*(3), 237–250.

Rugman, A. M., & Verbeke, A. (2004). A perspective on regional and global strategies of multinational enterprises. *JIBS, 35*(1), 3–18.

Rugman, A. M., & Verbeke, A. (2007). Liabilities of regional foreignness and the use of firm–level versus country-level data: A response to Dunning et al. (2007). *JIBS, 38*(1), 200–205.

Rumelt, R. (1984). Towards a strategic theory of the firm. In R. Lamb (Ed.), *Competitive strategic management* (pp. 556–570). Englewood Cliffs.

Safari, A., & Chetty, S. (2019). Multilevel psychic distance and its impact on SME internationalization. *IBR, 28*(4), 754–765.

Sagafi-Nejad, T., & Dunning, J. H. (2008). *The UN and transnational corporations: From code of conduct to global compact*, United Nations Intellectual History Project Series. Indiana University Press.

Salomon, R., & Wu, Z. (2012). Institutional distance and local isomorphism strategy. *JIBS, 43*, 343–367.

Santangelo, G. D. (2012). The tension of information sharing: Effects on subsidiary embeddedness. *IBR, 21*(2), 180–195.

Santangelo, G. D., & Meyer, K. E. (2011). Extending the internationalization process model: Increases and decreases of MNE commitment in emerging economies. *JIBS, 42*(7), 894–909.

Santangelo, G. D., & Meyer, K. E. (2017). Internationalization as an evolutionary process. *JIBS, 48*(9), 1114–1130.

Santos, T. (1970). The structure of dependence. *American Economic Review, 60*(2), 231–236.

Sarabi, A., Froese, F. J., Chng, D. H. M., & Meyer, K. E. (2020). Entrepreneurial leadership and MNE subsidiary performance: The moderating role of subsidiary context. *IBR, 29*(3), Article 101672.

Saranga, H., Schotter, A. P. J., & Mudambi, R. (2019). The double helix effect: Catch-up and local–foreign co-evolution in the Indian and Chinese automotive industries. *IBR, 28*(5), Article 101495.

Sarasvathy, S. D. (2008). *Effectuation: Elements of entrepreneurial expertise.* Edward Elgar.

Sartor, M. A., & Beamish, P. W. (2020). Private sector corruption, public sector corruption and the organizational structure of foreign subsidiaries. *Journal of Business Ethics, 167*(4), 725–744.

Scalera, V. G., Perri, A., & Hannigan, T. J. (2018). Knowledge connectedness within and across home country borders: Spatial heterogeneity and the technological scope of firm innovations. *JIBS, 49*, 990–1009.

Schaan, J-L. (1983). *Parent control and joint venture success: The case of Mexico*, Doctoral Dissertation, London, Ontário: University of Western Ontario.

Scherer, A. G., & Palazzo, G. (2011). The new political role of business in a globalized world: A review of a new perspective on CSR and its implications for the firm, governance, and democracy. *JMS, 48*(4), 899–931.

Schleimer, S., & Pedersen, T. (2014). The effects of MNC parent effort and social structure on subsidiary absorptive capacity. *JIBS, 45*(3), 303–320.

Schmid, D., & Morschett, D. (2020). Decades of research on foreign subsidiary divestment: What do we really know about its antecedents?' *IBR, 29*(4), Article 101653.

Schmid, S., & Schurig, A. (2003). The development of critical capabilities in foreign subsidiaries: disentangling the role of the subsidiary's business network. *IBR, 12*(6), 755–782.

Schmid, S., Schurig, A., & Kutschker, M. (2002). The MNC as a network: A closer look at intraorganizational flows. In M. Sarianna & M. Lundan (Eds.), *Network knowledge in international business* (pp. 45–72). Edward Elgar.

Schmid, S., & Wurster, D. J. (2017). International work experience: Is it really accelerating the way to the management board of MNCs? *IBR, 26*(5), 991–1008.

Schuit, R. (1985). The EIBA conference in Rotterdam. *EIBA Newsletter*, June, 3–4.

Schwens, C., Zapkau, F. B., Brouthers, K. D., & Hollender, L. (2018). Limits to international entry mode learning in SMEs. *JIBS, 49*(7), 809–831.

Servan-Schreiber, J-J. (1967). *Le Défi Americain.* Denöel.

Shaver, J. M. (2013). Do we really need more entry mode studies? *JIBS, 44*(1), 23–27.

Shenkar, O. (2001). Cultural distance revisited: Towards a more rigorous conceptualization and measurement of cultural differences. *JIBS, 32*(3), 519–535.

Shenkar, O. (2004). One more time: International business in a global economy. *JIBS, 35*(2), 161–171.

Simões, V. C. (1992). European integration and the pattern of FDI inflow in Portugal. In J. Cantwell (Ed.), *Multinational investment in Modern Europe: Strategic interaction in the integrated community* (pp. 256–297). Edward Elgar.

Simões, V. C. (2003). Networks and learning processes. A case study on the automotive sector in Portugal. In J. Cantwell & J. Molero (Eds.), *Multinational enterprises, innovative strategies and systems of innovation* (pp. 206–233). Edward Elgar.

Simões, V. C. (2018). If Dunning were writing now: The Eclectic Paradigm in an age of platform capitalism. Paper delivered at the 44th Annual Conference of EIBA, Poznan, December.

Simões, V. C. (2020). Implications of Covid-19 for international business: The case of platform companies. Opening Panel EIBA 2020, in *Implications of Covid for International Business*, Online Conference. December 10th.

Simões, V. C., Rocha, J. P., Piepenbrink, A., Cantwell, J., & Gugler, P. (2023). *The evolution of IB research: A topic model analysis of EIBA conference papers.* Paper delivered at the 49th Annual Conference of EIBA, Lisbon, December.

Sinkovics, R. R., Penz, E., & Ghauri, P. N. (2008). Enhancing the trustworthiness of qualitative research in international business. *MIR, 48*(6), 689–713.

Sinkovics, R. R., Yusuf, K., & Sinkovics, N. (2018). The effect of matching on perceived export barriers and performance in an era of globalization discontents: Empirical evidence from UK SMEs. *IBR, 27*(5), 1065–1079.

Slangen, A., & Hennart, J-F. (2008). Do multinationals really prefer to enter culturally distant countries through greenfields rather than through acquisitions? The role of parent experience and subsidiary autonomy. *JIBS, 39*(3), 472–490.

Slangen, A. H. L. (2013). Greenfield or acquisition entry? The roles of policy uncertainty and MNE legitimacy in host countries. *GSJ, 3*(3), 262–280.

Smale, A., Björkman, I., Ehrnrooth, M., John, S., Mäkelä, K., & Sumelius, J. (2015). Dual values-based organizational identification in MNC subsidiaries: A multilevel study. *JIBS, 46*(7), 761–783.

Song, J., & Shin, J. (2008). The paradox of technological capabilities: A study of knowledge sourcing from host countries of overseas R&D operations. *JIBS, 39*(2), 291–303.

Song, S. (2014). Subsidiary divestment: The role of multinational flexibility. *MIR, 54*, 47–70.

Spender, J-C. (1996). Making knowledge the basis of a dynamic theory of the firm. *SMJ, 17*(52), 45–62.

Stahl, G. K., Maznevski, M. L., Voigt, A., & Jonsen, K. (2010). Unraveling the effects of cultural diversity in teams: A meta-analysis of research on multicultural work groups. *JIBS, 41*(4), 690–709.

Stahl, G. K., & Tung, R. L. (2015). Towards a more balanced treatment of culture in international business studies: The need for positive cross-cultural scholarship. *JIBS, 46*(8), 391–414.

Stahl, G. K., Tung, R. L., Kostova, T., & Zellmer-Bruhn, M. (2016). Widening the lens: Rethinking distance, diversity, and foreignness in international business research through positive organizational scholarship. *JIBS, 47*(6), 621–630.

Stallkamp, M., & Schotter, A. (2019). Platforms without borders? The international strategies of digital platform firms. *GSJ, 11*(1), 58–80.

Steensma, H. K., Tihanyi, L., Lyles, M. A., & Dhanaraj, C. (2005). The evolving value of foreign partnerships in transitioning economies. *AMJ, 48*(2), 213–235.

Stewart, F. (1979). *International technology transfer: Issues and policy options,* World Bank Staff Working Papers No. 344. Washington DC: World Bank.

Stiglitz, J. E. (2002). *Globalisation and its discontents.* Allen Lane.

Stiglitz, J. E. (2006). *Making globalization work.* W. W. Norton.

Stoian, C., & Mohr, A. (2016). Outward foreign direct investment from emerging economies: Escaping home country regulative voids. *IBR, 25*(5), 1124–1135.

Stopford, J. M. (1974). The origins of British-based multinational enterprises. *Business History Review, 48*, 303–335.

Stopford, J. M. (1976). Changing perspective of investment by British manufacturing multinationals. *JIBS, 7*(2), 15–27.

Stopford, J. M., & Haberich, K. (1976). Ownership and control of foreign operations. *Journal of General Management, 3*(4), 3–20.

Stopford, J. M., & Wells, L. (1972). *Managing the multinational enterprise. Organisation of the firm and management of the subsidiaries.* Basic Books.

Strange, R., & Humphrey, J. (2019). What lies between market and hierarchy? Insights from internalization theory and global value chain theory. *JIBS, 50*(8), 1401–1413.

Sunkel, O. (1972). Big business and dependencia: A Latin-American view. *Foreign Affairs, 50*, 517–531.

Sunkel, O. (1981). Development styles and the environment: An interpretation of the Latin American case. In H. Muñoz (Ed.), *From dependency to development: Strategies to overcome underdevelopment and inequality* (pp. 93–114). Westview Press.

Sutherland, D., Anderson, J., & Hu, Z. (2020). A comparative analysis of location and non–location-bounded strategic asset seeking in emerging and developed market MNEs: An application of new internalization theory. *IBR 29*(2), Article 101635.

Tallman, S. (1999). The multiple roles of alliances in competency-based multinational strategies. *MIR*, *2*, 65–81.

Tan, A., Brewer, P., & Liesch, P. (2018). Rigidity in SME export commencement decisions. *IBR*, *27*(1), 46–55.

Tang, F. (2020). China urged to focus on domestic economy in next five–year plan to counter more hostile world. *South China Morning Post*, May 8. Retrieved February 8, 2022, from https://www.scmp.com/economy/china–economy/article/3083563/china–urged–focus–domestic–economy–next–five–year–plan?module=inline&pgtype=article.

Tang, L., & Koveos, P. E. (2008). A framework to update Hofstede's cultural value indices: economic dynamics and institutional stability. *JIBS*, *39*(6), 1045–1063.

Tang, R. W., & Buckley, P. J. (2020). Host country risk and foreign ownership strategy: Meta–analysis and theory on the moderating role of home country institutions. *IBR*, *29*(4), Article 101666.

Taussig, M. (2017). Foreignness as both a global asset and a local liability: How host country idiosyncrasies and business activities matter. *JIBS*, *48*(4), 498–522.

Taveira, E. (1984). *Foreign direct investment in Portugal: The present structure, and determinants of future evolution after the accession to the EEC*, Unpublished Doctoral thesis. Reading: University of Reading.

Teece, D. J. (1976). *The multinational corporation and the resource cost of international technology transfer*. Ballinger.

Teece, D. J. (1977). Technology transfer by multinational firms: The resource cost of transferring technological know-how. *The Economic Journal*, *87*(June), 242–261.

Teece, D. J. (1981a). The multinational enterprise: Market failure and market power considerations. *SMR*, Spring, 3–17.

Teece, D. J. (1981b). The market for know-how and the efficient international transfer of technology. *Annals, AAPSS*, *458*, 81–96.

Teece, D. J. (1986). Profiting from technological innovation. Implications for integration, collaboration, licensing and public policy. *RP*, *15*, 285–305.

Teece, D. J. (1998). Capturing value from knowledge assets: The new economy, markets for know-how, and intangible assets. *CMR*, *40*(3), 55–79.

Teece, D. J. (2007). Explicating dynamic capabilities: The nature and microfoundations of (sustainable) enterprise performance. *SMJ*, *28*(13), 1319–1350.

Teece, D. J. (2014). A dynamic capabilities-based entrepreneurial theory of the multinational enterprise. *JIBS*, *45*, 8–37.

Teece, D. J., & Pisano, G. (1994). The dynamic capabilities of firms: An introduction. *ICC*, *3*(3), 537–556.

Teece, D. J., Pisano, G., & Shuen, A. (1997). Dynamic capabilities and strategic management. *SMJ*, *18*(7), 509–533.

Tenzer, H., Pudelko, M., & Harzing, A-W. (2014). The impact of language barriers on trust formation in multinational teams. *JIBS*, *45*(5), 508–535.

Thams, Y., Chacar, A., & Wiersema, M. (2020). Global strategic context and CEO appointments: The importance of a global mind-set. *GSJ*, *10*(4), 676–699.

The Economist. (2000). The world's view of multinationals. *The Economist*, January 29. Retrieved March 4, 2019, from https://www.economist.com/leaders/2000/01/27/the–worlds–view–of–multinationals.

The Economist. (2020). Chaguan: Globalisation under quarantine. *The Economist*, February 29, *434*(9183), 50.

The Economist. (2023). Training days: China is educating engineers around the world. *The Economist*, October 19. Retrieved October 31, 2023, from https://www.economist.com/china/2023/10/19/china–is–educating–engineers–around–the–world, accessed on October 31st, 2023.

The Guardian. (2019). Donald Trump denounces 'globalism' in nationalist address to UN. *The Guardian*, September 24. Retrieved May 18, 2024, from https://www.theguardian.com/us–news/2019/sep/24/donald–trump–un–address–denounces–globalism.

Tian, X. (2007). Accounting for sources of FDI technology spillovers: evidence from China. *JIBS*, *38*(1), 147–159.

Triki, D., & Mayrhofer, U. (2016). Do initial characteristics influence IJV longevity? Evidence from the Mediterranean region. *IBR*, *25*(4), 795–805.

Trompenaars, F. (1995). *Riding the waves of culture*. Nicholas Brealey.

Tung, R. L., & Stahl, G. K. (2018). The tortuous evolution of the role of culture in IB research: What we know, what we don't know, and where we are headed. *JIBS*, *49*(9), 1167–1189.

Tung, R. L., & Verbeke, A. (2010). Beyond Hofstede and GLOBE: Improving the quality of cross–cultural research. *JIBS*, *41*(8), 1259–1274.

Tung, R. L., Zander, I., & Fang, T. (2023). The Tech Cold War, the multipolarization of the world economy, and IB research. *IBR*, *32*(6), 102195.

Turkina, E., & Van Assche, A. (2018). Global connectedness and local innovation in industrial clusters. *JIBS*, *49*(6), 706–728.

Uhlenbruck, K. (2004). Developing acquired foreign subsidiaries: The experience of MNES in transition economies. *JIBS*, *35*(2), 109–123.

UNCTAD. (1977). *Elaboration d'un Projet de Code International de Conduite pour le Transfert de Technologie*, TD/AC.1/6/Add.1. UNCTAD.

UNCTAD (1996). *World Investment Report 1996: Investment, trade and international policy agreements*. United Nations.

UNCTAD. (2000). *World Investment Report 2000: Cross-border mergers and acquisitions and development*. United Nations.

UNCTAD. (2003). *World Investment Report 2003: FDI policies for development: National and international perspectives*. United Nations.

UNCTAD. (2005). *Transnational corporations and the internationalization of R&D*. United Nations.

UNCTAD. (2013). *Global value chains: Investment and trade for development*. United Nations.

UNCTC. (1978). *Transnational corporations in world development: A re-examination*. United Nations.

UNCTC. (1983). *Transnational corporations and world development: Third survey*. United Nations.

UNCTC. (1991). *World Investment Report 1991: The triad in world investment*. United Nations.

United Nations. (2019). *Global Sustainable Development Report (GSDR) 2019: The future is now: Science for achieving sustainable development*. United Nations. Retrieved October 30, 2023, from https://sdgs.un.org/gsdr/gsdr2019.

United Nations. (2023a). *Take action for the sustainable development goals*. Retrieved October 30, 2023, from https://www.un.org/sustainabledevelopment/sustainable–development–goals/.

United Nations. (2023b). *Times of crisis, times of change: Science for accelerating transformations to sustainable development*. United Nations. Retrieved October 30, 2023, from https://sdgs.un.org/sites/default/files/2023–09/FINAL%20GSDR%202023–Digital%20–110923_1.pdf.

United Nations (2023c). *World Investment Report 2023: Investing in sustainable energy for all*. United Nations. Retrieved October 30, 2023, from https://unctad.org/publication/world–investment–report–2023.

Vahlne, J-E. (2020). Development of the Uppsala model of internationalization process: From internationalization to evolution. *GSJ*, *10*(2), 239–250.

Vahlne, J.-E., & Ivarsson, I. (2014). The globalization of Swedish MNEs: Empirical evidence and theoretical explanations. *JIBS*, *45*(3), 227–247.

Vahlne, J.-E., & Johanson, J. (2017). From internationalization to evolution: The Uppsala model at 40 years. *JIBS*, *48*(9), 1087–1102.

Vahlne, J.-E., & Johanson, J. (2020). The Uppsala model: Networks and micro–foundations. *JIBS*, *51*(1), 4–10.

Van den Bulcke, D. (1991). *Report on the activities of the European International Business Association–EIBA*, Miami.

Van Dyck, G. (2017). *Interview with Vítor Corado Simões*. Brussels, October 25.

van Hoorn, A., & Maseland, R. (2016). How institutions matter for international business: Institutional distance effects vs institutional profile effects. *JIBS*, *47*(3), 374–381.

van Kranenburg, H., Hagedoorn, J., & Lorenz-Orlean, S. (2014). Distance costs and the degree of inter-partner involvement in international relational-based technology alliances. *GSJ*, 4(4), 280–291.

van Tulder, R., Grøgaard, B., & Lunnan, R. (2023). *Walking the talk? MNEs transitioning towards a sustainable world*. Emerald Publishing.

van Tulder, R., Ruigrok, W., & Baven, G. (1991). *The globalization of glocalization of the car complex?* Paper delivered at the Monitor/FAST meeting on Globalisation of Economy and Technology, Brussels.

van Tulder, R., & van Mil, E. (2022). *Principles of sustainable business: Frameworks for corporate action on the SDGs*. Routledge.

Vanninen, H., Kuivalainen, O., & Ciravegna, L. (2017). Rapid multinationalization: Propositions for studying born micromultinationals. *IBR, 26*(2), 365–379.

Venaik, S., & Brewer, P. (2010). Avoiding uncertainty in Hofstede and GLOBE. *JIBS, 41*(8), 1294–1315.

Venaik, S., & Brewer, P. (2013). Critical issues in the Hofstede and GLOBE national culture models'. *IMR, 30*(5), 469–482.

Venaik, S., Midgley, D. F., & Devinney, T. M. (2005). Dual paths to performance: The impact of global pressures on MNC subsidiary conduct and performance. *JIBS, 36*(6), 655–675.

Verbeke, A. (2020). Will the COVID-19 pandemic really change the governance of global value chains? *BJM, 31*(3), 444–446.

Verbeke, A., & Greidanus, N. S. (2009). The end of the opportunism vs trust debate: Bounded reliability as a new envelope concept in research on MNE governance. *JIBS, 40*(9), 1471–1495.

Vernon, R. (1966). International investment and international trade in the product cycle. *The Quarterly Journal of Economics, 80*(2), 190–207.

Vernon, R. (1971). *Sovereignty at bay*. Basic Books.

Vickery, G. (1997). Crecimiento,y globalizaciónde la indústria del automóvil. *Economia Industrial, 314*, 27–61.

Villar, C., Alegre, J., & Pla-Barber, J. (2014). Exploring the role of knowledge management practices on exports: A dynamic capabilities view. *IBR, 23*(1), 38–44.

Waldman, D. A., de Luque, M. S., Washburn, N., House, R. J., Adetoun, B., Barrasa, A., Bobina, M., Bodur, M., Chen, Y-J., Debbarma, S., Dorfman, P., Dzuvichu, R. R., Evcimen, I., Fu, P., Grachev, M., Duarte, R. G., Gupta, V., Den Hartog, D. N., de Hoogh, A. H. B., et al. (2006). Cultural and leadership predictors of corporate social responsibility values of top management: A GLOBE study of 15 countries. *JIBS, 37*(6), 823–837.

Wan, F., Williamson, P., & Pandit, N. R. (2020). MNE liability of foreignness versus local firm-specific advantages: The case of the Chinese management software industry. *International Business Review, 29*(1), 101623.

Wang, C., Hong, J., Kafouros, M., & Wright, M. (2012). Exploring the role of government involvement in outward FDI from emerging economies. *JIBS, 43*(7), 655–676.

Wang, C., & Kafouros, M. I. (2009). What factors determine innovation performance in emerging economies? Evidence from China. *IBR, 18*(6), 606–616.

Wang, D., Hain, D. S., Larimo, J., & Dao, L. T. (2020). Cultural differences and synergy realization in cross–border acquisitions: The moderating effect of acquisition process. *IBR, 29*(3), Article 101675.

Wang, S. L., Luo, Y., Lu, X., Sun, J., & Maksimov, V. (2014). Autonomy delegation to foreign subsidiaries: An enabling mechanism for emerging–market multinationals. *JIBS, 45*(2), 111–130.

Weerawardena, J., Sullivan Mort, G., Liesch, P. W., & Knight, G. (2007). Conceptualizing accelerated internationalization in the born global firm: A dynamic capabilities perspective. *JWB, 42*(3), 294–306.

Wei, Y., & Liu, X. (2006). Productivity spillovers from R&D, exports and FDI in China's manufacturing sector. *JIBS, 37*(4), 544–557.

Wei, Z., & Nguyen, Q. T. K. (2017). Subsidiary strategy of emerging market multinationals: A home country institutional perspective. *IBR, 27*(5), 1009–1021.

Welch, C., Piekkari, R., Plakoyiannaki, E., & Paavilainen-Mäntymäki, E. (2011). Theorising from case studies: Towards a pluralist future for international business research. *JIBS, 42*(5), 740–762.

Welch, D. E., & Welch, L. S. (2006). Commitment for hire? The viability of corporate culture as a MNC control mechanism. *IBR, 15*(1), 14–28.

Welch, D. E., Welch, L. S., & Piekkari, R. (2005). Speaking in tongues: The importance of language in international management processes. *International Studies in Management and Organization, 35*(1), 10–27.

Welch, L. (1985). The international marketing of technology: An inter-action perspective. *IMR, 2*(1), 41–53.

Welch, L. S., Benito, G. R. G., & Petersen, B. (2007). *Foreign operation methods: Theory, analysis, strategy*. Edward Elgar.

Wells, L. T. (1983). *Third world multinationals*. MIT Press.

Wernerfelt, B. (1984). A resource-based view of the firm. *SMJ, 5*(2), 171–180.

Westney, D. E., & Van Maanen, J. (2011). The casual ethnography of the executive suite. *JIBS, 42*(5), 602–607.

Westney, D. E., & Zaheer, S. (2001). The multinational enterprise as an organization. In A. M. Rugman & P. Brewer (Eds.), *The Oxford handbook of international business* (pp. 349–379). Oxford University Press.

White, R. E., & Poynter, T. A. (1984). Strategies for foreign-owned subsidiaries in Canada. *Business Quarterly, 49*(2), 59–69.

White, R. E., & Poynter, T. A. (1990). Organizing for world-wide advantage. In C. A. Bartlett, Y. Doz, & G. Hedlund (Eds.), *Managing the global firm* (pp. 95–113). Routledge.

Wikipedia. (2018). *European Foundation for Management Development – EFMD*. Retrieved February 1, 2018, from https://en.wikipedia.org/wiki/European_Foundation_for_Management_Development.

Wilkins, M. (1982). American–Japanese direct foreign investment relationships, 1930–1952. *Business History Review, 56*(4), 479–518.

Wilkins, M. (1988). European and North American multinationals 1870–1914: Comparisons and contrasts. *Business History, 30*, 8–45.

Williamson, O. E. (1975). *Markets and hierarchies*. Free Press.

Williamson, O. E. (1985). *The economic institutions of capitalism*. The Free Press.

Williamson, P. J. (2016). Building and leveraging dynamic capabilities: Insights from accelerated innovation in China. *GSJ, 6*(3), 197–210.

Wionczek, M. S. (1981). El mundo subdesarrollado y las corporaciones transnacionales: El conflicto acerca de la transferencia de tecnologia y sus principales puntos negociales. *El Trimestre Económico, 48*, 45–85.

Witt, M. A. (2019). De-globalization: Theories, predictions, and opportunities for international business research. *JIBS, 50*(7), 1053–1077.

Witt, M. A., Lewin, A. Y., Ping Li, P., & Gaur, A. (2023). Decoupling in international business: Evidence, drivers, impact, and implications for IB research. *JWB, 58*(1), 101399.

Witt, M. A., & Redding, G. (2009). Culture, meaning, and institutions: Executive rationale in Germany and Japan. *JIBS, 40*(5), 859–885.

Wolf, J., & Egelhoff, W. G. (2013). An empirical evaluation of conflict in MNC matrix structure firms. *IBR, 22*(3), 591–601.

Wolf, M. (2023). *The crisis of democratic capitalism*. Penguin.

Xu, D., & Shenkar, O. (2002). Institutional distance and the multinational enterprise. *AMR, 27*(4), 608–618.

Yamin, M., & Andersson, U. (2011). Subsidiary importance in the MNC: What role does internal embeddedness play? *IBR, 20*(2), 151–162.

Yan, A., & Gray, B. (2001). Antecedents and effects of parent control in international joint ventures. *JMS, 38*(3), 393–416.

Yan, H., Hu, X., & Liu, Y. (2020). The international market selection of Chinese SMEs: How institutional influence overrides psychic distance. *IBR, 29*(4), Article 101703.

Yeniyurt, S., & Carnovale, S. (2017). Global supply network embeddedness and power: An analysis of international joint venture formations. *IBR, 26*(2), 203–213.

Yildiz, H. E., & Fey, C. F. (2012). The liability of foreignness reconsidered: New insights from the alternative research context of transforming economies. *IBR, 21*(2), 269–280.

Yildiz, H. E., & Fey, C. F. (2016). Are the extent and effect of psychic distance perceptions symmetrical in cross–border M&As? Evidence from a two-country study. *JIBS, 47*(7), 830–857.

Yli-Renko, H., Autio, E., & Sapienza, H. J. (2001). Social capital, knowledge acquisition, and knowledge exploitation in young technology-based firms. *SMJ, 22*(6–7), 587–613.

Yoshino, M. Y., & Rangan, S. (1995). *Strategic alliances: An entrepreneurial approach to globalization*. Harvard Business School Press.

Young, S., Hamill, J., Wheeler, C., & Richard Davies, J. (1989). *International market entry and development*. Harvester Wheatsheaf/Prentice Hall.

Young, S., Huang, C-H., & McDermott, M. (1996). Internationalization and competitive catch-up processes: Case study evidence on Chinese multinational enterprises. *MIR, 36*(4), 295–314.

Zaefarian, R., Eng, T-Y., & Tasavori, M. (2016). An exploratory study of international opportunity identification among family firms. *IBR, 25*(1), 333–345.

Zaheer, S. (1995). Overcoming the liability of foreignness. *AMJ, 38*(2), 341–363.

Zahra, S. A., Duane Ireland, R., & Hitt, M. A. (2000). International expansion by new venture firms: International diversity, mode of market entry, technological learning, and performance. *AMJ, 43*(5), 925–950.

Zander, I. (1999). How do you mean "global"? An empirical investigation of innovation networks in the multinational corporation. *RP, 28*(2/3), 195–213.

Zander, I., McDougall-Covin, P., & Rose, E. (2015). Born globals and international business: Evolution of a field of research. *JIBS, 46*(1), 27–35.

Zander, U., & Kogut, B. (1995). Knowledge and the speed of the transfer and imitation of organizational capabilities: An empirical test. *OS, 6*(1), 76–92.

Zanfei, A. (2000). Transnational firms and the changing organisation of innovative activities. *CJE, 24*(5), 515–542.

Zhang, F., Jiang, G., & Cantwell, J. A. (2015). Subsidiary exploration and the innovative performance of large multinational corporations. *IBR, 24*(2), 224–234.

Zhang, J., Zhou, C., & Ebbers, H. (2011). Completion of Chinese overseas acquisitions: Institutional perspectives and evidence. *IBR, 20*(2), 226–238.

Zollo, M., Bettinazzi, E. L. M., Neumann, K., & Snoeren, P. (2016). Toward a comprehensive model of organizational evolution: Dynamic capabilities for innovation and adaptation of the enterprise model. *GSJ, 6*(3), 225–244.

Zollo, M., Reuer, J. J., & Singh, H. (2002). Interorganizational routines and performance in strategic alliances. *OS, 13*(6), 701–713.

INDEX

Printed in the USA
CPSIA information can be obtained
at www.ICGtesting.com
JSHW050846031124
72668JS00003B/2/J